D0520536

DATE DUE

Social Sciences and Public Policy in the Developing World

Social Sciences and Public Policy in the Developing World

Edited by
Laurence D. Stifel
Ralph K. Davidson
The Rockefeller Foundation
James S. Coleman
University of California,
Los Angeles

LexingtonBooks
D.C. Heath and Company
Lexington, Massachusetts
Toronto

Library of Congress Cataloging in Publication Data
Main entry under title:

Social sciences and public policy in the developing world.

Bibliography: p.
1. Policy sciences—Addresses, essays, lectures. 2. Underdeveloped
areas—Social sciences—Addresses, essays, lectures. I. Stifel, Laurence
Davis. II. Davidson, Ralph Kirby. III. Coleman, James Samuel, 1926–
H97.S64   361.6′1   81-47748
ISBN Casebound: 0-669-04824-0   AACR2
        Paperbound: 0-669-04825-9

Copyright © 1982 by D.C. Heath and Company

Published simultaneously in Canada

Printed in the United States of America

International Standard Book Number:
    Casebound: 0-669-04824-0
    Paperbound: 0-669-04825-9

Library of Congress Catalog Card Number: 81-47748

Contents

Acknowledgments

The editors wish to express their appreciation to the many people who assisted in the preparation of this book. With the exception of the article by Paul Streeten, the chapters were all presented and discussed at a conference entitled "Strengthening Social Science Capacity in the Developing Areas," which was held in Bellagio, Italy, October 10–15, 1980. The editors and authors benefited from the rich discussion by the other conferees, distinguished social scientists from North and South: Bernard E. Anderson (United States), The Rockefeller Foundation; Claudio de Moura Castro (Brazil), Coordenação do Aperfeiçoamento de Pessoal de Nível Superior (CAPES); Cristina C. David (Philippines), University of the Philippines at Los Baños; Victor P. Diejomaoh (Nigeria), University of Lagos; José Encarnacion (Philippines), University of the Philippines; Reginald H. Green (United States), Institute of Development Studies at the University of Sussex; Roushdi Henin (Egypt), University of Nairobi; Harry T. Oshima (United States), University of the Philippines; Samuel Paul (India), Indian Institute of Management at Ahmedabad; Ammar Siamwalla (Thailand), International Food Policy Research Institute; Theodore M. Smith (United States), Agricultural Development Council. At The Rockefeller Foundation, the editors are particularly grateful to Henry Romney, director of Information Service, for the arrangements leading to this publication, and to Patricia Harris, program associate, for her characteristically efficient management of the process.

Acknowledgments

Introduction

As areas of knowledge integrally part of the modern university, the social sciences became internationalized through the university's worldwide diffusion as an idea and as an institution. The globalizing forces have included modern Western colonialism, carrying the full ensemble of Western institutions to much of the developing world; the rise of nationalism and the universalization of the nation-state, causing universities to be valued as necessary national institutions; the worldwide striving toward modernization, causing universities to be regarded as strategic and indispensable agencies; and the expansion of international aid, easing and accelerating the transfer from the North (including the USSR and Eastern Europe) to the South of those technologies and institutions considered necessary for both full independence and modernization. Although in many Third World settings universities were established during the colonial period, the introduction and expansion of the modern, differentiated social sciences were phenomena mainly of the terminal-colonial and immediate postcolonial periods. The 1950s marked the beginning of the great wave of their development.

Several kinds of external agencies—international, bilateral, and private—have promoted diffusion of the social sciences during their expansion and ever-greater differentiation in the developing world. The principal ones include UNESCO, as sponsor of regional social-science centers of diffusion; the development banks, particularly the Inter-American Bank, with its major loans for university development, and the Economic Development Institute of the World Bank, whose training of government officials has generated demand for economic research; the United Kingdom's Inter-University Council for Higher Education Overseas, the United States Agency for International Development, and Canada's International Development Agency and International Development Research Centre, each of which has emphasized university institution building; and two U.S. philanthropic foundations—the Ford Foundation and The Rockefeller Foundation. In chapter 3, the experience of the latter's philanthropy is examined as a case study of efforts by an external agency long concerned with the development of the social sciences in the North to promote their growth and institutionalization in the South.

In the dialogue engendered by the North-South transfer of social-science knowledge and its associated modes of inquiry and analysis of the human condition, three themes take prominence. One is the continuing evaluation by the southern inheritors—the social scientists of the developing world—about just how relevant, how useful, indeed, how benign, are the imports. Another is the continuing reassessment by northern social scientists of the categories, frameworks, and theories that they once presumed to be universal and have sometimes uncritically exported during the past three decades. The third theme centers on the emergence of a new, genuinely international community of social-science scholars who accept the facts that there are enduring dimensions of cultural relativity and that heterodoxy has its virtues, but who seek also to collaborate in research and in the quest for the identification of new universals.

Criticism of the social-science inheritance by some indigenous scholars of the South—joined by some scholars from the North—has tended to focus on three interrelated points. The first is that Western concepts, models, and paradigms, particularly the ideas and propositions imbuing the "modernization" paradigm in political science and sociology (which gained a brief ascendancy in the 1960s), not only grossly distorted realities but also imposed a developmental framework in which everything Western was by definition "modern," "developed," "secular-rational," and therefore presumptively superior, whereas everything non-Western was "traditional," "underdeveloped," "irrational," and presumably inferior. The socialization of scholars from the developing countries into this paradigm, with its implicit dominant-subordinate connotation, created and perpetuated, it is argued, an attitude of self-deprecatory dependence.

A second criticism is that the concepts and paradigms imported (primarily from the United States) are inherently value laden and ideologically biased toward conservatism, elite-centrism, inequality, and capitalism. Structural functionalism, systems analysis, neoclassical economics, Parsonian pattern variables, game theory, and exchange theory—these and others all tend, the argument runs, to be based on assumptions favoring stability and the status quo and to suppress, or at least conceal, the actual and potential dynamics and conflicts in both domestic and international society. Thus, they provide the rationale for neoimperialism and the perpetuation of dependency. This criticism is central to both Marxian and non-Marxian theories on dependency. Some social scientists in the South are also critical of the imported Marxist concepts as value laden and ideologically biased.

A third criticism is that Western theories, concepts, and paradigms are inherently and demonstrably culture bound. From this perspective, the developed countries' claims about the universality of Western social science are chimerical, if not arrogant. This criticism stems not from the existence of a peculiarly Western infirmity, but from the perspective of the sociology of knowledge that all thought is culturally and contextually relative. Thus, the "national" revolt against the presumed universalism of Western (mainly American) social science is not only a Third World phenomenon; the demands, for example, for a "Nigerian" or an "Indian" or a "Chinese" sociology are matched by similar self-assertions among some sociologists in

Scandinavia, France, Canada, and other nations and culture areas of the North itself.

Both Kenneth Prewitt (chapter 1) and Paul Streeten (chapter 2) review the nature and effect of the Third World critique—its identification of the ethnocentric bias in the modernization hypothesis and the questionable assumptions of universalism in Western paradigms and theories when exposed to realities of the developing world. Prewitt stresses that the critique has been a salutary corrective to some fundamental assumptions of predominantly American social science; he views as healthy the self-criticism it has provoked among northern social scientists, and their resulting greater humility and sensitivity to culture and context. This interaction, Prewitt feels, illuminates the growing maturity and confidence of the social-science enterprise in the Third World; and he sees an increasing reciprocity in ideas and the emergence of a genuinely international community of social-science scholars. Streeten also reviews sensitively the southern evaluation of the northern export and agrees that it is legitimate "to criticize orthodox Western models for their excessive claims" as well as to talk of "African," "Asian," or "Latin American" economics, politics, or sociology—but only with reference to the content (concepts, models, premises, paradigms, and theories). In his opinion, the laws of logic and the criteria of truth must remain universal. This judgment reinforces Prewitt's caution regarding the danger of carrying indigenization (in a regionalist or nationalist sense) to the extreme of methodological relativism and historicism—a hazard that he believes is recognized by concerned Third World social scientists as well.

In part II, the state of social science as a profession is examined in five regions: Southeast Asia, East Africa, West Africa, Latin America, and China. This is not a comprehensive survey of the developing areas; this coverage, however, is sufficiently broad to illustrate major similarities and differences.

One striking feature of the social sciences in the developing world is the regional variation in their pattern of development. Huan Xiang (chapter 5) describes their early flowering in the People's Republic of China, their demise during the Cultural Revolution, and current efforts to rebuild them almost from scratch. In contrasting Southeast Asia and India, Warren Ilchman (chapter 4) notes that whereas the latter has the older national-university culture and an established infrastructure for advanced social science, because of a deliberate government policy of indigenization Indian social scientists are less in touch with the international social-science community than their Southeast Asian counterparts. The more extensive development of the various disciplines in the Philippines reflects the close historical links between American and Philippine university cultures.

Latin America differs from other developing regions in terms of its longer history of university development. Jorge Balán (chapter 9) emphasizes its relatively early independence, its greater cultural continuity, and the successive waves of diffusion that have influenced its scientific and intellectual culture over the centuries. The social sciences were formally established in the University of São Paulo in the early 1930s (but also in Thailand and China at the same time), and anthropology was fairly well developed in Mexico and Peru some time before World War II. Yet despite these deeper roots and longer gestation, the emergence of the modern empirical social sciences in Latin America, and particularly of economics as a discipline differentiated from law, is, as elsewhere, largely a post–World War II phenomenon, as described in the chapters by Eduardo Venezian (chapter 8) and Jorge Balán.

A second characteristic of most developing areas is the comparatively greater development and strength of economics among the social-science disciplines. This is true of the five Southeast Asian countries surveyed by Warren Ilchman, of India, of West Africa (described by Akin Mabogunje in chapter 7), and of Latin America (described by Eduardo Venezian). Among the likely explanations are its higher prestige as a "harder" science, the greater utility for public policy that government officials presume it to have, and its promise of providing materially more rewarding careers through consultancies.

Another feature of the social sciences in the Third World is that everywhere their growth has occurred during an epoch in which the dominant ethos has been developmentalism. Commencing in the so-called development decade of the 1960s, when most of the modern social-science communities of the less developed countries (LDCs) were in gestation, international organizations, aid agencies, and national governments insisted on the developmental mission of the university. Exhortations that Third World universities must be demonstrably relevant for and committed to national development imbued all rhetoric about the role and responsibilities of social scientists. The result has been a marked orientation toward practicality and applied "problem-solving" research, and, consequently, vastly expanded opportunities for salary supplementation through contract research. The surveys in part II underscore the prevalence of this orientation.

A related common feature is the ever-increasing penetration of the state's power and supervision into all sectors, including universities. Increased governmental intervention in and control over universities is, of course, a worldwide phenomenon, as true of the industrialized North as of the developing South, and as true of pluralistic democracies as of monistic authoritarian regimes. In most developing countries, members of the university professoriat are legally or functionally considered employees in the public service. This status has a constraining effect on academic freedom; it can also have negative effects on emoluments and other entitlements of social scientists in universities. It underscores the imperative of service in the interest of national development and operates to dissuade critical analysis and judgment. Universities tend to be the major base for social scientists with advanced degrees and, with the notable exception of countries having a private university sector (such as the Philippines, Colombia, Brazil, and India), most Third World universities are public institutions.

Social scientists in most of the developing countries face material conditions and problems of professional status that hinder professional motivation and achievement. It is generally true that, economists aside, the prestige of social scientists is lower than or declining in comparison with that of academics in more scientific disciplines or in the professions or even that of educated personnel in other sectors (particularly the private sector) of their societies. In some countries, they share with all other members of the professoriat the effects of a devaluation of higher education by governing groups: low salaries force them to moonlight and to engage in contract research; and poor working conditions in terms of library facilities, equipment, infrastructure, and support services limit their opportunities for professional self-renewal and advancement. Both prestige and working conditions, however, are variable both between countries and, over time, within countries. Everywhere the social demand (and hence, the political imperative) for university education remains high, and in not a few countries, universities continue to receive favorable if not preferential treatment.

Variations also exist among less developed regions and countries as to how the social sciences are structured within the university. Where American influence has been significant (as in the Philippines), the social sciences are organized into individual departments and collectively into faculties of social sciences. Where British tradition remains dominant, the social sciences may have their own departments but usually remain under the faculty of arts. Where the Dutch and French have been most influential, law is regarded as a social science, but in both the Ivory Coast and Indonesia, separate faculties of economics have been created. In Latin America prior to the 1950s, economics was taught in faculties of law (the French tradition), but with the explosive growth of economics under American assistance, separate departments of economics emerged, followed by the other social-science disciplines. In rebuilding its universities, the People's Republic of China is having to re-create sociology and econometrics, which were abandoned during the Cultural Revolution. In most regions and countries, however, there is an effort to adapt the diverse inherited models to national-university cultures.

The development of postgraduate studies in the social sciences has necessarily been a second-generation phenomenon. Multiple pressures of varying intensity have promoted the launching of postgraduate programs despite shortages of professionally qualified staff (as in the Philippines). These pressures have included the drive for indigenization; needs to economize, to upgrade and expand the numbers of academic staff, or to conduct research on local development problems; and an assumption that postgraduate studies are a necessary complement of any self-respecting, status-seeking university. In universities influenced by the British tradition, the research doctorate continues to obtain (for example, in India and anglophonic Africa); increasingly, however, universities have gravitated to the American advanced-course-work pattern in graduate studies. The master's degree via course work has been introduced in several regions (Southeast Asia, India, Africa, and Latin America, most notably in Brazil). The doctorate via a combination of course work, research and dissertation has been much more selectively introduced (for example, in economics at Gadjah Mada University in Indonesia; at São Paulo, Rio, and Brasilia in Brazil; and at the University of Ibadan, Nigeria). The continuing attraction of the foreign (that is, northern) Ph.D.—for reasons of prestige, avoidance of inbreeding, or absence of local professional competence—remains strong, but varies from country to country.

The three chapters in part III provide perspectives on how the expanding social-science communities in Latin America, India, and East Africa have contributed to improved policies and national development. The vast majority of social scientists staff government agencies, colleges, and private firms; relatively few—mostly with graduate degrees—are engaged in research intended to have a direct or indirect effect on policy. Working in universities, government agencies, research institutes, or private consulting firms, these social scientists are involved with the production of knowledge about society that, in the words of Kenneth Prewitt, can "extend the observational powers of the state" and enlarge the information base upon which policies are formulated. In the many developing countries where limited avenues for articulating political views at lower levels impair the vision of centralized decision makers, social scientists may serve the function of surrogate legislators reporting on conditions in the rural areas and urban slums.

In all three regions, research social scientists have been deeply engaged in studying the development process. They have produced information at varying levels of generality: (1) development of an information base—the essential early step of systematically describing and classifying empirical evidence, including augmentation of data by means of surveys and censuses; (2) evaluation of public projects and programs—short-term studies, required by governments and donor agencies, which consist both of prospective feasibility analyses, often in the cost-benefit mode, and of appraisals of project impact over time; (3) assessment of the relation between public-policy instruments and policy objectives—medium-range studies on the effects, intended and otherwise, of current and alternative government policies, conducted to inform the political process and improve policy formulation; (4) discipline-centered investigations of a problem area—less-structured, open-ended, and autonomous research rooted in a discipline that may widen intellectual perspectives and provide fresh hypotheses leading to clearer understanding of the problem and to new theoretical frameworks; and (5) basic or theoretical research without a preconceived relation to social problems—to develop new methodological tools or deepen the conceptualization of a discipline. Though rare in Third World countries, basic research is mentioned here to complete the typology of social-science-generated knowledge; its social payoff is long term, a decade or more if the experience in the medical and natural sciences is relevant.

Chapters 10, 11, and 12 by Edgardo Boeninger, Myron Weiner, and David Court, respectively, confirm the remarkable diffusion and acceptance of problem-oriented research noted by Prewitt in chapter 1. Most of the research conducted by social scientists in LDCs falls within the second and third categories above, particularly short-term project studies often conducted under contract from governments or international organizations. Technocrats in the bureaucracies and development agencies are knowledgeable consumers of social-science research. Drawing heavily on the quantitative skills of the economists, they incorporate requirements for research into the expanding array of their operations. The central importance of project research is illustrated by Weiner's summaries of a sample of important policy studies at major research centers in India. In all except the very large developing countries like India, the demand for contract research and lucrative consultancies outpaces the supply of qualified indigenous social scientists.

The social sciences in the LDCs thus appear singularly successful in contributing to public policy. These contributions are the reason for the acceleration of their growth over the past two decades. Governments perceive a need for such research, and their effective demand signifies social utility. The social scientists' direct engagement with practical social problems has mitigated official apprehensions about a professional propensity toward academic irrelevance or—ostensibly the greater evil—criticism that may be subversive of national goals. Dependence on foreign researchers has been reduced and indigenization of the social sciences realized, at least in the sense that professional studies are now conducted primarily by nationals.

The success of the social sciences in responding to urgent current priorities deflects attention from the costs of the short-term time horizon typical of the profession. Given the deterrents in the university structure, the compelling pressures to supplement income, and the paucity of funding for independent-research agendas, it is not surprising that the material rewards and prestige of contract research and consultancies exert such influence. The authors in this section—and others in the volume—point out three weaknesses of social-science research, all of which result from excessive commitment to short-run problem solving for official agencies: a threatening erosion of standards, diversion from research on more profound social questions, and atrophy of the critical function of scholarship.

Erosion of Standards

The social sciences can be useful in helping to solve problems when there is underlying strength in the disciplines, and under ideal circumstances the research process and disciplinary vitality are mutually reinforcing. But when the principal consumer of research is the government, the process tends to circumvent the conventional scientific review of research quality and to undermine the source of renewal, the disciplinary base in the universities. The quality of problem-solving research is normally evaluated not by professional peers but by government officials seeking politically useful, unambiguous solutions to set problems. The research question defines the answer, which is frequently narrow, sometimes even trivial. Economists, for example, devote enormous amounts of time to performing the benefit-cost analyses that are routinely required for the approval of development projects, but the studies invariably produce "answers" greater than unity, thus confirming the economic viability of the projects. The scientific quality of the work may also be subordinated to such compelling criteria—justifiable, given its purposes—as adherence to schedules and conformity to research budgets.

In many countries social-science research has shifted from universities to specialized, often multidisciplinary research institutes and agencies because of the deterrents in the university structure and the need for organizational flexibility to bring different disciplines to bear on problem areas. This redirection, however, tends to erode scientific standards further; not only is disciplinary review of the research product on the supply side frequently weakened, but also the best social scientists are siphoned off from teaching and thus from replenishing the supply of social scientists in the universities. The result is a vicious circle of greater pressure on qualified researchers, further distortion of the incentive structure, and increased attrition in the universities. Moreover, the impairment of the natural feedback from research into training and the delayed indigenization of the curriculum constitute a heavy burden on the many students enrolled in undergraduate and graduate classes.

Although these results are not inevitable, David Court, in chapter 12, extends his earlier description of the social sciences in East Africa (chapter 6) to show the force of contract research upon a small, recent, and still-fragile community of scholars. He is apprehensive that the indigenous scholars who have finally gained control of the social-science enterprise in Kenya may not be able to institutionalize disciplinary research standards of neutrality and autonomy in the face of such corrupting influence.

Diversion from Research on More Profound Social Questions

Social-science research is the study of individual and social behavior. Though not an exact science, it is designed to deepen understanding of social relationships. In the development ethos of the Third World, the social scientists' contribution to the search for more-beneficial social arrangements will necessarily have a utilitarian value; however, their role remains a supporting one—to add to the fund of social knowledge so that political leaders can make better-informed decisions on public policies and action programs.

But preoccupation with short-term problem solving may jeopardize fulfillment of this professional function. First, such assignments frequently exceed the scientific competence of the social scientist, involving advice on strategies or policy directions that clearly belongs to the political arena. A second, more common disability is the limiting of the research question to the lower end of the descriptive–theoretical continuum of research-generated knowledge noted earlier. To the extent that the problem is narrowly defined, emphasis is on the application of existing knowledge (the engineering function) rather than on the extension of knowledge (the scientific function).

In either case, a tendency exists in many developing countries for the researchers to become overcommitted to such projects, driven by deadlines and prevented by shifting topics from achieving deep understanding in any substantive area. The absence of open-ended, autonomous research on a problem area has a social opportunity cost; few social scientists are widening intellectual perspectives, liberating society from its myths and illusions, or conceptualizing development issues. With the comfortable paradigm of modernization in eclipse, it is argued that social scientists should be creating knowledge that will be useful in the design of development strategies and programs to realize the complex, equity-oriented objectives that have been adopted throughout the Third World.

The misallocation of social-science resources to short-term problem solving reflects the incentive structure in Third World societies. Even though longer-term research on fundamental problems may represent a valuable public good, effective demand for its production is weak; potential consumers in government agencies and elsewhere often misconstrue its purposes and doubt its relevance to their needs. The problem of finding or

generating sources of support for such research confronts most societies—
U.S. social scientists' concern about increasing restriction of research
funding to transitory, politicized issues has been reinforced by the Reagan
administration's deep cuts in the social-science budget of the National
Science Foundation. Nevertheless, social scientists in the developing countries who have been indifferent to the application of their studies share
responsibility for the lack of support for autonomous research. It is argued in
part III that they should study how information enters the public arena and
affects policy, and direct a deliberate and sustained effort to communicating
the purpose and value of both short- and long-term research to a broader
audience.

Atrophy of the Critical Function of Scholarship

To the extent that their support derives from governments and development
agencies, the social scientists who conduct problem-solving research tend to
function as clients undertaking an official agenda, circumscribing the scope
of their research to assure focus on the problem and timely completion, and
avoiding critical analysis for fear of jeopardizing future research contracts.
At least in East Africa and India, the research results are the property of the
government, which frequently restricts release of conclusions not consonant
with prevailing policy. The social scientist thus can become a technocrat, in
the disparaging sense of the term as used in Latin America, with autonomy
curbed and limited influence upon public-policy issues.

The essence of the scientific process, in contrast, is the freedom to
pursue ever deeper understanding of an issue and to expose conclusions to
professional scrutiny and public debate. When focused upon broad public
issues, such research in the social sciences inevitably leads to critical observations about societal arrangements and to knowledge that is a source of
political power. Boeninger believes that genuine social inquiry can flourish
only in a free society that permits dissemination of conclusions to the
multiple actors in the policy process, including political parties, the military,
social organizations, and the church.

Authoritarian regimes that curb the exercise of the social sciences
vividly demonstrate their apprehension of the power of autonomous social
research. The dilemma of the social scientist's relation to government is
most starkly illuminated in the military regimes of Latin America. The issue
there is often not merely self-censorship engendered by potential with-
drawal of research funding, but the possibility of repression by measures
ranging from subtle to crude. The official view in such situations is that the
social-science community is polarized between useful technicians and radical critics. Many authoritarian regimes, however, are relatively permissive if

social scientists confine their activities to academic circles and do not seek to communicate to a wide audience or engage in political activism.

Is it possible for social scientists in the developing world to tread a useful but politically neutral path? Drawing on his experiences as a producer (university rector) and consumer (budget director) of research in the ideological maelstrom of Chile, Boeninger argues that the social scientist cannot be neutral, for the product of his research conveys political power and is based on value judgments about the nature of society. Of the two conflicting economic schools in Latin America, the Marxist and the neoclassical, even the latter, in the Chicago form dominant in the southernmost Latin American countries, is not without evident ideological roots. Although social scientists will continue to debate the relationship between doctrine and knowledge, Boeninger suggests it is possible to acknowledge explicitly the role of values in setting the research agenda and still aspire to scientific objectivity and truth. Moreover, he maintains that social scientists who seek to influence policy must match scientific knowledge with inspired social thought. Although economics has more analytical rigor, in Boeninger's view the softer social sciences may be more useful in informing social thinking and advancing the political debate from passion to reason. Social scientists clearly have no monopoly—and perhaps not even a comparative advantage—in social thinking, but Weiner and Court share Boeninger's concern that social scientists in developing countries are too often attacking problems at the margin of the social agenda and missing the broad landscape.

There is, then, a striking contrast between the massive resources devoted to development and the paucity of funding for critical analysis of the development effort and for deeper conceptualization of its relation to the tensions created by rapid economic and social change. Paradoxically, external funding for general support of the social sciences is declining sharply at a time when investment resources for development are enormous, disillusionment with conventional strategies of development widespread, and the recently launched social science enterprise in most countries not yet effectively institutionalized.

The volume concludes with an annotated bibliography, prepared by Elizabeth Brooks, listing selected journal articles from 1970 to 1980 on the social sciences in the Third World countries.

The editors hope that this book will illuminate the diverse and contradictory trends affecting the social sciences in the developing countries and deepen understanding of these young sciences—their role and potential for training and for generating knowledge for the well-being of the almost 3.5 billion people in the Third World.

Part I
The Internationalization of the
Social Sciences

1

The Impact of the Developing World on U.S. Social-Science Theory and Methodology

Kenneth Prewitt

Bringing an international dimension to American social science has produced changes in the institutions, the research questions, the methodologies and tools, and the core disciplines of social science. These changes go well beyond the boundaries of what traditionally in the social sciences have been thought of as *area studies*. The consequences of internationalization in the last three decades, from approximately 1950 to the present, are potentially as transforming for social science as the introduction of quantification in the prior three decades, from the 1920s onward. This argument, however, requires one overriding caution: the first principle of social science is that complex phenomena should not—and cannot—be explained with single-variable models. Social science is a complex phenomenon and no single factor, even one as multifaceted as internationalization, can begin to account for its scientific and institutional developments.

The Internationalization of American Social Science

There has been an extraordinary achievement in American higher education in the past three decades. The total number of faculty teaching international studies in U.S. graduate institutions in 1940 has been estimated at about 225. Robert Hall, in a 1947 report prepared for the Social Science Research Council, surveyed the condition of graduate training in various regions of the world. The following quotations convey the flavor of his report.[1]

> The Near East is completely neglected and there are few scholars in the country who know anything about the area except in the field of languages.

> It would be most difficult . . . to build a single major center on Africa.

> In the case of both India and Indonesia the lack of personnel is most appalling. Probably no center on either area could be adequately staffed with American personnel.

Thirty years later, area centers represent one of the proudest accomplishments of U.S. research universities. Numbers do not tell the full story,

3

but they indicate the magnitude of the accomplishment. It has been estimated that by 1979 there were 17,500 Ph.D.'s in international-studies fields.
Approximately half were trained in the social sciences, about 20 percent
were trained as historians, and the remainder were in the humanities disciplines. An examination of the faculty of twenty major research universities
revealed that a third of all nonscience faculty could be classified under the
rubric of international studies. In four leading universities (Chicago, Cornell, Harvard, and Stanford), half the faculty were so classified.[2]

Along with the numbers comes testimony to the quality of what has
been accomplished. Robert E. Ward, in an influential paper prepared for a
recent U.S. Presidential Commission on Foreign Language and International Studies, observes:

> The Commission recognizes that, as a result of joint private and public
> initiatives at both the local and national levels since World War II, the
> United States has acquired a very impressive array of advanced training and
> research programs in the international field. The basic purposes of these
> programs were to provide the country with a corps of academic specialists
> well trained in the languages and cultures of a broad range of largely
> non-Western societies that had long been neglected or ignored by the
> American educational system and with a fund of knowledge about those
> societies that would be useful for both scholarly and public purposes. In
> general these purposes have been well served and the programs richly merit
> commendation on these scores.[3]

The birth of area studies is usually dated from the early 1950s. And
though the international dimension of American social science is now much
broader than the scholarly activities encompassed by the term *area studies,*
much of what has happened in recent years builds upon, or occurs in reaction
to, area studies. The brief schematic history below provides the context for
my thesis.

The Research Site

As sociologists, political scientists, economists, and psychologists moved
away from geographic insularity and cultural parochialism and began to look
at societies beyond the borders of the United States, they had as models
historians and anthropologists, both of whose disciplines had "otherness" as
their subject matter. The historians studied other times, the anthropologists
other places. Historians and anthropologists shared the epistemological
inclination to extract from their foreign sites information relevant to already
formulated conceptualizations. An analogy frequently if incorrectly used
was that the foreign site was a laboratory for testing historical or anthropological theory. The historian, for example, was intent on demonstrating that

historical development was progressive and linear; the anthropologist needed ethnological cases to buttress, say, a general theory of structuralism or of
cultural transmission.

As political scientists, sociologists, psychologists, and economists adopted the approach of the historians and anthropologists, they tended to regard
the foreign country as a research site in which to examine hypotheses
exported from the United States. The considerable intellectual embarrass-
ment resulting from this approach is an issue I shall touch on briefly later.
For now, I shall simply identify the initial stages of the area studies movement.

Technology Transfer

Almost immediately, the scientific goals of the area-studies movement were
diluted by different, though not necessarily incompatible, motivations. It
became difficult to study foreign places without also becoming concerned
about the quality of the local research community—if, indeed, one even
existed. Readers will be familiar with the metaphors *indigenization, capacity
building, manpower training,* and *institution building.* American social-
science skills and values were not only taken abroad by the research community; they were also exported by foundations, for whom the missionary
impulse to do good was as important as the scientific goal of knowledge.
There were three important aspects of this technology-transfer dimension of
early international scholarship.

First, as articulated by American foundations and scholars, indigenization essentially meant the training of local personnel and the establishment
of research competence and facilities. Only later has indigenization come to
mean a locally led methodological and theoretical confrontation with many
key concepts of Western social science. Second, the metaphors were taken
seriously. Through such programs as The Rockefeller Foundation's University Development Program and the Ford Foundation's network of field
representatives, money was available to send large numbers of younger
Asians, Africans, and Latin Americans to American graduate programs. A
generation of local scholars was thus trained. Moreover, the foundations as
well as the government (primarily the Fulbright program) recruited Americans to teach abroad during the years when substantial numbers of local
scholars were still in training programs. A principal criterion for selection of
Americans to teach abroad has been the commitment to the values of
indigenization. Americans were expected to train their own replacements.
Most willingly did so. To be sure, the training, ideas, research methods, and
institutional models were largely American. The United States was the
exporting nation or, if you prefer, the hegemonic community; and most
Third World countries were the importers or, if you prefer, the dependent
clients.

The third characteristic of the technology transfer period is especially important. Inherent in the training emphasis, in contrast with the earlier research-site emphasis, was the notion that local scholars could and should become colleagues. Moving American scholars to Third World countries and Third World trainees to U.S. graduate programs established the principle of international collaboration. As a result, the area-studies community soon included scholars from the areas studied. This has proved to be a major step toward establishing an international community of scholars, which is the emerging characteristic of the current phase of internationalization.

International Community of Scholars

From the perspective of an American social scientist it appears to me that the present phase of internationalization can best be understood in terms of a change in the balance of trade in ideas. Growing modesty on the part of American scholars and growing maturity on the part of Third World social scientists have combined to change the context in which American scholarship takes place. The modesty of U.S. scholars expresses itself in the recognition that Western-generated theories and methods are not necessarily adequate for the comprehension of social phenomena elsewhere. The maturity of Third World scholars expresses itself in the development of indigenous hypotheses to account for local conditions, in the tendency to export as well as import ideas and methods (dependency theory being the classic illustration), and in the skepticism shown toward some Western social science. Although hemispheric asymmetries in resources and personnel will persist for some time, the North American/European research communities will now import as well as export, and the Asian/African/Latin American scholars will increasingly produce ideas that will be absorbed by an international community of scholars.

One specific way in which we see this happening is through the international diffusion of the idea of area studies. Certainly, the American social-science community pioneered the development of area studies, though some disciplines (such as anthropology) from other Western countries (such as Great Britain) were strongly international well before the area-studies movement of the postwar period. By now, of course, it is commonplace for scholars from various countries to study societies other than their own. Area studies are beginning to develop even in the Third World universities, a point to which I shall return below.

Another development in the current phase of internationalization is scholarly collaboration outside the area-studies movement itself. International conferences of sociologists, economists, or psychologists are addressing questions central to their respective disciplines, such as the history of the family, the economics of local markets, or the emotional development of infants. Scholars are addressing these disciplinary issues by applying data from various cultures, but the organizing principle is disciplinary theory, not the extension of knowledge about a particular area of the world.

Illustrating the Impact of the International Dimension

Today, it is no longer possible to identify a U.S. social science in the same sense that it could be identified before the emergence of area studies and the consequent introduction of an international dimension in many aspects of the social sciences. Some fundamental assumptions of U.S. social science have been shaken. The intellectual presumptions and methodological strategies that prevailed in the 1950s are now so transformed as to be hardly recognizable, as social scientists accommodated themselves to what they encountered and what they learned. Of course, not all the major changes in the social sciences can be traced to internationalization. Subdisciplines, such as mathematical sociology and public-choice analysis; research strategies, such as the empirical study of social change; theoretical currents, such as the Marxian tradition; and particular emphases, such as policy studies, have resulted from developments within the United States itself or from intellectual commerce with other advanced industrial societies. But although the growing density of intellectual exchange with Western Europe and Japan is part of internationalization, the intellectual importance of relations with Third World societies can be illustrated with reference to two issues, one methodological and one theoretical. These two issues—the discovery of boundary conditions and the collapse of the modernization paradigm—illustrate a significant change in U.S. social science that can be attributed at least partly to scholarly contact with Third World societies.

The Discovery of Boundary Conditions

In the 1950s American scholars were enamored of natural-science analogies. Quantification either was well established (in economics) or was becoming so (in sociology and political science). Accompanying quantification was the promise of experimentation (already established in psychology). If social science could quantify and experiment, why could it not also develop a deductive science and, in the process of testing rigorously formulated hypotheses, confirm lawlike generalizations about social behavior and social process?

    With the benefit of historical perspective, we now see that social scientists frequently encountered the natural-science model through philosophers, such as Popper and Cohen and Nagel, rather than through direct contact with physical or biological scientists. Perhaps this helps explain why our understanding of the discovery process in science was initially so naive. The early collapse of the unrealistic analogy with the natural sciences has contributed to the state of epistemological anarchy in the social sciences with which we are now struggling.

To understand the role of internationalization in the epistemological twists and turns of the last quarter-century we need to place in opposition two traditions: the search for a scientific language that would describe the invariant features of social behavior, and the search for an ever deeper understanding of a particular culture. Talcott Parsons typifies the first tradition. He constructed his theory of society on analytical abstractions. Norms (universalistic versus particularistic), status (achieved versus ascribed), and role relations (diffuse versus specific) were among the abstractions that facilitated classification and comparison of different societies. The abstractions of Parsonian theory, necessary if science were to attain precision of language and cross-cultural explanatory generalizations, were not well received by area studies scholars, despite the efforts of persons such as David Easton or Gabriel Almond to provide, at least for political science, common categories of analysis.

Area scholars were sensitive to time and place, to what we might call the boundary conditions of phenomena. Local conditions, cultural traditions, and historically rooted habit seemed not to fit comfortably with the abstractions of general theory. Under prodding from area-studies scholars, social science turned from abstractions to history, from invariant processes to highly variable behavior, from generalizations back to observation.

At this point we should take special note of the term *indigenization*. In its initial use, as already suggested, it referred to the importance of training local staff and placing institutions under local control. This emphasis on personnel and institutions has been superseded. Indigenization has come to mean development of local theories and appropriate methodologies. "It is now commonplace," reports one eminent observer of Asian social science, "to view Western theories from the vantage points afforded by the distinctive historical characteristics of our own societies. We examine the applicability of these theories with all of our critical faculties and spare no labor in unfolding indigenous theories which fit our own societies."[4]

Hwang San-duk is repeating a theme that has now attained cliché status in social-science communities around the world—the fashioning of concepts and methods of analysis that are appropriate to the histories, social realities, and immediate problems of particular societies.

The epistemological danger in the indigenization of social-science theory is recognized even by its own proponents. Hwang San-duk, in the address already cited, goes on to warn against the extremes of methodological relativism and of historicism. It was the specter of the latter that contributed to the search for analytic categories that would permit a science of society. Thus, the decline of Parsonian functionalism calls for an epistemological alternative to historicism.

While I am not expert enough to unravel the epistemological ferment stirring up the contemporary social sciences, some of the more promising developments can in significant ways be traced to the internationalization described earlier. One example is the revival of a classic theme in sociological analysis, which bears the modern label *ecological analysis*. This is the sensitivity to the context of social behavior which, among other accomplishments, has revealed the limits of social behaviorism. Although the ecological perspective can itself become a new form of determinism, in its more respectable formulations it maintains at the forefront of sociological analysis the critical role of history and context, both of which are defining characteristics of area studies.

More generally, we are witnessing the birth of what is called interpretative social science, in which the significance and meaning of lived-in worlds is replacing such conventional social-science metaphors as behavior, action, or institution. Interpretative social science draws on hermeneutics and textual analysis, on phenomenology and the social construction of reality, on the Critical Theory of the Frankfurt School, and on a new theory of culture being worked out by anthropologists such as Clifford Geertz, Marshall Sahlins, and Bernard Cohn. Geertz, for example, has written a celebrated sentence, "Man is an animal suspended in webs of significance he himself has spun." He continues, "I take culture to be those webs, and the analysis of it to be therefore not an experimental science in search of law but an interpretive one in search of meaning."[5] Thick description is the methodology. Symbol systems and the meanings that people attach to the informal logic of the events that constitute their lives can be empirically assessed by inspecting those events. This sounds descriptive and atheoretical, but an interpretative social science is resolutely theoretical. The small facts of thick description "speak to large issues, wink to epistemology, or sheep raid to revolution, because they are made to."[6] According to Geertz, "The essential task of theory building here is not to codify abstract regularities but to make thick description possible, not to generalize across cases but to generalize within them."[7]

It is not my task, nor is it my talent, to synthesize the epistemological currents at work in contemporary social science. If we reach into statistics and mathematics for the skills of quantification, we also reach into linguistics, literary criticism, history and comparative religion for guidance on the skills of interpretation. In doing so, where we are epistemologically cannot be divorced from where we have been internationally. Thus, although it would be easy to assign too much credit (or blame) to area studies and the gradual internationalization of the social sciences, it would be wrong to overlook the obvious difficulties that analytic abstractions encountered in the fieldwork that characterized area studies.

The Modernization Hypothesis

The fate of the modernization hypothesis illustrates how U.S. social-science theory has been challenged by the international experience. First, the intellectual collapse of the modernization paradigm was a direct result of social realities that persisted in contradicting the hypotheses embedded in the paradigm. It was a clear case of social events refusing to give way. The Lipset hypothesis, for example, maintained that democratic political stability and economic development were mutually reinforcing. Yet economic development has covaried as often or more often with authoritarian regimes (Taiwan, South Korea, Argentina, South Africa, pre-Khomeini Iran) than with regimes based on competitive elections and First Amendment freedoms. More to the point, economic development has proved not to be linear, Rostow's stages of economic development notwithstanding. There has been no inevitable progression in the growth of gross national product in many Third World countries. Economic decay or stagnation occur, as do economic growth and development.

More important, *interpreting* the failure of the modernization hypothesis has largely been the task of non-Western scholars, dependency theory as fashioned by Latin Americans being the best example. Despite its now-recognized shortcomings as a comprehensive explanation of Third World economic life, dependency theory alerted social science to a fundamentally different way of looking at the economic transactions between the industrial West and the nonindustrial societies of Latin America, Africa, and Asia.

At a deeper level, with the collapse of the modernization hypothesis came profound doubts about the progressiveness of history and, indeed, about the superiority of Western civilization. Anthropologist Bernard S. Cohn has cogently argued the link between modernization theory—the twentieth century's version of social evolutionism—and attempts at politico-economic dominance. Modernization theory, in making the present of one civilization the past of another, says to Asians, Africans, or Latin Americans: "What you are today we have been in the past; you may become what we are today, but by that time we of course will be something else because we will have gone on."[8] This is to impose on history a temporal analytic scheme that both locates the dominators and the dominated and helps justify that order.

Cohn reviews the (largely negative) consequences of modernization theory for anthropology and history, including the tendency to view culture and society as composed of "aspects, indicators, bits and pieces of things, which can be scaled and ranked to build indices of modernization" in which meaning is ignored and the integrity of culture denied. In this example and in others, the collapse of a Western theoretical construct, when confronted with the realities and the interpretations of non-Western societies, has liberated the affected social-science disciplines from what can be seen in retrospect as intellectual constrictions.

The growth of Marxist scholarship within American social science has been one of the most dramatic developments of the past two decades. Obviously, the introduction of Marxian analysis owes much more to contact with European scholars (and in this sense is related to internationalism) and to the critical protest politics of the 1960s and 1970s than to the facet of internationalism treated in this chapter. Still, area studies have made an interesting if indirect contribution by helping to renew concern with theories of the state.

From the 1920s to the 1950s, American social science concentrated on methodological developments, especially on the incorporation of quantification. This concentration led in turn to an emphasis on micro studies—for example, voting behavior in political science, social mobility in sociology, or labor behavior in economics. Largely absent were holistic social theories that dealt with the classic questions of the relations between the state and society.

There has now been a renewal of interest in theories of the state, led in large part by Marxists. But students of Third World countries have also made their contribution. Area-studies scholars often take the entire nation-state as their unit of analysis; they write scholarly books about countries, including Nigeria, Ghana, Burma, and Mexico. This form of scholarship has been rare among social scientists, who applied the techniques of quantification to various aspects of American society. Insofar as social-science scholarship in and about the United States thought about the state, it was mostly to argue that the state was a reflection of other social forces: pluralism, with its view that the state was only a referee for policy, which emerged from the variety of demands generated by numerous social groups; or elitism, with its view that the state primarily served the needs of a dominant, even conspiratorial, minority.

These earlier theoretical views have now given way to the idea that the state can be a relatively autonomous actor, influencing as well as being influenced by the social structure. We now have theorists who use the term *state strength* or *state capacity* in order to focus attention on whether a given state can perform any of numerous tasks expected of it—not only the traditional tasks of protecting territorial boundaries and maintaining internal order, but also the developmental tasks of transforming social structures or reallocating society's wealth. The view that states have varying capacities to promote economic development or to affect how income is distributed comes as no surprise to area-studies scholars, who from the beginning have had to concern themselves with how effectively new nations could transform the social structures and social values deposited by the mix of colonial practice and precolonial culture. The renewed interest in theories of the state no doubt has many origins. But certainly some of the credit for its growth belongs to the area-studies focus and the consequent internationalization of the social sciences. Area studies intellectually prepared the way for regarding the state as a discrete institution, more or less capable of acting on its own to promote or retard social change.

Current Development and Future Prospects

Thus, in its international activities U.S. social science has moved from area studies, in which the host country is primarily a research site, to an emphasis on skill transfer (the missionary impulse) and collegiality with local scholars, to a fundamental reshaping of the balance of trade in social-science ideas and approaches. Certain core concepts and methodologies in U.S. social science have been reformulated as American scholars have accommodated their institutions and their science to the international experience.

There is no reason to presume that we have now completed the process of internationalization. Of the several major current trends, such as the epistemological innovations already cited or the revival of questions concerning state and society, I will concentrate on the worldwide growth of a research-and-development or problem-solving emphasis in social science. This emphasis, which is international in scope, has far-reaching consequences for the traditional disciplinary base of the social sciences and for the utility and vulnerability of the enterprise we call social science.

Problem-Oriented Research

The activity I discuss has many different labels: social R & D, applied research, policy analysis, action-oriented studies. These various labels share a common assumption: the *research problems* selected come from the pool of *social problems* with which the society is coping. Systematic social inquiry—both the kind of data collected by social-science methods and the analytic techniques available to the social sciences—is expected to contribute relevant knowledge to the mission agencies, private or public, that are responsible for coping with poverty, hunger, unemployment, disease, crowding, and so on. Here, the word *expected* is critical; one of the defining characteristics of the research is the motivation of sponsor and scholar. Both are motivated by a concern for the social problem at hand, a concern that supersedes the traditional instinct of disciplinary research to choose as research problems those with the greatest promise of furthering the theoretical frontiers and skills of the discipline.

Problem-oriented research is frequently conducted under contract with a government-mission agency, although in Third World countries the sponsor or contractor is often an international-aid agency. The researchers are sometimes in government-research bureaus, and increasingly in consultancy firms and for-profit research corporations.

New methodologies and research strategies have been devised: program evaluation, cost-benefit analysis, impact studies, social experiments, and analytic techniques for dealing with longitudinal data sets. In some nations, certainly in the United States, specialized training programs have been designed. Initially these training programs supplemented traditional graduate training in the discipline-based social sciences, but increasingly they have come to substitute for traditional graduate work.

One of the most remarkable aspects of problem-oriented research is its rapid and extensive diffusion around the world. It is one of the few major developments in the social sciences that does *not* covary with the economic development of a nation or even with the maturity of the social science community within the nation.

This is quickly apparent from a comparison of area studies with problem-oriented research, both social-science inventions that have matured since World War II. Only the United States has a really advanced area-studies emphasis within the social sciences, although it is closely followed by other advanced industrial nations that have strong social-science communities. Japan has a rich tradition in sinology and in more recent years has developed world-class programs in Southeast Asian studies. Britain and France and, to a smaller extent, Belgium and the Netherlands, have long been associated with studies in and of their former colonies. The Soviet Union has invested in area studies where this served its strategic needs, including, of course, a major effort in American studies (which the United States has reciprocated). Less economically advanced nations, even those with strong social-science traditions such as India, South Korea, and Brazil, have not mustered extensive area-studies efforts, although they have often developed strong regional programs that have taken scholars somewhat outside their national boundaries. The general pattern is clear. The economically most advanced nations tend to have the most extensive and best-financed social-science programs, and extensive and well-financed programs tend to include research and training on a large number of nations other than one's own.

The tendency for development in the social sciences to covary with the level of national development characterizes not only area studies; postdoctoral-research opportunities, specialized journals, multiple-year research funding and national research facilities such as data archives, field staffs, and sampling frames for national studies are attributes of social science more likely to be found in the economically advanced than in the developing nations.

Problem-oriented research, in contrast, is not more pronounced in the more developed nations. A comparison of the United States and China, Japan and South Korea, Great Britain and India, Sweden and Kenya reveals a slightly negative correlation between the level of national development and the proportion of effort and investment within the social sciences that is devoted to policy studies, even though the absolute level of social-science resources would be higher in the more developed countries. Whereas, historically, inventions in the social sciences (theoretical, methodological, or institutional) have diffused from the more to the less developed nations, this pattern has been broken by the nearly simultaneous development of problem-oriented research communities around the world.

The reasons for this development have not been adequately investigated, but three factors are probably important. The social sciences were introduced into most developing countries at a time when the concept of development dominated public discourse. The atmosphere created by the language of development—rural development, educational development, economic development, and the like—focused scientific attention on the impediments to development, which quite naturally led to research on specific problems. Second, and closely related, is the emphasis on indigenization and its accompanying theme of a "social science for local problems." That is, the creation of an indigenous social science in theory and methods as well as personnel has not only liberated the local research community from Western concepts but also directed it to immediate social conditions. Commentary from and about Third World social science is heavily laced with the sentiment that social science has a responsibility to help the country develop, to contribute solutions to the problems of poverty, illiteracy, and so on.

A final reason for the extensiveness of problem-oriented research in many developing countries is the incentive structure for research. Here the role of international-aid agencies should be noted. Although they are not solely responsible for establishing a reward system for problem-oriented research, these agencies have substantial resources for social-science research. They also have internal requirements that investments in Third World countries be independently evaluated, if at all possible, by local researchers. Insofar as these investments are in social-service programs, the evaluation effort will claim the skills of the local social-science community. This creates a market demand for the skills and training associated with applied social research.

For the purposes of this chapter, the reasons for the worldwide growth of problem-oriented social research are less important than some of the potential consequences. Problem-oriented research, to be successful, must become self-consciously change-oriented. It is social inquiry that identifies policy alternative, considers implementation strategies, and assesses the probable consequences associated with different policies and implementations. Such a social science will combine the traditional disciplines in new and potentially innovative ways. For example, it might draw its research questions from economics and political science and select its research strategies from anthropology and history, thus linking the theoretical questions of choice-behavior and incentive structures with interpretative and historical methods of inquiry. How do cattle-raiding practices among the Boran of Kenya affect decisions about cattle marketing? How do ancient political rivalries among Peruvian peasants affect agricultural production? How do traditional belief systems affect whether the rural poor seek health treatment through ritual, herbs, witchcraft, or modern biomedicine? These political, economic, and cultural questions will require answers if problem-oriented research is to make a contribution to development strategies.

In these illustrations we see the promise of a social science designed to help Third World nations overcome the frustrations of failed development schemes. Our excitement about the promise of a problem-oriented social science should, however, be tempered. Three observations should give us pause: the possible deterioration of scientific standards, the inherent limitations of problem-oriented research, and the potential loss within the social sciences of a home for social criticism.

Scientific Standards

There are some signs that a problem-oriented focus within the social sciences is growing at the expense of disciplinary research. This does not by definition damage scientific standards, but it is worth remembering that improved methodologies and measurement strategies have traditionally been developed within the disciplines. It is also within the disciplines that increasingly complex understandings of social processes and social behavior have been advanced. It is disciplinary research that has tried to insulate social science from politicization by resolutely insisting on peer review and open publication. Historically, the disciplines have been the bearers of the scientific standard, have concerned themselves with adding to our stock of research skills and tools, and have been dedicated to cumulative research tradition.

In principle, there is nothing to prevent these traditional goals and standards from being absorbed by the problem-oriented research community. But as social science is turned toward a research agenda set by the problems of society rather than by the unanswered questions of a discipline, it will be tempting to gravitate toward the engineering model (find the solution that promises the best and quickest result) and away from the scientific models (seek research problems that place the most exacting demands on our scientific methods and theories). If social science drifts away from standard scientific goals, it will do so at the risk of creating a fragmented and noncumulative social science. In the decades to come, our theories will take on an ad-hoc, problem-specific character and our skills will not keep pace with the increasing demands placed upon them. Disciplinary research will suffer; so, too, will problem-oriented research. The quality of applied research is nearly always associated with whether it is rooted in the best theories and methods available from the traditional disciplines. Loosening problem-oriented research from its disciplinary moorings, which would be inevitable if the disciplines are weakened, risks creating a superficial social science. David Court's account of East African social science, presented in chapter 6, documents how rapidly scientific standards can be attenuated.

Whether scholars can simultaneously protect scientific standards and fashion a problem-oriented research strategy is one of the major challenges facing the international community of social scientists. Failure to meet this challenge will exact a heavy cost. Fortunately, some of our better scholars are beginning to wrestle with the various dimensions of the challenge, which range all the way from the most perplexing intellectual questions about the relation between policy intervention and social behavior, to issues of appropriate institutions, research procedures, and standards.

Inherent Limitations of Problem-Oriented Research

Freud spoke of those "impossible professions" in which one can be sure beforehand of achieving unsatisfying results. To his list of impossible professions—education, government, analysis—we certainly would add a social science designed to contribute to the development process of Third World nations. It is not an enterprise likely to realize spectacular results, or even very satisfying ones. This is partly because problem solving has its own dynamic, which continuously replenishes the store of problems confronting science or a society.

Only in a limited sense is a scientific problem solved; scientific inquiry necessarily leads to new problems and puzzles, and in this sense there is no end to a problem-solving activity. Science expands simultaneously the boundaries of what we know and what we do not know. Learning something about the workings of the human mind, the complexities of an organization, the history of a society, or the dimensions of culture will always lead to new questions.

The same is true of social-problem solving; with solutions come new social conditions that create other problems. People like to build on past accomplishments; therefore, their aspirations have no fixed limit. Research on an acceptable standard of living, for example, suggests that what is acceptable for any given population group is a product of its recent past. People generally want a little more than what they have. Moreover, what they want varies with what their neighbors have. Comparisons with past accomplishments and with visible neighbors exert an upward pressure on aspirations. Aspiration-level mechanisms (themselves a discovery of social-science research) redefine the issues with which societies, including their sciences, must cope. The fact that tuberculosis is no longer a killing illness does not make us patient with the slow progress of cancer research. The human engineering research that helps mere mortals fly jumbo jets also increases the complexity of the technical systems that humans are supposed to manage. The complexities of the problems for which the social sciences might be useful will always be one step ahead of our problem-solving abilities: social scientists work with the world as they find it, and the world moves, changes, progresses, and reverses direction. New problems rest on previous and therefore temporary solutions, if, indeed, *solutions* is the correct term at all.

It is for this reason that we speak of coping with rather than solving social problems. A problem-oriented social science may "solve" a research problem in the narrow sense, but about all it can offer the unsolvable social problem is intelligence that can be used by institutions that are practiced in coping. In understanding the limits of social research, we advance its ability to contribute. We also protect its scientific integrity. To claim for social science what it cannot provide, to expect it to be a substitute government or a substitute market mechanism, is to subject it to double jeopardy. First, it will fail as a problem-solving enterprise; second, it will fail as a science.

Social Science as a Client Community

Problem-oriented social science is often organized in terms of its relationship with the state. Social scientists work on research problems that are largely set by the agenda of the government. The research setting is often a government agency (a planning bureau or an intelligence agency) or a specialized research institution supervised by a government agency. Where the research settings are not themselves part of the state, client-oriented social science operates in consultancy firms and contract houses. Government solicits research through procurement arrangements that do not differ much from the methods used to procure typewriters, military hardware, building and contracting services, or numerous other products and services.[9] Training programs stress the skills that equip investigators for research on public-policy questions. Research norms stress schedules and budget-monitoring, for a government needs information on a timely basis and within the agreed-upon budget. Researchers talk in terms of "deliverables" rather than "findings," of reports and executive summaries rather than articles and books. Carried to an extreme, the client emphasis would transform social science into a profession of social engineers seeking sociological fixes for the problems with which government is coping. Although this extreme is so far nonexistent, many of the features that could lead to this transformation are pronounced tendencies in various nations.

A social science that is "under contract" to government is not likely to provide a home for broad, critical thinking about social issues. Yet this too is a task of a change-oriented social-science community, as Edgardo Boeninger documents and elaborates in chapter 10. Boeninger persuasively argues that social science must connect with the policy process at multiple levels, not only at the technocratic level but also at the level of setting global political goals and development strategies. This more general task is hampered unless at least part of the social-science enterprise is drawing its intellectual strength from philosophy and history, and these are not disciplines likely to be supported as social science increasingly turns its attention to the specific problems of development.

What is at stake, then, is the relationship between ideas and authority. We cannot assess social science around the world without reaching a deeper understanding of how power uses ideas and how ideas shape the purposes to which power is directed. This issue is itself a priority research question for social inquiry.

What we conclude as scholars and how we subsequently behave as foundation officers and science administrators has consequences for the vitality and utility of an international social-science community. In my view, we have not adequately understood either aspect. The increasing internationalization of the social sciences provides a remarkable opportunity to address both issues—how to maintain an autonomous science that can expand its skills and augment its theoretical understanding, and how to connect what we learn with attempts to improve the functioning of societies and the life conditions of individuals. On these issues, there is no developed world and developing world. There is an international social science that must collectively deal with the *social* and the *science* in the social sciences.

Notes

1. Robert B. Hall, *Area Studies: With Special Reference to Their Implications for Research in the Social Sciences* (New York: Social Science Research Council, 1947), pp. 81–87.

2. Elinor G. Barber and Warren Ilchman, *International Studies Review, A Staff Study* (New York: Ford Foundation, September 1979).

3. Robert E. Ward, "Statement on Advanced Training and Research in International Studies," in *President's Commission on Foreign Language and International Studies: Background Papers and Studies* (Washington, D.C.: Government Printing Office, 1979), p. 147.

4. Hwang San-duk, South Korean minister of education, in the inaugural address to the Second Conference of the Association of Asian Social Science Research Councils, *Asian Social Scientists,* no. 2 (1979), p. 11.

5. Clifford Geertz, "Thick Description: Toward an Interpretive Theory of Culture," in his *The Interpretation of Cultures* (New York: Basic Books, 1973), p. 5.

6. Ibid., p. 23.

7. Ibid., p. 26.

8. Bernard S. Cohn, "History and Anthropology: The State of Play," *Comparative Studies in Society and History* 22 (April 1980):212.

9. Indeed, social science in the United States is often procured according to administrative rules and procedures initially designed for the procurement of aircraft engines, weapons systems, and similar military components. Needless to say, such procedures have not transferred very effectively from the procurement of engine parts, which can be tested against exact and exacting standards, to the procurement of ideas and interpretations.

2

The Limits of Development Research

Paul Streeten

Introduction and Summary

In this paper,[1] I examine some of the problems that arise when research on social and economic development is carried out by scholars from rich countries with established and comparatively well endowed centers of learning. Research is itself a social activity, though social scientists tend to neglect the analysis of their own activities.[2] Here the social sciences will be treated as a form of (intellectual) technology.

Technology has been defined as the "skills, knowledge and procedures for making, using and doing useful things."[3] In spite of this broad definition, which covers, in addition to technical knowledge, knowledge of organization, administration, and management, the concept is not entirely appropriate for applied social science. Although there are some similarities with commercial technologies, there are also important differences. I shall ask what are the scope and the limits of the use and transfer of development research and what social, political, philosophical, and moral problems arise when scholars from one set of countries carry out social research on and in substantially poorer foreign countries.

In the second section, I contrast the linear, stages-of-growth, missing-component view of development with the view that underdevelopment is partly the result of the system of international relations, whether through malign exploitation or benign neglect on the part of the developed countries. Research itself can then be regarded either as providing a missing component or as being part of the oppressive or neglectful system. The role of rich-country support is radically different according to which view is accepted.

In the third section, I examine critically the charges that have been made by developing countries against research on their problems and in their territory by scholars from rich countries. The five main charges are (a) academic imperialism; (b) irrelevance, inappropriateness, and bias of concepts, models, and theories; (c) research in the service of exploitation; (d) domination through a superior and self-reinforcing research infrastructure; and (e) illegitimacy.

I conclude that basic knowledge is a common good in use but not in production. Its pursuit unites scholars across national frontiers. Truth cannot be nationalized, but there exist bias, distortion, and intellectual imperialism in a quite different sense from the one often decried, the correction of which is demanded by true scholarship. Scholarship rejects diplomacy and tact, though sensitivity is essential in social studies and tactics are in order if implementation is desired. The infrastructure of research is subject to increasing returns (both physical and intellectual), so that polarization, dominance, and dependence will tend to be established. There is an infant-industry argument for encouraging research in developing countries even, initially, at lower standards. This argument should, however, be clearly distinguished from arguments for parceling up what is the unity of scholarship. All ideas should be exposed to worldwide scrutiny and criticism.

In the fourth section, I distinguish between different arguments for collaboration in research between rich and poor countries and try to separate different reasons for such collaboration. These motives range from using the local institute in a subservient capacity to participatory theory construction. Collaboration between rich- and poor-country scholars, like joint business ventures, may be merely a facade for domination, but this can be avoided by first building up research capacity and then entering into genuine joint ventures. But the choice between capacity and quality raises difficult problems of objectives, time, discount rates, and risk. As there are grounds for collaboration, there are also grounds for specialization. But the economically appealing rule that countries should specialize according to their relative intellectual and physical endowments cannot be applied to research.

The fifth section discusses the question whether research in rich countries should confine itself to the interface of rich-poor relations or whether development research is an indivisible whole. The arguments for confining it to the interface are: (a) this is an area in which rich countries can act; (b) this escapes the charge of academic imperialism; (c) it avoids the paradox of rich-country institutions propagating indigenous capacity building; and (d) it avoids the impropriety and counterproductivity of advocating radical solutions for others. Objections to confinement to the interface are: (a) since not everyone can be prevented from doing research on the domestic issues of the poor countries, balance demands that anyone should be free to correct a possible imbalance; (b) attention by foreigners to domestic issues of poor countries may be a correction to internal brain drain and encourage domestic work on relevant issues; (c) international and internal variables interact and a division is methodologically impossible; (d) free research should not be limited by national boundaries. In spite of these objections, interface issues are in the present climate particularly suited for rich-country research. The section also discusses, as part of the interface, research on questions of international cooperation, confrontation (conflict), and LDC self-reliance.

The sixth section deals with problems arising from the origin and organization of research funds, the questions whether and when money is tainted, whether there should be concentration or dispersal of sources of funds, and how to bridge the gap between the requirements of policymakers and the freedom of academic research. It warns against sacrificing the important to the urgent.

The last section contains a brief warning against oversimple quantification in an attempt to emulate the "hard" sciences. It ends on the skeptical note that we still do not know what are the springs of development, and a warning that we should not sacrifice the important to the manageable.

Whence Do We Come? Where Are We? Where Do We Go?

Our perception of development has undergone a radical change in recent years. The thinking of the fifties and sixties, codified in the Pearson Report, was dominated by W.W. Rostow's doctrine that development is a linear path along which all countries travel. The advanced countries had, at various times, passed the state of "takeoff," and the developing countries are now following them. Development "was seen primarily as a matter of 'economic growth,' and secondarily as a problem of securing social changes necessarily associated with economic growth. It was taken for granted that organizing the march along the development path was the prime concern of governments."[4]

The linear view begged a host of questions about the nature, causes, and objectives of development. It tended to focus on constraints or obstacles, the removal of which would set free the "natural" forces making for the steady move toward ever higher incomes. This view is reflected, for instance, in the "General Principles Governing the Award of ODA Grants for Economic and Social Research in Developing Countries." The first sentence states: "The fundamental criterion is that the research proposed must be related to the problems that *impede* the social or economic progress of developing countries" [italics mine].

Applied to the areas of international relations, this view calls on the rich countries to supply the "missing components" to the developing countries and thereby help them to break bottlenecks or remove obstacles. These missing components may be capital, foreign exchange, skills, or management. Research itself and its technical and commercial applications also can serve to provide these missing components. The doctrine provides a rationale for international capital aid, technical assistance, trade, private foreign investment. By breaking bottlenecks, rich countries can speed up the development process in underdeveloped countries.

This linear or stages-of-growth view has come under heavy fire. It was criticized on logical, moral, political, historical, and economic grounds. Logically, it should have been clear that the coexistence of more and less advanced countries is bound to make a difference (for better or worse) to the development efforts and prospects of the less advanced, compared with a situation where no other country was ahead or the distance was not very large. The larger the gap and the more interdependent the international system, the less relevant are the lessons to be learned from the early starters. Morally and politically, the linear view ruled out options of different styles of development. Inexorably, we were all bound to pass through the Rostovian stages, in the words of the famous limerick, like a tram, not a bus.

There is another view which has gained adherents with the spreading disenchantment about development and about the international contribution to it. According to this view, the international system of rich-poor relationships produces and maintains the underdevelopment of the poor countries. In various ways, malignly exploitive or benignly neglectful, the coexistence of rich and poor societies renders the efforts of the poor societies to choose their style of development more difficult or impossible. Certain groups in the developing countries—entrepreneurs, salaried officials, employees—enjoy high incomes, wealth, and status and, constituting the ruling class, they perpetuate the international system of inequality and conformity. Not only Marxists but also a growing number of non-Marxists have come to attribute a large part of underdevelopment to the existence and the policies of the industrial countries of the West, including Japan and the Soviet Union.

This shift from a linear theory of missing components to some version of a theory of neocolonialism was accompanied by a change in emphasis of what constitutes the meaning and measure of development. Economic growth by itself was found to be largely irrelevant, and the eradication of poverty, reduced inequality, the need for more, securer, more diversified, and more satisfying jobs and livelihoods took the place of growth.

A third shift in interest and emphasis was away from the specific problems of development and toward the world's common problems: resources and, in particular, energy; the environment and its global pollution; the sea and the seabed; world population. Here again, the new emphasis was on scarcity and interdependence, on potential interest conflicts and hence the need to evolve a world order that resolves them.

These shifts in the perception of development were accompanied by a change from the abounding optimism about development and the potential contribution to it by the rich, in the fifties and sixties, to a deep pessimism in the seventies.

These shifts also affected the view of the role of research. In the linear, missing-components view, research in rich countries or by rich-country scholars can contribute bits of knowledge and thereby remove a particular constraint. In the neo-Marxian view, research may itself be part and parcel of the international oppressive, or at least impeding, system, depriving the developing countries of brains, or diverting the attention of their brains to irrelevant problems, or inducing them to produce apologias for their ruling class and the unjustifiable world system. The new view has been reflected in growing tensions and difficulties encountered in research relationships and resistance to the admission of social science researchers to developing countries.

In several places in this paper, and particularly in the next section, I shall try to analyze how this shift of perception affects the role of the research donor. What should be noted here is that irrespective of the scientific status of the new view, the mere fact that influential people in developing countries hold it is bound to make a difference to the research relationship between rich and poor.

But in addition to this fundamental shift, there have been shifts in fads and fashions. Just as fashion setters emphasize, display, and conceal at different times different parts of the female anatomy (though, presumably, all are there all the time), so economic and social research tends to be preoccupied with different aspects of the variables in the social system, to the neglect of others. Certain subjects or views, at any given time, have "sex appeal." The explosive interest in equality at the expense of economic growth can be regarded as such a fashion. Other cycles are the emphasis on industrial import substitution, followed by recommendations of industrial export promotion, and now, the beginnings of some disenchantment with industrial export-led growth and a new turn to primary export restrictions. Another fashion cycle is the switch from investment in physical capital to investment in formal education, followed by disillusion in formal education and a turn to informal education and motivation; also the swings between functional literacy and mass literacy campaigns. Another cycle is that between pessimism and euphoria about world food production. The debates on agriculture versus industry, large-scale versus small-scale techniques, formal versus "informal" sector, deteriorating versus improving terms of trade, material versus social objectives, growth versus the environment, and others have found, in turn, a clustering of views round alternating sides of the pendulum. The importance and the irrelevance or damage of development aid, as viewed by both donors and recipients, represent another swing. One could go on.

To the extent that these swings of the pendulum are indications of important underlying forces, research donors should clearly be concerned with them. But often they bypass the important issues, and looking back even only a few years, or even months, one is astonished at the problems that vexed the profession. With the wisdom of hindsight, it is now clear that the really important issues lay elsewhere. It would be nice to be able to predict where the next breakthrough in research is going to be, so that we can prepare ourselves for it. Yet, such a forecast would involve a logical contradiction. If I, or anyone else, knew where the *next* breakthrough was going to be, we should already have performed it and it would be the *last* breakthrough.

One insurance against becoming a mere follower of fashion is to continue to support research on unfashionable topics. Who knows, they might hit the headlines tomorrow. Energy has ousted the conventional ways of looking at security, money, and trade; concern with the environment has driven out old-fashioned growth; and the politics of bargaining is upsetting the assumption of atomistically competing units. A project on "Man (or, better, Woman), energy, the environment, and equality" sounds at the moment of writing as irresistible as the well-known best seller entitled *I Made Love to a Goat for the CIA and Saw God*. Yet, the burning issues of the 1980s may be quite different ones.

The Role of the Social Sciences and the Social Scientist in Development Studies

Development research in the developed countries has been criticized on several grounds.

1. First, there is the charge of academic, scientific, intellectual, or cultural imperialism or colonialism.[5] The critics see a close parallel between the operations of the more ruthless mining companies and the developed-country research teams. These teams move into the country with their already designed research projects, trying to "mine" for data and statistics, using locals for semiskilled activities like interviewing, filling out forms, and interpreting, but preserve for themselves at headquarters the monopoly-rent-earning activities of basic research design, processing, and publishing. The "researched" country, having been stripped of its data, suffers the humiliation of seeing the results published in the journals or books of the advanced industrial countries, adding prestige and glory to the foreign professors and their institutions. Sometimes, as in the case of certain multinational firms and the CIA, mining is combined with undermining; the research is used to interfere with the democratic processes of the country and to further the aims of foreign powers.

2. Second, there is the charge that "Western" concepts, models, paradigms, and the questions asked—both the agenda for research and the filing cabinets—are inappropriate for understanding the utterly different

circumstances of developing societies. Here again, an analogy is drawn between the inappropriate industrial and agricultural techniques and the concepts, models, and methods of economics and other social sciences. These alien concepts and models determine inappropriate policies and either divert attention from the real problems (e.g., corruption) or become apologies for existing power structures (when the charge becomes the one discussed under 3). Excessive sophistication, esoteric irrelevance, ignorance, and false beliefs conveyed by these doctrines are opportunistic and serve vested interests. Heavy emphasis on capital/output ratios, savings and investment ratios, the notion of unemployment and employment, aggregate income, and others have, it is argued, misled policy makers (or strengthened them in their narrow class interests) and have concealed the importance of institutional and other structural changes, such as land reform, corporate reform, tax reform, credit and banking reform, the creation or strengthening of an independent, honest, and efficient administrative service, or an egalitarian educational system. The paradigms of "Western" social science serve as blinkers or escape mechanisms, preventing scholars and policy makers from seeing and acting upon the strategic fronts.

3. A stronger version of the charge of opportunistic irrelevance is the view that advanced-country research is part of the system of international capitalism, in which underdevelopment makes possible the growth of the capitalist countries of the West. Private foreign investment, the multinational enterprise, international trade, international monetary arrangements, universities, and, indeed, research itself all reinforce the position of the advanced, industrial countries, together with a small class of privileged people in the underdeveloped countries, and serve the exploitation and the continuing underdevelopment of the majority of people in the poor countries. The framework of research is essentially an apology and justification for the neocolonial apparatus of exploitation.

4. Fourth, there is the charge of domination and dependence in a rather different sense. The complaint here is not that the developing countries are exploited (as in the charge of intellectual imperialism or neocolonialism), nor that the concepts and models are inappropriate or ideological. The trouble is simply that as a result of the concentration of funds, greater scope for specialization, and the accumulation of skills, the scholars from the developed countries have gained a superiority and this superiority, combined with the institutions and attitudes derived from it and reinforcing it, prevents research institutions and attitudes in the developing countries from growing to strong and independent status. Both the incentive and the capacity to generate new ideas and to carry out indigenous research on relevant problems are weakened by the operations of the foreign scholars and institutes. The relationship between the foreign professor and the local workers is often that of patron and protégé. The patron will try to get jobs,

write references, arrange a fellowship to the metropolitan country for his protégé. But the relation is one of dependence of the developing-country researcher on the favors of the foreign patron. Only more inward-looking policies toward research (it is argued), more cooperation with countries at similar levels of development, and the pulling down of a curtain against the stunting influence from outside hold out hope for the growth of realistic and relevant research, based on self-reliance, self-confidence, and autonomy. It is a kind of intellectual infant-industry argument.

The economic analogy can be extended. What is needed (it has been argued) is import substitution in research, the elimination of stultifying foreign competition, the establishment of a temporary domestic monopoly.

5. Fifth, there is the charge of illegitimacy. If this amounted merely to saying that scholarship should be confined to the territory within a scholar's national boundaries, it could be dismissed without further discussion. But a question of moral (though not intellectual) legitimacy is raised when research leads to the recommendation of actions, the cost of which is borne entirely by other people. There is something, if not illegitimate, at any rate distasteful in people from safe and comfortable positions recommending revolutions or painful reforms, or, for that matter, the maintenance of the *status quo*, to others.[6] This is, of course, a much more general point, not confined to research on poor countries. It raises the much discussed question of the moral responsibilities of the scientist. But it arises in particularly acute form if the subjects of investigation are countries on whose government we have no influence.

To what extent are these five charges justified? The analogy between mining or quarrying and searching for knowledge is surely false. The more nickel, copper, or gold I have, the less is left for you. This is not so with knowledge. We all can draw on the stock of knowledge, and my discovery does not normally deprive you of intellectual profits from it, though it may deprive you of recognition for the discovery.

More important, there are common standards of scholarship, which assert their universality and the solidarity of any one scholar with the international fraternity of other scholars. Commitment to the search for knowledge, to scientific objectivity, and to telling the truth as one sees it knows no national frontiers. In addition to the intrinsic value of this commitment, loyalties to universal values that cut across frontiers have their political value in an age when nationalism, a powerful Christian heresy, and ideologies have become dominant secular religions. In this sense, therefore, there cannot be African, Asian, and Latin American criteria for truth or validity. Mining companies can be nationalized; criteria for truth cannot.[7]

However, the problem is complicated and sometimes confused by people mistaking economics for a form of logic, truth for logical validity, and criteria of truth for its empirical content. For if economics is equated with a form of logic ("the logic of choice"), it would follow that there is only a single, universal economic science from China to Peru and no separate economics for Africa, Asia, or Latin America.[8] Yet, clearly, if we turn from the standards and criteria by which we judge evidence, methods, and conclusions to the content of our work, it should be plain that very different propositions are likely to be true for different societies. In this sense, it is perfectly legitimate to speak of "African," "Asian," or "Latin American" economics or politics or sociology. It is this confusion between logical validity and truth, to which some economists have themselves contributed, which is partly responsible for what appear to be nationalistic attacks on the "legitimacy" of "Western" social science.

It is part of scholarship to recognize the limitations of the propositions established and possibly applicable to one region (or period) but not, or not without modification, to another. It is understandable that territorial and temporal claims of the validity of certain theories have tended to be excessive and that there is, for this reason, an element of "imperialism" in the generalizations of social science. But this sense of "imperialism" is, of course, entirely different from the one discussed above. Thus, it can be argued that important elements of "scientific socialism" are an extrapolation and universalization of the experience of industrial England between 1780 and 1840, when inequalities increased and when, in the midst of fairly rapid industrial progress, the poor may, for a time, have become poorer. Ricardo and Malthus universalized the temporary pressures on land of the rapidly growing population of England, while technical progress lagged behind. The so-called General Theory of Employment, Interest, and Money is a rather special theory, applicable to the grossly underutilized resources in industrial countries during the Depression of the 1930s. Neoclassical economics, with its nicely calculated little more and little less, its assumptions of maximizing behavior and atomistic competition, may be regarded as a generalization of certain principles of petty-bourgeois housekeeping. And so one could go on. Not only the Ricardian theory of distribution, the Malthusian theory of population, the Marxist theory of the increasing misery of the masses, the Keynesian theory of employment, but also various theories of secular stagnation, secular inflation, secular shortages of dollars, food, or raw materials, or secular doom may all be projections onto a vast historical screen of the snapshots of a few years or decades and the magnified protests and responses to which these short-run experiences give rise. The designers of these theories suffer from a high elasticity of expectations or, less politely expressed, hysterical reactions.

If these doctrines had made more limited territorial and chronological claims, if they had confined themselves to their time and place, nobody would have paid much attention. They derive their interest and their significance from the grand design, the magnificent extrapolation, the large screen, from magnifying the trivial into the false. But it is quite legitimate (in the service of universal truth) to criticize orthodox Western models for their excessive claims, for their "intellectual imperialism." It is in the interest of honest work to assert that in Africa, Asia, Latin America, at very low levels of development, in another demographic setting, in tropical climates, in a different international system, and so on, they order things differently.

Yet, such limitation of excess claims, if it is legitimate, must be recognized as legitimate by scholars wherever they may be. There have been sociologists (like Karl Mannheim), anthropologists (like Lucien Lévy-Bruhl), linguists (like Benjamin Lee Whorf), and philosophers of science (like Thomas Kuhn) who have argued that the criteria of truth and validity cannot be dependent on social, cultural, linguistic, or other existential factors, indeed that even asking questions about differences between beliefs and theories presupposes logically universal and fundamental criteria of truth.[9]

Those who claim that bias enters into social paradigms and theories and that "Western" social science is an apology of exploitation or a diversion maneuver are not always clear about the precise manner and form of entry. There appear to be at least four possibilities.[10]

1. Bias determines the *content*, and thus the *validity*, of the analysis *psychologically*.

a. The analysis is consciously false; the propositions are lies.
b. The distortion is semiconscious; there is wishful thinking, special pleading, a degree of self-deception.
c. The distortion is subconscious or unconscious; the conclusions are rationalizations.

It may, of course, be that one group of men implants what it knows to be false notions into the minds of others by manipulative efforts. If the victims are not aware of being manipulated, their beliefs would fall under 1*c*, while the activity of the manipulators (propaganda, conditioning) falls under 1*a*, at least as long as they do not believe their own lies.

Freudian rationalization is a method of resolving conflicts peculiar to the individual, whereas rationalization here considered serves to resolve social conflicts. Ideology is for society what the resolution of guilt through self-justification is for an individual. But tensions in the structure of society will tend to manifest themselves in the psychological problems of individuals, and the two spheres are not strictly separable.

In all three cases, *a*, *b*, and *c*, only *false* statements are contaminated. Ideology is defined as "false consciousness." Bias may provide a motive for finding a *logical* (as well as an illogical) basis for a desired conclusion, but the analysis is not then distorted. There is a sphere of objective thought.

The Archimedean point (i.e., the point from which the doctrine of biased determination is itself lifted into objectivity) is given by exposing the motives. (There is, however, a danger that this effort itself is contaminated by unexpressed bias.)

2. Bias determines the *content* and thus the *validity* of analysis by affecting the structure of thought (categories, presuppositions, premises, paradigms). Contamination is not a matter of individual or even social psychology, but everyone in a given situation who thinks at all has to think in a certain biased way. Probing of motives cannot eliminate implicit bias, for it is an essential condition of all thought.

Nowadays, a similar point is made by stressing the manner in which language influences the way we see, select, and analyze events, and thus opens the door to bias. First, it enters not only—as is generally recognized—into the selection and criticism of evidence, but also into our classifications and frames of reference. Particularly in social studies do we take our vocabulary from the field of study itself. Thus, the valuations of the market-place and of the political arena are carried unobtrusively into scientific analysis.

Second, language introduces a bias by adopting identical terms for situations that are similar in some respects, dissimilar in others. To use the same concept or model or metaphor to refer to different situations is a source of both danger and opportunity. Danger, because the reference may distort or misrepresent the facts; opportunity, because it may enlarge our vision by drawing attention to hitherto unnoticed features.

Third, there is the danger of seeing real essences behind terms of mere classification.[11]

In whatever manner we analyze the seepage of bias into analysis, it follows that not only false but *all* statements under this second heading are "ideological" and hence logically suspect, unless areas are cleared which are claimed to be exempt from bias. Thus, some writers say that (*a*) only certain historical *periods* (e.g., in a class society), or (*b*) only certain *fields of study* (e.g., social studies), or (*c*) only certain *classes* (e.g., the bourgeoisie) are subject to contamination, have "false consciousness."[12]

But the corollary that only certain periods, fields of study, classes, or men are free from bias can, of course, itself be a fruitful source of ideology. Combining *a*, *b*, and *c*, we arrive at the Marxist view that there is a proletarian social science in the late stages of capitalism to which truth is guaranteed. Particularly Georg Lukács has argued that only proletarian class-conscious thought represents reality "adequately." Mannheim (in his earlier work) believed that only the "socially unattached" (i.e., radical) intellectuals can seek the required "dynamic synthesis," a "total perspective," that overcomes the inadequate, partial, and biased conceptions of other groups. Hegel thought that reason revealed itself to philosophers (particularly Hegelian philosophers) at a certain stage of history. Nearer home, Marshall, Pigou, and others in the tradition of Benthamism imply that in the midst of interest clashes, only the state is an agency that can see and promote disinterestedly the public good.

On the other hand, some authors argue that it is not only valuations and bias, but other extraneous spheres that determine thought, e.g., social or economic *conditions* (as contrasted with *interests, aspirations, valuations*), natural environment, nationality, race, generation, geopolitical region. This determination may be conceived either as causal or as an expression of some kind of unity, like that which links the characteristics of a personality.

The Archimedean point cannot be reached empirically or logically, but only metaphysically. The "intellectuals," "the working class," the "Third World," the "wretched of the earth," or "action," "commitment," "a synthesis," or "an absolute sphere of values," guarantee objectivity. Or, using the linguistic approach, only a "perfect language" that exactly fits the facts could enable us to pull ourselves up by our own bootstraps. The attempt to save the theory from self-contradiction succeeds only through an arbitrary step into metaphysics. The choice lies between dogmatism and absurdity.

3. Bias has merely *selective* significance. It does not affect the content or validity of thought, but its direction.

a. It may be *positively selective*: bias determines *that* a proposition is made then and there. The questions asked are value-determined, but not the answers. The relation between bias and theories is not causal, but similar to the kind of determination by which a question "determines" an answer.

b. It may be *negatively selective*, preventing certain propositions from being made in certain situations. Thus, questions relevant to developing countries may never be asked by social scientists from rich countries. Research on such questions as tribalism, power structures, and corruption is ignored or neglected.

An Archimedean point is not here required, for validity is independent of valuations. The distinction, however, between type 3 and type 2 ideology is blurred when we remember that an inadequate, partial conception of reality may lead to bias not by commission but by omission. The Archimedean point would consist in scaling down the claims of the theory to less generality, but then it often loses all interest.

4. Valuations determine whether certain propositions are understood, recognized, publicly accepted. Again, no Archimedean point is required.

According to which of these views (1 through 4) is held, the role of criticism is (*a*) to show up and make explicit the more or less sinister motives in the false explanations of the opponents, or to psychoanalyze their theories, (b) to analyze the structure of their thought, (c) to fill in gaps in the selection, or (d) to relate ideas to their social setting. It is also obvious that these four views have radically different implications for the question as to what extent unexpressed value premises invalidate social theories. Yet, eminent exponents of these theories of ideology have shifted uneasily between self-destructive and fairly trivial positions. To say (a) that the tests of logic change with one's values is open to the old objection to skepticism: if the theory is untrue, no more is to be said; if true, its own objectivity must be denied. On the other hand, to say (b) that we meet with obstacles in our attempts to be impartial in thinking about social and political matters, especially in different settings, serves as a useful reminder that social scientists, too, are human. But the ambiguity between these two views lends apparent force to many theories that reject all "Western" paradigms.

It is likely that the limitations shown up by those combating the excess claims and correcting the distortions of biased ideologies will ultimately benefit work in and on the developed countries themselves. There is mutual illumination which a shutting off and "going it alone" would impede. This is a bonus, but even if it were not so, theories with excess claims are not "true for Europe but not true for Africa": they are simply not true.

I conclude that although the laws of logic and the criteria for truth must be universal, the concepts, models, premises, assumptions, paradigms, theories, or questions in the social sciences are in some respects peculiar. *There may be an African economics, distinct from a European economics; there can be no African truth.*[13] By rigorous analysis, by accumulation of evidence, and by explicitly bringing out value premises, errors and biases can be reduced. But there will always remain a residual of ideology. And this residual element may be particularly misleading if transferred from the experience of industrial countries to developing countries. It is for this reason that the assertion of the universality of the criteria for truth must be qualified, although the remedy cannot be found in "indigenous" theory construction or in erecting a barrier against "alien" doctrines.

One important element of truth in the charge of "Western" intellectual domination is the ideological component of "Western" theories just discussed. There is a second element of truth in these charges.

While the stock of fundamental knowledge is a public good, to be drawn on by anyone anywhere, the resources that enable scholars to conduct research are, of course, scarce, and the recognition, prestige, and fame that are the reward of successful work are competitive and by no means a free good. A scientific discovery can be used by anyone, but only one man can make it. And he reaps the monopoly rent of recognition.[14] Moreover, recognition attracts funds and funds make it possible to gain recognition: a cumulative process that will tend to penalize ill-endowed centers of learning.

No money: no ability to train and attract a high quality and a large quantity of scholars: no scope for specialization for good work: no recognition: no money. It is then understandable if institutions starved of funds in the developing countries should resent the well-endowed foreigners who use their work in the developing country to gain further recognition and hence even more funds to attract more and even better scholars. If this invasion is then accompanied by concepts, models, and paradigms that are irrelevant, unrealistic, or ideologically biased, if these concepts, models, and paradigms make excessive claims, if the behavior of the foreigners is tactless, insensitive, or patronizing, it is understandable that the indigenous scholars will charge the foreigners and their doctrines with being dominant and arrogant and that they will wish to bar them.

There is also a feeling that opportunities to present, exchange, develop, and communicate ideas and to implement them are much greater in the developed countries. Doers and thinkers meet at beautiful country houses like the Villa Serbelloni in Bellagio or in Ditchley Park or in Bürgenstock or in Königswinter or at Wilton Park, and from these meetings, clusters of ideas and policies emerge.[15] In rich countries, there is a continuing generation and exchange of ideas between policymakers and scholars from which paradigms and programs are crystallized. Nothing comparable exists in the Third World. Different paradigms, incorporating variables that are omitted, especially political and social factors, would create a different picture of reality and different programs for action. It is felt that existing opportunities for such a crystallization are inadequate or absent and that, in particular, the United Nations bodies have failed to generate the ideas on which policymakers could draw.

All this constitutes an argument for institution building in the Third World, to which I shall return. But the analogy with international trade, just like the analogy with quarrying and mining, is surely false. "Import substitution," the exclusion of foreign competition, and the establishment of a local monopoly in research, even if they were feasible, would not generate the kind of ideas that could eventually face international competition. The pursuit of knowledge is not like the pursuit of profits.

Finally, there is clearly some justification in the fifth charge, namely, moral illegitimacy, though the term "illegitimacy" is unfortunate. It is all too easy, and therefore exceedingly difficult for those who take their social responsibility seriously, to be a radical, a revolutionary, a reformer, or, for that matter, a conservative, for another country.[16] The moral commitment to objective research may conflict with the noncommitment to action or the commitment to nonaction.

But there is another side to it. Foreign support, whether financial or intellectual, is often welcome to scholars in developing countries because it gives them greater independence from the pressures of their own governments. What may appear from outside as illegitimate interference is then regarded, from inside, as a basis for autonomy, for critical detachment. It has been reported that authoritarian governments which applied strict political standards to the research financed by themselves did not interfere with externally financed research, even when it was critical. The universal commitment to scientific research and to presenting its conclusions as one sees them is not only fundamental to all scholarship, but its institutional expression through foreign support for research also has a political aspect. It may be one way in which critical and uncongenial views can be developed and expressed in a repressive regime. It follows from the commitment to objective research that the scholar, in presenting the results of his work, will not be concerned with tact, tactics, or diplomacy. He will not keep silent merely to spare feelings and he will not mince words. It would be a form of inverted snobbery and condescension if scholars from developed countries thought it necessary to treat "sensitive" problems of the developing countries with kid gloves, although this is what has largely happened, even in the very terminology of this sentence. Such diplomacy and inverted snobbery have reduced the intellectual standard of work in this field. Tact and diplomacy are, of course, necessary if recommendations are to be adopted by governments. But this must not affect the content and presentation of basic research, partly because it offends against the principles of scholarship and partly because policies based on blinkered analysis are bound to fail.

Such frankness and even bluntness is entirely consistent with, indeed is demanded by, empathy with and imaginative understanding of the problems analyzed, though not necessarily sympathy for all that is done. Some outside criticisms have, it is true, failed in their sensitivity to the social complexity. But then, some sycophantic or "diplomatic" work is at bottom patronizing and hence equally insensitive.

Are Western scholars more liable to impose biased or inappropriate concepts and models than scholars from the developing countries? Many of the "alternative" models used by Third World intellectuals have, of course, Western origins. Marxism is a Western doctrine. So are intermediate technology, structuralism, planning, cumulative causation, and growth poles.

Myrdal, Singer, Perroux, Ivan Illich, and Fritz Schumacher are all "Western" thinkers and Prebisch is only marginally an "underdeveloped" scholar. As illustration of "innovative economic contributions based on indigenous conditions and talent," Padma Desai quotes the early Soviet economists Evgenii Preobrazensky and G.A. Fel'dman, the Chinese shift from the Marxist emphasis on the revolutionary potential of the industrial proletariat to that of the rural masses,[17] and the Indian efforts at evolving an intermediate technology such as the Ambar Charkha and the Chinese campaign to produce steel from backyard blast furnaces, though both attempts were unsuccessful.[18] These are not altogether good examples of indigenous innovations of ideas and, in any case, the social science research content of the Chinese and Indian innovations is small, whereas the Russians are surely for this purpose "Western."

Perhaps more relevant are the studies carried out by the Economic Commission for Latin America (ECLA) in the fifties on import substitution, the structural theory of inflation, the relations between the "center" and the "periphery" and *dependencia*.

But with these exceptions, the new patterns have grown more out of praxis and experience than out of systematic research. Indeed, those who take a non-Keynesian view of the relation between the power of ideas and the good sense of practical experience see evidence that solutions to social problems are worked out by men and women going about their daily work, by politicians, party officials, farmers, businessmen, union officials, administrators, teachers, extension workers, and that the grand theories distill these practical experiences.[19] It would be arrogant, as well as wrong, to believe that only research is the source of new knowledge.

Paradoxically, the doctrine of the limits of transference may itself be regarded as a typically Western product and therefore as nontransferable.[20] This line leads us to the dilemma of the Cretan liar. More sinister, there is a short step (it might be argued) from the doctrine of the need to evolve alternative styles of thinking to the doctrine of "separate but equal" and from there to apartheid. It is quite easy to give the call for alternative sytems of thought a nasty racialist ring. The doctrine of nontransferability may be interpreted as an unpleasant form of Western neocolonialism. But, at least logically, this trap holds no danger. If nontransference must not be transferred because it is Western, transference is O.K. Rejection leads to acceptance.

I conclude that knowledge itself is a common good and that its pursuit unites scholars across the world;[21] that scholarship rejects diplomacy and tact, though sensitivity and imaginative understanding are essential in social studies and tactics are in order if implementation is desired; but that the concepts, models, and theories are often partial, inadequate, irrelevant, or biased in a manner which ignores or distorts the relevant problems; that while the *consumption* of knowledge is free, its *production* can be monopolized; and that the infrastructure of research (seminars, conferences, country houses, institutes, universities, travel, grants, sabbaticals, etc.) is subject to increasing returns, so that polarization, dominance, and dependence will tend to be established and reinforced. There is an intellectual and economic infant-industry argument for encouraging research in the weak periphery, even if it is initially of a lower standard than research carried out in established centers, but there is no argument for a local monopoly and against exposing ideas to worldwide scrutiny and criticism.

Equal or Unequal Partners in Research

Clearly, the commitment to universal standards of scholarship in no way reduces the need to encourage the growth and self-confidence of indigenous research institutes. It is now a cliché to say that research in developing countries must be sensitive and must be collaborative. When in Rome, do as the Romans do; better still, get a Roman to do it!

Although research links with department or institutes in LDCs are now generally advocated and, less widely, adopted, it is not always clear what the purpose of these links is. One might distinguish between the following objectives *from the point of view of the scholar in the developed country*. (Different objectives would be listed if we looked at joint ventures from the point of view of the developing country or its scholars.)

1. In order to conduct research in a particular country, a link with a domestic institute is helpful. It provides a source of data collectors, interviewers, interpreters, and other useful local resources. These are essentially ancillary services.

2. The link may be used for more or less blatantly political and tactical purposes. It may facilitate gaining approval from the authorities for conducting the project; it may remove criticism in the local press and by public opinion; it may make it easier to gain access to certain sources of information or it may be an essential condition for this.

3. A link may be thought necessary in assisting in the dissemination and application of policy-oriented research. Domestic institutes often have special links with government agencies and other policymaking bodies and the dissemination of research conducted in developed countries is facilitated when it is channeled through these institutes.

4. In some cases, the prestige of foreign institutions is greater than that of domestic ones in the developing countries. A link may then serve to add "respectability" and acceptability to the work of a local institute, even though the foreign link is only tenuous (perhaps confined to an occasional exchange of scholars, brief visits, or only a letterhead).

5. The link may be intended to build up and strengthen indigenous research capacity, whether of individual skills or of whole institutions. It is generally recognized that such capacity is highly desirable in itself and is a necessary condition for development. Outside links may then be a useful form of promoting this. If it were thought that this could be done better through teaching and assisting in curriculum design, the reply would be that research is best learned and taught by doing it. Teaching by itself (without research) is less effective in teaching how to do research, and would also attract less well qualified people.

6. A link may be desired in order to improve, through the association, the teaching capacity of the sponsoring institution.

7. Finally and ideally, the local institute may contribute professional

expertise at the highest level. The indigenous scholars, being more familiar with the society and the local problems, may improve the design of the research project, may help to ask the right questions and prevent errors, and may contribute to the right balance of emphasis. One may be even more ambitious and aim at what Susanne Hoeber Rudolph calls "participatory theory construction," an attempt to overcome the partial and fragmented vision of all social theory by complementing a "Western" approach by an "Eastern," a "white" by a "black" and "brown."[22] If what I have said about the imperialist claims of partial social theories is correct, such participatory theory construction has remedial value and can contribute to a more comprehensive and truly universal theory of society. Just as the vision of a mountain changes according to the point from which we observe it, so African, Asian, Latin American, or European partial visions may be brought together. An approach that joins different partial visions can give us a more accurate picture of reality. Participation may be the cure not only for political discord but also for intellectual distortion.

Some of the above objectives may be pursued jointly, but conflicts may arise. Collaboration agreements and joint ventures, in scholarship as in business, may be forms of window dressing. They may pretend that dominance and dependence do not exist where they do.

In such a situation, objective 5, help in building up research capacity (which may include help in reducing a heavy teaching load or help in reducing the time spent on supervising and organizing research of others by the few who could be better employed in doing the research themselves), may have to precede objective 7, genuine collaboration.

This roundabout way of strengthening research capacity raises important and difficult issues. The problem is sometimes presented as a trade-off between strengthening indigenous research skills and research quality. At least three questions should be asked.

1. What is the purpose of the support? Is it research or training for research? If training, is the intention to create or improve individual skills or whole institutions?
2. What is the time horizon? Is it important to have results of the highest quality soon or is it preferable to forego speedy results for the sake of more and better results later?
3. What risks is the donor prepared to take? The results of backing underdeveloped research in order to strengthen its capacity are even more uncertain than backing highest-quality research. Some projects will fail or be disappointing. Is there a case for diversification in order to spread risks; or, resources being scarce, should they be concentrated to reduce the risk of failure?[23]

If it were merely a question of timing and risk taking, the problem would be simple. The real difficulty is that there is an inconsistency between the teacher-pupil relationship and the equality implied in international collaboration. It is not arrogance, nor intellectual neocolonialism, nor the assumption of superiority, but the *fact of superiority* which is at the root of the trouble. No amount of sensitivity, tact, and courtesy can get round this unpalatable fact, which may be more important in causing hostility and resentment than the propagation of wrong models or the existence of superior material resources. Ironically, the contribution of foreign scholars, where it is most realistic and relevant, may be most resented. For it is uncomfortable to be told by foreigners what is right and to have one's errors corrected by them.

The most fundamental argument for international cooperation in development is that human beings, wherever born, should be able to develop their capacities to the fullest extent, both in order to fulfill themselves and to contribute to the common heritage of civilization, of which the stock of knowledge is part. In the light of this, the so-called trade-off between quality and capacity appears as an intertemporal choice with an element of risk. But, human beings being what they are, how the fact of initial superiority and inferiority can be acknowledged and removed is a much more difficult question.

For objectives 1 through 4, collaboration is often more honest and more practical if both partners get something out of it. There is no objection to introducing an element of trading: you help me in getting data and I help you with designing a curriculum or in giving lectures and in reducing your teaching load. Arrangements for mutual benefit, not all of which need directly relate to the research project, are possible and often desirable.

A practical conclusion for donors who desire joint ventures in research is that funds may be required for consultation and for preparing the ground for cooperation. A particularly suitable area for feasibility or preinvestment or pilot studies would be grants for the exploration of suitable scholars and institutes for cooperation in research and the precise conditions for collaboration.

Another practical conclusion is the need to encourage and finance scholars from developing countries to conduct research in developed countries on the problems of these countries and on the problems generated by the world system of international relations. Only through such reciprocal and symmetrical arrangements can the idea of international cooperation of equal partners in research be realized.

So far, I have talked about links in general. Should there be *specific* links between *particular* universities or departments and institutes in developing countries? There are arguments for and against. The case for such links is that there is stronger commitment, a clear responsibility, advantages of continuity and of getting to know one another well. On the other hand, it may mean reduced flexibility, so that one is bound to accept students or staff members from the linked institutions to the exclusion of others who might contribute more, or that one engages in a series of joint research projects for which other partners would have been more suitable.

If participation and collaboration achieve complementarity, can there also be specialization, a divison of labor between research in developed and in developing countries? Basic research being a human-capital-intensive activity and often also equipment-intensive, it might be argued that most of it should be conducted in countries where sophisticated human capital and institutions are relatively plentiful and that developing countries should confine themselves to adopting and adapting basic research from the industrial countries and direct their own efforts at research that can be applied quickly and can best be done locally. Yet, such a conclusion would be misleading. First, the ability to adopt and adapt requires a research capacity not too dissimilar from that in the developed country. Workers must be able to appraise critically what is useful and what is not, and how the useful can be adapted. This ability presupposes research capacity of the same order and of the same depth as that of the original workers. Second, in view of the international market in professional social scientists, developing countries may have to attempt to match, or nearly match, the research opportunities their best brains are offered abroad if they wish to keep them. And keeping them may be a necessary condition for carrying out useful applied research with quick-yielding results. For both these reasons—the need of an indigenous basic research capacity in order to adapt and the need to plug the brain drain—developing countries cannot simply confine themselves to applied, quick-yielding, locally relevant research plus adaptation of research from abroad.

But there remains the question of balance and direction. If scholars are induced not to leave the country but carry out the kind of irrelevant, esoteric, excessively sophisticated, abstract work that gains prestige in the centers of learning of the developed countries, little is gained. To rechannel the external brain drain into an internal brain drain brings no benefit to the community. How this can be prevented raises difficult questions of academic prestige, social concern, conflicts between social and professional priorities and individual motivation. On these grounds, a case might be made for some closing in of the scholars of the developing countries, for reduced contacts with the international community of scholars, if such turning away encourages attitudes more in line with social priorities. On the other hand, if the scholars in the developed countries recognize that what is regarded as "the best" in one setting might be the enemy of the good in another and adjust not only their research priorities but also their pecking order of recognition and prestige, the objections to international cooperation across wide-open frontiers are weakened or removed. Paradoxically, by lowering the claims of prestigious subjects and "standards of excellence," by making analysis more flexible, standards less universal, and policy recommendations more diverse, greater universality and better international collaboration can be achieved.

Implications for Research Priorities

If research on LDCs is a sensitive area for rich-country scholars to become involved in, should they perhaps confine themselves to the interface between rich and poor countries? Should donors be cautious about the type of research they are willing to underwrite? What limits, if any, should be imposed? Several responses to these questions are possible. One would be that we should identify the priority areas and then tackle them jointly, by rich- and poor-country cooperation. In particular, the interaction between (a) signals and incentives; (b) structural changes in the distribution of assets, access to power, and access to education; and (c) technology could provide an agenda for joint, international, multidisciplinary research.

The other approach would be to say, yes, these are the important problems, but they are not suited for joint research. Purely domestic issues should not be on the research agenda of rich-country scholars and institutes for four reasons. First, there is little rich countries can do to implement policies for wholly domestic matters of the developing countries, whereas rich countries *can* act in the international arena. Second, research on purely domestic issues gives rise to the charges of mining and possibly undermining, discussed above. I have argued that such charges are often based on a confusion, but the political and psychological obstacles are nonetheless real.

Third, there is something paradoxical (though not contradictory) in foundations, agencies, or institutes from rich countries advocating the need to strengthen indigenous research capacity as an important ingredient in development and then doing the work themselves. I have argued that a somewhat Böhm-Bawerkian approach[24] can make the two consistent, but again some resistance may remain.

The fourth objection is the most serious one and I am schizophrenic about it. It links up with the discussion of "legitimacy" in the section "The Role of the Social Sciences and the Social Scientist in Development Studies." Assume a careful analysis leads to the conclusion that a radical redistribution of assets and power is a condition of progress. Can we then tell citizens of other countries to adopt these radical changes which may require a revolution? At the level of independent, objective analysis, there is nothing wrong with saying such changes are necessary, where they are seen to be.[25] But if said by an outsider, this may be condemned not only as an easy option (I have already said that nothing is easier than to be radical for another country), but also as counterproductive. These changes, by definition, are going to hurt some people. If these people can point to the outside agency as the source of inspiration of these changes, this may make it more difficult for the progressive group to carry out its intentions. What some may regard as supporting and well-wishing outside pressures, others will see as the kiss of death, or at least as an embarrassing embrace. So here is the dilemma. Honest research bids us expose the political constraints and point to the radical solutions, but it may be both improper and counterproductive for foreigners to recommend painful and possibly bloody domestic reform.

Equally, if the analysis were to lead to the conclusion that the costs of a revolution in terms of human suffering are too great and that reforms should be brought about gradually, can we then tell the country to refrain from violent change, even if this means that many will continue to suffer extreme poverty and deprivation? May not such recommendations again be both facile and counterproductive, by encouraging the advocates of violent change to say that foreign research supports the existing power structure?

Some of the issues raised here are just part of those usually discussed under the heading "the moral responsibilities of scientists" and are not different from those faced by atomic or genetic scientists. But the dividing line between the subject of research and its application is less sharply drawn in the social sciences. The subject matter itself is influenced by the study, and the interaction between academic and moral considerations is therefore closer. Further, scientists can influence actions of their own governments as citizens—but much less the actions of other countries' governments.

The second approach (ruling out domestic issues) leads to the conclusion that the appropriate area for research by scholars from rich countries, whether they work on their own or jointly with scholars from the developing countries, is where the actions of rich countries impinge on the poor countries, what in the current jargon is called the interface: international trade, including adjustment assistance, aid, capital movements, the multinational enterprise, international monetary reform, energy, the environment, the sea and the seabed, migration, transfer of technology, the direction of research and development expenditure in rich countries, science policy, international taxation. These are areas in which data are available without intrusion and in which analysis and concern by the rich can lead to action and improvement by the rich. International issues could therefore be regarded as those suited par excellence for development research in and by developed countries.

There are objections to such an ordinance of self-restraint. The self-restraint can work properly only if it is obeyed universally. For if scholars not obeying the ordinance move into a developing country, advocating a partial solution, such as the importance of getting prices right, without stressing the other components of the strategy, they might inflict more harm than good. Balancing action to neutralize such damage might then be needed. Equally, if the (partial) conclusion were reached that a revolution is a necessary condition for development, would it not be facile to permit this to be presented to another country without work on the details of other policies that would have to accompany the radical reforms? Since not everybody can be prevented from working on internal problems of the developing countries, anybody must be free to do so, if only to counteract one-sided and biased research.[26]

Secondly, if, as has been argued, preoccupation with prestige-endowed topics that are irrelevant to the development efforts of the developing countries leads to internal brain drain,[27] attention to relevant, though domestic, topics by scholars from rich countries may stimulate interest in these topics and attach indigenous prestige to them. Work by a foreign scholar on income distribution in Brazil has, if not initiated, certainly provoked a good deal of excellent domestic work.

Thirdly, foreign observers are often much more illuminating than those submerged in their own societies. Probably the best book on the British economy is that written by a group of American scholars and edited by Richard Caves.[28] Outsiders can bring a freshness of perception to bear on a country's problem that nationals of that country cannot.

Fourthly, the distinction between international and internal topics is analytically untenable. The international system penetrates national affairs and vice versa.[29]

Fifthly, the best research is inspired by what the researchers think they can do best and what interests them. It would be a pity if there were no funds to back these efforts.

Finally, I have argued that scholarship has its standards, which ignore the maxims of etiquette, diplomacy, and tact. If, after honest research, in the light of the evidence, politically sensitive conclusions emerge, they should not be suppressed, dressed up or softened. But it is well to remember that cooperative research calls for standards of cooperation.[30] Jagdish Bhagwati, in his contribution to the panel discussion "What We Need to Know," at the Princeton Conference on International Trade and Finance (March 1973), tells the story of how Frazer, the great anthropologist from the pre-Malinowski, pre-Radcliffe-Brown era, when asked if he had ever visited the exotic areas he wrote about, replied: "I only write about savages, I don't mix with them." Bhagwati goes on to note that the foundations, USAID, and the World Bank, supported by the jet, had removed any obstacles and Frazerian inhibitions to the pursuit of knowledge, if not pleasure. But there may be a conflict between opportunities and objectives. Just as the hordes of tourists in search of exotic sights destroy the very mysteries they have come to see, so scholars may interfere harmfully with the processes they have come to study.

In addition, there is a certain process of selection at work, encouraged by high living standards abroad and the relative absence of equally high academic standards. Some years ago, Dudley Seers wrote a memorable article, "Why Visiting Economists Fail." Perhaps the time has come to write a companion piece, "Why Failed Economists Visit." T.N. Srinivasan, in his already-quoted Belgrade paper, "The State of Development Economics," notes, rather generously and politely, that "there are situations in which the value of the contribution of the resident foreign economist covers his marginal cost."[31]

I find it difficult to give a clear answer to the questions about the limits of research by scholars from rich countries, except that research into international issues, and particularly those areas in which action by rich countries can contribute to development, is in some respects more appropriate and safer, in spite of the objections mentioned, than research into entirely domestic issues of the poor countries. The "adjustees" of adjustment assistance are more appropriate subjects for research than the victims of a foreign revolution. But if the "interface" penetrates into largely domestic issues, no barrier can halt the progress of research.

Yet, there is another problem. Even where national interests coincide, and where appropriate policies would lead to common gains (such as access to imports from LDCs), there is a question about the division of these gains. In other areas, national interests may clash. Certain gains for the developing countries may be available only at the expense of developed countries. Are such problems of bargaining, and possibly confrontation and conflict, appropriate areas for rich-country research? Alternatively, there might be schemes of self-help, where the best policy would be for developing countries to turn away from the rich and encourage arrangements among themselves (regional integration, payments unions, etc.). Could such problems be studied in developed countries?

In spite of the suspicion that such research may be nationally biased and self-interested, I can see good reasons why it could be usefully conducted by rich countries in cooperation with poor. First, until the work has been done, it is not always clear whether the game is a zero-sum one or whether positive sums may be available for distribution. It is quite legitimate to investigate the conditions in which private foreign investment, freeing trade, or permitting immigration help both groups of countries and when they are beneficial to one at the expense of the other.

Second, even where interests clearly conflict, informed bargaining is often to the advantage of both partners. Representatives of multinational enterprises often insist that they prefer to negotiate with well-informed, hard-headed officials from developing countries to having to face ignorant and incompetent ones (though OPEC may have gone too far for them). The short-term advantages that may be gained from the latter, they argue, are not worth the recriminations, regrets, and retaliatory actions that spring from the later reactions to ill-informed bargains.

Third, developed-country scholars are quite capable of detaching themselves from the narrow national interest of their own country and of analyzing conflict situations that can be resolved to the advantage of the developing countries. Some of them are eager to do this. The exploration of areas of potential bargaining power is only beginning. What is needed is more information about this power and greater solidarity between competing developing countries to exploit it jointly. A preliminary list of areas to be investigated would include the following:

1. Commodity agreements combined with restrictions of supply in commodities or groups of commodities for which world demand is price-inelastic, so that producing countries can jointly raise the price of the agricultural commodity or mineral or a group of such commodities in order to reduce substitution and improve their income terms of trade.
2. Contracts with the multinational enterprise, covering a host of clauses, containing conditions for foreign operations.
3. The threat not to sign patent, trademark, or copyright conventions.
4. The threat of confiscation or nationalization of foreign-owned assets or restrictions on new investment or the imposition of various conditions on such investments.
5. The threat of refusing or slowing down or tying debt service on past debt or of refusing continuing freedom to remit profits and repatriate capital.
6. The threat to diversify monetary reserves, to shift them across frontiers, or to demand conversion into gold.
7. Alliances with developed-country interest groups, such as independent retail chains or importing agencies, wishing to import low-cost commodities, combined, possibly, with "dumping."
8. The threat to deny overflying rights to airlines.
9. The use of bargaining power based on ability to prohibit the presence or passage of troops.

Other areas might include refusal to cooperate on the control of narcotics or in the prevention of global pollution or refusal of military facilities.

One would hope, however, that areas of cooperation will give more scope than areas of confrontation and conflict. There are ways in which the talk of international cooperation can be backed by action. One way to give reality to this notion is for the rich countries to encourage exchange of ideas and experience between developing countries. In many respects, they can teach one another more than developed countries can in such areas as export promotion of labor-intensive products, family planning programs, rural development, including smallholder schemes. Countries which have recently undergone an experience are much better equipped to communicate it than countries that had gone through this experience decades or hundreds of years earlier, in quite different demographic, climatic, international, and social conditions. This is another important argument for the encouragement and finance by developed countries of "offshore" research on an international or interregional basis.

The upshot of this discussion is that international and "interface" issues are more appropriate items on the agenda for research of rich-country institutions than purely LDC domestic ones, but that this is subject to a number of qualifications. More particularly, (a) development is a complex process in which international relations cannot be severed from domestic ones; (b) self-restraint will never be universal, and if one group of researchers (possibly belonging to the same school of thought) occupies itself with these issues, balanced scholarship requires that their work be subject to the criticism of others in the professions; (c) focusing interest in high-prestige centers of learning (the United States, Europe) on purely LDC domestic issues may correct the internal brain drain (the diversion of efforts to irrelevant prestige topics) and stimulate indigenous, relevant research in the developing countries; (d) outside observers often have a better insight; and (e) the universality of scholarship draws no political frontiers, though the existence of such frontiers may impede the work and color the outlook of scholars. On the other hand, work on international issues may be as suspect as work on domestic issues, precisely because the national self-interest of rich countries is involved. In spite of these qualifications, I would conclude that the emphasis of rich-country research in rich countries should be on "interface" issues.

Money: The Root of All Good

Quoting proverbs is like reading tea leaves: you can always find what you are looking for. Proverbial wisdom is wise because it hedges its bets. It is irrefutable, because it is self-contradictory. "Many hands make light work" seems to offer advice to a catering manager wishing to determine the number of staff he should recruit. But proverbial wisdom protects itself by coupling with the proverb its antidote: "Many cooks spoil the broth." Similarly, the impecunious scholar turning his troubled conscience to sources of finance finds ambiguous advice from "*Pecunia non olet*" and "He who pays the piper calls the tune." In principle, it should make no difference where research money comes from, as long as no intellectual, moral, or political conditions are attached to the methods and conclusions of the work. In practice, what matters is not only freedom from ties but also whether outsiders, on whose cooperation the work depends, see it in this light.

However self-effacing the CIA or the U.S. Defense Department or, indeed, any American source may be, many Latin Americans regard *all* U.S. money as tainted. Yet, the rational reaction to suspect sources is not to reject them but to demand full and open disclosure of the purpose, methods, and origins.

At one time, it was possible to distinguish between public and private (charitable) sources of finance. Public sources clearly insisted on, or were thought to insist on, returns on their money, which meant support for their policies. Private charitable sources were regarded as more disinterested, more prepared to support genuinely independent research. This distinction, if it existed, broke down with the revelation of the various private foundations that the CIA had used for channeling funds for its purposes. On the other hand, government departments may genuinely divest themselves by channeling their funds through independent bodies, such as the University Grants Committee in Britain or the various science research councils, so that academic freedom and public accountability are reconciled. For reasons such as these, the public-private distinction does not coincide with that between heteronomy and autonomy.

Another distinction may be drawn between national and international sources. National sources might be thought to be concerned with promoting the interests of the nation, international sources those of the world community. But international organizations have their own partial and vested interests, and it is doubtful whether they are inclined to support more independent research than some national bodies; and some national bodies may take a genuinely international view.

More important, in my view, than the source or channel of funds—in other words, whether they come from public or private bodies, from national or international ones, or whether they are channeled directly or indirectly (through intermediate bodies)—is the question whether they are highly concentrated or whether there is genuine, not just legal or formal, dispersal. There are obvious advantages in concentration. Wasteful duplication of effort and overlaps can be avoided; attention can be drawn to gaps in our knowledge; data, concepts, and methods can be standardized. But there are also dangers in concentration. The principal danger of heavy concentration and centralization of research funds is that diversity, originality, criticism, and heterodoxy are liable to be discouraged in favor of a uniform and possibly premature orthodoxy or a swinging with fads and fashions. The pressures of the professionalization of a subject in the direction of conformity to the standards evolved by the profession are, in any case, powerful. If they are further strengthened by a single grant-dispensing research council, the chances for critical, independent work are weakened.

Against the obvious benefits of concentration and centralization must be set the less obvious losses resulting from weaker questioning of the prevailing orthodoxies. The safeguard of original, independent, critical research must therefore be sought in a multiplication of channels of funds between which the applicant has a choice and an encouragement of small, independent, uninhibited scholars. An additional safeguard is not to entrust the decision solely to established academics working in the same field as the applicant. Academics from other fields, officials, politicians, and other laymen may be useful members of grant-awarding bodies and appointments committees. They can help to break through the crust of conformity. Multiplication of channels in turn calls for a single place where these sources are listed, so that potential applicants are fully aware of the opportunities.

Should research be commissioned by grant-giving, policy-making bodies according to their needs and priorities as they see them, or should the initiative come from the researchers? The arguments are by now well rehearsed. On the one hand, the flicker of original, first-class ideas is such a rare thing and depends so much on individuality and autonomy that any spark that is struck should be carefully fanned. Interference or even requests that impose conditions may extinguish these precarious and precious flames. Again, innovation and originality do not usually thrive under the straitjacket of officially commissioned projects. Donors are preoccupied with the urgent problems of the day and the near future; researchers are better at raising more fundamental issues of greater importance in the more distant future. The conflict is between the urgent and the important, between the short-term and the long-term, between the simple rule of thumb and the complex web, and between getting answers and raising questions. Further, useful and applicable knowledge often grows unexpectedly out of what may at first appear to be esoteric and useless knowledge. For these reasons, the purposes of policy are often best served by leaving scholars free to identify the problems and set about solving them in their own way. At least there should be an area in which such free pursuit is vouchsafed.

On the other hand, problems of action *are* urgent, and data and analysis are needed for informed policy. Unless the donor and customer (the policy-making department) can specify what precisely he requires from the contractor, there will be waste, gaps, and a failure to focus on what is usable.

This dilemma can be overstated. There is no need to opt between, on the one hand, a clearly specified take-it-or-leave-it attitude, when the customer lays down clear specifications, and, on the other hand, complete laissez-faire. If universities and research institutes are represented on the grant-giving bodies or their committees by men and women who understand the needs and attitudes of scholars, and if the needs and priorities of the policy-making bodies are spelled out clearly, the gap can be greatly reduced. Many good, competent scholars and even more graduate students look for appropriate topics to work on, and if ministries, councils, international agencies, or foundations make it known on what topics they require more information and analysis, many are eager to respond. Letting priorities be known and continuing a dialogue between policy makers and researchers, perhaps on joint committees and through informal contacts, will greatly contribute to bridging the gap between the needs of policy makers and the incentives and temperaments of independent scholars.

Science and Crypto-Science

If the social sciences are a "soft" technology compared with the "hard" technology of the natural sciences, development studies have been regarded as the soft underbelly of "economic science." I have heard it equated to economics minus logic. In the attempt to emulate the colleagues practicing "hard" economics, mathematical methods have sometimes been brought to bear on issues for which they were not appropriate.

Growing concern with social objectives—employment, equality, the environment—has led to calls for the "dethronement of GNP," which (erroneously) has been regarded as an *economic* objective. But if there was a fault in the preoccupation with GNP, it was excessive attention to a simple quantitative index, irrespective of the valuation implicit in its sets of weights—in other words, of its composition, distribution, and the manner in which it was produced. We are in danger of repeating this very same fault in attempting to extract simple indexes for the social objectives. The proportion of the GNP earned by the bottom 40 percent and the Gini coefficient are just as inadequate and, by themselves, misleading measures of what we are getting at when we try to reduce inequality, as GNP is an inadequate measure of productive capacity. Inequality of income distribution touches only a small portion of the vast, multidimensional problem of inequality. There is inequality of ownership of assets, of access to earning opportunities, of satisfaction from work, of recognition, of ability to enjoy consumption, of access to power, of participation in decision making (cf. n. 29). The call for greater equality, for a genuine community of equals, cannot be answered simply by measures that reduce the Gini coefficient or any other simple measure of inequality, which are inadequate even in expressing what concerns us in unequal income distributions. It is possible to envisage a technocratic society, where decisions are highly centralized and in which a few enjoy the satisfaction from power and creativity while the many carry out boring and disagreeable tasks in a hierarchic structure and in which the Gini coefficient is zero.

The danger of social science research that attempts to emulate the "hard" sciences is that it focuses on the measurable and neglects the rest. Some of the most important obstacles to the eradication of poverty and the promotion of greater equality lie in areas in which measurement is still very difficult or perhaps impossible. Among these are the following:

1. Unwillingness of governments to grasp the political nettles: land reform, taxation, labor mobilization, widening access to education.
2. Linked with this, elitism, nepotism, corruption.
3. Behind these again, various forms of oligopoly and monopoly power: the power of large landowners, of big industrialists, of the multinational enterprises.
4. In a different field, but sometimes equally disruptive, the power of organized labor unions and the obstacles to an incomes and employment policy. In some countries, the government could be described, not as the "executive committee of the bourgeoisie," but as the executive committee of the trade unions.
5. Restricted access to educational opportunities and the imbalance in education and the resulting job certification that both reflect and reinforce the unequal structure of power and wealth.
6. Weak entrepreneurship and defective management and administration of public-sector enterprises, of private firms, and of the civil service.
7. Lack of coordination between central plans and ministries, central plans and regional, local, and project plans; too many countries are long on planning, short on administration.
8. The weakness of the structure, area of competence, recruitment, training, and administration of the UN agencies charged with development combined, sometimes, with a narrowly technocratic approach, encouraged by the origin and organization of these agencies and their politically "noncontroversial" approach.
9. There are, of course, also the terrible facts of mass slaughter of ethnic minorities (often entrepreneurial and therefore hated) and political opponents, imprisonment without trial, torture, expulsion, the large sums spent on armies and the police, and other horrors.

The list is not exhaustive but merely illustrative. It shows that the temptation to select the quantified and the quantifiable at the expense of other, possibly more important, areas should be resisted. The important question is: What are the springs of development? Many would stress the importance of entrepreneurial and managerial motivation, attitudes, and education. We do not know what characteristics make for the social selection of an innovating, entrepreneurial group. Neither innate characteristics nor education nor religion can explain why some societies at certain periods are better and quicker at innovating than others at other times. Innate characteristics are distributed according to normal distribution curves; the level of scientific education is quite high in many societies in which innovation is poor, and vice versa; and all kinds of religion have proved to be consistent with innovation. What we need is an explanation of why, with the right education, innate characteristics, and religion, the ablest and fittest, the "best and the brightest," the creative innovators, are not attracted to business but, instead, to politics, universities, or the civil service.

Economists have chased for hundreds of years the sources of economic growth and development. Land and natural resources (the Physiocrats), labor (John Locke and the classical economists), capital (Marx, Harrod, Domar), education (T.W. Schultz, Gary Becker), achievement motivation (David McClelland), and, most recently, research and development have, in turn, been scrutinized and, when examined in detail, found wanting. The experts looking at the facts tell us in each case that the factor they investigated is not very important for development. Consequently, we must confess that we do not know what causes development and therefore lack a clear "agenda for research." But we must try to resist the temptation to behave like the drunk who has lost his key and looks for it not where he dropped it but under the street lamp—because this is where the light is.

Notes

1. The paper is an exercise on the sociology of research and of international relations. As an economist, I have no particular advantage in writing about these issues. I am aware of the philosophical shortcomings of my argument and of the lack of thorough empirical evidence to support some of my suggestions. I have benefited from comments and criticisms of an earlier draft by Irma Adelman, Peter Balacs, Ronald Dore, Edgar Edwards, Unni Eradi, Michael Faber, Anne Gordon, Keith Griffin, Seev Hirsch, Jill Rubery, Ernest Stern, Frances Stewart, Hugh Stretton, B.R. Virmani, Gordon Winston, and Howard Wriggins. To these, and to a research seminar at Queen Elizabeth House, I am very grateful. I am also grateful to the Economic Development Institute of the World Bank and its director, Mr. Andrew Kamarck, for having provided the facilities and stimulating atmosphere for the early stages of this work.

An earlier version of this paper was presented at a conference in Bellagio on the financing of social science research for development, February 11–16, 1974, sponsored by the Ford Foundation, the Canadian International Development Research Centre, The Rockefeller Foundation, USAID, and the World Bank.

2. While it may appear odd of social scientists not to examine the social origins and implications of their own activities, it is quite consistent with what might be called the blind spot of autoprofessionalism (or, by Gunnar Myrdal, "The Beam in Our Eyes"): psychologists' children are crazy mixed-up kids, and the suicide rate among psychiatrists is the highest; dentists have bad teeth; experts on management cannot manage their affairs nor marriage counselors their marriages; planners are quite incapable of

planning their own lives; and the London School of Economics, that power-house of social science, was in difficulty about its own structure. So it should not surprise us that social scientists have somewhat neglected the social determination and implications of their own professional activities.

3. Frances Stewart, "Technology and Employment in LDCs" (Paper for Ford Foundation Conference on Technology and Employment, New Delhi, 1973, where she quotes R.S. Merrill, "The Study of Technology," in the *Encyclopaedia of Social Sciences*).

4. Colin Leys, "The Role of the University in an Underdeveloped Country," *Education News* (Department of Education and Science, Canberra), April 1971. For a critique of the linear theory, see Dudley Seers and Leonard Joy, eds., *Development in a Divided World* (Hardmondsworth: Penguin, 1971), chap. 2.

5. This charge can be interpreted broadly, when it covers also the subsequent two charges, or narrowly, when it is confined to "mining."

6. Ronald Dore remembers "being at a conference in Singapore when the sociologist Wertheim gave a paper on the obstacles to development, which he identified as landlords and capitalists, ending with the stirring prediction that the masses were already awakening and that the duty of the scholar was to help them sweep away their enemies. An Indonesian there was somewhat indignant: 'Fine for you, Professor Wertheim. But I'm the sausage that's going to be fried in the fire—though I'm neither landlord nor capitalist.' " Ronald Dore goes on to say (in private communication) how the same point arises when we preach income redistribution in even a mild form to our colleagues from poor countries, whose reference group is the international academic community rather than peasant incomes in their own countries.

7. Michael Faber reminded me of John Austin's "*In vino*, possibly, '*veritas*,' but in a sober symposium '*verum*'." "What needs discussing rather is the use, or certain uses, of the word 'true:' " J.L. Austin, *Philosophical Papers*, ed. J.O. Urmson and G.J. Warnock (Oxford: Clarendon Press, 1961), p.85. But for the sense in which I use it, Pilate's question holds no terror; "true" will do for my purposes.

8. This is the view of, for example, Lionel Robbins: "It has some-times been asserted that the generalisations of Economics are essentially 'historico-relative' in character, that their validity is limited to certain histor-ical conditions, and that outside these they have no relevance to the analysis of social phenomena. This view is a dangerous misapprehension." *An essay on the Nature and Significance of Economic Science*, 2d rev. ed. (London: Macmillan, 1935), p. 80. See also Ludwig von Mises, *Human Action* (New Haven: Yale University Press, 1949). Sir Geoffrey Wilson tells me that about 20 years ago, when he was in Ceylon starting up the Colombo plan, he

sent to Sydney Caine, who was then vice-chancellor of the University of Singapore, a memo suggesting that the economics of the countries of Southeast Asia might better be studied locally than at the London School of Economics and that an institute might be set up for the purpose in South India, where, incidentally, foreign scholars might find a home and see what it was like to work in local conditions. Caine's reply "led me to think that I had blasphemed in church—economics was economics, whether in London, Delhi, Tokyo or the moon, etc., and I retired covered in confusion at ever having had such an unclean thought."

9. See Steven Lukes, "On the Social Determination of Truth," in *Modes of Thought: Essays on Thinking in Western and Non-Western Societies*, ed. Robin Horton and Ruth Finnegan (London: Faber & Faber, 1973).

10. The classification follows closely my introduction to Gunnar Myrdal's *Value in Social Theory*, ed. Paul Streeten (London: Routledge & Kegan Paul, 1958), pp. xxxvi−xli.

11. Insofar as only the *emotive* use of words is stressed, the linguistic analysis should be classified under 1. Bias enters at the psychological level and could be eliminated by a purged language.

12. The expression occurs in one of Engels's letters to Mehring. Cf. Franz Mehring, *Geschichte der deutschen Sozialdemokratie* (Stuttgart: Dietz, 1921), *1*:386.

13. Spelled out less aphoristically, this means: there exists a set of propositions about social and economic phenomena and their relations which is generally true of Africa (at least for the time being), but not generally true elsewhere; but there can be no set of exclusively African criteria for what is true.

14. "The comparison that Lagrange made of Newton is worth repeating in this connection: Assuredly Newton was the greatest man of science, but also the luckiest. For there is but one system of the world and Newton was the one who found it. Similarly, there is but one grand concept of general equilibrium and it was Walras who had the insight (and luck) to find it." P.A. Samuelson, "Economists and the History of Ideas," *American Economic Review* 52, no. 1 (March 1962):3−4.

15. Michael Faber tells me that "when Danilo Dolci held a conference of notables on his problems of development, he chose Palma di Montechiaro (the true home of the fictional Gattopardo), where the heat was intolerable, the village hall was filled with the stench from the open gutters outside, the din from the square made the speakers inaudible, and the fragile electricity supply could be counted upon to break down."

16. See the section "Implications for Research Priorities," below.

17. But Bakunin, a thinker with intuition in many respects superior to Marx's (though greatly inferior as a theorist), had seen the revolutionary

potential of the peasants and predicted revolutions, not in the most industrialized countries, but in underdeveloped rural societies like Spain, Russia, and China.

18. Padma Desai, "Third World Social Scientists in Santiago," *World Development* 1, no. 9 (September 1973):63–64.

19. A synthesis of the Marxian and Keynesian view of the respective influence of interests and ideas is presented by Max Weber: "Interests (material and ideal), not ideas, dominate directly the actions of men. Yet the 'images of the world' created by these ideas have often served as switches determining the track on which the dynamism of interests kept the action going." *From Max Weber: Essays in Sociology* (New York: Oxford University Press, 1947), p. 280.

20. In an interesting report on a seminar in Poona, Andrew Shonfield reported that he "was frankly surprised at the violence of the antipathy shown by the Westerners towards the Western way of life" compared with the enthusiasm for large-scale facilities to produce cement, electricity, and steel of many "Easterners." Fritz Schumacher "emphasized the need to protect, above all else, the process of 'organic growth.' Planning of development on this view would be as much concerned to avoid the introduction of new manufactured products...which would put the established [producers] in the villages out of business." "Whereas Schumacher foresees spiritual disaster in any attempt to speed up development through a programme of large-scale industrialisation, [Colin] Clark asserts flatly that it cannot be hurried up at all." "Alternatives to Backwardness," *Encounter*, no. 99 (December 1961), p. 60.

Similarly, the "decision to introduce English education was taken not without an acute controversy. The story of this controversy, known as the controversy between the Orientalists and Anglicists, is quite familiar to all students of the history of Indian education. The curious fact is that the Orientalists were almost all Englishmen in the service of the Company, whereas almost all Indians of repute were Anglicists....It was the strong position taken up by Macaulay that forced the issue in favour of the Anglicists." G. Ramanathan, *Educational Planning and National Integration* (Bombay: Asia Publishing House, 1963), p.21. And Macaulay wrote in his famous "Minute on Education": "I am quite ready to take the Oriental learning at the valuation of the Orientalists themselves. I have never found one among them who could deny that a single shelf of a good European library was worth the whole native literature of India and Arabia." In *Sources of Indian Tradition*, comp. Theodore de Bary, Stephen Hay, R. Weiler, and Andrew Yarrow (New York: Columbia University Press; London: Oxford University Press, 1958), pp. 596–597.

In spite of some Western critics of Western modernization (since joined by Ivan Illich), Max Weber identifies the claim to a single universal future as an important characteristic of Western civilization. "A product of modern European civilisation, studying any problem of universal history, is bound to ask himself to what combination of circumstances the fact should be attributed that in Western civilisation, and in Western civilisation only, cultural phenomena have appeared which (as we like to think) lie in a line of development having *universal* significance and value." Max Weber, *The Protestant Ethic and the Spirit of Capitalism* (London: George Allen & Unwin, 1930; New York: Charles Scribner's Sons, 1958).

21. It is this unity of scholarship that gives us the right, beyond a general appeal to human rights, to send petitions to foreign governments to protect the life and work of colleagues in danger of being imprisoned or tortured for their ideas. If this were not so, such petitions, based on professional solidarity rather than human rights, would be a form of intellectual imperialism.

22. "Reflections of an Indian Scholar," mimeographed.

23. In his discussion of this problem, Edgar Edwards makes the additional point that policymakers in developing countries "should regard research by their own nationals, particularly on sensitive issues, as being better grounded in local knowledge and possibly more concerned with national welfare and long-term implications than research conducted abroad or by visiting scholars." "Employment in Developing Countries," mimeographed, p. 75.

24. Böhm-Bawerk was a famous Austrian economist who reasoned that greater production later resulted from devoting current resources to more "roundabout" methods of production—for example, rather than training students, training trainers of students.

25. There is a school of thought that advocates "participatory observation," "participant intervention," the role of "militant-cum-observer," and "liberation anthropology." Without going into the merits of this case, such activities are bound to remain a minority interest.

26. Another example is some of the currently fashionable doctrines of project appraisal. These profess to cover domestic social objectives, such as reducing inequality in income redistribution and raising savings rates. Yet, if propagation of these doctrines were to proceed, while the critics of these methods kept silent, the analysis and policy would be one-sided and biased.

27. T.N. Srinivasan, "The State of Development Economics," in *Planning Income Distribution. Private Foreign Investment.* International Meeting of Directors of Development Research and Training Institutes, Belgrade, Yugoslavia, August 28–30, 1972 (Paris: Development Center of the Organization for Economic Cooperation and Development, 1972), pp. 189–190.

28. Richard E. Caves and associates, *Britain's Economic Prospects* (Washington, D.C.: Brookings Institution, 1968).

29. Thus, British aid to overseas education can be analyzed only in the

context of the educational systems of the developing countries. International trade policy cannot be isolated from the domestic allocation of resources. And so on.

30. Here again, work on the Brazilian data of income distribution has a moral. The complaint in Brazil is that officials sympathetic to a critical analysis provided a foreign scholar with the data but that he, without reference to them and without consulting them, published them speedily in a foreign journal. Revolutionary or radical mining and imperialism are regarded as just as objectionable as conservative mining.

31. Srinivasan, "The State of Development Economics," p. 191.

3

Agencies of Diffusion: A Case Study of The Rockefeller Foundation

Laurence D. Stifel,
Ralph K. Davidson, and
James S. Coleman

The social sciences were not among the first interests of The Rockefeller Foundation after its creation in 1913. They came on scene serendipitously sixteen years later (and, in the foundation's program in developing countries, nearly another three decades later). There were two main reasons for the initial exclusion. One was the strong personal opposition of Frederick T. Gates, principal adviser in business and philanthropy of John D. Rockefeller, Sr., and a dominant figure in the original board of trustees. Despite early explorations—including the trustees' appointment of a committee of economists in 1914 to recommend important economic problems to be studied— Gates persuaded the board not to enter the social sciences; he deeply distrusted them, being convinced that medical science was the sole key to human welfare and progress. Largely because of Gates's influence, Raymond B. Fosdick notes, "by 1920 the Foundation had to all intents and purposes been captured by the doctors."[1]

The other reason for this early neglect was that, commencing in 1923, those fields had become the major focus of effort of the Laura Spelman Rockefeller Memorial, established by Mr. Rockefeller as a memorial to his wife, whose personal interests were in social welfare. Beardsley Ruml, a psychologist and the first and only director of the Memorial, has been called the "father of social sciences in America." Ruml passionately believed that any progress in the field of social welfare "shows as a primary need the development of the social sciences and the production of a body of substantiated and widely accepted generalizations as to human capacities and motives and as to the behavior of human beings as individuals and in groups."[2] Acknowledging the immaturity, limitations, and the extreme difficulty in furthering the development of the social sciences, he nonetheless argued that "unless means are found for meeting the complex social problems that are so rapidly developing, our increasing control of physical forces may prove increasingly destructive of human values."[3] Ruml's forceful advocacy of the case for investment in the social sciences prevailed. It followed his own recent conversion, as he later described:

> I was never a social scientist. . . . I joined the company of social scientists abruptly in 1923, without invitation and without asking permission. . . . The fact is, I had foundation trouble: a large fund, some $75 million dedicated to the advancement of human welfare but without policy or program. The trustees of the [Laura Spelman Rockefeller] Memorial did not hire me because they wanted to go into social sciences; they decided to go into social science because they found that the reasons which were persuasive to me were persuasive to them also.[4]

Under Ruml's vigorous leadership, by the time the Memorial was merged with The Rockefeller Foundation in 1929 approximately $41 million of its income had been spent in promoting development of the social sciences both in the United States and abroad. The Memorial's legacy of commitments and ongoing activities was a critical element in the solid establishment of the social sciences as one of the major divisions within the reorganized Rockefeller Foundation of 1929, a position they have maintained—with varying prominence and sometimes even precariously—for over fifty years.

Objectives and principles established during Ruml's leadership of the Memorial were adopted by the foundation trustees at the time of the 1929 merger and have been further developed in the ensuing decades. They have remained dominant guidelines for the foundation's program in the social sciences. One has been the primacy accorded the discovery and support of the best minds, wherever found. During three decades, Ruml and his two successors (Edmund E. Day [1929–1937], former professor of economics at Harvard, and Joseph H. Willits [1939–1954], former dean of the Wharton School of Finance and Commerce) pursued a global talent search, "scouting for talents, just as the big leagues do," as Willits put it, adding, "I would break any rule in the book for a chance to gamble on talent. . . . May we never invest in the reproduction of mediocrity!"[5] Hundreds—and, ultimately, thousands—of fellowships or grants were awarded over the years to selected budding and established social scientists, first throughout the United States and Europe, then in other parts of the world, for advanced study and professional development. One indicator of the effectiveness of this strategy is that all but one of the seventeen Nobel laureates awarded in economic sciences since the program commenced in 1969—coming from five different countries—have been former foundation fellows or grantees.

A second enduring principle initiated by Ruml and continued by his successors has been emphasis upon applied—what would now be called development-oriented—research in the social sciences. "The Memorial," Ruml stressed, "had no interest in the promotion of scientific research as an end in itself. . . . The interest in science was an interest in one means to an end, and the end was explicitly recognized to be the advancement of human welfare."[6] In 1934, and again in 1945, a committee of foundation trustees reaffirmed this principle. Grants were given to a wide range of institutions in the United States and abroad for work in applied economics; these included the National Bureau of Economic Research, the Institute for Advanced Study at Princeton, the Brookings Institution, the Stanford Food Research Institute, the London School of Economics, the University of Oslo, and the Dutch Economic Institute. As Ruml put it in a subsequent reminiscence, "Through the promotion of the social sciences it was felt that there would come a greater knowledge as to social forces and a higher objectivity in the development of social policy."[7] This emphasis upon practicality—upon the *application* of social sciences to human and social problems—has been both implicit and explicit in the developmental focus of the foundation's University Development program, launched in 1961.

A third, and related, long-standing objective stemming from the Ruml Memorial era, and one repeatedly reaffirmed, is scientific empiricism. Ruml believed that the social sciences had been retarded in their development because they had remained largely speculative, bibliographical, or literary in character, and that this was due to lack of opportunities for social scientists to have immediate personal observation of the social problems or social phenomena under investigation. In the absence of other sources, the Memorial and subsequently the foundation took the position that this obstacle could be overcome only by providing scholars with funding for travel, leaves of absence, statistical and clerical assistance, and "other means of placing the investigator in more intimate contact with this problem." This pattern of assistance, aimed at inculcating and fostering the ethos of empiricism, has remained central in the social-science program of the foundation. It is a position not everywhere acclaimed; in the early 1950s the foundation was under attack by a committee of the U.S. Congress for having too much empirical emphasis. The committee felt that such emphasis could cause the knowledge of social phenomena to be reduced to applied science.

Interdisciplinarity, both among the social sciences and between them and the other sciences—however inherently limited, seemingly rhetorical, and imperfectly realized—has also been a declared desideratum from the beginning. One of the major scientific objectives of Ruml's Memorial was "to promote the study of social problems by the various academic departments in collaboration in the belief that the present categories in social sciences—economics, political science, sociology, anthropology, psychology—are essentially artificial, that their usefulness as a basis for social research is limited, and that a synthesis is necessary."[8] This explains the extensive support provided by the Memorial to Yale's interdisciplinary Institute of Human Relations and to the Social Science Research Council.

At the time of the 1929 merger, the new president, Dr. Max Mason, emphasized that the foundation had essentially only one program, "directed to the general problem of human behavior, with the aim of control through understanding."[9] Although Fosdick later characterized the structural reorganization aimed at implementing this program to be "a well-intentioned gesture which had no effect,"[10] the principle had been doggedly reaffirmed over the years and repeated efforts made to realize it concretely—for example, in the North China integrated rural development program (1935–1938); the Crete Survey, conducted jointly by the Health and Social Sciences Divisions (1947–1951); and the University Development/Education for Development Program (1961 to the present).

Internationality was explicit in the grandiloquent goal—"the well-being of mankind"—of the foundation's benefactor; it was also an explicit objective of the Memorial during its lifetime: "The development of twelve or fifteen well rounded centers of social science research throughout the world with possibilities of easy interchange of faculty and students was undertaken, both because of the evident values in the advancement of social science and because of the indirect effect upon international good will and world understanding."[11] The extensive worldwide activities of the International Health Division between 1913 and the early 1950s established the foundation's genuine commitment to internationality. During the first twenty years of its existence more than 43 percent of the foundation's appropriations (approximately a quarter of a billion dollars) were for programs outside the United States. By 1950 it had engaged, or was then involved, in programs in ninety-three foreign countries, fifty-seven of them among what are the developing countries.

These long-standing objectives—furthering excellence wherever found, scientific empiricism, the application of knowledge, interdisciplinarity, and internationality—have served as guidelines in the evolution of the social-science program of the foundation. They remain operative guidelines today. Other enduring principles, goals, and mechanisms used to attain them have included insistence upon the professionalism of the foundation officers (the advantages of which are presumed to outweigh the limiting biases of the specializations of incumbents); concentration on the development of "centers of excellence" (while remaining mindful of the dangers of institutional bias from too-narrow commitments); the centrality of universities as recipient institutions (Willits: "Universities are places of infinite hope and infinite despair, but they are the West Points where social scientists are germinated and their educational and professional standards determined");[12] nonintervention in a recipient activity once support has been provided (Fosdick: "cut the strings when the gift is made");[13] and awareness of the need for long-term commitments as well as their "orderly termination," juxtaposed with a preference for immediacy, quick results, and shorter-term, more catalytic pump-priming role ("Get in and get out").

During the early 1930s emphasis continued on the development of selected major university centers of advanced training in the social sciences in the United States and abroad, and on the extensive use of fellowships for training a new generation of social scientists. In addition, three broad fields of major interest for more-intensive support were international relations (including the Foreign Policy Association, Council on Foreign Relations, London's Royal Institute of International Affairs, Paris's Centre d'études politiques étrangères, and Geneva's Institute of International Studies); economic stabilization (including the National Bureau of Economic Research, Social Science Research Council, Brookings Institution, and London School of Economics); and public administration (Harvard's Graduate School of Public Administration, the Public Administration Clearing House). By the mid-1930s, after extended review it was decided to phase out general support for university research centers and to focus on supporting scholars or projects of exceptional merit. This more flexible program was intended to promote strategic advances in fundamental knowledge in the social-science disciplines and to encourage concentration upon emerging problems of great urgency. Special emphasis was given to pioneering studies in economics (particularly national-income measurement and quantitative conceptual models of the economy) and in the methodology of survey research (particularly the work of Lazarsfeld and Merton at the Bureau of Applied Social Research at Columbia University).

Until the mid-1930s The Rockefeller Foundation's major thrust in the social sciences was capacity building of both personnel and institutions, mainly in the United States but also in selected centers in Europe. Its first serious—albeit limited and brief—engagement in promoting the social sciences in developing countries was in China. From its launching in 1913, the foundation had a strong interest in China, the first country outside the United States in which it undertook a major program and commitment. During the first two decades, health and medical education dominated the China program, at the center of which was Peking Union Medical College, the single greatest institutional investment in the country ($40 million). From 1932 through 1937, when the Japanese invasion halted development throughout China, the foundation became the major external financial supporter of the Nankai Institute of Economics, China's leading center of research and postgraduate training in economics, modeled initially on the London School of Economics. Both the institute's program and the foundation's rationale for supporting it were in many respects forerunners of the social-science component of the foundation's University Development Program launched in the LDCs thirty years later on a global scale. The objective was to build and maintain a center of excellence to serve all China. The emphasis was on combining teaching and research (the institute was both a highly productive research center and offered China's first quality postgraduate-degree program in economics); on "teaching through research" (selected areas of Shantung Province became field stations for research by postgraduate students); on staff development through both foreign and local scholarships; and on the development of teaching materials. The program's ethos was "indigenization"—to "Chinafy economics" both for its own sake and for the influence it could exert on China's government and national economic development.

China was also the locale of the foundation's first major interdisciplinary effort in integrated rural development. A new president who had taken office in January 1930 had serious misgivings about the foundation's commitments and activities in China, particularly the enormous sums that had been and continued to be expended on the Peking Union Medical College and the broad diffusion of grants to many mission universities, colleges, and hospitals. The trustees were equally concerned about overconcentration on China; indeed, a trustees' committee that had conducted a major new appraisal of foundation programs in the early 1930s queried:

> Is the welfare of mankind best served by enlarging our investment in China? Is China the outstanding strategic point in which we ought to push our attack? . . . We would point . . . to the possibilities that lie in a country like Mexico. . . . The South American countries like-wise present an inviting field. India is another conceivable opportunity.[14]

At the meeting to discuss the committee's report, the trustees also considered an ambitious report by Selskar Gunn, then the foundation's vice-president in Europe (and later Asia), recommending modification and extension of the program in China. This followed an extensive survey he had made of the China program during the preceding two-and-a-half years. The trustees approved the recommendations, noting that it would be both expensive and of long duration ("If we embark, we embark for the voyage, and we must contemplate a trip of considerable duration if any significant contribution is really to be made").[15] There were three reasons for the decision to continue concentration in China. One was to conserve and to capitalize upon previous foundation investments there; the institutional capacities that had been developed over the years should now be applied to the practical problems of national development. The second reason, which was to become familiar two decades later as the vast sweep of ex-colonial countries asserted themselves, was to pursue the ideas of plasticity and an experimental laboratory.

> The plastic condition of [China's] life and institutions at the present moment is an inviting challenge to a positive kind of service. Indeed there is a sense in which China might become a vast laboratory in the social sciences, with implications that would be international in scope.[16]

The third reason was to take advantage of what Gunn argued to be an unparalleled opportunity for a meaningful interdisciplinary effort by all divisions of the the foundation (the active participants were Health, Agriculture, and Social Sciences) to concentrate on a single developmental challenge and problem, namely, the reconstruction of a rural-experiment county in China (Tinghsien). The instruments for this experiment were to be the institutions of higher education, many of which the foundation had already been assisting. What became known as the China Program involved support for a consortium of Chinese universities organized under the rubric North China Council on Rural Reconstruction. China's leading universities in the social sciences were participants (Nankai in economics, Yenching in sociology and political science, and Nanking in agricultural economics). In conception and in promise, the experiment has been judged among the most imaginative approaches to "integrated rural development," a program objective that was reborn and acquired wide currency three decades later. More than a million dollars had been expended on the China Program when, in 1939, the war forced its termination.

Up to 1945, the geographic distribution of the foundation's expenditures for the social sciences was: North America, 80 percent; Europe, 18 percent; China and Japan, 2 percent; and the developing countries, 0.4 percent (Latin America, $47,641; Near East, $136,117; and Africa, $368). This Americo-Eurocentric concentration contrasts with the medical sciences, where the distribution was: North America, 37 percent; west Europe, 19 percent; and China, 39 percent; and with public health, where 16 percent of the expenditures before 1945 went to the developing countries, not including China. The brief exposure of the social sciences to China during 1932–1939 was in the nature of a first probe.

From the mid-1940s on, three developments were of special significance for the status and future orientation of the social sciences in the foundation. One was the initiative in a special 1945 report of the trustees' Committee on Policy and Program, chaired by Chester I. Barnard, which had completed a global review of the foundation's programs (the first since the trustee review in 1934). It noted the fundamental changes in the world produced by the war and identified one of three major new objectives as the "Understanding of Human Behavior." The committee felt that a disproportionate amount of foundation resources during the previous decade had gone to the health sciences (45 percent, compared with 18 percent for the social sciences), and that accordingly there should be reallocations among the divisions and expanded support for the social sciences. The foundation should attempt positive, constructive leadership in this field, with special emphasis on the new behavioral approaches:

> There should be a leadership effort to promote fundamental scientific research in the field of social psychology and social anthropology [and sociology], i.e., the reaction of men to the reactions of other men; the behavior of men as members of groups; the behavior of groups as wholes; the psychology of formal organizations; the characteristics, determinants and effects of customary behavior; and communication.[17]

This new programmatic direction was approved; in the ensuing years, there was a modest increase in grants in this area; but by the early 1950s it petered out. For this there are two explanations. First, in 1950 the Ford Foundation inaugurated its new major behavioral-science program with far larger sums at its disposal in a growth area of limited talent. Second, in 1952 Chester Barnard retired and was succeeded by Dean Rusk, whose interests (and those of others) in the social sciences were somewhat different. During roughly the first two decades following World War II—until the University Development Program got under way—the disciplinary emphasis in the social sciences remained predominantly in economics and international relations, with less support in other areas (population, legal and political philosophy, and area studies). Support for public administration had been phased out during World War II.

A second development was another brief excursion by the social scientists into interdisciplinarity and a developing country. The foundation's International Health Division (IHD) received a request in mid-1947 from the Greek government for assistance in preparing a ten-year overall development plan for Crete, by all indices an underdeveloped area. From its long experience in the Third World, the IHD was convinced that little could be done to improve public health without sound general economic, social, and political foundations. They therefore invited the Social Sciences Division (which accepted) to participate in an operational program (the first in the history of Social Sciences) in Crete. The rationale, according to then Social Sciences director Willits, was to enable the social sciences to see more clearly from a "grass roots" base "the ways by which the knowledge and skills of the industrialised countries might serve the orderly evolution of the unindustrialised countries without damaging their cultural and political integrity."[18] A systematic economic and social survey was made in collaboration with individual and institutional Greek counterparts, new ground was broken in the development of special sampling and statistical techniques, a report was made to the Greek government (and later published), and the foundation's involvement ended. In his final evaluation Willits concluded from the experience that technical-assistance programs would most likely fail "due to the ineptness, incompetence and naiveté of our own [Western] efforts."[19] Accordingly, the foundation should pursue three main objectives: (1) support the development of a cadre of several hundred social scientists with extensive field experience in the LDCs "to advance the competence of this country in the next fifty years to deal intelligently in its relations to less developed countries";[20] (2) analyze and distill from past experience what lessons have been learned; "otherwise, we merely repeat mistakes—and find new ones";[21] and (3) help the LDCs to help themselves.

Early in 1948, the foundation's social-science officers had already launched an intensive in-house review about what could and should be done regarding the escalating interest in, attention demanded by, and needs of the developing areas. Other foundation divisions were similarly engaged; but Health and Medicine already had extensive Third World experience, and Agriculture was by then deeply involved in its expanding program in Mexico and elsewhere in Latin America. This in-house debate and assessment among the social scientists continued until the mid-1950s. In the meantime, actions along the lines of Willits's recommendations were initiated. Several grants were made to support Third World area-studies programs in the United States (such as Near Eastern Studies at Princeton, Southeast Asian Studies at Cornell, and Far Eastern Studies at Washington and Columbia) and fieldwork by individual Northern Hemisphere scholars in Southern Hemisphere settings—all aimed at enhancing a capacity better to understand the societies, cultures, and economies of the latter. Also in 1951 came the first post-Nankai capacitation grant to a Third World social-science institution—the Gokhale Institute of Politics and Economics in Poona, India, for demographic, social, and economic research. Pressure to do more was mounting on all sides. Norman Buchanan noted that according to trustee mandate, The Rockefeller Foundation had an obligation to contribute to the development of the social sciences worldwide.

In December 1954 John D. Rockefeller III, then chairman of the board of trustees, wrote to foundation president Dean Rusk stating that it was becoming increasingly obvious that the underdeveloped areas would play an increasingly important part in the world of the future and suggesting that they be added as a distinct new program area of the foundation. A few months later, in an overall review of the foundation's program, Rusk observed that there already had been a shift of orientation in the program toward the underdeveloped countries. Appropriations for the LDCs had increased steadily from $3.5 million in 1953, to $4.5 million in 1954, to $6.5 million in 1955. But more had to be done, particularly by the social sciences, which have "not been active south of the Rio Grande and it now seems necessary to close the gap."[22]

In December 1955 Rusk secured the approval of the board of trustees for an officers' proposal that under an "Expanded Program" the foundation use $5 million per year of capital funds for a period of five to ten years specifically earmarked for the LDCs, in addition to sums for the LDCs already in the "Regular Program" budget—thus bringing the total to $9–11 million per year. He observed that, given the enormity of the needs and the magnitude of activities by other donor agencies, even this was a pittance. However, he argued, the foundation did have some special nonfinancial assets that, applied at key leverage points, could make a large contribution. These included officers and staff with long service in develping countries; total flexibility in recruiting; a reputation for political disinterestedness; capability for acting promptly; preparedness for long-term involvement;

and extensive experience in training leadership for scholarship and public service. As to the financial effect these outlays would have on the foundation, Rusk noted that the market value of securities held by the foundation had increased from $270 million in 1950 to $557 million in 1955; therefore, spending into capital was feasible.

In a seminal staff paper circulated the following month, Social Science director Norman S. Buchanan proposed that, by their very nature, the key leverage points in the LDCs for the developmental epoch immediately ahead were universities and institutes. As the "main citadels of protection for the 'disinterested' scholar or scientist . . . they are the most appropriate centers for RF support."[23] Buchanan noted that the major programs of other larger donors were "tending to stress highly immediate needs and the practical necessities of the moment to the neglect of the more basic but less obvious foundations on which a country has to rest its capacity for improving the well-being of its people. . . . RF's resources," he concluded, "do not allow it to compete with these large-scale programs of other agencies. But could it not perform a singularly important role in development if it were to bring a few universities in these countries to a level of excellence?"[24] Key operative concepts in the Buchanan formulation were "concentration" on a few selected universities, development of them as "centers of excellence" to serve as poles of emulation and diffusion, and the combination of "teaching and research" and strengthening of the universities as a whole, not of just a single department or activity within them.

For the next six years the Expanded Program was in full swing, and the social sciences began extending their coverage throughout the developing world. Developmental and capacitation grants were made to, among others, the Indian School of International Studies; the Institute of Public Administration and the Department of Economics of the University of the Philippines; the Center of Latin American Monetary Studies, Mexico City; the Faculty of Economics of the University of Chile; the Economic Research Institute of the American University, Beirut; the Institute of Economic Research of the University of the Andes, Colombia; the Brazilian Institute of Economics of the Getulio Vargas Foundation, Brazil; the Faculty of Economics of the University of Nuevo León,Mexico; the Economic Research Center of the Catholic University of Chile; the Faculty of Economics of the University of Rio Grande do Sul, Brazil; and the Center of International Studies of El Colegio de México. Grants were also made to U.S. centers for research on economic-development problems of the Third World, as well as for improving the training milieu in the United States for foundation scholars and fellows pursuing advanced studies there.

During the Expanded Program phase, the LDC selected-universities strategy as a focus for coordinated effort in the Third World was the subject of much in-house discussion, dominated by such central issues as whether it should be foundation-operated (following the tradition of Health and Agricultural Sciences); incentives and modes of recruitment of expatriate staff; special arrangements for engaging American universities in the enterprise; and, above all, criteria for selection of the few LDC universities in which there would be interdisciplinary across-the-board concentration.

In December 1961 the new president, J. George Harrar, presented the trustees with a proposal for a new University Development Program (UDP), to be initiated in the Third World at an estimated cost of $100 million over a ten-to-fifteen-year period. The program would embody the concepts of concentration on a few selected universities (as against previous diffusion among many); of interdisciplinarity among the participating foundation divisions; of concern with the selected universities as wholes; and of preparedness to provide support for at least ten years, although no guarantee would be given in advance. In the months prior to the trustees' meeting, interdisciplinary teams of officers had visited all major Third World regions to make on-site evaluations of a large number of universities, from which a short list was compiled. From the latter would be selected, if the program was approved, six to nine UDP universities. The board approved the proposal "without blinking an eye," as Kenneth Thompson put it, and the University Development Program was officially launched.

From its beginning the University Development Program (the name was changed to Education for Development in 1974) has had one overall objective: to help a selected number of universities in Third World countries become centers of excellence, largely staffed by indigenous scholars and engaged in teaching and research relevant to national and regional needs. The program recognized that such countries—many of them on the threshold of independence in 1961—faced complex problems of social and economic development beyond solution by mere transfer of knowledge from the industrialized West. A major requirement, therefore, seemed to be strong universities within these nations, having research capacity not only for adapting existing knowledge to local situations, but also for creating essential new knowledge, as well as the development of teaching programs to educate the substantial numbers of individuals essential for social and economic development.

For almost two decades the University Development/Education for Development (UD/EFD) Program has been the foundation's primary mechanism for promoting the social sciences in the Third World. This program differs from the past less in the amount of resources allocated to this purpose than in the distinctiveness of the model or strategy that guided the foundation's support at each university. The precise institutional program was worked out cooperatively with relevant individuals in each institution. The crucial elements in the new approach were: (1) concentration on a few universities, (2) emphasis on long-term staff development, (3) temporary appointment of professional expatriate field staff to the participating universities, (4) long-term commitment to each cooperative project, and (5) support for applied research on national problems.

Before elaborating on each of these elements, it should be pointed out that the relative significance of the foundation's inputs is difficult to determine precisely and that in all cases there were many sources of funding. It is extremely difficult to unravel the fortuitous juxtaposition of forces—internal and external—that can so dramatically affect a Third World university's progress or decline.

1. Concentration on a few universities. The decision to work in only one or two locations in an entire continent was a distinctive feature of the new program, designed to maximize its effect. Such concentration provided a framework for encouraging and assessing proposals and conveying the boundaries of the foundation's interest. The support for a single institution in a country or region, however, made the cooperative program vulnerable to the volatile political currents and disruptions that have characterized a number of Third World universities. Private foundations have a comparative advantage over bilateral government donor agencies in being able to ride out short-term political disruptions, and most of the cooperative programs have experienced fluctuations during the period of the program.

Aside from general guidelines (that a university selected should be neither so good that it did not require assistance, nor so hopeless that funds would be wasted; and that there be geographic diversification), there was inevitably a large subjective element involved in the selection of specific institutions. The UD/EFD experience demonstrates forcefully that in the selection of centers of concentration, strength is built upon strength. Some of the most successful university projects have been those where prior investments by other donors, sometimes including The Rockefeller Foundation, had already started to build a physical and human infrastructure that enhanced the productivity of the foundation's contribution.

2. Emphasis on long-term staff development. A very heavy emphasis was given to indigenous-staff development through fellowships awarded for study, usually in the United States or Europe, to promising staff members recommended by the university. Whenever appropriate, doctoral candidates were enabled to pursue research in their home country or region in order to enhance the relevance of the research to national needs. A careful selection and counseling process has contributed to a high retention rate of returning fellows by the UD/EFD universities. Each university now has a core of well-educated, capable local scholars. Some former fellows have moved to government positions, where they have strengthened key agencies and have the potential to enhance understanding and support of the universities.

The increased cost of graduate education in the West and the development of new educational programs in the Third World suggest the importance of different patterns of support for staff development, and the foundation has provided support as a part of staff development for local fellowships, postdoctoral study, shorter-term fellowships for defined purposes, and some study abroad combined with local postgraduate programs. However, Third World postgraduate programs—despite their otherwise-powerful rationale—are not effective substitutes if classes are too large, thesis supervision inadequate, or language problems unresolved. In the longer run, however, strengthening Third World postgraduate programs in the social sciences is essential in the creation of local capacity for teaching and research.

3. Temporary appointment of professional expatriate field staff. The appointment of professional staff members of the foundation to regular faculty or administrative positions in each university, following normal university appointment procedures, provided interim teaching and research support, as well as continuity to the overall program. They were supplemented by visiting professors and researchers from universities in the United States or abroad for shorter-term appointments requested by the university leadership. The effectiveness of expatriate professors depended on several variables, some beyond their control. Those with prior international experience generally adjusted more quickly and were more effective than those on their first assignment. Assignments of two years or longer were more effective than one-year or briefer assignments. The provision of interim expatriate professors in the early stages of the program, particularly in the newer African universities, was indispensable, not only to set standards and provide leadership, but also to sustain and upgrade academic programs while their indigenous successors were completing their postgraduate education abroad. But the acceptability of substantial numbers of visiting staff exercising leadership positions was a function of a particular time, situation, and phase of receptivity that has now passed in much of the Third World, and with the substantial increase in the numbers of Third World scholars it is no longer needed.

4. Long-term commitment to each cooperative project. Although no guarantees were provided in advance, the foundation was prepared to furnish support for at least ten years to each university in the program. If doctoral programs require four to five years, the project must span the period from the selection of fellows to their full professional integration into the academic program a decade or more later. The foundation normally entered into a general agreement of cooperation with each university, with the foundation as a guest and a junior partner in the relationship. Based on an understanding of what the foundation was prepared to contribute, the university requested support for the combination of activities it felt was appropriate and most useful. This has varied significantly among universi-

ties and within a single university over time. When the program began in East Africa, for example, only 10 percent of the university staff was African, whereas in Thailand faculty members in the three cooperating institutions were all Thai. Consequently, in East Africa the emphasis was on identification and training of future staff, whereas in Thailand more resources were allocated to providing opportunities for further education of existing staff.

5. Support for applied research on national problems. One of the UD/EFD Program's major purposes was to contribute to the creation and application of knowledge by indigenous scholars in areas of critical importance to the Third World. Support was provided both to teaching departments and to research institutions; continuous efforts were necessary to moderate the inherent tensions that exist between them, in order to relate effectively the teaching and research function. The foundation has also encouraged students enrolled in local graduate programs, primarily at the master's level, to undertake applied-research projects for their theses.

Although strengthening the university as a whole has always been the primary concern, the interdisciplinary participation of foundation staff has necessarily led to an emphasis on their areas of professional specialization, namely, agriculture, health, and social sciences. Multidisciplinarity was an objective of the program from the beginning and saw the greatest realization in the support of development-oriented research. Approximately 45 percent of the total foundation expenditure of approximately $125 million over a two-decade period was made in support of the social sciences—and for most of that time, the chairman of the committee that implemented the program was a social scientist. The following project descriptions deal only with the development of the social sciences: political science; economics, including agricultural economics; sociology, including rural sociology; anthropology; geography; and, in a few instances, business administration, psychology, education, and linguistics.

Universities in East Africa

Higher education in East Africa began in 1921 with the creation, at Kampala, Uganda, of a technical-training institution named Makerere College. Makerere was subsequently expanded to include elementary training in medicine, but plans to upgrade it to university level were not fully realized until 1949, when it became the University College of East Africa. Meanwhile, a technical school in Nairobi, Kenya, had developed into East Africa's main source of qualified engineers and architects at a subuniversity level; renamed the Royal Technical College in 1958, it eventually became the University College, Nairobi.

In the late 1950s, with independence for Uganda, Kenya, and Tanganyika obviously near at hand, British and local authorities accelerated discussions aimed at establishing a multicampus, single University of East Africa to serve the region. The new institution, federally structured, would consist of the University College of East Africa (Makerere College), Kampala; the Royal College, Nairobi; and a new college, to be created in Dar es Salaam, Tanganyika. Whereas each college would have its own fully developed arts-and-sciences programs, the more expensive professional faculties would be maintained and shared at only one location.

Foundation officers were impressed with the potential of this plan, and shortly after formal inauguration of the University of East Africa in July 1963, UD/EFD cooperation began under an agreement that included substantial support for the social sciences. Ultimately this federal structure did not survive political developments and each country sought instead to develop its own comprehensive national university.

To increase the initially small numbers of East African staff, the foundation from the outset placed heavy emphasis on staff development for the various social-science departments, an endeavor that may well rank as its most lasting contribution to higher education in the region. More than 60 percent of the East Africans who completed graduate studies under Rockefeller Foundation fellowships now occupy positions of academic leadership in these departments.

Concurrently, the foundation sought to strengthen undergraduate teaching, in part by encouraging the production of locally based curricular materials; and, as East African faculty returned from studies abroad it collaborated in establishing graduate programs in economics (Nairobi) and education (Dar es Salaam) and a diplomacy training program at Nairobi.

To promote another objective, the expansion of applied social-science research focused on development issues, the foundation supported activities in the Makerere Institute of Social and Economic Research and the creation or development of three other research arms: The Institute for Development Studies at Nairobi, and the Economic Research Bureau and the Bureau of Resource Assessment and Land Use Planning at Dar es Salaam. All four have been fully incorporated into their respective university establishments and continue to attract as much national and external funding as they can handle, except for the Makerere Institute in the post-Amin period. By demonstrating how a university's intellectual social-science resources can be applied to problems relevant to shaping policy, they have become models emulated by other countries.

University of Ibadan, Nigeria

In 1962 the University of Ibadan, a newly independent entity after some fourteen years as a college in "special relationship" with the University of London, actively sought Rockefeller Foundation assistance for its plans to become a major research and training center serving Nigeria and West Africa. To foundation officers the university seemed a natural choice for UD/EFD activities, and cooperation began the same year. Staff development was a fundamental goal, but from the outset the foundation also gave special attention to innovative programs of research bearing on national and regional needs and to strengthening graduate education. Indeed, a significant portion of its support through 1979 related directly to the university's "indigenization, practicalization, and out-reach efforts." In addition to the health sciences, agriculture, and the humanities, the cooperative program at Ibadan emphasized the social sciences.

Over the years, the university's department of economics has become one of the strongest within the Faculty of Social Sciences, steadily improving its undergraduate teaching and developing a first-class master's-degree program (1969) and, more recently, a Ph.D. program. Part of the research in economics is carried out jointly with the Nigerian Institute for Social and Economic Research, an agency largely financed by the Nigerian government. All told, the foundation supported 137 fellows under the sponsorship of the university and this institute; about 75 of them are today on the Ibadan staff; 42 others hold appointments at other Nigerian universities or scientific and research institutions. Elsewhere in the social sciences, the foundation assisted progress in the departments of political science, sociology, geography, and agricultural economics.

In 1978–1979 the university experienced a series of crises, involving not only student unrest—leading to confrontations with police and closing of the campus—but also continuous problems arising from its financial situation. Despite these difficulties, Ibadan still has the best-qualified staff of any university in tropical Africa; among Nigerian universities, furthermore, it has the largest graduate program and a continuing potential for expanding and improving its graduate teaching and research. The specific programs that the foundation helped initiate have, to a remarkable degree, been institutionalized and are continuing with full Nigerian support.

By the time cooperative UD/EFD activities terminated in 1979, enrollment at the university had grown from about 1,500 to more than 8,000. Concurrently, Nigeria's university system had expanded to encompass thirteen universities, with a combined enrollment of about 60,000. The contribution made by the University of Ibadan to the leadership and staffing of the new institutions has been substantial.

University of the Philippines

Various considerations favored the University of the Philippines as the location for the first UD/EFD center in Southeast Asia. Founded in 1908, it was patterned on the American system of education; it had received extensive previous assistance from the foundation, dating back to 1922; the lower ranks of its faculty included a group of able young scholars; and of its attached professional units, both its medical school and college of agriculture had earned good reputations. Furthermore, although the university in 1962 was still essentially an undergraduate college, it had by then adopted the goal of becoming a major center of graduate education in a broad range of disciplines.

Cooperation under the UD/EFD Program began officially in April 1962, a time of political stability in the Philippines. By the mid-1960s, however, a movement of national radicalism had emerged, and by the end of the decade, bowing to pressure from a minority on campus who regarded the program as an intrusive American presence, university and foundation officials agreed that the cooperative efforts should be largely terminated. The one exception to this decision was the School of Economics, whose dean and faculty members strongly urged continuation of the partnership. As a result, the foundation has maintained its assistance in economics, providing general support until it became unnecessary in the late 1970s and, more recently, making grants for a new area of graduate specialization, demographic economics.

The School of Economics came into being in 1965. Merged in it at that time were the university's department of economics, established in 1926 and offering a master's-degree program since 1932; and a 1957 creation, the Institute of Economic Development and Research. In the year of the merger, the school commenced a nondegree program in developmental economics for Philippine government officials, under which over 500 midlevel technical personnel have since earned certificates. Three years later, in 1968, the school established a doctoral program in economics.

Today the school's graduate training and research program is recognized as the best in Southeast Asia, and substantial numbers of its students come from elsewhere in the region. Demand for services of the graduates is high, both by government ministries and by the private sector. The research arm of the school, the Institute of Economic Development and Research, continues to acquire public and private support for its work which includes current studies regarding international economics, human resources, population, income distribution and poverty, regional and rural development, money and finance, and development-impact analyses. Since 1975, moreover, the government-created Philippine Center for Economic Development has directed its efforts to providing financial support for research, teaching, training, and other activities of the school.

Reviewers have suggested that foundation assistance under the UD/EFD Program, by reason of its timing and duration, contributed significantly to the school's development and helped bring about the present level of funding.

Universidad del Valle, Colombia

The Universidad del Valle, a public university of the department of Valle del Cauca, was founded in 1945 and first attracted The Rockefeller Foundation's attention in the early 1950s, when the young leaders of its medical school began experimenting with new educational methods and approaches, including the distinct innovation for Latin America of full-time rather than part-time faculty. As of 1961, the foundation had made several grants in support of the medical school, and it was to some extent because of this experience, but also because the university had by then demonstrated good overall potential for responding to the problems of Colombian society, that it was selected in that year as a UD/EFD center.

Cooperative efforts were directed to (1) developing a modern medical school in which all the health sciences would be promoted; (2) creating a social-science faculty to provide instruction in economics, political science, and sociology as keys to the understanding of the structure and dynamics of society; (3) expanding the existing faculty of philosophy, literature, and history into a full-fledged Division of the Humanities; and (4) introducing approved techniques of administration and strengthening the library. Concurrently, the university set about developing departments in the physical and biological sciences and mathematics (now comprehended in the Science Division), and consolidating several professional units into a single Engineering Division.

By 1977, the final year of foundation cooperation under the UD/EFD Program, the university had grown from a small, promising institution into a major teaching and research center, and in the same period had exerted a substantial influence on Colombian society. Indeed, outside observers have credited the university with playing a major role in bringing the economy of the Cauca Valley to its present prosperous condition.

The performance of the Economics and Social Science Division has, however, been a disappointment. One persistent problem during the period of cooperation was the high rate of turnover in the deanship, which not only meant lack of coherent leadership but also left the division poorly situated to retain its full-time teachers in the face of career opportunities offered by the public sector in Bogotá and the private sector in the university's home city of Cali. At the start of the 1970–1971 academic year, the shortage of teaching personnel had become so severe that the students—also dissatisfied on other grounds—declared a strike, which continued through 1972.

The division managed to survive this turmoil and today maintains its teaching staff and a modest research program. Although in the 1960s it established master's-degree programs in both agricultural economics and industrial management, the former did not survive the upheaval in the early 1970s and the latter has since been transferred to the Engineering Division. Nevertheless, by assisting the Economics and Social Science Division in its early years to create a body of relevant teaching materials—in Spanish and directed to Colombian problems—the foundation undoubtedly helped bring about the present research emphasis on Colombian development issues.

Universities in Bangkok, Thailand

In launching UD/EFD activities in Bangkok in 1963, The Rockefeller Foundation resumed a cooperative relationship with Thailand that had begun nearly fifty years earlier with grants primarily in medical education. Selected for the new undertaking were three of the country's leading educational institutions: Thammasat University, founded in 1933 as the University of Moral and Political Sciences, which concentrated on the humanities and the social sciences; the University of Medical Sciences, founded in 1942 and subsequently renamed Mahidol University; and Kasetsart University, founded in 1943 and devoted to the agricultural sciences.

By the formal termination date of December 1981, the cooperative program in Bangkok will have proved the most extensive of all the foundation's UD/EFD efforts, involving at one point, for example, the assignment there of about thirty-five foundation field staff members and visiting professors. Although at the outset foundation officers had encouraging discussion with leaders of the three universities about the development of a common graduate program, this concept was never realized.

In the social sciences, the foundation provided support for economics, political science, sociology, and anthropology at Thammasat, and for agricultural economics at Kasetsart. The main focus at Thammasat was the Faculty of Economics, and because in 1963 the university was undergoing fundamental changes, circumstances favored a long-range cooperative plan for the economics faculty. This plan involved strengthening undergraduate teaching through staff development and curricular reform, inaugurating an English-language master's-degree program in economics, and, finally, creation of an effective research program.

This order of priorities reflected the faculty's situation at the start: a staff composed of only six full-time and some sixty part-time members drawn from government agencies; very large classes; and instruction based largely on lectures, with little reading assigned and no writing required. As a result of staff development via scholarships and fellowships, some fifteen staff members completed master's-level training at the University of the Philippine's School of Economics, and some thirty earned the doctorate in studies abroad, primarily in the United States. Concurrently, foundation-supported visiting professors—on both short- and long-term assignment—helped with curricular reform, in particular the development of teaching materials that reflected the Thai economy and society.

The English-language master's program in economics began in the summer of 1969, and by 1975 most responsibility for teaching and thesis supervision, as well as for the undergraduate program, had been taken over by returning Thai staff. Most of the over 100 theses completed under the English-language master's program and its Thai-language counterpart were focused on development issues in Thailand. Together, these papers represented probably the best collection assembled anywhere of empirical and analytical material on the Thai economy.

Founded during the transition from an absolute to a constitutional monarchy in the 1930s, Thammasat University has seldom been out of the political limelight. This was particularly true during the 1970s, when students from Thammasat and other universities and technical schools formed a protest movement that led to the overthrow of the military government in October 1973. During the turbulent years that followed, students in general, and Thammasat in particular, were identified with the problems of political instability—accentuated by the collapse in 1975 of the U.S.-supported war in Vietnam. Military rule was reinstated after a bloody attack on the students at the Thammasat campus, and the university's rector, Dr. Puey Ungphakorn, the nation's leading economist, was forced into exile at the peril of his life.

The Thammasat staff members who earned their Ph.D.'s abroad in the 1970s returned to a campus that until recently was highly politicized. Nevertheless, progress toward the final objective for the Thammasat Faculty of Economics, the creation of an effective research program, has continued slowly. At present, the faculty is recognized as a valuable resource for the study of national social and economic problems.

Gadjah Mada University, Indonesia

Founded in 1949 during Indonesia's struggle for independence, Gadjah Mada is the oldest of the universities established by the Indonesians themselves. It started out under an inherited tradition of relatively autonomous faculties, minimal contact with the community, and curricula unrelated to national problems—a mold that proved difficult to break. By 1971, however, the university's leaders had resolved on gradually transforming Gadjah Mada into an institution capable of serving national needs, and on this basis, cooperative UD/EFD activities began.

In the social sciences, The Rockefeller Foundation has focused its attention on two faculties and two multidisciplinary but essentially social-science-oriented research institutes. For the Faculty of Economics, staff development was stressed from the outset, through both foundation administered fellowships and funds provided to the university for this purpose. Initial cooperation with the faculty included implementation of an agricultural-economics workshop designed, at the ministry of education's request, to upgrade staff at provincial universities in economic theory, analytical tools, and research methodology. After five years this objective had been largely accomplished; moreover, the number of faculty staff with advanced training was increasing. Accordingly, in 1976—again at the ministry's request—the faculty initiated Indonesia's first structured Ph.D. program based on course work and a dissertation. Although the process of staff development is still far from complete, the faculty today is the leading economics faculty in the country and plays an important role not only in training staff for provincial universities but also in conducting research and consultancies for government ministries.

In the case of the Faculty of Social and Political Sciences, the foundation has stressed the production of appropriate undergraduate teaching materials, those available in Indonesia being extremely limited in scope. So far, four books of selected texts have been published. Here, too, staff development remains a prime requirement, and it is therefore an encouraging sign that younger, better-trained staff are choosing to help build the faculty.

The Institute of Population Studies was established in 1973 with three main objectives: to contribute to an understanding of Indonesia's population problems; to create public awareness of the nature and extent of these problems; and to help devise means for their solution. Headed by an internationally recognized Indonesian scholar, it has grown into one of the most active and respected research centers in the country and, because of the quality and relevance of its work, readily obtains funding for major research projects from the government as well as international donors. The students in the Institute's training programs come from population-studies centers throughout Indonesia, government ministries, provincial universities, and family-planning organizations.

The Institute of Rural and Regional Studies, also established in 1973, focuses on rural-development issues. In addition to a training program for the staff of regional planning boards, the institute conducts a considerable amount of research under the financial auspices of the ministry of internal affairs and the provincial planning ministry.

The UD/EFD Program at Gadjah Mada still has several years to run. Much more time must elapse before its full contribution to development of the social sciences in Indonesia can be assessed.

National University of Zaire

The foundation began this cooperative program in 1972. Zaire—third largest of the African countries in area, fourth largest in population, and French-speaking by colonial inheritance—was then in the middle of a period of relative economic prosperity and seemingly determined on a course of cultural and economic nationalism. Reflecting this trend, the government in

1971 had nationalized all institutions of higher learning and amalgamated them into a single system, The National University of Zaire (UNAZA), with campuses at Kinshasha, Lubumbashi, and Kisangani. Under the government's plan, each campus was to specialize in a separate set of disciplines, thereby avoiding duplication of effort; moreover, the ambitious reorganization plan called for drastic revision of curricula and degree programs to make them relevant to the country's needs.

In subsequent years, the downturn in world copper prices exposed the fragility of Zaire's economic base. The consequences for UNAZA were a massive reduction in financial resources, sharply diminished professional salaries, disruption of scientific activity, and deterioration of its logistic infrastructure. Fully aware in 1972 of these eventualities, The Rockefeller Foundation nevertheless took on the challenge of cooperating with the university as a UD/EFD center in the fields of health, agriculture, and the social sciences.

In the social sciences, which were broadly defined, support has been provided for the Faculty of Economics at Kinshasa, the Faculty of Social Sciences at Lubumbashi, and the Center of Interdisciplinary Research on the Development of Education (CRIDE) at Kisangani, with the scope of the program adjusted in each instance to local circumstances.

For junior Zairean faculty members sent abroad under foundation auspices—either on short-term training courses or to carry out doctoral studies, sometimes completed overseas and sometimes involving defense of their dissertations at UNAZA—reintegration into the university on return home has been generally smooth in academic terms. Staff development aside, however, the record of achievement is disappointing.

Although significant changes in university curricula were introduced after 1972, to help students acquire immediately applicable skills and thus become directly employable even if they left the university after completing only two years, implementation of these changes remains spotty. Likewise, the quality and volume of research performed at UNAZA have declined in recent years, owing mostly to the lack of resources. Only the units given foundation support are still carrying on useful work, most notably CRIDE at Kisangani. At the Lubumbashi campus, where one of the chief contributions of foundation-supported visiting staff (now departed) was the establishment of graduate programs, resources for their continuation no longer exist.

In view of the immense difficulties encountered in Zaire because of logistic and financial problems, the foundation is terminating this cooperative program earlier than planned, using the final grant to help reintegrate additional UNAZA staff members returning from training overseas.

The challenge posed by UNAZA still exists, but whether Zaire can make effective use of its human resources, given its current economic and political situation, remains a question.

Federal University of Bahia, Brazil

Cooperative activities with the Federal University of the State of Bahia began in mid-1973. University leaders were eager to modernize the traditional approach of the then twenty-seven-year-old institution, and the program that they jointly planned with foundation officers featured not only a reorganization on interdisciplinary lines but also an emphasis on community- and regional-development issues. Although this innovative and ambitious concept is yet to be realized, foundation support has contributed to progress with existing faculties and departments in the fields of health, agriculture, and social sciences.

One specific achievement is the establishment of a master's-degree program in economics, begun on a trial basis in 1973 and equipped with a substantially revised curriculum in 1974. The continuing shortage of well-qualified Brazilian staff is still a problem; however, two members of the teaching staff have now returned after earning the doctorate abroad on foundation fellowships, and the university is maintaining efforts to recruit additional economists from elsewhere in the country. Also worthy of mention is the current university requirement—novel for Brazil—that students enrolled in this graduate program participate in teaching undergraduate economics; some fifty past and present graduate students are currently either teaching in the Federal University or other universities in Bahia, or working in government institutions. Although the research function of the program has lagged because of staff scarcity, the master's theses completed are proving to be a valuable source of information and analysis regarding developments in Bahia. As more Brazilian staff return from studies abroad, it is expected that the pace of research will increase.

The foundation has also provided support for a master's-degree program in the social sciences that includes the disciplines of anthropology, sociology, political science, and social and economic history. Created in 1968 with the objective of training graduates for research and university-level teaching, this program has until recently been strong only on the theoretical side. Now, however, as better-qualified social scientists are returning to the faculty, it is acquiring a broader base and commencing empirical research on real problems facing Bahia's rural and urban regions.

As previously noted, when President Harrar first proposed a University Development Program to the trustees in 1961, he indicated that it might be a twelve-to-fifteen-year undertaking and might cost up to $100 million. In 1977, just fifteen years after formal establishment of the UD/EFD Program, the board decided to complete it as a separate program within the period required for orderly and responsible termination. Although cooperative projects at three major universities were then still at midpoint, the trustees and officers agreed that once support for these was brought to a close by the end of 1983, the original objectives would largely have been realized. Thus, the program would stand as a $125 million, twenty-year achievement.

In 1977 the trustees also agreed that a comprehensive review should be made of the program—the largest single interdisciplinary undertaking in the foundation's history. Its objective would be to understand the historical experience in order to generalize what has been learned that might be relevant to the foundation and to other international organizations concerned with strengthening higher education in the developing world. The results of the review will appear in two volumes: the first, a critical case study of the program; the second, a more general analysis of this experience within the context of post–World War II development of higher education in the Third World.

Foundation officers believe that it was appropriate and, given its comparative advantage, highly desirable for the foundation to undertake a program to strengthen the social, agricultural, and health sciences in universities in the developing countries for the two decades beginning in the early 1960s. The program was a timely intervention, for if it had been launched earlier, it would have confronted colonial regimes in Africa and Indonesia; launched later, it would have encountered a less receptive climate for the university-development type of approach. The two-phased concept of first developing the university as a strong institution (UD) and then fostering its developmental capacities and role (EFD) was valid. After meeting the basic institution-building requirements, a stronger emphasis on developmental activities became possible as increased numbers of local staff returned to their institutions after completing postgraduate education. The strong expatriate presence was essential in the early phase, and the foundation's professional field staff was successful in establishing standards, largely because of its long-term commitment and professionalism. The primacy given to local-staff development through the fellowship program was the critical factor in establishing a capacity in the universities to continue to expand and strengthen their teaching and research.

In summary, the Social Science Division of The Rockefeller Foundation, fifty-two years old in 1982, has its roots in the Laura Spelman Rockefeller Memorial, whose director, Beardsley Ruml, has been called the "father of social sciences in America." This chapter describes the foundation's role in the creation of the modern empirical and quantitative social sciences in the United States and their extension abroad. The balance shifted to the developing countries under the Expanded Program, launched by Dean Rusk in 1955. This was followed by the establishment of the UD/EFD Program in 1961, which became the primary mechanism for support of the social sciences over the past two decades. Although this phase of the foundation's engagement with building the social sciences in the developing countries is nearing conclusion, the task is not finished. The succeeding chapters in this volume describe the varying stages of institution-alization of the social-science communities in different regions of the Third World and the strong forces impeding the full realization of their professional potential. Common to all regions is frustration with the pace of development and its failure to benefit vast segments of the population. Social scientists require continuing support and encouragement if they are effectively to confront the challenges posed by these conditions and increase understanding of the development process and how it can be channeled to meet urgent social and economic needs.

Notes

1. Raymond B. Fosdick, *The Rockefeller Foundation* (New York: Harper & Brothers, 1952), p. 193.
2. Beardsley Ruml, Memorandum to the Trustees, October 1922, Laura Spelman Rockefeller Memorial Files, Rockefeller Archive Center.
3. Ibid.
4. Beardsley Ruml, Final Report of the Laura Spelman Rockefeller Memorial, 1933.
5. Joseph H. Willits, Memorandum to Raymond B. Fosdick, November 10, 1942, Rockefeller Archive Center.
6. Ruml, Final Report, p. 9.
7. Ibid.
8. Ibid.
9. Fosdick, *The Rockefeller Foundation,* p. 142.
10. Ibid., p. 145.
11. Ruml, Final Report.
12. Joseph H. Willits, Memorandum to Raymond B. Fosdick, November 10, 1942.
13. Fosdick, *The Rockefeller Foundation,* p. 293.
14. Special Trustee Committee Report, 1934, Rockefeller Archive Center.
15. Selskar Gunn, Outline of China Policy, January 23, 1934, Rockefeller Archive Center.
16. Ibid.
17. "Report of the Special Committee on Policy and Program of the Rockefeller Foundation," December 1946, p. 13, Rockefeller Archive Center.
18. Joseph H. Willits, "Preliminary Conclusions from the Study of Crete," March 8, 1949, Rockefeller Archive Center.
19. Ibid.
20. Ibid.

21. Ibid.

22. Dean Rusk, Memorandum, May 1955, Rockefeller Archive Center.

23. Norman Buchanan, "A Note on the Rockefeller Foundation Program for the Underdeveloped Areas," January 3, 1956, Rockefeller Archive Center.

24. Ibid.

Part II
The State of the Art:
Selected Regional Surveys

4

Hybrids in Native Soil: The Social Sciences in Southeast Asia

Warren F. Ilchman

Teachers and the Taught

Since seeing as a youth the play *The Corn Is Green,* I have kept in my heart the tales of successful teachers. These tales serve to inspire the weary to continue the often unfriendly task of making the strange familiar to those accustomed only to what they already know. Some of the names are familiar, like Miss Moffat, Lord Jowett, and Thomas Arnold. Others in this hagiography are more recent, such as Wijoyo Nitisastro of Indonesia. In the early 1960s, Wijoyo and his colleagues, all recently educated in the United States, found themselves in virtual intellectual exile while Sukarno led the country. A year before Sukarno outlawed the teaching of "Western economics," Wijoyo and his University of Indonesia colleagues had begun to teach economics to the Indonesian military in Bandung. A few years and a coup later, the same economics lecturers found themselves government ministers and Wijoyo head of all state planning. Since Aristotle and Alexander, this was the ultimate in respect paid by a student to his or her teacher, and it was paid not only to these Indonesian economists, but also to their American teachers in Berkeley and Pittsburgh and to the teachers of their teachers in the two Cambridges.

Other subjects of these heroic tales are whole societies or places as inspired teachers, inspired because they were so successful in choosing apt pupils who seemed to learn their lessons well. The Japanese, for example, during their occupation of Malaya in World War II, established two schools (Syonon Koa Kunrenjo and Malai Koa Kunrenjo) and a Rhodes-like Tokugawa scholarship program taking the best students to Japan to ensure future national leadership of high quality, sympathetic to the Japanese. The curric-

The intellectual debts I owe on this chapter are many. In four years, I spoke with hundreds of social scientists in Southeast Asia. If I could, I would acknowledge them all. As I cannot, I would like to acknowledge the contributions of four: Somsakdi Xuto, Raul de Guzman, Kernial S. Sandhu, and Selo Soemardjan. My former colleagues in the Ford Foundation in Southeast Asia have made a major contribution to the ideas and judgments contained here; in particular I want to name Peter Weldon, Sidney Jones, Reuben Frodin, Ted Smith, Dave Pfanner, Michael Morfit, Pepe Abueva, John Cool, Peter Geithner, Gerry Fry, Barry Gaberman, David and Frances Korten, and John Bresnan. So many ideas for this paper came from David Szanton of the U.S. Social Science Research Council that I probably should have made him a coauthor. Needless to say, I bear responsibility for any misinterpretations of what they so intelligently conveyed.

ulum stressed discipline, overcoming hardships, and rigor *(seishun)*. The names of the students in this enterprise read now like a *Who's Who* of contemporary Malaysia—ministers, even prime ministers, vice-chancellors, and judges. The Japanese apparently chose well and educated thoroughly. Their only flaw was that, like most teachers, they were not around to enjoy the benefits of their efforts.[1]

An example of a place's being a teacher is Paris. Until the end of World War I, King Rama VI forbade Siamese youths on King's Scholarships from going to Paris to study, so fearful was he of the infectiousness of the idea of revolution. After 1918 this prohibition was relaxed and a group of young Siamese went to Paris, mostly to study law. These young men, under the leadership of their fellow student from Paris Pridi Banomyong, joined with the military to stage the constitutional revolution of 1932. It was clear that Paris taught her political lessons well, perhaps even including the lesson of governmental instability.

Though I would not necessarily hold with Keynes that statesmen are all subject to the ideas of some academic scribbler of an earlier era and that their ideas were learned while the statesmen were relatively young (it is true that older statesmen sometimes act as if they believed it; the publication of the first volume on the Thai economy by Phraya Suriyanuwat in 1911 resulted in the King's banning the teaching of economics for some period), I do believe that education counts and that, at least at the outset and in later refreshment, it is always foreign in origin. To discuss one case of that sharing and naturalizing process—the social sciences in Southeast Asia—it is neces·sary to put the process in the general context of the diffusion of the idea of the university and, more particularly, of the rise in the contemporary university of a secular faith in social positivism. Both provide the set of constraints within which Southeast Asian institutional development took place; both were the origin of the available social technologies; both act as the point of departure and the source of criticism for the naturalizing process.

The Idea of the University

Of man's many achievements, the spread of the idea of the university may be one of the most persistent, pervasive, and notable. Since the first band of scholars was recalled home from Paris to establish Oxford, there has been continuous and relentless diffusion and replication of the concept of an institution that would simultaneously foster learning for its own sake, the *studium generale,* and adapt learning to the needs of the local environment. The fifteenth century saw the idea spread to Germany and Scotland; the sixteenth century, from Spain to the Southern Hemisphere of the New World, to Lima, to Guatemala, to Mexico City, and across the ocean to

Manila; the seventeenth century, from Britain to the Northern Hemisphere of the New World, to Cambridge; from the latter, to the denominational colleges on the eastern seaboard in the eighteenth century and to the Midwest in the early nineteenth century and then as land-grant institutions across the United States for the remainder of the century and into the next. The nineteenth century saw the idea also spread to Australia and New Zealand and in 1857 to three places in India, to Bombay, Madras, and Calcutta.[2] A decade later, the Japanese found their model in the German universities, and a few decades later the Siamese found theirs in both the French and the British.

The twentieth century has seen an unprecedented diffusion of the idea of the university. Recent decades have been marked by the establishment of universities by the hundreds: from Berkeley to the multicampuses of the University of California, from teachers' colleges to comprehensive universities, from nothing to Shady Valley Community College, somewhere in Southern California. The process was recapitulated everywhere: in Europe, Asia, Africa, and Latin America. Some new countries built new universities; some established institutions in the capital assisted new institutions in the provinces. The case of Thailand is typical: from Chulalongkorn University in 1917 to Thammasat in 1933, to Silpakorn and Kasetsart universities in 1943, to Sri Nakharinwirot in 1954, to the Asian Institute of Technology in 1959 and Mahidol in 1960, and then to the provinces with the three universities in 1964 and 1966, and then the "open"university in 1971, with a second university about to begin.

An action repeated so often in such diverse and often unpromising settings requires a model, or template, as Eric Ashby calls it. This model is necessary to guide the organization of knowledge, the way learning is imparted, and the determination of the population at whom the education is aimed and the objectives for which their education should prepare them. Possessing a model helps to economize on necessary choices and eliminate the possibility of reinventing existing processes. The model can also hinder institutional creativity in adapting to local needs and in overcoming what is wasteful in the model internationally. But a model there is. It was once provided by the church; later, by whatever empire of which one's country was a colony. Today, given the replication of the idea of the university hundreds of times, perhaps even a thousand, in the last two decades, a World University Model has emerged. Each new university bears remarkable resemblance to those before it and to those developing contemporaneously with it. Few innovations seem to persist; what initially appears as an experiment in, say, the organization of knowledge (e.g., a college of comparative studies) proves to be a transitional device until money and personnel permit the proper implementation of the World University Model. Where once the church and empire diffused the idea of the university and determined the model by which it was replicated, the present World University Model is encouraged by the returning foreign-educated, by what has recently been developed in a neighboring country, and by the ministrations of foundations, national aid-givers, and international organizations such as UNESCO and UNDP.

The model has seven main features. First, the primary target group for university education is young adults, and the university is to serve as society's gatekeeper for these young adults to assume positions of prestige and responsibility. Second, the state is the main source of structured decisions about the institution and the responsible agent to ensure its proper performance. Third, knowledge is to be organized by disciplines. As far as I know, there have been virtually no attempts to organize knowledge differently—perhaps by problems or purposes to be served. The array of disciplines is also substantially uniform: so many varieties of social sciences, humanities, and natural science, and so many forms of engineering, areas of medicine, constituents of business management, aspects of agriculture, and so on. When finances and/or personnel preclude the full array, what is lacking becomes a deficiency that needs remedying, and chairmen, deans, vice-chancellors, and aid givers never cease to remind those higher in authority about the problem. Fourth, research within the discipline is the means of advancing knowledge. Fifth, a fundamental responsibility of those fulfilling instructional roles is to participate in the international exchange of knowledge as equal professionals and, at the same time, make their learning available for local needs that are deemed legitimate by the authorities. Sixth, the experience of students is to be organized hierarchically by a degree structure that culminates in the degree required to teach the subject. Transitionally, those in lower positions in the degree structure can teach, but this is only a temporary dispensation. Finally, a nation should seek to be self-reliant in producing all the skills required to maintain its universities. Borrow advanced education while you must, but do not remain a cultural debtor.

When universities in Southeast Asia were developed, the World University Model prevailed, and still does. The social sciences in that region must be understood in the context of their universities (and their compulsions). To understand the urgings for improvement, the designs for change, and the analysis of what is deficient and why, the World University Model and its Southeast Asian manifestations must be taken into account.

The Rise of Social Positivism

The contemporary university has been characterized by the rise of a secular faith in social positivism. When Clifford Geertz proposed a program of improving social-science research in Indonesia, he concluded by saying,

> For Indonesians to cultivate the social sciences is to join one of the great movements of contemporary thought, to become part of an intellectual endeavor which, though it began in the West, is more a product of an age than a place. It is to enter, for better or worse, into a critical . . . aspect of twentieth century civilization, a civilization marked, among other things, by a tremendous self-consciousness concerning its own foundations.[3]

In its university context, what Geertz is referring to is the rise and differentiation of the social sciences as part of the legitimate curriculum of the university. What motivated this effort was the belief in the legitimacy of understanding based on social positivism, an idea inspired by social philosophers in the late nineteenth and early twentieth centuries and by empiricists in our own era. Belief in social positivism made necessary for its adherents the bursting of moral philosophy as a discipline to make way for economics and psychology; the same belief made history too confining for those who wanted political science to exist as an autonomous discipline. From those social sciences and other sources, people who felt the social reality they wished to understand and teach about was not adequately treated called into existence the disciplines of anthropology and sociology. The more applied social sciences followed shortly thereafter. Once the disciplines were differentiated, their proponents in different parts of the world lobbied for recognition and eventual parity as faculties and providers of equivalent degrees. Now a part of the World University Model, this remarkably recent concept of social sciences—in a sense a development of the post–World War II period—is diffused along with other aspects of the model whenever universities are created or improved.

I call it the rise in the contemporary university of a secular faith in social positivism. By that I mean that those who profess to be social scientists and who are concerned about the division of labor and the social means of reducing scarcity share with each other—and not necessarily with those who profess to be other than social scientists—a conviction that what counts in explaining social phenomena is what may be observed directly or indirectly, that behind individual acts is a knowable process—an economy, a polity, a society, a personality—about which knowledge can be cumulative, and that this process can be understood and communicated through the use of numbers and metaphors. The better the numbers, the greater the likelihood of finding the truth. It is a secular faith in that its adherents believe human relations can be explained in their own terms, without reference to the supernatural. It also holds that certain things that might be known about social relations can be acted upon with the prospect of changing social relations. These articles of faith are seldom tested or even testable. The chief form of piety is not to hold them up to the null hypothesis, but to do research. Research is to the social scientist what prayer is to the religious. The outcome of the research is less important than the activity itself.

In terms of Southeast Asian social scientists, this idea of the rise of a secular faith in social positivism helps us appreciate the tensions between and among disciplines, the variable sense of legitimacy in the university curriculum, the urge to participate in public policy as a test of knowledge, and the concern about the adequacy of research methodology and the infrastructure to count social things.

The Social-Science Community

The worldwide diffusion of the idea of the university and particularly the rise in those universities of a secular faith in social positivism explicitly affected the social sciences in Thailand, the Philippines, Indonesia, Malaysia, and Singapore is the subject to which we will now turn. The best way to begin is to meet members of that social-science community.

A Pioneer

I am one of the first holders of a Ph.D. in the social sciences in my country. Against the opposition of the colonial rulers and my parents, I left my country for the United States shortly before the Second World War. My parents assumed I would be a lawyer and join them in the call for the legislative rights of our people against the metropolitan power. I wished to be a scholar. Because I had studied English in school and read English often and well, I felt I could catch up with my American classmates. I also believed the United States was friendlier than other white countries to foreign students.

The graduate university I attended was one of the few U.S. institutions I had ever heard of; fortunately, it was a good choice. Many professors were away to the war, but I got sufficient quality attention to become well grounded in the discipline—at least as it was then taught. My dissertation, which I finished in late 1945, was on an aspect of colonial occupation of my country. Although I wrote this on a university fellowship (a great honor for a foreign student), I had all sorts of jobs in financing my way through my doctorate. At these various jobs, I met some of my most enduring friends.

I returned to my country shortly after the war. Liberation had already come. I had hoped my dissertation would have served that cause, but I was too late and could only hope it would now be published so that the young could know about colonialism. I returned to the elite university in the capital where I had been an undergraduate; the acting rector immediately hired me—not simply as professor but as chairman of the department! One of my first tasks was to usher out the colonial teachers (my teachers!) and to arrange a curriculum for our nationalist future. I was sorry to see my teachers leave, especially given what they had experienced at the hands of the Japanese, but it was important to bring the most modern learning to our people and they did not have it. I naturally borrowed heavily from the program through which I had gone, but I also had the help of two recently returned and recently hired M.A.'s. They both hoped to return for their doctorates, but had decided to commit themselves to the job of building a nation.

The three of us had to teach the curriculum, hire a faculty, and develop a plan for staff training. As I couldn't spare the M.A.'s, of course, slowly we began to send our colleagues off for further study. I tried to ensure that they went to the States, though sometimes scholarships came from Australia and elsewhere at the point we needed them and so we sent people where we could. Some years after I gave up the chairmanship, a grant from USAID (or whatever it was called then) sent even larger numbers to the United States. Under any circumstances, as we waited for our young colleagues to return, those who remained taught what we knew and sometimes were only a page or two ahead of the students in subjects we didn't know at all.

In the mid-1950s, I thought we had the department going relatively well. Only three M.A.'s and one Ph.D. had returned, but more were expected with every year. The young staff awaiting opportunities for graduate work had begun almost to master our discipline's syllabus. We had also helped several other colleges establish a similar department. It was fortunate that we had had the experience of developing a curriculum, for our colleagues in other colleges had never been outside of the country. I was also active in establishing a professional society and holding our discipline's first conference. The papers were mostly short and formalistic, but we had made a beginning. We even launched a journal, but after a few issues we suspended publication.

At that point I thought it was time to do some real research. My dissertation seemed dated and I saw no purpose in revising it. I decided that I should leave the country for a year and take my family to a foreign university where I could read and write. I had been abroad several times since returning to my country, usually to international conferences where one wrote papers on subjects like "the role of education in national development." But the experience of research I knew as a doctoral student was what I sought again.

I hoped to go to the United States, for my children were becoming quite proficient in English. Through a Fulbright, I was eventually invited by my alma mater to return as a visiting professor. Before I could take the professorship, however, the change of government forced my rector to resign. As the senior professor and chairman, and known by my facility in English and my Fulbright to have good relations with Americans, I was appointed rector. Indeed, my first act was to negotiate a major staff development grant with Midwestern University in the States.

My chief responsibility was to develop six satellite campuses of the university in the provinces, and this I succeeded in doing. For six years, through expansion of the branches, through student riots and two army occupations of the campus in the capital, through epithets and charges of protecting Communists, my colleagues and I kept higher education going and kept our idea of the university alive.

By then it was clear to me I had used up all my capital with the regime, especially after its shift to the right, and had to step down. In my resignation, I stated my desire to return to scholarship and was allowed to resume my professorship. I looked forward to teaching again and to finding where the discipline had gone. By then, several colleagues had returned with their doctorates and I engaged the brightest of them, a former student of mine who went on to a brilliant career as a graduate student in the States, to tutor me on changes in the discipline. He had written several important papers, published internationally, and had been to many conferences abroad. Indeed, one of our department's problems, given our low salaries, was to keep this young scholar from joining an international agency. In any event, after a few sessions with him it was clear my background in mathematics and statistics was inadequate; I couldn't even ask the right questions or understand what he gave me to read. I was embarrassed, as was he, and we tacitly let my reeducation lapse.

Thus, when the UNDP offered me a two-year contract in Africa, I accepted, relieved that I would at least be able to do something for which I had expertise. What I achieved there is not of interest, but shortly before the contract expired and I was negotiating to stay on with UNESCO, a change in government at home—this time slightly to the left—brought me back as minister of state for higher education. My job was to develop the branches of the university into comprehensive universities serving their regions. A second job was to keep the students out of the way of the military.

This was, I feel, a successful period in my life. The campuses became autonomous; we introduced the semester system, unit courses, and grading by the instructor. We also launched our first in-country post–B.A. program. Although we always had the legislation to do so, that year we began the American system of course work for the master's and laid the plan for an in-country course-work doctorate. I also inaugurated a program of in-service improvement of social science staff through our newly formed Social Science Research Council. My chief accomplishment (or stroke of luck) was that the students and the military did not clash, despite growing unemployment among the educated, the Vietnam War, inflation, and some rather brutal infractions of citizens' liberties. The Chinese and *bumi*[a] radical students were split on the issue of Sino-Soviet relations and spent their time undercutting each other rather than on higher education or the regime.

When the government shifted again, I was brought in as minister of education. I found myself out of my depth and without a real political constituency. Over the issues of control of primary education (I lost the authority to the ministry of the interior), the selection of deans (the earlier-established principle of election, which I favored, was replaced by appointment by the rector), and a huge budget cut in education to fund the military to fight insurgents, I resigned and was permitted to return to the university. As I had no real discipline any longer, I was made Distinguished University Professor. I lecture annually on semihistorical and cultural topics; there are some students who take my courses and, above all, I teach them to respect the disinterested search for knowledge. I attend some occasions, especially when English-speaking foreigners are there. I am chairman of our national U.S. friendship committee and I take an interest in issues of human rights.

A Modern

I am a professor in the social sciences at the major university in our capital. The university is the oldest in the country and pioneered my discipline shortly before the Second World War. I am forty-five years old.

Formerly an undergraduate and junior instructor at my university, I went to the United States in the late 1950s for my doctoral work. I was one of thirty from my university in various fields who did their degrees at roughly the same time at Midwestern University under the auspices of USAID (or whatever it was then called). Some of us felt that MU was not where our discipline was best developed and that it might have been advantageous to get the perspectives of many universities. But we were grateful to be there together for mutual support, especially as our English was not too advanced at the outset and we could also share meals. (Our wives didn't come until the second year.) In addition, the young hotshots in the field were at MU and so we got a taste of how the discipline was changing. Many of my MU professors are now at Harvard and Berkeley. Of the seven graduates in my field at MU, six got their doctorate degree and one had to stop at the M.A. level. Four of us eventually returned to our home university and three of us (myself, another Ph.D., and the M.A.) are still on the faculty. One has joined the government and another is about to join an international orga-

---

[a]Original settlers, the dominant majority; for example, the Malays and the Indonesians.

nization in Geneva. Both say they want to return to teaching but I don't think they will.

My dissertation involved working out a model using certain coefficients relating to activities in my country. It was the first time this very advanced methodology (advanced for the time, anyway) was used with LDC data and I had some difficulty making it work. Several papers got published from the dissertation, a joint one with my supervisor in an international journal, and the others in our discipline's national journal. The latter, fortunately, publishes in English, so I didn't have the usual time gap between research, translation, and publication. I then pioneered this field in the university in my country. All the people who are using this methodology for the government are my former students.

As you may know, our academic salaries are very low and because we live in the capital our expenses are very high. This means I can't rely on my university salary for my livelihood. Fortunately, my wife, who studied information science at MU while I was working on my doctorate, also carries on her profession and this helps. I am also principal investigator on two projects: one with the IDRC and the other with the Friedrich-Ebert-Stiftung. I do some consulting with the private sector and with government. I am found especially useful for proposals to the World Bank (a fellow foreign student at MU from another country is now the loan officer at the bank for my country). Last year, I was made a member of our delegation to UNCTAD (UN Conference on Trade and Development). What with friends in Geneva and a generous per diem, I can save a bit there, too. I am also able to buy things on trips; I was able to get our present car while I was a specialist at the East-West Center three years ago. Needless to say, all these outside efforts to earn an adequate living cut into teaching time. Fortunately, I have a young instructor and a teaching assistant to help me.

Revising the curriculum is also a problem. So much has happened in my own field that I fear my students are not keeping pace with current developments. Indeed, with all my obligations, I really need some time to catch up myself. But our general field is also in need of attention. Enough people have returned home with their degrees that we should have a first-class curriculum worthy of a master's and, next year, a doctoral program. In fact, already I think our master's requirement in statistics is at least as hard as it was at MU—when I was there.

One of our problems, of course, is those faculty members who did not go abroad for their degrees or who did so long before the discipline really changed. One tries hard not to embarrass these people, but it is difficult to have what is in effect a two-tier faculty and not to let the students know who is "with it" and who is "out of it." It's also unfair to the students, especially if they wish to go on to further graduate work abroad, and I expect our very best to go to the States or Australia for a long time to come.

Research is what is really important to me. It has changed for me, however, in the last few years. I used to be involved in the whole process. Now I help formulate the problem and do not come in again until the data need interpreting. I often visit the provincial universities to encourage people there to do research. There is little tradition or incentive for research in these universities, so it is important to convey to them the newest methodologies and to tell them that research will advance national-development goals. I have been told that visits like mine are found to be very useful. In fact, our national social-science group has organized a research network of faculty in provincial universities to collect data for national research. It gives them good experience and helps us in our work.

I have also been president of our discipline's professional society and coedited our journal for two years. In addition, I have tried to publish a few papers each year, for international conferences. After my dissertation, I had intended to write a text in my field (one was and is badly needed), but I never got around to doing so. Also, few students read English with facility; as a result, many have difficulty reading my assignments or even fully understanding my lectures. I really must write that text someday.

What I need most of all is a year away. I have rejected several offers from international agencies to join their staffs permanently. I'd like to go to the States or perhaps Australia (they have begun to do very good work in my field in Canberra) to catch up and do some sustained research. There are problems in leaving, however. It would not be easy for my wife to take leave from her work, and my children are getting ready to sit for the examinations that will determine whether they will get into my university. The university is also starting its doctoral program and I will be needed for that. Moreover, in the event the government moves to the right, I may well be called on to be an adviser, perhaps even a minister.

A Provincial

I am a lecturer in the social sciences at a provincial university. I am thirty years old. I was formerly a student here, and began teaching the term after I stood first in the M.A. class. All of my colleagues also attended this university as students. The subject I teach is not the one I wish to teach, but it is a course required by the ministry of education, which sets our syllabus.

Our campus is very new and only partly built. Of the faculty, four have Ph.D.'s: the former rector (who is now with the government in the capital), the present rector, and the deans of veterinary science and engineering. We have a list of eligibles for doctoral study; some of my colleagues have been on that list for twelve years. I am one of the few who were educated abroad. With funds from my family and a loan from an uncle in Seattle, I spent two years in the States and received my M.A. from Southwestern University, near Los Angeles. SU allowed me admission without requiring that I take the Graduate Record Examination and with a low TOEFL [Test of English as a Foreign Language] score. While my first year was pretty much a loss because I was not proficient in English, I improved in the second year and wrote, I thought, a good master's thesis on policies of the recent government in my country. I had requested that I be allowed to continue to the Ph.D., but SU had no fellowship money and I was not fluent enough in English to be a teaching assistant. The decision was ultimately all right with me, however: I was needed back on this campus, my father had been sick, and my family had chosen a bride for me. I learned a great deal in those two years. It has really made a difference in what I teach, and I think my students appreciate the fact that I have been abroad for my graduate education.

The conditions for teaching here leave much to be desired. I have to teach fourteen to eighteen hours a week. The classes are crowded and noisy. There are few books and virtually no place to sit down to read them. I have my lecture notes cyclostyled and I have put on library reserve the books and reprinted articles I bought at SU. They are, to say the least, in a rather perilous state by now, even though so few of my students know enough English to read the material with real understanding. Our library gets no foreign social-science journals regularly. Because I share my office with four other lecturers, I seldom see students outside of class; in fact, I leave the campus after my lectures. There used to be cultural events—debates, lectures, and student plays—that once kept me on campus. But since the military have become wary of meetings where students are present and because the martial-law curfew is relatively early in the evening, the campus tends to shut down by midafternoon. In fact, it is hard for me or the students to get a bus there after 5 P.M. The exams are set by the ministry, and so far my students have done well. They memorize the names of leading Western social scientists and occasionally drop them in their essays. That impresses the examiners in the capital.

At SU, I came to appreciate research and have tried to continue it since my return. I translated a chapter of my thesis into our language and had it published in our university's annual publication. It received great praise from my colleagues and from the rector. I submitted two other pieces of my empirical research to our discipline's national journal. One was lost and the other was turned down on the ground that I hadn't addressed the Scott thesis about morality in peasants. I don't know that author and I haven't found his work in my country. Still I continue and I try to have at least one article a year in our university publication. Because our library is poor, I try to visit our capital once or twice a year to use the library of the university there. But that library is not even as good as SU's, which was very bad. Indeed, if I had not been able to use a countryman's UCLA ID card, I would have had difficulty completing my master's.

Most of my research is empirical. I have worked on changing attitudes toward adopting new crops. For WHO in the capital, I have surveyed attitudes toward the use of contraceptives in the region and I participated on the team that assessed the value of children. I am not a demographer and had no interest in the subject until I did the survey, but now I find it interesting. I visited the capital when all the results were tabulated. There I met my countrymen who were the professors in charge of our nation's team and the Canadian and German professors who had overall responsibility for bringing all the national studies together. Given the difficulty I had administering the questionnaire, I didn't envy them that task.

Occasionally, professors from the capital come to lecture on the newest research methodologies in the West and on the importance of research. I always attend the lectures and encourage my colleagues to do the same. These professors use many special words and I try to help my colleagues to understand, as they are a bit embarrassed to ask questions. Our countrymen also encourage us to address our national problems in our research and to ensure that foreign models are not used indiscriminately. With these points I am very much in agreement.

Doing research, however, sometimes takes a back seat to earning a living. Since my salary as a lecturer covers my family's needs for only about a third of the month, I must hold several jobs. Fortunately, my father left me a small business, which my brother and I run; we also look after some land we have in the next province. I have been doing some feasibility studies for some local Chinese merchants who need to have such a study done to get a government loan. Recently, with the arrival of the new regional decentralized-planning office, I have heard that the government will offer opportunities to do studies for them on development programs. Given all the problems I had in the study I participated in for the government two years ago (because of all kinds of payments to people who didn't do any of the work, we ran out of money and had to volunteer our time at the end), I will be suspicious for a while.

In my most realistic moments, I have to admit that I will probably never return to America to finish my Ph.D. I would have accepted a fellowship to work on it in New Zealand, but that was eventually given to a person in animal science. I have been told that the university in the capital is beginning a new Ph.D. program and perhaps I will consider going there. It would be especially hard to leave now, however. The department and the university are still growing and I am one of the few foreign M.A.'s on the staff. I have a family, and my wife speaks no English; I wouldn't want to leave them behind. My brother also needs me in the business. Perhaps the next generation will have the doctorates. Under any circumstance, I like teaching our young people; I believe I am serving the purposes of national development, and I enjoy the status of being a university person.

A Student

I am a third-year student in the social sciences at the other university in the capital. I am nineteen and a girl. Although I have a national name, my family is Chinese.

Most of my classmates in the social sciences are also girls, though all of my teachers are men. The reason there are mostly girls is because students' highest preference is for medicine, then technology, science, business, social science, and, last, humanities. *Bumi* boys and girls get most of their preferences. For instance, in the social sciences, they fill up economics classes at the major university in the capital and even accounting-economics classes at my university. We are able to take what is left. The sorting out really begins earlier though, when certain students—usually *bumi* boys—go to the secondary schools in the exact sciences and take advanced mathematics, sciences, and English. The rest of us don't get enough of these subjects—unless our parents are very rich and powerful—and hence take university courses that don't require them.

But I am glad I am in the social sciences. I find my courses very interesting. When I finish, I hope to have a position in the civil service and I think my studies will help me. I am also thinking about going for my master's part-time. You see, positions and promotions in our civil service are related to degrees.

My teachers come to lecture and then they disappear. They often lecture at the other university as well, just as some of its teachers come to teach us. Although we don't see our teachers very much, we can buy their lectures. Because we are turning to a system of instructor evaluations, it will be important to memorize the lectures. Some teachers have also put together books of readings in our field. I wish there were more textbooks. With all the students who study the subject, you would think we would have more texts.

There are assignments in the library, many of which I have to skip because I often can't find a seat or the book I need is out or has been stolen. Sometimes I can't follow the assignment's English. Although I have had four years of English in the state schools, I still cannot read rapidly enough to make going to the library worth my time. The library is also open too few hours and my parents want me home rather early in the afternoon. Since the university was closed for a month by the military last year, there have not been many acivities on campus after 3 P.M. anyway.

In the final year, each student participates in a research project. I am going to do a survey of attitudes of students toward a voluntary student service. The teaching assistant will help me develop the questionnaire and then show me how to interpret the results.

My parents will be proud if I graduate from the university and receive a post in the civil service. I will be proud too.

A National-University Culture

The four people we have just met are composites of many hundreds I have met and they resemble, I am sure, hundreds more I have not met. Give or take an emphasis here or a fact there, they could be social scientists in any one of the five countries about which we are speaking; our modal colleagues would find the culture of social science in each country quite recognizable. What might be unfamiliar to them are the practices deriving from the larger national-university culture that affect the disposition of professional effort and the sources of ultimate authority. This national-university culture emerged during the colonial era, when the idea of a university was either brought to the colony for implementation or was the subject of vigorous debate between the colonial authorities and the leaders of the nationalist movement. In the case of Thailand, which was never formally a colony, there were special treaty relationships at the time the first university was established, and these colored the choice of models and continued to do so after those treaty relationships were ended.

In their national-university cultures, the five countries resemble their former colonial authority or powerful ally more than they do one another, though in key respects they are very much alike. The differences go beyond the issue of nomenclature—for example, whether the head of the institution is called vice-chancellor, president, or rector—and they are often specific to the social sciences. For instance, where Britain was the colonial power or significant early influence, geography as a subject is important in terms of numbers of faculty and students. Where Britain was not a factor, the subject of geography barely exists. The social sciences are also part of an "arts faculty" and not more autonomous. There are also specific legacies. The Faculty of Economics and Administration at the University of Malaysia is modeled after the London School of Economics, and the School of Comparative Studies at the Universiti Sains Malaysia after the University of Sussex. Where Dutch and French have left their influence, law is a social science and is treated as such in research and teaching. Where the United States had political preeminence, as in the Philippines, the subjects of sociology, anthropology, and social psychology have a legitimacy they lack in those countries that experienced tutelage from others. In the latter, these subjects entered indirectly via programs such as Malay studies or languish in the humanities or in schools of education. The same is true of the applied social sciences of communications, demography, and public administration, developed so early in the United States. They have a legitimacy in the Philippine University curriculum that they lack elsewhere.

The important aspects of the national-university culture transcend the social sciences and pertain to the conduct of all university activity. Even where a subsequent major power exercises a strong effect on one of the Southeast Asian nations in its university development, such as the United States in encouraging the semester system or instructor evaluation, it is against this dominant culture that the new proposals must contend. At the risk of oversimplification, the components of this national university culture can be compared among the five Southeast Asian nations and with their former metropolitan powers. It should be remembered that the items enumerated in table 4−1 are comparisons and not absolute descriptions (what may seem important in the national-university culture may appear less important when compared with how the same item is treated in another national-university culture).

Table 4−1 shows that the clusters of characteristics in the national-university cultures of Southeast Asian nations are remarkably close to those prevailing in these nations' former colonial associations. Given the elitist orientation toward admissions in Thailand (and Great Britain), it is not surprising that an open university is chosen as the vehicle to respond to demand. Nor is it surprising that Indonesia has begun national doctoral education before Thailand, Singapore, or Malaysia (apart from the British "thesis" degree), or that the Philippines is considerably advanced, with a doctoral program at the University of Santo Tomas without even a single full-time faculty member. Nor is it a matter for surprise that selecting a dean is an issue for discussion in Thailand and Indonesia, whereas the issue seems relatively settled in the Philippines. In the case of the problems of part-time students, the Philippines (with such competition in the educational market, a college must be responsive) can be expected to work hardest to resolve them, with Indonesia coming second, though reluctantly. The inadequate differentiation of professorial ranks (too few relative to the number who might occupy them) is a characteristic feature in Europe, where a single grand professor dominates a faculty. Only in the Philippines could a lay board of trustees be the ultimate authority, or the private sector be given such scope; these conditions obtain also in the United States. When issues of change are involved, these derivative but naturalized characteristics are factors that aid or resist what is needed or demanded.

A Comparative View of the Social Sciences in Southeast Asia

At the operative level, the national-university culture creates differences among countries. In the main, however, the culture of the social sciences in

Table 4-1
National University Cultures Compared with Former Colonial Powers

Characteristic	Britain/Malaysia, Singapore, Aspects of Thailand	Holland/ Indonesia	France/ Aspects of Thailand	United States/ Philippines
Emphasis on post-B.A. education (or its equivalent)	low	medium	ambivalent	high
Tolerance toward private sector in higher education	low	low	low	high
Degree of elitism in university admission	high	high	ambivalent	low
Degree to which university teaching and research are mixed (vis-á-vis research confined to nonteaching research institutions)	medium	low	low	high
Requirement of full-time residence for advanced work	high	medium	high	low
Responsiveness to "consumer demand" (whether of students or employers)	low	low	ambivalent	high
Degree of closeness to the responsible government ministry	high	high	high	low
Autonomy of faculty governance (e.g., selection of deans)	high	high	ambivalent	low
Number of professors in faculties	low	low	low	high
Faculty control over examination process	low	low	low	high
Extent of "fit"	high	high	medium	high

Southeast Asia is relatively uniform across the five countries. For all five, the social sciences are relative newcomers to the university curricula. Economics and political science as we would recognize them were first taught in Thailand in 1933. Social and economic sciences began at Gadjah Mada in 1949 and at the University of Indonesia in 1950. The University of Malaya introduced economics in 1949 with the establishment of the university, then in Singapore. The University of the Philippines started a course in sociology in 1911, though sociology and anthropology remained a subdepartment until the 1950s. Indeed, when we correct for the pressure of expatriate teachers in various universities, it might be argued that the full introduction of national teaching of the social sciences really dates to the 1950s.

This can be seen by the age of the first Ph.D.'s. Most are still teaching and, at the most, are only now reaching the end of their careers. Although the first Philippine Ph.D. sociologist received his degree in the late 1930s, the first anthropologist (then a Jesuit from the United States) in the Philippines received his degree in 1957 and the first Philippine anthropologist in 1962. The first Dutch-trained Indonesian Ph.D. economist received his degree in 1955, the first sociologist Ph.D. (trained in the United States) in 1962.

All five countries also have in common the same disciplinary hierarchy. Economics is the strongest discipline in terms of the selectivity of students, the number of faculty in the capital and increasingly in the provinces with advanced degrees, the number of aspiring professionals undergoing advanced training, the viability of a professional organization and journal, the number of and attendance at national post-B.A. programs, the number of texts in the national language, and the published achievements of scholars. What is true nationally also holds at individual institutions, although there are universities in the Philippines and Indonesia unable to secure and retain faculty in economics and hence do not offer courses.

After economics, there is national variation. Geography is a strong second discipline in Malaysia and Singapore, political science in the Philippines and Thailand. Indeed, with their penchant for crafting constitutions and designing political order, Thai political scientists almost rival economists in numbers, strength, and quality. In Indonesia, after economics, the remaining social sciences are equally weak. In both Malaysia and Indonesia, political scientists have been considered for some time a relatively undesirable addition to the social sciences.

The distribution of Ph.D.-level social scientists is also similar in the five countries. They are disproportionately concentrated in the major institutions in the major cities. In Thailand, for example, 13 percent of all social-science faculty hold doctorates, and two institutions in Bangkok in 1975 had 52 percent of those doctorates. Of the total Ph.D. social-science faculty in Thailand in 1975, about 95 percent were employed at Bangkok universities.[4] Similar concentrations occur in Indonesia and the Philippines. These concentrations are also self-perpetuating. In Indonesia, between 1970 and 1977, only 17 percent of opportunities for doctoral work abroad went to candidates outside of Java. Within Java, over 65 percent of these opportunities went to faculty at the five major universities.[5] In addition, there is a heavy concentration everywhere of Ph.D.'s in economics.

Another commonality is that most Southeast Asians holding advanced degrees in the social sciences completed their work in the United States. Of

130 Thai economists who had studied abroad for advanced degrees by 1975, 52 percent received their degrees from the United States, 12 percent from Australia, 13 percent from the Philippines, and 20 percent from Europe.[6] Of the 14 Ph.D.'s at the University of Singapore, 11 were in the Department of Sociology and all but one of this group had taken the doctorate in the United States.[7] In 1974, it was estimated that 92 percent of the foreign-educated Philippine political scientists had taken their degrees in the United States.[8] Only in Malaysia does there appear to be a deliberate attempt to restrict experience in the social sciences in the United States; there, the preference is for the United Kingdom.

A rather distressing commonality is the relatively low demand for social sciences. The prestige, and hence, popularity of the social sciences is considerably lower than that of science, technology, medicine, and business; they are more sought after only in relation to the humanities and education. In countries where education of women is common, women predominate in the social sciences, even in economics. There is other evidence. For instance, in 1970 at Gadjah Mada University, 78 percent of those enrolled in the economics program were doing general economics, 4 percent accounting; in 1976, 81 percent were doing accounting, 15 percent general economics, and 3 percent agricultural economics.[9]

The inferior status of the social sciences can also be seen at the master's level. Throughout Southeast Asia, master's programs or post-B.A. degrees are marked by exceptionally high attrition, indicating little demand for social-science graduates, especially economists, or for graduates in general. Only through fellowships is it possible to secure a cohort of students for the duration of the degree. The high attrition in social-science degree programs also accounts for the universities' reluctance to initiate doctoral education. The clientele in this case is assured from ambitious faculty, but, as everywhere, doctoral education will need heavy subsidization for students through fellowships.

Given all five countries' planning orientation the deficiency of basic socioeconomic knowledge about their populations, and the increased presence of research foundations and social-science-related international organizations, research and consultancy opportunities abound for senior faculty who are foreign-educated and associated with the major universities in the capital. With the removal of any one factor, however—senior status, foreign education, association with a major university, or residence in the capital— the number of opportunities declines. Junior faculty in major universities in capitals are often associated in the research of senior faculty. Junior faculty with foreign training are more likely to be breaking into their own funded research opportunities. The increasingly decentralized perspective in state planning and "the-poorest-of-the-poor" orientation of international organizations and research foundations mean that senior foreign-educated faculty in research universities outside the capital are increasingly privy to research and consulting opportunities, and these entail staff opportunities for junior faculty. Because the provincial networks are fairly fragile, there is still a tendency for governments and international organizations to decentralize their research by way of national-research consortia emanating from senior foreign-educated faculty in major universities in the capital.

The subjects for research are seldom ones the researchers would have selected had they been able to determine their own research agenda in terms of important problems in their discipline or even in their country, or in terms of questions of intrinsic interest or as part of their agenda for continuous self-education to be a better teacher-scholar. The research agenda is set from outside the university social-science community. It is true that government officials seeking research to be done by others often consult with likely executors of that research; but the subjects leave much to be desired. Not only are they usually unrelated to the scholar's intellectual needs or desires, but the research that is usually commissioned is of a data-gathering sort with minimal requirements for interpretation and analysis. Secondary analysis of earlier efforts is almost nonexistent. Moreover, once the required number of reports is sent to the responsible agency, whether national or international, the prospects are bleak that findings, let alone interpretations, will make their way back to the national social-science community. Peer review of findings or their utilization is uncommon. Finally, the process lacks the means of sustaining a scholarly appreciation of the research enterprise. Because much of the research that is supported requires considerable gathering of data, both junior and senior faculty are engaged in only small portions of the total process.[10] Although analogues to this experience of social-science research exist everywhere, it is difficult to believe that the segmentation and subcontracting of research on subjects chosen by others is a healthy atmosphere in which to nurture self-educating scholars.

There are exceptions, such as the research programs of the Thai National Research Council and the National Science Development Board of the Philippines, where faculty propose research of their own choosing and where a scholar usually controls the process from problem definition to interpretations of results. Financial support for these projects is small and restrictions as to the use of funds substantial.

All research opportunities, however, whether from government or international organizations and research foundations, are financially important to all who can secure them. The universities in Southeast Asia provide their social scientists with less than they require for their personal needs and aspirations (in Thailand in 1976, they received $150 a month gross, no house or car, and earned another $50 a month by teaching at other institutions; in the University of the Philippines system, junior faculty earn $140 to $220 a month, with some assistance for housing, while full professors receive $234 to $276 a month; Indonesia pays roughly the same as the Philippines, though there are several allowances that increase the sum; Malaysia and Singapore have similar pay scales: in Malaysia, a Ph.D. earns $637 monthly and an M.A. $558).[11] I have never met a senior foreign-educated social scientist in a major university in a capital who did not supplement his income in some fashion. In four of the five countries, faculty are, by and large, civil servants, complicating the payment for research purposes. But each country has overcome that problem in one way or another, and only Malaysia penalizes a social scientist for earning more than a certain sum for doing research. With the large number of international supporters of social-science research, it is very difficult for a dean or rector to know the extent of faculty research commitments. Each country has also evolved a way of awarding overhead and indirect costs to the institution so that administrators will be willing to have research done by their faculty. Foreign observers, confused by the way indirect costs are handled, often misinterpret the system; still, the practice in Indonesia of employing as consultants to the project those who funded the project does indeed appear to stretch the indirect-costs rationale.

All five countries have established an infrastructure for trying to ensure professional renewal and improvement of standards. Economists were first, in most cases, with a professional society and a relatively regular journal. In the Philippines, the other disciplines have also been organized (political science in 1962, sociology and psychology in 1963, linguistics in 1969), and journals are appearing on an increasingly regular basis. An umbrella organization, the Philippine Social Science Council, was founded in 1968 to assist the professional associations and to mediate changes in the social sciences elsewhere to Philippine social scientists. Thailand and Indonesia have established omnibus societies for noneconomists (and Thailand an omnibus journal) to facilitate professional exchange and improvement of standards.

It is in the improvement of standards that the practices evolved in Southeast Asia are quite instructive. Many ways have been tried to improve the quality of the supply of existing social scientists. There are efforts in the Philippines and Indonesia at "flying professors," whereby the country's better professors are transported from the leading universities to teach at provincial universities for brief but scheduled times and to provide role models. Indonesia has developed disciplinary consortia to determine the syllabus for the curriculum in the social sciences. Each country seeks to improve its method by stretching quality resources more extensively. Efforts at individual improvement are also marked. With a government intent on quality institutions of higher learning and blessed with considerable foreign exchange (and the need for racial affirmative action), the policy in Malaysia is for advanced training abroad for faculty. In Thailand, the Philippines, and Indonesia, the efforts at improving social-science faculty are largely domestic ones. For ten years the National Research Council in Thailand has run a summer social-science methodology workshop where a number of faculty gather for lectures on trends in the disciplines, methodology, and statistics. They participate in a group-research project, largely derivative from survey research, and return to their universities with the council's hope that the exposure was useful. To my knowledge, this effort has never been evaluated. The summer workshops, however, have been supplemented by efforts of the Social Science Association of Thailand, through visiting short-term professors, to take the concern for improving methodologies and professionalism in research to the provincial universities and teachers colleges directly.

The Philippine Social Science Council took responsibility for professional improvement in that country and organized social scientists by region into a research network. Once the network members were trained in survey-research methodologies and statistics, the council conducted a series of annual national surveys, which simultaneously enriched the social-science knowledge of the country and the experience of the social scientists in participating in empirical research. Even though there are other methodologies that might assist the improvement of social scientists, and despite the fact that participants have expressed a feeling of exploitation by the senior foreign-educated faculty from major universities in the capital who supervised the exercise, the council members have not been persuaded to evolve different approaches. The feeling of exploitation may continue until the various research centers in the network begin to have their own projects.

The third approach for improving the existing social-science faculty is the one taken by the Indonesian Social Science Council, the Jajasan Ilmu Ilmu Sosial. On the basis of recommendations from Clifford Geertz, the Jajasan sponsored the establishment in 1974 of three research stations, located at or near university campuses, where a total of 36 (12 at each station) social-science faculty (selected to include education, religious studies, law, and history) from throughout the archipelago attend an academic year-long research workshop. They are under the supervision of a senior Indonesian social scientist and a foreign scholar, who assist them in developing and implementing research designs of the student-cum-fellow's choosing. This nondegree program is aimed at giving experience in research, and emphasizes the role of one's own research agenda in the process of sustaining and improving one's skills and understanding. The tangible product is a research report publishable in a professional journal. Needless to say, much of the education arises from the mutual education of the participants and from the interaction between the participants and the subjects of their empirical research. About 200 have completed this program.

Finally, all five countries have favorable implicit social-science policies. Social scientists, known as professionals in the discipline, serve in cabinet or subcabinet positions in each country. Professional social scientists predominate on planning boards and in relevant ministries and appear in authority in positions that require considerable interaction with foreign nationals. All five governments employ social scientists for explicit professional positions—in central banks, bureaus of statistics, population programs, tribal affairs offices—and often maintain domestic or foreign training programs to improve their skills. Social scientists are asked to consult, sit on commissions, and do policy-oriented research. When universities are built or expanded, the social sciences are included (eventually all disciplines). Existing faculty are encouraged by incentives to improve their qualifications, and foreign advanced education is either subsidized, formally encouraged, or not obstructed. The five governments issue passports and travel permits to national social scientists traveling to sustain professional contacts, and visas are usually accorded to foreign social scientists to undertake research within the countries, all of which indicates a favorable policy toward idea migration. Finally, public research funds are available and there is every prospect that these will increase.

A Comparison with India

Given that the conditions for social science in the five Southeast Asian nations are similar, it may be helpful to compare what has been achieved in any one Southeast Asian nation with what has been achieved elsewhere. The usual comparison is between what is modal in an LDC with what is the very best in, say, the United States. More instructive might be a comparison with what has been achieved in India, with the proviso that some judgments will necessarily be qualitative and interpersonally nonverifiable.

Certain basic features of the comparison need noting. First, the national-university culture in India is older. The first three Indian universities—Madras, Bombay, and Calcutta—were established in 1857, long before their Southeast Asian counterparts. The first indigenous Ph.D. was awarded in India the same year that Harvard awarded its first Ph.D., and in 1930 an Indian physicist working in India received the Nobel Prize in physics. Second, the infrastructure for advanced social science has been in place longer and more substantially in India than in Southeast Asia, thanks to both the British and nationalist governments. A census, district gazettes, cumulative national-income accounts, and a flawed but unique national-sample survey conducted since the early 1950s all provide the grist for serious research and teaching. In Southeast Asia all those features are less advanced and more recent; some are nonexistent. Third, comparison is deceptive given the size of India compared with that of any one nation in Southeast Asia (India is roughly fifteen times larger than Thailand or the Philippines). In numbers alone, there are many more social scientists in both absolute and relative terms. Indeed, in 1976 there were more unemployed advanced-degree-holding social scientists in India than employed social scientists in Indonesia.[12] This fact should not be surprising given the ubiquity of Indian social scientists in international organizations and in the universities of West Africa and the Middle East.

If we control for size and the capacity to aggregate human and economic assets in a place such as Delhi, it could be argued that relative to a comparable social-science population in India, Southeast Asian social scientists come out quite well. For example, if we compared the intellectual achievements of the last ten years in the social sciences in Thailand or the Philippines with those of Maharashtra (a state with roughly the same population), we could rather quickly conclude that on the basis of number of international professionals, published work of international quality, access to library collections, infrastructure of curriculum and research centers, acknowledged pertinence to public policy, knowledge of methodologies and computational technologies, and other factors, the social sciences in Thailand or the Philippines are considerably ahead of the social sciences in Maharashtra, as Malaysia is ahead of Kerala, Kashmir, or Assam, and Indonesia ahead of Uttar Pradesh.

One reason for this may be that, unlike Southeast Asian social scientists, Indian social scientists have experienced a quiet cultural revolution. By deliberate government policy in the late 1960s, Indian social scientists were cut off from their international, largely Western, counterparts. They were forced to turn to each other for stimulation and to provide the proper professional peer group. An indigenous route to the doctoral degree had to be nurtured and appreciated, as advanced education outside of India was confined to a few non-social-science fields. Leading Indian social scientists with world reputations were excluded—through denial of visas and, often, opportunities—from vigorous participation in international social science. Little activity outside India was encouraged; the admission of foreign scholars was severely circumscribed. Painful but probably necessary, this cultural revolution has produced a relatively vigorous national social-science community, considerably more out of touch with international social science than the social-science leaders in Southeast Asia. It is perhaps appropriate that the world proponents of indigenization (one Thai wag said this was a euphemism for "Indianization") are Indians.

Apart from a brief period under Sukarno and an occasional minister of education in Thailand, such as Pinyo, or interior minister in Malaysia, such as Shafie, there is little public leadership in Southeast Asia for a cultural revolution of the sort experienced by Indian social scientists. There are rumblings about the need for a national interpretation of social phenomena that would replace the dominant models of "loosely structured social relations" for Thailand, the prevalence of the requirement for smooth interpersonal relations in the Philippines, and the *abangan-santri-prijaji* trinity pertaining to Indonesia (or Java).[13] But these rumblings come from within the community of social scientists and serve as preliminary healthy goads to national interpretations. Few social scientists in Southeast Asia call for a national criterion of truth or a Third World reality that only those in the Third World can perceive. Foreign scholars are generally welcome; participation in international conferences is eagerly sought. Indeed, a consequence of this internationalism is the comparative retardation of local education at the doctoral level in the social sciences; hospitality to advanced education abroad remains substantial. A benefit is the growth of cosmopolitan professionals faster than in the more hermetically sealed India.

Afterthoughts

So far in this chapter, social scientists in Southeast Asia have been discussed as if they were primarily professionals, university-level scholar-teachers, and participants in an international community of individuals articulately self-conscious about society's foundations. They are also very much part of their own national political scene. Whatever formal politics they espouse, social scientists in the five countries are political in fulfilling their professional roles in ways not always appreciated by observers. All five countries have truncated legislative processes and a press without a tradition of independent investigative reporting. The debates in which social scientists engage as professionals in their discipline cast them in the role of a surrogate legislature, and in their popular writings are as close as their countries come to investigative journalism. Questions of policy choices, degrees of devolution, monitoring policy performance (whether it be population, land reform, or water rights), and other issues are raised by social scientists in environments where nonofficials seldom raise any questions. In rural areas this political role becomes more explicitly legislative. Social scientists who conduct research in rural areas and then publish their findings in effect become representatives of those who are outside the polity. Even if they are not sympathetic, they introduce the views of these nonvoting constituents into the discussion of those in authority. Without exaggerating, it can be argued, for example, that in the Philippines, what never could be said in the press or politically about corruption was said by an IDRC-supported study, about distribution of income by a study from CAMS (Council of Asian Manpower Studies), about the integrity of the 1979 referendum by a Friedrich-Ebert−supported study, about water rights by a Ford Foundation−supported study, and about the delivery of services by a Philippine Social Science Council national survey.

Social scientists are political and also human. As the four portraits earlier in this chapter indicate, social scientists in Southeast Asia are subject to considerable conflicting pressures. As a community, they are called upon in ways and to extents that their Western counterparts seldom experience. They are engaged in developing departments, sustaining universities, establishing research centers, founding professional associations, launching journals, facilitating international associations, assisting their governments and their colleagues, and trying to carry on lives as teacher-scholars. If Western social scientists had to respond to the same demands and expend the same levels of energy, the productivity of Western social sciences would increase manyfold. Yet Southeast Asian social scientists must fulfill these multiple demands with exceptionally scarce resources, including, and especially, the resource of time. So compromised are they by these scarcities that they often appear to unsympathetic Western observers to have low scholarly standards or inadequate training. In most instances, these charges seem to me to be utterly wrong.

But there is no surcease from these responsibilities in sight. Indeed, there are some on the horizon that I think should be accepted and on which well-wishers should pledge their assistance in any way that is appropriate. The first is the further development of quality domestic Ph.D. programs. Some progress has been made, and there are stirrings everywhere in the region of more initiatives to come. Many of these initiatives are as solidly grounded as the hundreds of new doctoral programs that emerged in the United States in the 1960s and 1970s. Although I have some misgivings about the number of social-science disciplines and the accompanying waste—human and economic—of maintaining existing disciplinary distinctions (I have found it increasingly difficult to know, from the problem chosen, the methodology employed, or the audience intended, what the researcher's discipline is; I would prefer, in all candor, having two disciplines in the social sciences—economics and noneconomics, though I appreciate that it is too tardy a wish to see fruition), the prospect of offering doctoral-level education (in addition to the largely honorific thesis degree currently authorized) will be the chief item on the agenda of social-science departments in major universities in capital cities in the region. The issue is not whether, but when and how.

To facilitate the most constructive resolution of these efforts, well-wishers in the international social-science community can assist in many ways. They can provide plural models for consideration, visiting short-term faculty in key subjects, transitional opportunities for a year of course work, and postdoctoral opportunities for graduates of these national doctoral programs. The next five years may be the most creative and demanding in social-science graduate education in Southeast Asia and a period when external assistance can be most creatively utilized.

A second responsibility that will further stretch the already overextended community of Southeast Asian social scientists is the need to develop a public tradition of research, a protected, figurative, public space where social scientists can share their findings, mutually educate, and acquire the constructive habits of peer criticism. Although considerable research is being conducted in the region, there is nowhere yet a tradition that encourages and protects the autonomous and responsible sharing of research results, that sees research as a constructive activity in its own terms. Research is perceived as being performed in the service either of the regime or of those who oppose the regime. Important efforts in the direction of a public tradition of research include *Prisma* in Indonesia and the *Social Science Review* in Thailand. More efforts, I believe, will be required.

In this, well-wishers in the international social-science community can be of assistance in two ways. First, they can cease insisting that research be policy-relevant; all forces within the society, with the exception of religion, militate in that same direction. Whether what is done as policy research (or as government-sponsored research for specific purposes) in Southeast Asia is useful for policy is a moot question, but there is no lack of it. Indeed, what many scholars would like (and need) is a release from relevance in order to pursue questions that have importance for them as social scientists. Whereas we sometimes must exhort Western social scientists to pay attention to public matters, Southeast Asian social scientists must stand at attention almost all of the time. Supporting research for its own sake may well be more useful in strengthening the university of social scientists than efforts, from inside and internationally, to engage social scientists more completely in the service of public policy.

The international community of social scientists can also nurture an autonomous public tradition of research by engaging their counterparts in mutually agreed-on subjects for research and conferencing. A model for this might be the current collaboration between the Social Science Research Council of the United States and the Indian Council of Social Science Research. I would, however, add two caveats. In doing this, well-wishers should not choose the topics in advance. They should not seek Southeast Asian collaboration on topics primarily of interest to Western scholars. Second, their collaborations should not always be focused on the region. Social scientists in Southeast Asia do not want to be mediated to the world of scholarship by the Southeast Asianists. Nor do they perceive their growth in the discipline as proceeding exclusively from their intimate knowledge of the region.

A third responsibility is to develop a genuinely national contribution to the social sciences. I mean that in three ways. First, although I reject any notion of a special Thai or Indian or African truth, I do believe that social scientists from different traditions can expose as mere convention what many of their colleagues consider "nature." There has been too little contribution from Southeast Asian social scientists in this direction. Rather than demonstrating alternative allocations of social value as found in their societies, the social scientists have at most questioned the right of foreign social scientists to preempt the descriptive task. Second, there has not been forthcoming from any Southeast Asian social scientist, except Dr. Soejatmoko, a holistic view of any society in the region. There are no national successors to Clifford Geertz. Of course, there are no successors to him in the West either, where the tradition has been monographic and single-problem oriented. But the need for the attempt is important, to nurture a more mature community. Third, no contributions to social-science methodology have arisen from the region. Social scientists in Southeast Asia are net borrowers methodologically. On the other hand, the terms could be reversed. Why a major contribution to survey research has not been made by social scientists in the exquisitely stratified societies of Thailand and Java is beyond my understanding. A vital, mature social science in Southeast Asia can exert a strong influence on, for example, how differences in social rank can be used in empirical research—a problem faced in research everywhere.

International social scientists can also help to encourage more-creative national contributions to the social-science disciplines. First, external support should be forthcoming to gifted people able to make contributions. Long-term, high-risk assistance for creative social scientists is scarce indeed. Second, the international social-science community should refrain from overwhelming these individuals with demands for attention and delaying their creative work. That thought, finally, brings us to the title of this chapter. Everywhere, social science is a hybrid, and its adaptation to native soil is nowhere assured. As social scientists, we are protected by the institutional equivalents of the inputs that assure performance in high-yielding seeds. We are protected by the structure of the university system, the "rent" the possessor of a degree can charge, and the subsidizations governments and the rich make available. We promise what the native variety, or, in the case of social matters, common sense, seems deficient in producing. In enough instances, this promise is fulfilled. Occasionally, in relation to such issues as inflation and unemployment, our intellect and education seem no more productive than common sense.

In the adaptation of this hybrid to Southeast Asia, there is an opportunity that should be among the responsibilities of Southeast Asian social scientists, though not theirs alone: the opportunity to adapt social sciences to other than elite conditions. To qualify to be a social scientist requires a long, costly, and privileged apprenticeship. Teaching and research are conducted at universities and for government where the social scientist is surrounded by elite audiences and associates. How social scientists would fare if they had to adapt to less than elite conditions is a question about which I have some fears for social scientists everywhere, but for Southeast Asian social scientists in particular. Could our fellow professionals improve on common sense problem solving for ordinary people? Could they, for example, organize a water cooperative, develop a marketing strategy for street peddlers, apply cost-benefit analysis to very small enterprises or public works, forecast the demand for food or commodities for smallholders? Can social-science technologies deal with issues of varying scale? Can the talents to deal with them be acquired without the costly apprenticeship? Is there the equivalent of the "barefoot social scientist," able to improve on common sense with methodologies and appropriate intellectual technologies that will assist problem solving, at least until a specialist can be obtained? That is real native soil. Without adaptation to it, the hybrid may be subject to rust.

Notes

1. Yogi Akashi, "The Koa Kunrenjo, 1942–45; A Case Study of Cultural Propagation and Conflict under the Japanese Occupation of Malaya" (Conference on Southeast Asian Studies, Kota Kinabalu, 1978), mimeographed, *passim.*

2. Eric Ashby, *Universities: British, Indian, and African: A Study in the Ecology of Higher Education* (Cambridge: Harvard University Press, 1966), chaps. 1–2.

3. Clifford Geertz, "A Program for the Stimulation of the Social Sciences in Indonesia" (Report to the Ford Foundation, Princeton, August 1971), mimeographed, p. 30.

4. Gerry Fry, "Education and the Social Sciences in Thai Universities: An Overview" (Draft report to the Ford Foundation, Bangkok, February 14, 1977), mimeographed, p. 19.

5. Selo Soemardjan, "Manpower Development for Social Sciences in Indonesia" (Draft report to Jajasan Ilmu Ilmu Sosial, Jakarta, January 1, 1980), pp. 7–9.

6. Chattip Natsupha, "Economics Discipline in Thailand," Social Science Association of Thailand, mimeographed, 1975; also see Malcolm Gillis and Stephen Guisinger, "Economics in Thailand and the Ford Foundation," *Ford Foundation Economics Review,* November 30, 1975, mimeographed.

7. "Department of Sociology, University of Singapore," Department of Sociology report, 1976.

8. Elmer Viglia, "Some Observations on the Teaching of Political Science as a Discipline," *Philippine Political Science Journal* 1 (1974): 69–74.

9. Malcolm Gillis, "Economics in Indonesia and the Ford Foundation," *Ford Foundation Economics Review,* November 30, 1975, mimeoaphed, p. 12.

10. I am much indebted here to the draft papers on the social sciences in Indonesia by Michael Morfit.

11. Roger Montgomery, "A Report on Visits to Five Southeast Asian Universities with Graduate Programs in Economics and Agricultural Economics" (Draft, Jakarta, April 1978), mimeographed.

12. The data appear in Warren Ilchman, "The Social Sciences in Southeast Asia" and "The Social Sciences in South Asia" (Reports to the Ford Foundation, March 1977), mimeographed.

13. The dominant cultural characterizations of three principal countries in the area derive from John F. Embree, "Thailand—A Loosely Structured Social System," *American Anthropologist* 52, no. 2 (1950), pp. 181–193; Frank Lynch, S.J., *Four Readings on Philippine Values,* 2d ed.(Quezon City, Philippines: Ateneo de Manila, 1964); and Clifford Geertz, *The Religion of Java* (New York: Free Press, 1960). In the case of the Javanese "trinity," *abangan* refers to the peasant, animistic tradition, *santri* to the urban Islamic orthodox merchant class, and *prijaji* to the Hindu-Buddhist educated civil-servant class.

5 Social Science and the Modernization of China

Huan Xiang

China, as one of the developing countries, has faced and continues to face many problems in common with other developing countries. The overwhelming majority of these developing countries have successively won national independence and entered a new historical era. All of us face the tasks of developing the national economy and culture, defending national independence, and promoting social progress. These aims inevitably give rise to a series of new questions in fields ranging from economy, politics, culture, and education to national defense and foreign affairs, all of which require answers from social scientists in these countries. Our research work should thus go beyond practice to provide orientation and policy suggestions. Social-science research has an important bearing, then, on the accomplishment of these tasks, which in turn promotes the development of the social sciences. This has been repeatedly borne out by the modern history of mankind. Our part of the world once produced brilliant ancient civilizations and made significant contributions to the progress of mankind. Today, the social scientists of these countries must strive to absorb and adapt all the achievements of the natural and social sciences to their own traditions, thus making new contributions to the advancement of the social sciences, to national development, and to human civilization.

The Role of the Social Sciences in China

The social sciences, in the modern sense of the term, have existed for less than a century in China. However, the study of social phenomena and social problems for purposes of administering the country dates back to ancient times. China's early "social scientists" experienced a golden era in the Spring and Autumn and the Warring States periods over 2,300 years ago. The academic traditions of China have always attached importance to the personal conduct and social responsibility of individuals. Many of our ancient works still sparkle with wisdom today. Until the sixteenth century, China was one of the most advanced countries in the world, and Chinese culture was greatly admired. Modern science and culture budded in China at approximately the time of the Renaissance in Europe, but the feudal autocracy and subsequent brutal aggression by foreign powers trampled and crushed these buds, and Chinese society fell behind.

The social sciences in modern China followed a tortuous course of development. After 1840, China gradually became a semifeudal, semicolonial country facing a grave national crisis. This compelled Chinese progressives and reformist scholars to look to the social sciences of the West to help rescue the nation. The liberal reformist ideas represented by Kang Youwei and Liang Qichao and the democratic revolutionary ideas represented by Sun Yat-sen successively exerted widespread influence and played an important role in promoting change in the traditionally static Chinese society.

However, it was only with the introduction of Marxism that China began to have social sciences in the true sense of the term. Various branches of the social sciences that take Marxism as their theoretical basis sprang up and developed vigorously after incorporating the realities of China. The victory of the Chinese revolution was the result of the blossoming of social sciences there. The founding of the People's Republic made it possible for social sciences in China to flourish in an all-around way. Inheriting the tradition of combining theory with practice, a tradition which formed during the period of the democratic revolution, China's social-science research has always been closely linked with national construction in the economic, political, and cultural fields. The state attached great importance to the social sciences, and the findings of social-science research, in turn, facilitated the rapid progress of the country in the 1950s.

It must be admitted, however, that the social sciences in China also suffered from dogmatism. This dogmatism, partly imported and partly "homemade" is in essence subjectivism divorced from reality. It not only hampered the social sciences but also led to grave mistakes in the work of national construction. This was true particularly during the ten years from 1966 to 1976, when Lin Biao and the Gang of Four imposed their cultural autocracy on the people, suppressing academic freedom and creative thinking; social-science research was disrupted to the point of stagnation and even retrogression, while China's national economy was pushed to the brink of collapse. It was only after the fall of the Gang of Four and their cultural autocracy in 1976 that social sciences in China were able to flourish again. As people's minds were emancipated, our economic construction and the life of the entire nation began to get on the right track.

Our experiences in those years have helped people in government service on the one hand and in the academic world on the other to see clearly that only when the social sciences prosper can people find the theories and methods best suited to the conditions of their country, and that only then can the nation and society develop. If the social sciences are disrupted, social development will surely suffer. Thus, the pivotal role of social science is given much more emphasis, and consequently, social scientists assume a greater responsibility for their country.

The Social Sciences and China's Modernization

Following the downfall of the Gang of Four, China entered an entirely new period, with socialist modernization as the paramount task for the coming decades. The modernization of industry, agriculture, national defense, science, and technology is an arduous undertaking. A series of wide-ranging and deep-reaching reforms will be necessary to ensure steady economic growth and the material and spiritual well-being of China's people; to give full scope to socialist democracy, thus enabling the people fully to exercise their rights; to consolidate political stability and national unity; and to improve government administration and leadership training. Modernization places even higher demands on the Chinese social scientists, challenging them to study the nation's past experience and present situation and to provide answers to the new problems that will emerge over time.

To keep pace with the development of the country and also as a result of the removal of cultural autocracy and dogmatism, social science in China is undergoing tremendous changes, which are shown in the liveliness of academic life, in the swift development of new ideas, and in the breadth and depth of the problems explored. Along with the vigorous advance of social sciences, the contingent of researchers has quickly expanded and grown in strength. In 1977, shortly after the downfall of the Gang of Four, the Chinese Academy of Social Sciences (CASS) was founded. It now has 25 research institutes in various disciplines. In addition, social-science academies have been set up in most of the twenty-nine provinces, municipalities, and autonomous regions, with a total of 83 research institutes. There are also 64 social-science research institutes and 245 research units in universities and colleges. The ranks of professional social-science researchers have thus multiplied, and a good number of them are scholars whose attainments have only recently come to prominence. Nearly 100 social-science periodicals are being published, and the publishing house of the Chinese Academy of Social Sciences alone put out 150 titles in 1979 and 1980. These publications shed new light on virtually all the branches of social science. At the same time, a growing number of scholarly works by academics of other countries are being translated into Chinese. Moreover, our academic exchanges with other countries have reached a level not known in the last thirty years. People can see that social science in China is experiencing a new era of "letting the hundred flowers bloom and the hundred schools of thought contend."

The Chinese Academy of Social Sciences is an important part of this new intellectual fermentation. Since it was founded, its members, together with the other social scientists in China, have engaged in extensive rethinking and self-criticism. As a result of this process of critical reexamination of the present state of Chinese social sciences and how they should be revived and strengthened, three main points have emerged.

The first is that we must abandon dogmatism. Some Chinese attribute present problems to the Cultural Revolution. However, although the Cultural Revolution hurt China disastrously, that period does not provide a full explanation. The Chinese have a tradition of dogmatism deriving from Confucianism. The feudalistic and bureaucratic elements in the Confucian tradition prevailed in China until the revolution and the overthrow of the Kuomintang regime. The bureaucratism of the Chinese is far worse than that of any other people in the world. Another form of dogmatism that came in with the Revolution and was strongly influenced by the Soviet Union is to treat Marxism-Leninism in a dogmatic way. The Cultural Revolution was the inevitable consequence of this type of dogmatic thinking.

In the latter half of 1978 the Chinese social scientists, under the leadership of the Chinese Communist party, declared that praxis should be the sole criterion for testing the truth. Truth must be derived from practice—from the facts. From facts, Chinese social scientists concluded that their adherence to dogmatism during the past thirty years has been wrong. Although Marxism has been and still remains the accepted theoretical base and framework of the government, it provides no specific formula for establishing socialism in a backward, rural country like China. Creative thinking is required in order to construct a Chinese socialist society.

The second point is that Chinese social scientists, again under the leadership of the party, have been preoccupied with questions of what kinds of changes should be made in China's political and economic systems to achieve the objectives of modernization. The party and the government decided to organize some study groups to study the nation's political and economic problems. Their membership was drawn from scholars of CASS, regional social-science associates, relevant government ministries, and workers and peasants in the factories and communes. These groups traveled throughout the country making their investigations. They then submitted to the government specific proposals for action.

In the political sphere, these proposals included the imperatives that the party and the government must be separate, the government must be elected by the people, and the party should attend to party affairs and not interfere with government affairs. Democratization of the political system must have the highest priority. These principles were adopted by the People's Congress in June 1980 and will be reflected in the revised constitution of the People's Republic of China.

In the economic sphere, Chinese economists are devoting much attention to two problems: planning and marketing, and centralization and decentralization. Many of the suggestions for reforms in these areas have been recommended by Chinese social scientists and will be set forth in a plan.

In the legal sphere, new codes are being written and the principle of the complete independence of the judiciary has been accepted.

The third point is that Chinese social scientists recommended that the people should educate themselves. Newspapers should not be solely instruments for propagating government decrees. Mass media should not only report news; they should monitor what the government is doing and serve as a forum for discussion of critical problems facing the nation, such as the reorganization of the economy, democratization of the political system, and so on. All the reforms mentioned above were fully discussed in the newspapers.

Recently, Chinese social scientists initiated an open debate in the newspapers on "What is socialism?" and "What is capitalism?" Under China's form of socialism today, it is possible for individual citizens to open small shops and small restaurants. Another question being debated in the media concerns the meaning of life. Many young men of the present generation believed in the slogans of the ultra-left. Some of them had become indifferent to things and lazy and undisciplined in their jobs. The media initiated an open debate on this serious problem. The Chinese welcome this debate: one newspaper is receiving 15,000 letters a day on these questions. The editorial office of a major youth magazine received 40,000 contributions from young readers in three months' time. This spirited public debate will help resolve the problem.

The tension between orientation to discipline and orientation to problems does not exist in social-science research in China at this time. Perhaps it will develop later.

CASS faces two major problems in its efforts to reconstitute and strengthen the social sciences in China. One is the training of social scientists, including both the retraining of the older generation and the training of the new generation. During the Cultural Revolution, a whole generation of Chinese social scientists was lost; there are very few between the ages of twenty-five and thirty-five. It is imperative to bring back, retrain, and update the social scientists who were sent to the factories and the rural areas during the Cultural Revolution. China must also train the upcoming generation. As part of this objective, specialists have been sent to China from the United States, the United Kingdom, Japan, and other countries to conduct seminars aimed at bringing the older generation of social scientists up to date on new trends. In the meantime, CASS has organized M.A. programs and, when members of the older generation return from retraining, CASS may also launch Ph.D. programs. There are only a few thousand highly qualified social scientists in China today, including those who obtained their

Ph.D. degrees in Western countries before 1949 and those who secured their M.A. degrees in the former Chinese universities prior to the Cultural Revolution. China thus lacks specialists in many fields.

The second major problem CASS faces is to revive certain disciplines that were abandoned during the Cultural Revolution. These include sociology, which will now be reestablished in six universities; econometrics (there are very few econometricians in China); and business management and administration, a field that has been completely neglected and must be adapted to Chinese conditions.

In being reinstated, all these disciplines must be adapted to the situation in China. How such adaptation is to be achieved is currently under study by CASS. China at this moment is at an important historical stage in its development. It is a phase of trial and error, of how to build a Chinese socialism, of how to retain Marxism as a base but not be bound by Marxist dogma. In dealing with this problem, China will no doubt encounter many successive practical difficulties. However, its policy of complete open-mindedness and receptivity to suggestions and to the lessons of experience, learned by others, will help the nation overcome the obstacles.

Subjects previously neglected will be given special attention. Thus, there is to be an Institute of Sociology, as well as an Institute of Political Science Research. The Institute of World Religions is doing good work; there has been a revival of all the religions that were suppressed during the Cultural Revolution.

The revival of the social sciences in China will be carried out most effectively through the medium of the Chinese language. Many Chinese-Americans, Anglo-Chinese, and others have come as visiting professors to conduct seminars in Chinese. Recently, the University of Pennsylvania sent a group of American scholars, three of whom were Chinese-Americans. Another group of three Chinese-speaking scholars came from Hong Kong. The students are very receptive to these Chinese-speaking professors, because at this stage even the best students are unable to grasp more than 80 percent of English-language instruction.

China's policy of simultaneously seeking to restore discipline and a work ethic among certain elements of the younger generation and encouraging the principle of "letting the hundred schools of thought contend" does not, in our view, constitute a contradiction. The open debate we are now conducting on the meaning of life is for the benefit of the younger generation. Its purpose is to let people contend and draw their own conclusions. The Chinese experiment now in progress, with the successive challenges it must confront and overcome, will be one of the most interesting and important of this era. We believe we can find a way.

In the past there has been a very serious misunderstanding of the Russian experience. The Russians started twenty years ago to reorganize their economy according to the profit motive, and they have failed. Many

Russian scholars thought that Marxist principles could not be reconciled with this reorganization. We must understand the Russians—they were and are very insistent upon their own brand of Marxism. When they take one or two steps forward, their bureaucrats and party theoreticians accuse them of reviving capitalism, and they are then pulled back once again to their orthodoxy. That is the way they have zigzagged for twenty years, with no results. The Russians are interpreting Marxism in their way, and we must interpret it in our own way.

As we in China understand it, then, Marxism is a developing science rather than a closed system. It opens the path for us to seek truth rather than confining it. Therefore, it is a minimum requirement of Marxist theory that China proceed from realities instead of dogmas and put its knowledge and thinking to test in practice. Following this principle, Chinese social scientists are currently examining the theories, principles, and policies of their work in the past, distinguishing what is right from what is wrong to find the way for the future. Only thus can we free ourselves from the bonds of all old conventions and put our work on a genuinely scientific basis so as to promote the rapid development not only of our social sciences but also of our economy, politics, and culture as a whole.

In economics, the last two years have witnessed wide-ranging studies and animated discussions among Chinese economists on the reform of the nation's economic system and the readjustment of its economic structure. In 1978, Hu Qiaomu, president of the Chinese Academy of Social Sciences, published a treatise, "Accelerate the Four Modernizations by Observing Economic Laws," which gave enormous impetus to this discussion. China's economists hold that because no specific mode has been prescribed in Marxist classics for socialist economic construction, we must conduct theoretical studies and practical explorations ourselves in the light of conditions prevailing in China. Some detours and mistakes will therefore be unavoidable. Despite its considerable growth so far, China's economy is encumbered with several problems that cloud the superiority of the socialist system. The main problems are overcentralization of power and too rigid a control of the economy; excessive use of administrative methods rather than market mechanisms as a lever in the management of economy; little decision-making at the local level or opportunity for the enterprises or the workers to take part in the management; and failure to apply effectively the principle "to each according to his work" and that of material interest. The main problems with the economic structure are improper priorities and proportions among agriculture, light industry, and heavy industry, resulting in an overexpanded but internally imbalanced heavy industry and a sluggish development of light industry and particularly of agriculture; an addiction to high-speed growth that led to an excessive rate of accumulation; backward transportation, communications, commerce, and service trades; overextended capital construction and disharmony between productive and non-productive construction projects; insufficient attention to foreign trade and economic relations with foreign countries; and lack of corresponding development in culture, science, education, and public-health facilities.

These problems have aroused the serious attention of the government; hence the decision for readjustment, restructuring, and consolidation. Many of China's economists are working with officials of government ministries, looking into the existing problems and offering suggestions and drafts for readjustment and restructuring. China's long-term economic-construction plan will be mapped out on the basis of such investigations and study.

To facilitate the development of the national economy, Chinese economists have also studied and discussed many theoretical questions, including the aim of production, management efficiency in terms of economic results, and science's part among the productive forces. At the same time, we are also trying to learn from the experience of foreign countries in economic construction. For instance, the economy of the People's Republic was, from the beginning, modeled on that of a foreign country. The problems mentioned above arise partly from errors in China's own work and partly as a result of its economic model, from which the country has not yet freed itself completely. Only by studying its own experience and that of other countries can China determine its own course, revitalize its economy, and prosper.

Chinese social scientists are also contributing to the further development of socialist democracy. The victory of the Chinese revolution signified the coming to power of the downtrodden as well as the beginning of socialist democracy. However, because of the limitations of the domestic and international environment in the ensuing period, plus the influence of the centuries-old feudal autocracy and the shortcomings of the country's political approaches at the time, socialist democracy was not fully developed and was instead for a while seriously undermined. The nation's democratic system is still far from perfect. Therefore, one of the major tasks is to strive to reform the political system so that the people will become the real, not nominal, masters of the country and will be able to take a direct part in government administration. Philosophers and political scientists are studying this question intensively and offering their views and suggestions. Reforms implemented so far include separation of functions of the party and the government, deconcentration of power, establishment of an independent judiciary, abolition of lifelong tenure of cadre posts, conducting direct elections at the county level, working out systems to guarantee supervision of the government by the masses, and expanding the powers of workers' congresses in enterprises. China's scholars, including political scientists, sociologists, and jurists, have joined the people in trying to eliminate bureaucracy, patriarchy, and privilege seeking by some leading cadres, and other undemocratic practices. For a country like China, the task of establishing a genuine socialist democracy is immense.

For China, socialist democracy means not only political and economic democracy but also academic democracy. Academic freedom should be guaranteed; free expression of differing views should be not only permitted but encouraged. China seeks to implement the policy of "letting a hundred schools of thought contend," and to eradicate completely the remnants of cultural autocracy. In this view, no one should be allowed to use his position or power to coerce others. The slogan of Chinese social scientists today is "Science knows no taboo." This calls for breaking with all conventions that hamper efforts to explore new ideas, bringing forth those new ideas, and adhering to the principle that praxis is the sole criterion for testing truth. The practice of academic freedom is considered to be in line with Marxism, Mao Zedong Thought, and the principles of socialism. The new outlook has brought about an unprecedentedly lively atmosphere for China's social sciences. Misreading this, some people in the West term it "liberalization" or "de-Maoization." That is a great misunderstanding of the quintessence of Marxism, of Mao Zedong Thought, and of socialism.

So far, I have given a brief account of the part China's social sciences have played and will play in our modernization efforts. We are soberly aware that because of shortcomings and mistakes in our work in the past decade or so, our social sciences have fallen far behind. Many of our research projects were interrupted for a long time and our research institutions and data destroyed. Many of the older generation of scholars were long persecuted and prohibited from carrying on their work, and little was done to foster new talents. Data gathered today are scanty and their analysis as yet incomplete, and since we are unfamiliar with recent developments in the methodology of social sciences in other countries, we still have a number of blanks to fill. Thus, although social sciences in China have recently been reinvigorated and are thriving, they generally lag far behind the needs of the country and the level of attainment of many other countries. Chinese social scientists are therefore called on to make prodigious efforts, including learning from the achievements of their colleagues abroad.

Economic, political, and scientific developments have tied the whole world together. With many interests and problems in common, social scientists can no longer focus attention on a specific academic problem of their own country while neglecting the changes in the world situation or academic progress in other countries. Having the whole world in view means that we share a common responsibility toward the defense of world peace and the progress of human civilization.

We all need a peaceful international environment in which to develop our national economies and cultures. However, people today are increasingly alarmed by threats to world peace. A number of social scientists engaged in international and strategic studies even issue warnings about a third world war. This is by no means idle prophecy. With the armament race, aggression, and imperialism on the rise, the international situation is tending toward greater tension and turbulence. This imperialism is directed first of all at certain developing countries, threatening their independence and security. Social scientists of all countries, and particularly of the developing countries, are challenged to raise a unanimous voice in opposing hegemony, aggression, and war. Although they may study different subjects and probably belong to different schools of thought, the defense of world peace and opposition to hegemonism have become pressing tasks for all.

It is China's conviction that each country, large or small, has its own strong points and merits. Science transcends national boundaries. The achievements of any country in the sciences naturally contribute to the civilization of all mankind. All research projects that social scientists undertake, as long as they are relevant to the welfare of the people, will have a bearing on the development of their respective countries and at the same time contribute to human progress. Therefore, we look forward to more academic exchanges between countries. We shall not only learn from each other and make common progress in social-science research but also enhance mutual understanding and friendly cooperation among the peoples of the world. Let us join hands in advancing our research in the social sciences, furthering academic intercommunication, and making greater contributions to the civilization of mankind.

6

The Idea of Social Science in East Africa: An Aspect of the Development of Higher Education

David Court

The University of East Africa began with faith in social science. The years since the establishment of the University in 1963 have seen the growth of social science departments and research units at the successor national universities in Kenya, Tanzania and Uganda, which were founded in 1970, and the emergence of a self-conscious group of scholars committed to the development and application of knowledge about East African society.[1]

The establishment of social science in East Africa is an aspect of a broad process whereby forms of intellectual activity have been taken up in settings which differ markedly from those in which they originated.[2] Social science, like natural science before it, historically has developed at a series of different centres where the conditions have been most favourable over a given period of time. Elsewhere its appearance has been inspired by imitation, competition, rejection or adaptation.[3] There has been an interplay between factors responsible for bringing social science to the new environment and those forces in the home setting which determine the forms in which it is able to take root.

Social science in East Africa is an object of concern because it is a part of the system of higher education which has generally been criticised in recent years. In the past seven years, the contribution of higher education to mass welfare and the redistribution of resources, rather than the advancement of specialised technology and undifferentiated economic growth, has been much queried. Arguments for the primacy of the supply of food, health, shelter and the affirmation of cultural autonomy have given rise to bitter questions about the utility and appropriateness of higher education,[4] about the kinds of social science which are being pursued, and about the social responsibilities of social scientists.[5]

The social science activities of universities have been criticised from several viewpoints. In the first place, social science has been seen, actually or potentially, as a major means of reducing the distance of the universities from society and its development. This view stresses that social science is a universal technology which, with modifications to meet the local situation, can contribute to the understanding of the social conditions necessary for increased productivity and social welfare, and to the solution of fundamental problems of underdevelopment.[6] In contrast with the criticism made from this standpoint, which regards social science as a fundamentally valid intellectual undertaking in danger of going astray into abstraction and excessively academic concerns, the second kind of criticism challenges its legitimacy. It denies its claims to scientific objectivity, alleges that it is inevitably incapable of understanding African society because it is a Western creation, and deplores its stress on quantitative methods. As part of the doctrine which stresses continued dependency of the independent, formerly colonial, states on their former colonial rulers, it connects social science with a subservient national elite and declares it to be an instrument for alien cultural dominance over the rest of their society.[7] Both these criticisms accept that social science can be an aid to governments. They differ in their assessment of whether material improvements are best achieved through a dispersed, widely accessible knowledge and participatory methods, or whether the specialised quality of the knowledge confines it inevitably to a relatively small number of highly trained practitioners. A third view asserts that a day-to-day concern with the practical tasks of development is not the proper purpose of social science. This view declares that social scientists reflect on and interpret events and ask fundamental questions about society and the principles which govern it.

The tension between these practical and intellectual conceptions has been a constant feature of the short history of East African social science. There has been pressure for most of this period towards the reorientation of social science from a predominantly individual intellectual enterprise to the service of government, although very recently there have been signs of the resurgence of a desire for individual intellectual work. The history of social science in East Africa is the story of the formation of an academic community under conditions in which the centre of gravity has moved from individuals within the universities to government.

I myself assume that, for all its limitations, social science can be a useful aid for understanding the process of development. Its utility lies in its character as a distinctive means of understanding problems, based on systematic observation and analysis and distinguished from other forms of inquiry by its methodical procedures for gathering information and assessing the validity of observation and analysis. Its intellectual quality and its practical value depend upon its circumstances. In East Africa these circumstances differ markedly from those in which social science grew into its present state. Social science is a body of knowledge which has diffused from certain Western centres to East African universities; its adaptation, survival and influence in East Africa have been determined by East African circumstances. Within East Africa, circumstances have varied among the three countries. Uganda provides an example of an established institution, Makerere, with a tradition of sound social research, engulfed by the degeneration of the political and economic order which damaged it. Although in the long run it may offer important insights into the conditions of institutional survival, the extremity of recent disorder and the difficulty of getting exact information on what remains of Makerere prevent meaningful comparison with the sister institutions. Most of my analysis hence concentrates on social science at the Universities of Nairobi and Dar es Salaam.

The Origins of East African Social Science

The present pattern of social science activity is partly a product of the expansion of higher educational institutions. It has also been influenced by the changes in opinion among East African intellectuals and in the demands of government. There has been a steady expansion in the volume of work in social science and in the number of East Africans doing it.

Social science in East Africa had its origins in the Makerere Institute of Social Research which was founded in 1948 and developed a strong tradition of study in social anthropology under the leadership of Dr. Audrey Richards, the late Lloyd Fallers and Professor Aidan Southall. In 1958 the permanent staff of the Institute consisted of nine anthropologists, one sociologist and one economist. In the college itself at this time the disciplines of political science, economics and sociology had eight staff-members, whose courses were taught from within the department of social studies which in turn was part of the faculty of arts and sciences. This apportionment of resources compared with the departments of English, geography, history and religious studies, which had 27 staff positions among them. At this time there were two East African staff-members of arts and sciences.[8]

The acknowledgement of social science as distinct from the arts and humanities dates from the foundation of the University of East Africa in 1963. At this time a faculty of social sciences was created consisting of separate departments of economics, sociology and political science and public administration, with the East African Institute of Social Research being a constituent department of the faculty. The organisation of corresponding departments at Nairobi and Dar es Salaam set the stage for a development which has resulted in the establishment of social science departments and research institutes at all three universities (Table 6–1).

The proceedings of the annual East African Social Science Conference over the period 1959 to 1973 show the increasing volume of activity and the changes in its concerns.[9] In 1950, 10 papers were presented; by 1973 the number had increased to 142. In 1963 out of the 55 papers which were presented only one was by an East African author whereas, by 1969, 32 out of 121 were by local authors and by 1973 the number had risen to almost 100 out of 142.

Table 6−1

The Development of Social Science Faculties at the Universities of Nairobi and Dar es Salaam: 1964−1978

	1964	1970	1976	1978
University of Nairobi				
Undergraduate enrolment	113	848	460	571
Graduate degrees awarded to Kenyans	—	4	17	28
Social science staff	33	46	102	118
Kenyans on social science staff	5	21	50	67
Kenyans as per cent. of social science staff	15%	46%	49%	57%
University of Dar es Salaam[a]				
Undergraduate enrolment	90	955 (586)[b]	824 (516)[b]	995 (686)[b]
Graduate degrees awarded to Tanzanians	—	3	52	61
Social science staff	16	107	164	194
Tanzanians on social science staff	1	64	79	129
Tanzanians as per cent. of social science staff	6%	60%	48%	66%

SOURCE: *Annual Reports*, Universities of Nairobi and Dar es Salaam.

[a] The faculty of arts and social science at Dar es Salaam includes the departments of education and commerce whereas these are separate faculties at Nairobi.

[b] Excluding the department of education.

Accompanying the expansion of social science activity came increasing specialisation into disciplines and with it changes in the type of problem studied, with a shift away from anthropological investigations of institutions and practices in very small social units towards the study of current issues of economic and social interest on a national and regional scale. In 1950, all 10 papers which were presented reported anthropological studies of small ethnic communities. In 1963, papers presented at the annual conference were divided into disciplinary sections and since then the most significant trends have been the increase in those devoted to recognised practical problems, a similar expansion of those based on survey research methods, and a shift of concern from small communities to issues of national, regional and continental interest (Table 6−2).[10]

Along with the changes in disciplinary approach and subjects in the 1960s came, thirdly, a change in perspective and methods. At the time of the foundation of the University of East Africa the dominant strain of social inquiry reflected the British academic tradition on which the University was

Table 6−2

Topics of Papers Presented to the Annual East African Social Science Conference: 1958 and 1968

1958	1968
The Kamba trade in wood carvings	The public sector and development in East Africa
Kuria generation-sets	
Masai age-groups and some functional tasks	Patterns of industrial location and urban growth in East Africa: 1945−65
Preliminary observation on the Balokole movements, particularly among Bahima in Ankole District	Income policy in Kenya: need, criteria and machinery
	The problem of party leadership in Kenya
Efficiency against self-expression in local government	The adaptation of socialist goals to the economic and political realities of developing countries
The anatomy of administrative origins: Uganda 1890−1902	
Family *waqf* in Zanzibar	Fertility limitation among women in rural Kenya
Aspects of Nyamwezi witchcraft	
Some economic aspects of Kumam marriage and family	Child-rearing techniques and manifest curiosity among Baganda children
Piercing	
	Planning for development: a review of traditional rural settlement in Tanzania
	The returns on investment in higher levels of education in Kenya
	Prismatic theory and the emerging shape of African administration

SOURCE: Makerere Institute of Social Research, *Institute Publications: 1950−1970 (Kampala: Makerere University, 1972).*

based; it emphasised the study of history, philosophy and anthropology. This tradition was steadily supplemented and to some extent overshadowed by the "new" social science—rooted in the disciplines of economics, sociology and political science—which emphasised theory as the goal, individual behaviour as the unit of analysis and quantitative measurement as the mode of assessment.[11] The growth of this kind of social science was manifested in the titles of the new courses which appeared in university calendars, the new textbooks which they used and the increasing emphasis upon empirical, usually survey, research.

In political science, for example, courses in political development and political sociology appeared using such concepts as "political culture," "political socialisation" and "interest articulation"; this attention to the relationship between the political order and the attitudes and values of the populace began to intrude upon the earlier preoccupation with institutions and their forms. The bibliographies assigned for these courses drew upon the swelling stream of literature on the politics of developing countries which grew out of American political science and in which the work of David Apter, Gabriel Almond and James Coleman was most prominent in the field of African studies.[12] The interdependence of empirical research and general theory was a major premise for a succession of field studies in East Africa which were carried out mainly by American scholars and graduate students; these aimed to apply particular theoretical concepts by means of extensive sample surveys. For example, the Education and Citizenship Project which was inaugurated in 1966 from Makerere involved a survey of 13,000 primary and secondary school students in Kenya, Uganda and Tanzania.[13]

This shift of emphasis in the content of social science was largely a result of the expansion of the programme of international studies of American universities which brought East Africa into contact with the American traditions of social science and higher education. At Makerere, for example, the Fulbright programme of support for visiting professors, the institutional link with the department of political science of the University of Chicago and the programmes supported by the Ford and Rockefeller Foundations carried a thin but steady stream of American social scientists to Makerere, and later to Nairobi and Dar es Salaam, and a broader flow of East Africans in the opposite direction for graduate training. The Rockefeller Foundation was the largest single source of American support for the development of university social science. In the decade 1963–73, that Foundation contributed $10,000,000 in grants to social science departments at the three universities and, in addition, provided 85 scholarships for East Africans to pursue doctoral studies in social science overseas and made it possible for the universities to appoint 167 visiting social science professors during the same period.[14] Concurrent with the impact of American social science was the growing influence of empirical approaches at British universities, particularly those founded during the expansion of higher education of the 1960s; these universities continued to be the largest single source of foreign university teachers in East Africa.

The enthusiasm with which the University of East Africa embraced the "new" social science was justified by the belief of both its local and foreign promoters that it offered the prospect of a body of knowledge which was relevant to understanding the phenomena and problems of national development with which the political and intellectual leaders of the newly independent countries were preoccupied. Accordingly, the development of social science was justified from the outset by its ostensible utility for understanding and solving problems of development. For example, at the conference in Como in 1968 which brought together representatives of the East African governments, the University and its foreign patrons—and which in many ways charted the early course of development for the University—the case for social science was stated in these terms:

All the Colleges regard research in the social science as of special importance, for three main reasons: its value in making available information
essential to economic development; its indispensability for "Africanising"
the content of undergraduate social science teaching; and its contribution
to establishing a strong awareness of the richness of African life and
culture.[15]

Two years later the *Annual Report* of Makerere College stated the case
even more directly:

Lying somewhere between what has been termed the two cultures, that of
the technology of sciences and the arts, is a third culture, the social sciences.
Often this is not recognized for what, among other things, it is—the instrumental basis of government, administration and development planning.[16]

The Social Science Council of East Africa—which in 1966 took over the
annual social science conference—defined its objective as the promotion of
"the application of the social sciences to concrete problems of the social and
economic development of Eastern Africa."[17] In 1969, a memorandum
urging the importance of continued regional collaboration in the social
sciences went out of its way to stress the practical utility of social science:

The social sciences can thus be seen as an instrument of both knowledge
and action, not only for the daily management of society but for the
preparation of long-term policies. Oriented to the needs of society and
particularly to the demands of decision-making bodies, the social sciences
provide the information necessary for better understanding of the conditions, implications and objectives, necessary adjustments and interventions—they furnish, in other words the indispensable elements for more
discriminating and coherent courses of collective action.[18]

The most direct and substantial outcome of the utilitarian rationale for
social science was the establishment of centres of applied social science
research. The forerunner was the Makerere Institute of Social Research
which in 1965 succeeded the original East African Institute of Social and
Economic Research founded by Dr. Audrey Richards early in the 1950s.
This was followed by the Institute for Development Studies at the University
of Nairobi and the Economic Research Bureau in the same year, and by the
Bureau of Resource Assessment and Land Use Planning at the University of
Dar es Salaam in 1967. These units were intended to conduct organised
research relevant to policy; they were to concentrate on the urgent economic
and social problems of national development. These objectives were stated
thus by the principal of the University College of Dar es Salaam at the
time of the creation of the Economic Research Bureau:

To develop research activities in the subject in order to push further the knowledge of general economic questions of developing countries and to link the teaching of economics as closely as possible to East Africa and to assist in the solution of current economic problems of Government and business in Tanzania.[19]

While this utilitarian view of social science remains paramount, various trends are evident. These trends are part of the shift in thought in Western countries and in Africa about the character of development itself. They have been stimulated by the extent to which failures of the predicted development process in the past 20 years have led some scholars to look beyond the theory of modernisation which had hitherto dominated the study of development. The new outlook emphasises the relationship between development problems and characteristics of the national and international social structure.[20] This has led to increased interest in the historical antecedents of the present situation and is associated with emphasis on "political economy" and Marxist approaches. The writings of Samir Amin have been particularly influential in reflecting and reinforcing this trend; within East Africa the work of Justinian Rweyemamu, Lionel Cliffe, Colin Leys and John Saul has had a complementary impact, while Walter Rodney's book, *How Europe Underdeveloped Africa*, is probably the single most widely assigned set-book in introductory social science courses.[21]

The Social Science Community

Structure

East African social scientists can be divided into two main groups: those who hold positions in the social science departments and research institutes of the universities and those in the civil service and private sector who have graduated from university social science departments. It is difficult to estimate precisely the size of this latter group but an indication can be gained from the number of graduates who have specialised in social science. For example, in 1978, 185 students graduated from the University of Nairobi with a social science undergraduate degree.[22] In the same year, 94 full-time students and 21 part-time students were registered for M.A. degrees in the faculty of arts at the University of Nairobi. Thirteen per cent. of those completing an undergraduate social science degree at Nairobi concentrated their study in a single subject for the last two years of the three-year degree—the "3:1:1 degree"—and, for most, this concentration involved a third-year thesis. These are the students who are expected to obtain a high mark in examinations and to enter the pool for admission to postgraduate studies and preferential appointment to the civil service. The importance of this wider group of social science graduates outside the University is that they constitute the informed public opinion and potential public of social science. Their importance resides in the manner in which they support social science and in the extent to which they draw upon academic social science in their practical work. However, the most active section of the social science community is located in the universities.

The most visible achievement of East African social science has been the expansion and Africanisation of social science departments in the universities. They have in 10 years developed from small departments with mainly expatriate teachers into large university departments with no more than a minority of expatriates (Table 6−1). Although this university community has expanded rapidly, it is still small. East African social scientists at the three universities number less than two hundred. Virtually all of this number completed their bachelor's degree in East Africa and for the established first generation this was from Makerere followed by a doctorate from a university overseas. Of those on the staff of the social science departments at the Universities of Nairobi and Dar es Salaam in 1979, approximately 50 per cent. received their postgraduate training in the United States, 20 per cent. in Great Britain, a similar proportion at one of the East African universities and the remainder elsewhere.[23]

The primary unit of teaching and academic administration is the disciplinary department which is grouped with others in a faculty of arts and social science directed by a dean. The course of study is specialised. At Nairobi, for example, students study three subjects in the first year and either two or one for the remaining two years. The University of Dar es Salaam has a more complex structure which is organised on the basis of "vocational streams" and includes a compulsory course in "development studies" throughout the three years, but this still results in a more specialised programme of study than that required for most American undergraduate degrees.[24] The most important feature of departmental organisation is the concentration of administrative authority and responsibility in the head of the department. With a position on the university senate, control over the allocation of funds for research and teaching, and a determining voice in appointments and promotions, the departmental head dispenses valued resources and represents effective authority. While the style of individual chairmen differs in terms of willingness to delegate responsibility and engage in consultation with their subordinates, the hierarchical structure of university administration and the prevailing ethos have tended to reinforce this system of authority. There are few signs of a pattern of departmental organisation in which responsibilities including the headship are distributed and rotate among a number of members of the department. The University of Dar es Salaam has moved away from the British model of a single professor who is automatically head of the department. Both the Universities of Nairobi and Dar es Salaam have departments where the head is not a full professor and both have adopted the American rank of associate professorships, with several of such in each department. Nevertheless the table of organisation is a relatively hierarchical one (Table 6–3).

Diversified Roles

The profession of social science is probably a less exclusive vocation for most of its East African practitioners than it is in Europe or in the United States. Social scientists are subject to a variety of obligations which are in practice as demanding as the profession of social science. Among these demands are the financial responsibilities to family and community which are incumbent upon their educated members, the demand that the educated citizen put his talents at the service of government and the attractiveness of so doing, and the demands from various non-governmental agencies for consultative services. They produce a situation in which academic social scientists are simultaneously engaged in a variety of different activities and where few see themselves as necessarily academic social scientists for life.

Private economic enterprise or employment is prohibited for faculty members at the University of Dar es Salaam but it is fairly universal at Nairobi where social scientists are engaged in an exotic range of commercial ventures including the ownership of hotels, bars, abattoirs, ranches and consulting companies. By contrast, direct participation in governmental administrative planning—beyond that made through teaching and research—is more common at Dar es Salaam than at Nairobi. But in both places the heads of all social science departments and research institutes were, with one exception, members of at least two governmental committees or working groups in 1978. In both countries university staff-members have varying

Table 6–3
Teachers of Various Ranks: All Social Science Departments, Universities of Nairobi and Dar es Salaam: 1979

	Nairobi	Dar es Salaam
Professors	4	2
Associate Professors	4	6
Senior Lecturers	15	12
Lectures	32	30
Assistant Lecturers	11	42
Tutorial Fellows	10	15
Total	76	107

SOURCE: Staff lists of the Universities of Nairobi and Dar es Salaam.

degrees of obligation to their wider families and home community, which is made more demanding by their educational achievement and national prominence. This is probably more intrusive in Kenya than in Tanzania because the individual there has relatively greater resources at his disposal, and because the idea of individual financial contributions to collective undertakings is a more prominent feature of the traditional culture as adapted to modern circumstances. Thus many faculty members of the University of Nairobi are involved in the management, organisation and financing of projects, especially the development of schools, in localities from which they originally came.[25]

In addition to their direct service to government, social scientists are in demand as consultants to projects of various commercial and international agencies. The relatively small pool of social scientists, and the increasing demand on international agencies to make use of local as well as foreign experts, mean that social scientists in East Africa are often requested to provide advice across a wider range of topics than their counterparts elsewhere. The result is a tendency towards the dispersion of interests and attachments. For example, included among the published works of the most senior member of the department of political science at the University of Nairobi is a diversity of topics ranging from the role of women in rural development to technical education, East African literature and political theory; his present work includes a large-scale study of arid land agriculture for the United Nations Educational, Scientific and Cultural Organization.

Concomitant with the opportunity for diversified experience while on academic appointment is a correspondingly increased opportunity for employment outside the university. Of the East African social scientists on the staff of the Universities of Nairobi and Dar es Salaam in 1973, 30 per cent. are now employed outside the university. Among different types of social scientists, economists have the highest rate of departure for non-academic employment. Of the 40 persons who obtained a doctorate in economics at an overseas university on a Rockefeller Foundation scholarship in the period 1963–77—they were among the most outstanding undergraduate students of economics in the past 13 years and had been designated by the university as prospective members of staff—only 8 or 20 per cent. are still at a university.[26] The rate of attrition is similar for all three universities. The Ugandan academic economists have left their country as well as their university and are mostly to be found in international agencies. In Kenya, their scarcity in a capitalistic economy has enabled economists to obtain appointments at salaries which the university cannot match; in Tanzania salaries have been fixed at a uniform scale for all public employment which includes the university and since there are few opportunities for private employment, university economists tend to go into governmental planning offices.

Regional Identity and Associations

Social scientists have a strong sense of East African regional identity. This is partly a result of the fact that many staff-members of the social science departments took their first degree at Makerere during the days of the University of East Africa. This sense has been heightened by the dispersion of Ugandan social scientists occasioned by the repression in Uganda and their appointment to posts in departments at the other two universities. For example, in 1979 at the University of Nairobi four members of the department of sociology and five members of the department of government were Ugandan "refugees." Others have gone to the Universities of Dar es Salaam, Zambia and several universities in Nigeria.

The Social Science Conference which had been a most effective stimulus and means of regional social science communication succumbed in 1975 as a result of the strains being experienced within the East African Community which led to the demise of the Community itself two years later. Two more immediate reasons for the discontinuance of the annual conferences were the political tyranny in Uganda, which included the destruction of Makerere as a centre of learning, and the increasing divergence in political outlook and the consequent mutual suspicion which developed between Kenya and Tanzania. The result was a severe curtailment of intellectual contact among the social scientists of the three countries. Some communication is nonetheless maintained between Kenya and Tanzania and the wider region of East, Central and Southern Africa. The practice of exchanging external examiners for degree examinations keeps the social scientists of the region in some measure of contact. A group known as the East African Social Science Consultative Group, formed in 1974 by young social scientists who were aggrieved by the extent to which opportunities to attend conferences and do research were dominated by their elders—especially the department chairmen who controlled the executive positions of the then still existing East African Social Science Council—also operates to maintain some contact. Since 1974, with financial support from the Ford Foundation, this small group of young social scientists from the region have met periodically for the purpose of presenting scholarly papers or discussing particular themes. Because of the demise of the Social Science Council and the cessation of its annual conferences, the Consultative Group has become the main organised channel of communication among the social scientists of the region. A new organisation has latterly emerged under the title of The Southern African Universities Social Science Council which has a wider geographical scope, a less immediately practical focus as well as a more radical political bent than its predecessor. The titles of the two conferences which it has so far planned are: "The Politics and Liberation of Southern Africa" and "Imperialism and Class Struggle in Africa."

The Intellectual Life of the East African Social Science Community

Research

There has been a steady increase in research and publication on East Africa and much of it is being done by East Africans. Virtually all members of social science departments at the Universities of Nairobi and Dar es Salaam report that they are engaged in at least one research project and slightly more than half are involved in more than one. This work results in papers for departmental seminars and in locally published books and journals. The volume of literature on the East African economies is increasing by about 80 to 100 new publications each year.[27] In 1976, 10 books reporting research work carried out by members of the department of sociology at the University of Nairobi were published commercially in Nairobi.[28]

Despite the steady increase in East African authorship, it is still the case that foreign scholars predominate in research and publication. The balance on East African affairs is more uneven for some topics than others. Killick's bibliography of work on the East African economies, for example, cites 639 authors of whom only 84 or 13 per cent. are East Africans.[29] The changing trend is evident in the fact that whereas in 1963 only one of the 50 publications which appeared was by an East African, the ratio had risen to 23 out of 92 for the entries in 1975. Although similarly precise information is not available for other fields, it is evident that fields such as sociology and political science have developed to the point where East African authors numerically dominate in work done locally and are beginning to refer almost as much to each other as they do to foreign authors.

The intellectual concerns of most East African social scientists centre around the issues of development. Of the books, reports, articles and papers produced by East African social scientists less than 30 per cent. do not address a widely recognised issue of topical interest; the majority deal with rural matters.[30] A desire to treat East African conditions and to throw light on some practical problem of East Africa is a principal factor in the choice of research topics. Approximately 50 per cent. of all current social science research and virtually all research in the applied social science institutes—which do not offer a degree—aim to provide information and recommendations on a specific topic in response to requests from government and technical assistance agencies. There is also another second type of publication which does not make explicit recommendations such as might be required by contracts with government but which aims rather at delineating the situation to which a policy is to be applied. This kind of opportunity, for working in a relatively unprescribed manner within a given field, is made possible by the interest of technical assistance agencies in supporting research in broadly identified fields of interest to those concerned with framing and applying policies. Examples here include the joint Ford-Rockefeller Foundations' programme for research into the relationship between population and development; the Ford Foundation's sponsorship of research on roles and opportunities for women; the Rockefeller Foundation's interest in research on educational policy; the Swedish Development Agency's interest in research into "equity"; and the Danish Development Agency's concern with rural industrialisation. Research under this kind of sponsorship permits much more scope than the first type for more academic interests, but it tends to have the disadvantage of deadlines which limit the intensity of analysis.

A third type of research is that which is inspired entirely by individual scholarly interest and a concern for academic achievement. This is not inevitably inconsistent with socially relevant research, but it can be, and it therefore tends to rely primarily on university sources for its support, although the American foundations have supported some of this kind of research. Convenience is an important factor in determining the choice of research topic. Research workers choose topics which are manageable within available time and resources and as a result there is extensive reliance on questionnaires and surveys in contrast with research which uses more intensive interviews or participant-observation. Similarly, there is a bias in fiscal studies towards topics on local government finance as evidence of the same tendency to adopt topics which are manageable but not necessarily intended to have practical value.[31]

The expansion of social science research is a function of the demand for it and a corresponding willingness to provide the necessary funds. There are three main agents of demand for social science. In the first place is an increasingly well-established belief among the intellectuals that social science is important because it provides knowledge and understanding, whether this is to be used by government for the more effective execution of its policies or whether it is to provide the basis for criticism of government from a more or less Marxian point of view. Regardless of whether it is effective for either of these purposes, it is widely believed that it does provide "relevant training" and is hence an appropriate activity for universities.[32]

Second, as the East African governments have become increasingly devoted to planning they have desired to have information about the society being planned. They have sought out university research institutes and departments, established commissions of inquiry and expanded and intensified the work of official statistical offices. Several governmental reports of recent years have involved major undertakings of research and synthesis and have substantially augmented our knowledge of East African society. Notable examples are the *Report of the Training Review Committee* in Kenya and the *Report of the Management Training Study* in Tanzania.[33] Statistical agencies provide information on important situations which complement their regular statistical reports. A prominent example is the periodical *Social Perspectives* which is published by the Kenyan Central Bureau of Statistics and provides an analytical digest on topics of interest; the *Annual Manpower Report to the President of Tanzania* is a similar example. International agencies also commission and instigate research. Anxious that advice and expenditure should be informed and relevant, they tend to precede projects with feasibility studies and they follow them with evaluative studies which sometimes involve quite elaborate research. The work of the World Bank and the International Labour Office's *Employment, Incomes and Equality in Kenya*[34] are important works of synthesis and they have stimulated further work by social scientists on the economics of education.

These demands for research have led to the creation of institutions for its performance. The universities have encouraged research and established the applied research institutes to promote social science research. These institutes account for over half the research and publications on economic and social issues on East Africa in the past 15 years.

The steady stream of publications from the research institutes has supplied a sizeable volume of information on economic and social conditions. The research centres have carried out a variety of specific research and evaluative projects at the request of government and international organisations. Members of the Kenyan Institute for Development Studies conducted in 1978 the following investigations on contract:

> "Evaluation of the Foot and Mouth Disease Control Programme in Kajiado and Narok Districts" for the Veterinary Department, Ministry of Agriculture; "The Demand for Energy in the Modern Sector of the Kenyan Economy" for the National Council of Science and Technology; "Repayment Rates for Loans for Low-cost Housing" for the Nairobi City Council; "The Efficiency of Maize Marketing with special reference to the monopoly position of the Maize and Produce Board" for the Ministry of Agriculture; and "Guidelines for Donor Agencies considering support to projects in arid and semi-arid areas of Kenya" for the Ministry of Economic Planning.[35]

Social scientists also serve on a variety of governmental committees. Three members of the Kenyan Institute of Development Studies, for example, were consultants to the National Committee of Educational Objectives and Policies, which met over an 18-month period before completing in 1976 a report to define the course of Kenyan education over the next 10 years.[36] In addition, the knowledge and outlook provided by social science and research are diffused through memoranda and personal communication between some social scientists and the staff of government ministries.

The results of the work of the research units enter the work of the academic departments through the courses taught in the departments, other service courses in research techniques and the study of the publications in which the research is reported.

At the University of Nairobi, the distribution of funds for research is managed by a committee of deans and at Dar es Salaam it is handled by a committee of teaching staff. Kenya and Tanzania each has a National Scientific Research Council, established in 1977 and 1971, to coordinate research and promulgate lists and criteria by which research projects are to be chosen for support. As the volume of research has expanded, procedures for granting official clearance have been systematised in a committee of the Office of the President. Although delays, especially for foreign research workers, are not uncommon, the system is a relatively efficient one and, most notably in Kenya, relatively hospitable to research of all kinds.

Publication

While the research institutes and several departments have their own series of research papers which appear in mimeographed form, the opportunity for printed publication has been provided by two local publishing houses and two branches of British firms publishing social science work. These are the Oxford University Press, Heinemann, the East African Literature Bureau and the East African Publishing House. The lists of publication of these firms since 1970 contain a quite considerable number of titles in the social sciences and account for a fair proportion of the works on East African economy and society. There has also been a great increase in the number of social science journals specialising on East Africa. In 1978, there were 34 East African journals publishing science material.[37] Eight were in archaeology and cultural and historical studies; five in sociology; four in economics and statistics; four in political science; three in administration and management; two in agriculture and rural development; two in philosophy and religion; two in geography; two in education; one in linguistics; and one in science and technology.

A number of these journals are official organs of regional or national social science societies but they are published through the efforts of university-based social scientists under the responsibility of an editor who in almost all cases is an academic. Of the 34, eight began before 1965, 11 emerged between 1966 and 1970, and 15 have been created since 1971. Half of them print less than 1,000 copies of each issue and only two print more than 2,000.

The relatively large number of journals in East Africa has been made possible by the financial contribution of the East African Literature Bureau which was charged by the former East African Community to publish journals and books on East African topics. Unconstrained by commercial considerations, it has been able to publish manuscripts rapidly, although in so doing it sometimes showed limited concern for quality in either selection or editing. It published over half of the total number of social science journals and with some individual variation this required an annual subsidy to each journal of approximately $3,000. Of the other journals, four have been assisted by single grants from international bodies—the Ford and Rockefeller Foundations and the United Nations Educational, Scientific and Cultural Organization; some receive regular support from their sponsoring association and the remainder have to survive on subscriptions and subsidies from the universities.

The abundance of publishing outlets has made it possible for most authors to find a publisher. The problem is less that of finding material than of finding material of reasonably good quality. The important effect of this publishing outlet was to increase rapidly the number of publications with East African authorship and to demonstrate that if the facilities were available the material to be published would be forthcoming. Although the demise of the East African Community has jeopardised the future of several journals, the initial stimulus to production which it provided has been important and might find expression in the improved intellectual quality of publications in the future.

Teaching and Graduate Study

The strength of East African social science is to be measured not only by its production of works of research but also by the vitality of its undergraduate and graduate teaching. Some social scientists think that the principal purpose of their teaching should be to make their students familiar with methods of research. Others consider that the importance of social science lies in its part in general education, the transmission of certain types of knowledge and of a particular way of viewing the world. The courses in methods of research which are a staple of each social science department take two forms. The first and most popular has been the so-called "teaching through research programmes" which enable selected undergraduates to gain experience of research in a supervised project during the long vacation; it is now a common feature of social science teaching at both Nairobi and Dar es Salaam. The provision of opportunities for students to engage in research on their own part of society is intended to deepen their knowledge of society and its problems; it has also, through the resulting written reports, substantially enlarged the body of empirical research material about East Africa available for the use of future undergraduates. (Incidentally, a comparison of the lists of books and articles required or suggested for study in social science courses five years ago and today reveals the magnitude of this change. Five years ago East African authors were few and far between on these lists whereas today in many courses the majority of books are by African authors.) It should also be valuable to successive generations of students who will not necessarily go on to graduate research or academic careers, but will become civil servants; they will have gained an appreciation of research through experience in the collection and analysis of data, the construction and interpretation of tables, the discrimination of valid from invalid assertions and the understanding of the limits as well as the potentialities of various types of research. As future politicians and administrators, they should know what the university is capable of providing, and as that part of society which is literate about social science they may be able to make intelligent and pertinent demands for its provision and to assess its merits.

The development at the University of Dar es Salaam of a common course in methods of research to be taken by all social science students was an interesting innovation. The aim was to develop an integrated social science method drawing on elements common to the main disciplines. Despite its apparent logic, the course did not succeed in elevating itself above the independent desire of the individual departments to control their own courses on methods and they have now reasserted this previous control over the teaching of methods of research.

In Kenya, the teaching of social science has been oriented towards research. While this is also strong in Dar es Salaam, it has been supplemented there by an attempt to use it for a more general educational purpose and for developing and diffusing a certain attitude towards society. This is evident in the common framework of first-year geography, history, sociology and economics and was most notable in the course entitled "East African Societies and Environment," which until recently was taken by all social science students throughout the period of their stay at the University. This course and its successor, the course on "Development Studies," have aimed to convey understanding of the nature of underdevelopment in Tanzania, of the potential role of science and technology and to analyse the socialist approach to the surmounting of underdevelopment.[38]

Graduate Education

From their inception, social science departments in East African universities have offered M.A. and Ph.D. degrees but these degrees required only a dissertation and were taken largely by non-Africans. The important change was the emergence of M.A. degrees based on courses and examinations. At the University of Nairobi, for example, the first two-year courses of study leading to the master's degree were created in economics and sociology in

1973; at Dar es Salaam similar degrees emerged at about the same time in political science, economics and education. No department offers a doctorate which requires attendance at lectures and seminars but several East Africans each year received a doctorate through the submission of a dissertation.

Several factors account for the growth of graduate education. The most influential has been the demand from government ministries for training programmes which are more advanced than those provided at the undergraduate level and which can provide courses directed towards the practical tasks of particular professions. The establishment and maintenance of the programmes for the master's degree in economics at Nairobi and in education at Dar es Salaam, and the emphasis on social work in the graduate offerings in sociology and on management and administration in political science, are representative of such responses to governmental demands. In these cases, governmental officials participated in the formation of the programmes, and the relevant ministries have sent students to the courses, provided studentships to make this possible and have given incentives in the form of increases of salary on the successful attainment of the degree offered.

A second factor has been the university itself; training for the master's degree for prospective members of the academic staff has been provided in order to arouse their interest in local issues, to improve their qualifications for doctoral studies overseas and to serve as means of preliminary selection for staff-members. The universities have been able each year to attract their most able graduates to these staff-development training programmes because of the attractiveness of the prospect of doctoral study overseas.

The desire to attract graduate students from a wider radius has been another reason for the establishment of graduate work. The earliest and most ephemeral attempt was the programme for an M.A. in African studies at Makerere; it was an interdisciplinary course with lectures and seminars in which students took courses on African subjects in several departments simultaneously. The wives of expatriate visiting professors made up most of its student body. It foundered because of its failure to attract East African students and the desire of departments to teach single subject degrees; it was abolished three years after its inception. Part of the intention underlying the programme for the master's degree in economics at Nairobi was the idea of an outstanding regional centre, but the programme has not been able to attract students from the wider region. Neighbouring governments want a national rather than a regional framework for the teaching of applied economics for the master's degree and they are particularly suspicious of the Kenyan variant of that subject. The one-year Diplomat Training Programme at the University of Nairobi is one regional programme which has been successful in attracting students from other parts of Africa because the international character of Nairobi, and the large number of international bodies and embassies which are represented in the city, make it attractive for prospective diplomats. The programme for the master's degree in political science at Dar es Salaam was similarly successful in attracting students from a wide area because of its emphasis on development administration and the widespread interest in the Tanzanian approach to development, together with the presence of several well-known professors in the department.

Another impetus to the provision of graduate education is the belief that the university gains in status through providing such training. The members of departments are often eager to have graduate students. These motives vary among departments and universities. The preponderance of the government's demand is evident in the fact that the strongest graduate programmes are those which are in effect service courses—e.g., in economics and education—for which the majority of students are civil servants seconded to the course and paid for by government.

One handicap among others is the smallness of the size of departments in the East African universities. Graduate programmes require a variety of teachers and the larger the number of special objectives, the greater are the requirements. Interdisciplinary programmes offer the opportunity to circumvent this obstacle but at the same time heads of departments who are eager to keep their staff for their own departmental purposes resist the dispersion of their interests and loyalties to activities outside their departments.

Issues and Cleavages within the Social Science Community

At each university there has been some conflict between the social science research institute and the teaching departments. The relative freedom and access to funds of those in research institutes and their relatively light obligations in teaching have aroused the envy of their relatively more heavily burdened colleagues in teaching departments. The wish for ever greater degrees of financial and academic autonomy by the research institutes comes into conflict with the administration of the university which desires central control and uniform procedures. Disciplinary departments are part of the traditional academic pattern; multidisciplinary research centres are not. The debate over whether social science research should be based in an academic discipline, and therefore be located in a teaching department, or should be brought together in a multidisciplinary research institute, has been constant at all three universities. It was the failure to find a satisfactory formula for reconciling the different interests of research and teaching staff which was primarily responsible for the demise of the Makerere Institute for Social Research. The views of some academics that much of the work done by the research institutes has no legitimate place within a serious university coexists with the view of some government officials that the same work is excessively academic in conception and form. Such conflicting criticisms place the research institutes in a difficult position; it is hard for them to please both their academic colleagues and governmental patrons.

In the early years of social science research in East Africa, it was thought right to assemble able scholars and to permit their interests and assessments to define the research programme under the guidance of a responsible research director. As indigenous East African leadership emerged, and the universities and governments began to specify their ambitions and demands in research more clearly, a different and opposite mode emerged. The new model favoured a centrally prescribed research programme which defined who was to be appointed, instead of the older pattern in which the interests of staff determined the problems of research. In the face of this change of emphasis, most scholars were ill-equipped by virtue of their academic training to meet this kind of demand. The intellectual traditions acquired by academic training in major universities in the United States and Great Britain did not always make it easy for social scientists, both expatriate and East African, to conform with the demand for research oriented towards policy with definite programmes. Most such training had as its objective the fostering of understanding within the scientific discipline and of research which advanced knowledge within it. At the same time, it encouraged and depended upon a belief in academic autonomy and made academics uncomfortable with external demands for results within a specified period of time.

The "Generation Gap"

Most of the first generation of East African social scientists received their graduate training in Great Britain. They accepted the tradition of inquiry which prevailed there; many of them were drafted very quickly into administrative positions as part of the campaign to replace expatriates by East Africans in the civil service. The general consequence of this was to diminish their productivity in research and in some cases to end it completely. Some managed to continue to be associated with research, but as organisers of research rather than as investigators. The younger social scientists who are now making their mark on the universities tend to have received their training at American universities during the period when "political economy" and Marxist approaches were gaining ground. This difference in the types and tradition of training has fostered some tensions between the generations of social scientists. It is reinforced by the tendency of the older generation to dominate the patronage of research and opportunities for attendance at conferences. This is, however, only one tendency among others. Among the first generation of heads of social science departments in the universities only one has remained in his position for over five years; the rest have moved either outside the university or into administrative positions. At the same time, the research institutes have provided a safety valve for frustrated ambition by offering higher status to those whose promotion to professorial rank seemed blocked by relatively young incumbents in the academic departments.

More important than rigidity at the top has been the issue of quality in the middle. The rapid pace of Africanisation in the mid-1960s established in permanent appointments some individuals who were less able than succeeding waves of scholars who were the product of more rigorous selection and training. A member of this latter group has described the resulting danger to academic quality:

> Rapidly promoted [through Africanization policies] up the ladder of seeming academic achievements in their various disciplines, they attain titles whose academic demands neither their own intellectual formation nor their academic productivity can measure up to. The result is insecurity, a strong attachment to gerontocracy, and an unwillingness to confront other epistemologies in their own intellectual formation. Academic mediocrity is then reflected in the constant urge to fight ideological battles (natives versus expatriates, socialists versus nationalists) and not theoretical battles.[39]

The existence of a single national university excludes alternative opportunities; it causes the intellectually insecure to be obsessed with preserving their position rather than to be concerned with issues of intellectual substance.

New issues have been brought to the fore by a small group of hard and energetic social scientists, most of whom have returned from overseas, usually the United States, during the past five years. Animated by an awareness that they are representatives in their own country of a foreign culture, they are trying to adapt themselves and the task of social science to the poverty which surrounds them. They incline towards non-disciplinary approaches to research; they insist that the "Third World" is the proper unit for analysis, and frequently espouse Marxist explanations of underdevelopment. They bridle at evidence of humiliating bonds of intellectual dependence and proclaim the necessity of specifically African forms of scholarship.

Intellectual Concentration versus Practical Involvement

East African social scientists are caught up in a debate about the extent to which poor, still largely illiterate societies can afford and justify institutions which concentrate the intellectual powers of the societies in order to nurture exceptional intellectual abilities in investigation and analysis. Professor Ali Mazrui has put the issue in the following terms:

> The philosophy of intellectual concentration is one which believes that the business of a student at a university must be strictly that of a student. He should concentrate his efforts on intellectual pursuits and attempt to make maximum academic use of his limited stay at this institution of higher training. The philosophy of practical involvement however argues from the belief that a student's career is not complete unless he displays a readiness to get involved in some practical affairs of his society. It is not enough that he engages in study and thought; he must also respond to the needs of the masses around him by a display of practical sympathy, and react against the ills of his community and his world with a moral commitment to reform.[40]

The issue is a universal one but it is intensified in the setting of extreme poverty such as prevails in East Africa. The University of Dar es Salaam has taken several measures to develop an ethos of community service and practical involvement among staff and students alike.[41] The most important was the change in admissions procedures in 1976 which broadened the criteria of eligibility so that admission to the University now requires not only the relevant academic qualifications but also several years of practical experience and favourable recommendations from a student's employer and the local branch of the political party. Complementing this is the requirement that part of each academic year be spent by students in a period of practical work. The intention of these and other measures aimed at the same end is that the experience should engender the understanding and maturity to impel students to use their higher education in a way which will increase their future contribution to their society. More fundamentally, it is hoped that it will help students acquire a sense of common cause with the mass of the population and reduce the sense of superiority which university students have been accused of possessing in the past.[42]

Scholarly Detachment versus Practical Involvement in Policy

At the University of Nairobi there have been intermittent discussions of schemes of national service for students to demonstrate the University's commitment to the community but few practical steps have yet been taken in this direction. The issue for social scientists and the university at large has been less that of working out ways of giving the students practical experience than of defining their own attitude towards the demands of government which is committed to the principles of "manpower-development" and "policy-oriented research." The viewpoint of some social scientists at the University of Nairobi departs from the still prevailing belief that the social sciences should be devoted to the service of government. They are often contemptuous of their colleagues whose tasks are prescribed by government or by consultancy-contracts; they argue that such colleagues inevitably affirm the policies of a particular political elite and strengthen it.[43] For them criticism and the discussion of fundamental questions, not the service of ministerial activities, are the proper purpose of social science. This role is not viewed as an abdication of national responsibility or retreat into the ivory tower but as a positive contribution to policy:

> That academics should have the freedom to analyse and criticize govern-
> mental programmes from all kinds of world view is a right that must be
> enjoyed by academics if policy makers have to confront real alternatives in
> the decision-making process. For it is only by trying to create a community
> of "home grown" researchers and scholars capable of initiating, organizing
> and executing their own research into indigenous socio-economic issues
> will we also have a local reservoir of social literates from which the state can
> recruit its planners and the university its researchers and teachers.[44]

Cultural Liberation and Nationalism versus Internationalism

The younger generation of social scientists in East Africa are discontented with the attachment of the universities to Western traditions. They wish to have autochthonous traditions. The attitude of these social scientists towards the prevailing international standard is at best ambivalent. Virtually all East African social scientists learned their profession directly or indirectly from British or American universities and thereby became part of an international profession sharing certain beliefs in common and acknowledging certain standards. To adhere to these beliefs and standards seems sometimes to continue a condition of dependency and leads to the claim that they are largely inappropriate to the East African situation. Many East African social scientists assert that, as they have learned it, social science has been part of a process of cultural imperialism. To some extent this argument is associated with individual unwillingness to master the theories and statistical skill contained in present-day social science knowledge; often the arguments use the Marxist idiom because it is a convenient means of dissent against the dominant intellectual tradition.

At the same time, reaction against "bourgeois social science" also represents an attempt to do intellectual justice to the particularity of the local situation. It finds expression, for example, in efforts to develop interdisciplinary courses of study.[45]

The resistance against the traditions which scholars have absorbed and to which they still adhere extends to techniques of research on the grounds that they oversimplify social reality, alienate respondents, and provide few paths to subsequent action. From this analysis have come claims for an alternative mode of research which stresses the need to understand society from the standpoint of those being studied, in a process of mutual discovery through "qualitative" and "participatory" approaches.[46]

The Institutional Environment of Social Science

The University

The East African universities have encouraged social science teaching and research because that is what universities in Great Britain and the United States did when the East African universities were established. They also did so because they were seen as means of Africanising the curriculum and of demonstrating through research the relevance of the university to its society. At both Nairobi and Dar es Salaam there has been steady and increasing support for the social science teaching departments and this is illustrated by the increase in established academic positions. Both universities have appointed their most able graduates as future members of staff. Each university has created special institutions for the promotion of research in social science. Subsequent university support for the research institutes has varied in magnitude because in the face of expanding enrolments the decisions of university administrators and heads of departments favour teaching rather than research. Furthermore, both the universities of Nairobi and Dar es Salaam have also emphasised the teaching of science as opposed to social science. Nevertheless, in the provision of resources and positions, the universities' support of social science for the period as a whole has been substantial.

Advancement within the universities has been determined by the traditional indicators of academic achievement in research and teaching. At Dar es Salaam the ease of shifting between teaching and administration has led to the incorporation of practical experience as a criterion in decisions about promotion. This complicates decisions about appointment because of the added difficulty of weighing different kinds of practical experience against particular types of academic achievement.

In the early years of the universities the development of social science was subordinated to the goal of replacing expatriates. "East Africanisation" tended to dominate discussions of appointments and to make it difficult for anyone who urged circumspection to avoid the charge of "using the artificial issue of standards" as a means of keeping out members of certain ethnic groups or unnecessarily retaining expatriates. In this period recruitment was largely a matter of encouraging prospective candidate for appointments back into the department which had sponsored them the moment they had completed their overseas studies. Appointments committees existed to formalise the appointment of individuals, who in the case of the University of Dar es Salaam had been listed as staff-members throughout the period of their training. Now that "localisation" is almost complete, appointments to available positions may involve a choice between several qualified East African applicants and hence the opportunity and necessity for applying criteria relating to the kinds of emphasis and interests which the department wishes to further.

There is dissatisfaction in the teaching staffs about the administration of the universities. They say that it is too centralised and oligarchical; they claim that strictly academic issues are decided by administrators. In 1978, the University of Nairobi decided to purchase a new computer system without any prior consultation with the academic departments concerning their requirements and the kinds of technology which might most effectively and cheaply meet their needs. More irritating because more frequent are situations in which individuals in the university administration are able to make decisions about expenditure, study-leaves, book orders, staff contracts and similar lesser and greater issues which impinge upon the autonomy of academic departments. The year 1976 was an especially difficult time for the University of Nairobi; the institution was closed on several occasions following student fights with police and political unrest associated with the assassination of a prominent and popular member of the National Assembly. During the longest period of closure, several faculties attempted to express their views through the faculty board. They pointed to the failure to consult with academic staff and students in matters central to the academic life of the University. For example, the faculty of arts, which includes the social science departments, drew attention to deficiencies of the existing organisations of authority; they criticised the political connections of the vice-chancellor, the domination of the university council by non-academics and the absence of consultation in the conduct of the affairs of the University. They contrasted this with principles of university government embodied in the act of parliament which established the University:

> In order for the University to achieve its goals, both the academic staff and students must be in a position to initiate, discuss and decide upon policy and other matters that relate to the academic well being of the University. The administration's duty is to service these functions and, for the University to operate efficiently, the administration must be subordinate to the academic side. Only if these fundamental principles are upheld can a University effectively service its community and the society as a whole.[47]

Whether or not this mode of university government is implied in the act of parliament which established the University, it has found limited expression in recent practice.

In Tanzania the government has viewed the transfer of staff between the University and the civil service as desirable. It is intended thereby to keep the University in touch with practical experience and to prevent university appointments from becoming a source of high social status. Many staff-members have been assigned, often at little notice, to posts in government and quasi-public organisations; flow in the opposite direction has also occurred although on balance there has been a greater movement from University to government. This has resulted in the periodic disruption of teaching programmes and contributed to a general air of instability. The prospect of imminent transfer to a post outside the university can weaken the sense of permanence and continuity necessary for the formation of an enduring attachment to that university and to the ideals necessary for effective teaching and research.

Within the framework set by the University's dependence on the government and the internal structure of the University, a further important influence has been that of visiting foreign social scientists. Throughout the seven years of existence of the University of East Africa and since, virtually all the social science departments at each constituent college were led and predominantly staffed by non−East Africans. They were the first bearers of social science; they established precedents and practices of departmental organisation and research, many of which are still very influential. In addition to the group of social anthropologists brought together by Dr. Richards at Makerere in the 1950s, there have been other identifiable expatriate groups such as the group of development economists at Makerere who were involved in a four-year study of the problems of development planning in the East African countries in the mid-1960s, and the group made up by John Saul, Lionel Cliffe and Walter Rodney and their colleagues at Dar es Salaam in the early 1970s.[48] Part of the achievement of these groups stemmed simply from the fact that a particular set of individuals happened to be together in the university at a particular period in time and developed an intellectual affinity which each found very stimulating. Such prominence of expatriates is unlikely to recur.

Problems have been experienced at Dar es Salaam in particular with such things as acquiring paper and maintaining typewriters; the procurement of teaching materials in Uganda under President Amin was at a virtual standstill. Nonetheless, the East African universities have on the whole established relatively effective printing, publishing and library facilities which are an aid to work in social science. Social science in East Africa relies much less on quantitative methods than it does in Europe or North America. In part this is a result of intellectual and political choice; in part it is a legacy of deficient teaching of mathematics in primary and secondary schools and the tradition of separating students into arts and science streams, which ensured among other things that few prospective social scientists had any mathematical skill. In part also it is a result of the pressures of computer salesmen who have sold antiquated or inappropriate machinery to universities. Despite efforts to make computers more accessible through the introduction of mini-computers and "software" programmes, such as the Statistical Package for the Social Sciences, which require only literacy for their use the universities have not been able to create among their social scientists widespread awarenesss of the potentialities of computer-technology. The use of computer facilities as an aid to social science analysis, which is pervasive in North American social science, is still largely absent in the work of East African social scientists, and the result is a barrier to international communication in the social sciences.

Government

In the past 15 years social science, along with the universities, has to a great extent become dominated by government. The growth of governments in size and complexity in this period and their large ambitions in central planning in all three East African countries have created a demand for personnel and information which universities have been expected to supply. The spirit of this change was perceived in 1972 by a visiting professor:

> Six years ago the university staff (largely expatriate) was trying to attract the attention of the larger society, and especially of course the Government. Such attention as I recall, was given grudgingly. What we were doing did not matter. As a result the university had considerable elbow room. The university does matter now, and much of that elbow room has been occupied by conditions and presumptions arriving from the outside. For example in the mid-sixties it was reasonable to spend our time asking about the role which universities *should* play in the development of their society. Today that question rings hollow. A more realistic question is how the university can play the role which is increasingly assigned to it.[49]

The faith of East African governments in the university as an essential element of a modern regime and a means of modernisation has led to high expectations on the part of governments. These expectations have encouraged governments to spend substantial sums of money on the universities and this has sharpened their expectations and made them very sensitive to the actions which take place in universities. They want much from the universities and they are suspicious lest the universities fall short of their expectations. Governmental expenditure on the national university in 1978 amounted to 10 per cent. of the educational budget for Kenya.[50] This financial investment combined with the fact that the government employs a large proportion of graduates—in Tanzania virtually all of them—gives government an acute interest in encouraging the university to teach and investigate what it thinks it needs to have taught and investigated. In response to governmental demands social science departments have striven to provide service courses adapted to declared governmental needs. The universities seek to meet these desires; for example, the programme for the B.Phil. in economics at Nairobi was inaugurated in 1967 in order "to give advanced training in economics to people who are or will be engaged in work as professional economists, particularly in government."[51] An interim external evaluation of the B.Phil. programme in 1973 summarised the extent of governmental cooperation:

> The B.Phil. programme has proved itself during its years of operation. It has won the approval of Government. The Government has participated actively in the programme, has elected its nominees to the programme with care, and has made discriminating use of its graduates.[52]

At the undergraduate level the emphasis on professional and vocational training has found most vivid expression in the reorganisation of the faculty of arts and social science at the University of Dar es Salaam in 1971. This replaced the existing system of disciplinary departments with one in which courses for students were organised not around the discipline but around the expected requirements of particular occupations. The argument was that the university must meet national "manpower needs." (The reorganisation around six central vocational streams has been subsequently modified by an expansion of alternatives and substreams to the point where it leaves little of the original intention and demonstrates the resilience of the disciplinary ideal in face of attempted innovation.) Yet although the new scheme of study had a vocational flavour, the courses required for the social science degree continued to have an academic content reflecting the interests of the profession and the realities of a situation where "manpower needs" could not, except in the most general ways, be translated into a particular required skill which could in turn become the basis for a university degree. Warning against this trend, the dean of arts and social science at the University of Dar es Salaam noted in 1971:

> The principal task for the Faculty of Arts and Social Science is to provide its students with a method for asking the right questions and of using the answers coherently. Undue preoccupation with career orientation could well hinder this principal task of social science.[53]

Because the universities do not wish to become vocational schools the governments of Tanzania and Kenya have established a number of institutions which do offer courses at different levels and of different duration which are intended only for purposes of professional training. Their purpose is indicated by names such as the Institute of Finance Management, the East African Management Institute and the Kenya Institute of Administration.

Governmental influence on research affects the choice of research topics, the style of research procedures and the form in which findings are presented. In both Kenya and Tanzania, the government sometimes publishes lists of desired research topics and a National Council of Science and Technology makes decisions about grants. In practice the main topics are worked out in discussion between university departments and research institutes and planning units of ministries while the actual conduct of the project tends to rely in some measure on individual initiative. Ultimate governmental control is assured by the requirement that projects receive official clearance.

More important than the influence of government upon the topics to be studied—in Kenya there is more official latitude—is the fact that evaluation increasingly has become the major type of research. For example, the government's desire for an evaluation of its Rural Development Programme drew so many social scientists to it that as a result other desired activities could not be carried out.[54] Specific project-evaluations are now the staple fare of the research institutes.

The advantage to government of social science in a university is that its slight distance permits a degree of reflection about issues without the distraction of day-to-day concerns. A good relationship with government will be essential to a vigorous social science community in the future and for that the personal channels of communication and the ability of social scientists to educate as well as simply serve the civil service are both necessary. The presence of officials on the governing academic boards of the research institutes is another arrangement through which this education can occur.

Much thought has been given to finding ways to prepare and distribute the findings of research in easily digestible form. The network of informal relationships which brings research workers, politicians and civil servants together is a more effective way of communicating findings and thinking about problems than printed papers and elaborate memoranda. The small scale and the centralised character of the political system and the small number of social scientists combine to render close connections more feasible than they are in larger societies.

Nonetheless, the East African universities are each single institutions located in the capital city and as a result their closeness to the seat of power and the centre of events gives social scientists a visibility and hence vulnerability which might be less if the universities were located elsewhere or if there were several other universities in the country. In these circumstances, the line between advocacy of hitherto unaccepted ideas and criticisms perceived as subversive is not always easy to define.[55] The social sciences are in a delicately poised situation in East Africa. Makerere is the most notable example. Few universities have suffered so much from governmental oppression as has Makerere under Idi Amin. In this period one vice-chancellor has been murdered and two dismissed; students and staff-members have been imprisoned and killed; the campus has been invaded and the student body physically harassed and humiliated; and virtually all qualified social scientists on the staff have been driven into exile, leaving the University a shell of its former self staffed by junior Ugandans and expatriates from the Indian subcontinent and the Middle East.

A better situation obtains at the Universities of Nairobi and Dar es Salaam, but even at these institutions governmental intervention has on occasions shown the weakness of the academic staff. In Nairobi there was a six-month closure of the University following a student demonstration in 1976; there were several occasions when the calling of riot police was the first response of the regime to demands by students; the chairman of the literature department was detained; governmental informers are present in particular social science courses. However, the academics have been able to do little about these kinds of measures.

At Dar es Salaam the relationship of the government with the University appears to be more positive. The intellectual stature of the president who is an active rather than a ceremonial chancellor of the University and a frequent visitor to the campus has something to do with this. The tension between town and gown is also less marked at Dar es Salaam than elsewhere. There is more support for the government among expatriates and Tanzanian staff-members. At the same time the government feels free to take liberties with the academics. The transfer of social science and other staff has on occasion been decided without any prior consultation with the individual affected or the university administration; in 1977, some social science members of staff were forced into retirement "in the public interest."

The universities have not yet managed to achieve that position of "equal among equals" which it has been suggested is an essential condition if the university and the social science activity it conducts are not to be permanently condemned to the periphery within their own culture.[56]

Technical Assistance Agencies

The early impetus to the development of social science was provided by the British Ministry of Overseas Development, the Rockefeller and Ford Foundations and the Carnegie Corporation. The rationale for their interest was their acceptance of the importance of understanding the social concomitants to economic development and a belief that social science could contribute to that understanding. In the past five years there has been a large increase in the funds available for social science research and training and in the number of organisations providing it. The list of international organisations currently providing support for social science research at the University of Dar es Salaam includes the U.N. Educational, Scientific and Cultural Organization, the Nuffield Foundation, the Population Council, the development assistance agencies of Sweden, Finland, Norway, Great Britain and the United States, the Commonwealth Foundation, the Friedrich-Ebert-Stiftung, and the Deutsche Akademische Austauschdienst, the International Development Research Centre, the Ford and Rockefeller Foundations, and several national and regional organisations.[57]

External support has contributed substantially to the emergence and growth of social science and whatever achievements are credited to it. Among the most obvious of such achievements are the vast increase in knowledge about East Africa and the expansion of books and papers by East African authors which can be used in teaching. Support for visiting social scientists has enabled local social science to keep in touch with external developments in the various branches of social science.

Financial support has not always had unqualifiedly beneficial effects. The external agencies are inclined to support research which is oriented towards practical problems and they like to see tangible results within limited and stipulated periods of time. Foreign governmental bodies are even more inclined in this direction than are the private philanthropic foundations which have especially earlier been concerned with training in fundamental subjects and are willing to take a long-term perspective. The foreign agencies, governmental and private, call upon East African scientists for advice, and although this is in principle desirable, it does divert those social scientists from research which they might themselves undertake otherwise. There are so few East African social scientists that, between working on behalf of government and helping the foreign institutions which are attempting to foster East African development, they cannot meet all the demands on them. If their numbers were greater that would reduce the need for expatriates, diminish the demands on the time of social scientists, permit greater functional specialisation and encourage more permanent careers whether in academic or practical work. In the meantime in Kenya a product of the demand for research information has been the emergence of a number of private firms of consultants which seek contracts with governmental and foreign bodies for the performance of applied social science. Four such companies, owned and run by Kenyans, were formed in 1978.

Because the members of technical assistance institutions are interested in the social sciences and in the controversies current in Western societies, they sometimes promote the study of these issues in the countries where they are working. Thus the study of such topics as "women's studies," population, environment and unemployment are emphasised by them in East Africa.

Much of the effort to assist the development of social science rests on the assumption that East African social science can be strengthened by the primary provision of opportunities for contact with foreign scholars. A survey of the extent to which senior East African university social scientists travelled outside their country in the year 1978 revealed that those above the level of lecturer averaged five opportunities for travel outside the country with almost half of these being to the United States or Europe. Nonetheless, it is possible that excessive provision for foreign travel can distract those it is intended to help. It takes them away from their work and from the situation in which they might do something useful. There could conceivably be too many opportunities for keeping in touch with international social science; the result might be a diminishing sensitivity to and interest in the local situation.

Opportunities to work overseas for extended periods in international agencies or foreign universities have attracted fewer East African social scientists than Nigerians who have emigrated in large numbers. However, it is instructive to look at the whereabouts and activities of the first indigenous department heads for the departments of economics, sociology and political science at the three East African universities. Of three sociologists, one remains in charge of his department, a second is director of the Council for the Development of Economic and Social Research in Africa, and the third is a professor at an American university. In political science the first head of the department at Makerere, Professor Ali Mazrui, is now a professor at the University of Michigan and in 1979 was also chairman of the African Studies Association of the United States. Both his East African counterparts are heads of international institutions dealing with public management and administration, one at the United Nations Centre for Research on African Development in Casablanca and the other at the East African Management Institute. Of the economists, two work for the United Nations in Nairobi and the third, having left the University to become economic adviser to the President of Tanzania, is currently with the secretariat of the Brandt Commission in Geneva. Although these appointments might confer prestige on East African social science, they represent the loss of a senior generation to university-based scholarship.

Achievements and Shortcomings

The effective development of social science depends in the first instance on intellectual power, the mastery of intellectual traditions and sensitivity, imagination and openness to new problems. It also depends upon the creation of institutions committed to the production of knowledge, the provision of financial support by governmental and other patrons, the expansion of public understanding of social science, and consensus about the purposes of social science and the means to their attainment.

In East Africa, the idea of social science has in the space of 15 years taken tangible shape through the foundation of university departments, the emergence of a small indigenous community of scholars who have by now produced a certain amount of writing on East African society. The creation of a social structure for social science—the departments and syllabuses, journals, graduate training, research institutes, relationships with the community—and the demands of teaching have inevitably preoccupied the first generation of East African scholars, sometimes at the expense of sustained research. Institutional roles in research do exist but are fragile, and the word research has been applied to a wide range of activities from fact-finding to journalistic commentary and uninhibited polemics. The energies and interests of social scientists have been dispersed across a wide range of activities. This has partially been a consequence of the availability of external opportunities for trained persons but partly also of a sense of national duty which has led social scientists to take on work which seems to have immediate practical relevance.

Social science in East Africa has not suffered from lack of financial resources. But it has not succeeded in the more difficult and more important task of establishing public appreciation for it. It began well in this regard but the original expectations about what social science could do went far beyond what it could achieve. The early expectation was that social science could produce both information and relevant policies for the solution of the practical problems of development. The pressure to provide "answers" and "recommendations" has led to a concentration upon factors which are subject to manipulation rather than on the more inaccessible institutional processes or more fundamental aspects of the social order. It has also provided a standing temptation to make spurious claims which ignore the political factors which determine the outcomes of policy. There are rare instances where social science research has been the basis for far-reaching policy; this has usually been when the same person did the research and then was able to decide the policy.[58] Most of the research done on East Africa has probably not had a significant effect on what has subsequently happened. The vulnerability of social science to criticism in East Africa has come from its failure to meet the claims of practical relevance which have repeatedly been made on its behalf.

Was it not perhaps too much to have expected these things of social science in East Africa? In dealing with a similar question about social science in Indonesia, Professor Clifford Geertz has said:

> The customary reply is to say: the country must modernise if it is to prosper; it can only modernise if certain major social problems are solved;

those problems can only be solved if certain sorts of knowledge are available; and social science can provide such knowledge. For my own part, I am dubious. As yet no country has modernised—whatever that term may mean—on the basis of the social sciences, and looking around at what knowledge those sciences have so far produced, I do not see a large prospect of any country doing so. Perhaps a finding here and there will help in avoiding errors; the habit of thinking abstractly and systematically about social affairs is a useful one for any people and dispassion is a trait in short supply in every political system in the world. But practicality, in the narrow sense, rather ends there. The argument for stimulating the social sciences must rest on other grounds than the faith that they will provide ingenious methods for transforming stagnation into movement. It must rest on the far deeper and stronger argument that they are a form of intellectual movement, that they are part of what we mean by modernity.[59]

The expectation that the main purpose of social science in East Africa should be to furnish answers to problems faced by the central government is being modified. One direction of modification is the demand that social science should be a part of the education and participation of the masses. The other is that social science should penetrate intellectually into the fundamental processes at work in African societies. These two views have somewhat different requirements. The furtherance of social science as scholarly understanding requires support for learned journals, long-term as opposed to contract-research projects, the analysis of data and not just their collection, and encouragement of reflectiveness.

It has also to establish a standard of what is acceptable intellectually. This applies equally to social science as fundamental understanding and as a component of mass participation. As interest expands in participatory research, it is important that efforts be made to define its potentiality and limitations. At present, the virtues of participatory research are expressed negatively in criticisms of the most evident limitations of survey methods. It too must develop a more positive standard of veracity.

Finally, it would be instructive to treat the relationship between research and policy as an hypothesis and to study this relationship in the case of some particular research projects or particular policies. Now that there is a sizeable body of social science research which has been carried out in the name of relevance to policy, we should have a more exact picture than we do now of the influence, if any, of this work, and the conditions which seem to have determined the forms and extent of its use. An alternative would be to start with a few major policies and discover whether they have drawn at all upon research, and if so in what ways.

Whatever the desired course of social science in East Africa turns out to be, attention to training is an urgent necessity. Despite the growth in graduate education of East African university departments it remains the case that a doctorate from an overseas university has the greatest prestige for prospective East African social scientists. The increasing costs of overseas training, coupled with the better ability of local departments to provide graduate training programmes, make it desirable to consider possible alternatives.[60] At this stage of East African social science, the society of most interest to East African social scientists should be their own; to take them out of it for four or five years seems not to be the best way of gaining social self-understanding.

Whether one approaches social self-understanding through the more traditional forms of scholarship and publication or through the untried project of "participatory research," there is a need to infuse the knowledge gained through social science into public opinion. The need, as Professor Hyden has emphasised, is to develop intellectual skills in the public, not for the purpose of providing practical answers to specific policy problems, but more generally to foster an intellectual atmosphere in which policies can be rationally assessed.[61]

Notes

1. East African social science is discussed in James S. Coleman, "Some Thoughts on Applied Social Research and Training in African Universities," *African Review* 2, no. 2 (April 1972), pp. 289–307; Ali Mazrui, *Political Values and the Educated Class in Africa* (London: Heinemann, 1978); Tarsis B. Kabwegyere, "What Kind of Social Science in Africa?" (paper presented to the Historical Association of Kenya, Annual Conference, December 1970); Anthony J. Killick, *The Economies of East Africa: An Annotated Bibliography with an Introductory Survey* (Boston: G.K. Hall, 1976); Anyang Nyongo, "The Teaching of the Social Sciences in East Africa: An Evaluation Report" (Dakar: Council for the Development of Economic and Social Research in Africa, December 1978); Akki B. Mujaju, "Political Science and Political Science Research in Africa," *African Review* 4, no. 3 (July 1974, pp. 339–358.

2. See Edward Shils, *The Intellectuals and the Powers* (Chicago: University of Chicago Press, 1972) pp. 85–94, 335–481; and "The Implantation of Universities: Reflections on a Theme of Ashby," *Universities Quarterly* 22, no. 2 (March 1968), pp. 142–166. See also Eric Ashby, *Universities: British, Indian, African: A Study in the Ecology of Higher Education* (Cambridge: Harvard University Press, 1966). On the transfer of social science, see Paul Streeten, "Some Problems in the Use and Transfer of an Intellectual Technology," *The Social Sciences and Development* (Washington, D.C.: International Bank for Reconstruction and Development, 1974); and Thomas Eisemon, "Educational Transfer: The Social Ecology of Educational Change," *Teachers College Record* 128, no. 3 (February 1975), pp. 359–369.

3. Joseph Ben-David, *The Scientist's Role in Society* (Englewood Cliffs, N.J.: Prentice-Hall, 1971).

4. There are several studies of university students at African universities but few which deal with university teachers. One which does is Pierre L. Van den Berghe, *Power and Privilege at an African University* (London: Routledge & Kegan Paul, 1973). Among other works which analyse the university in East Africa are David Court, "The Experience of Higher Education in East Africa: the University of Dar es Salaam as a New Model," *Comparative Education* 11, no. 3 (October 1975), pp. 193–218; Svein-Eric Rastad, "Issues of University Development in East Africa" (M.A. thesis, University of Nairobi, 1972); Roger Southall, *Federalism and Higher Education in East Africa* (Nairobi: East African Publishing House, 1974).

5. See, for example, Colin Leys, "The Role of the University in an Underdeveloped Country," *Journal of Eastern African Research and Development* 1, no. 1 (December 1971), pp. 29–40.

6. A lucid statement of this position is contained in Coleman, "Applied Social Research and Training in African Universities."

7. The issue of intellectual dependency is addressed in a chapter entitled "Cultural Liberation and the Culture of the Educated Class," in Mazrui, *Political Values and the Educated Class in Africa*, pp. 368–379. A brief but particularly pointed expression of the issue is contained in Atieno Odhiambo, "Whose Social Scientist are You? An Initiation into a Problem of Cultural Dependence," *Journal of East African Research and Development* 6, no. 1 (July 1976), pp. 85–88.

8. Makerere University College, *Calendar* (Kampala: Makerere University College, 1958).

9. Makerere Institute of Social Research, *Institute Publications: 1950–1970* (Kampala: Makerere University, 1972).

10. Ibid., pp. 17–19.

11. An analysis of the intellectual mainsprings of this trend, including a comparison of the British and North American social science traditions in relation to the study of development, is contained in Colin Leys, ed., *Political Change in Developing Countries* (Cambridge: Cambridge University Press, 1960), pp. 1–12.

12. David E. Apter, *The Politics of Modernization* (Chicago: University of Chicago Press, 1965); G.A. Almond and J.S. Coleman, *The Politics of Developing Areas* (Princeton: Princeton University Press, 1960).

13. This project is described and some of its results are presented in Kenneth Prewitt, *Education and Political Values* (Nairobi: East African Publishing House, 1971). Among other studies which have attempted to apply theories of "political development" to East Africa are Joel Barkan, *An African Dilemma: University Students' Development and Politics in*

Ghana, Tanzania and Uganda (Nairobi: Oxford University Press, 1975); and Göran Hyden, *Political Development in Rural Tanzania: A West Lake Study* (Nairobi: East African Publishing House, 1969).

14. David Court, *Rockefeller Foundation Assistance to Higher Education in East Africa 1963–1973: An Evaluation* (New York: Rockefeller Foundation, 1974).

15. Report of the Conference on the University of East Africa, held at the Villa Serbelloni, Bellagio, Italy, 21–25 October 1963, mimeographed (1963.).

16. *Annual Report* (Kampala: Makerere University College, 1965).

17. Draft Constitution of the Social Science Council of East Africa (mimeograph, 1969).

18. Draft memorandum of the Social Science Council of East Africa on Continued West Africa Regional Collaboration in Research and Training in the Social Sciences, mimeographed (1969).

19. Letter from the Principal of the University College of Dar es Salaam, 1965.

20. A comprehensive summary of this intellectual movement and its relationship to economic trends is presented in the report of the First Inter-regional Meeting on Development, Research Communication and Education: Organization for Economic Cooperation and Development. *The Development of Development Thinking* (Paris; OECD, 1976). See, for example, Samir Amin, *Accumulation on a World Scale* (New York: Monthly Review Press, 1973).

21. Justinian Rweyemamu, *Underdevelopment and Industrialization in Tanzania: A Study of Perverse Capitalist Industrial Development* (Nairobi: Oxford University Press, 1973); Lionel Cliffe and John Saul, *Socialism in Tanzania* (Nairobi: East African Publishing House, 1972); Colin Leys, *Underdevelopment in Kenya; The Political Economy of Neocolonialism* (London: Heinemann, 1975); Walter Rodney, *How Europe Underdeveloped Africa* (Dar es Salaam: Tanzania Publishing House, 1972).

22. University of Nairobi, "Summary of Undergraduate Student Population," mimeographed (1978); and "Postgraduate Nominal Roll 1978/79 Academic Year," mimeographed (1978); University of Dar es Salaam, "Students: Nominal Roll," mimeographed (1978).

23. Calendars for the academic year 1978–79 of the Universities of Nairobi and Dar es Salaam.

24. This structure is described in *The University of Dar es Salaam Calendar, 1978–1979*, pp.96–99.

25. This kind of role is described in E. Martin Godfrey and Cyrus G. Mutiso, "The Political Economy of Self-Help: Kenya's Harambee Institutes of Technology," in D. Court and D.P. Ghai, *Education, Society and*

Development: New Perspectives from Kenya (Nairobi: Oxford University Press, 1974), pp. 243–274.

26. David Court, "Scholarships and University Development: Some East African Issues," *Higher Education* 8, no. 5 (September 1979), pp. 535–551.

27. Killick, *Economies of East Africa*, p. 2.

28. University of Nairobi, *Annual Report 1975–1976*, p. 62.

29. Killick, *Economies of East Africa*, p. 4.

30. Institute for Development Studies, *Research and Publications* (Nairobi: University of Nairobi 1970–1978); Economic Reserach Bureau, *Annual Report* (Dar es Salaam: University of Dar es Salaam, 1970–1978); Makerere Institute of Social Research, *Institute Publications* (Kampala: Makerere University, 1973); and publications lists of Heinemann, Oxford University Press, East African Publishing House and East African Literature Bureau.

31. Killick, *Economies of East Africa*, p. 5.

32. Dr. Warren Ilchman makes this general point with reference to universities in South East Asia when he suggests that "In Southeast Asia and elsewhere, education in the social sciences, especially though not exclusively in economics, is the modern equivalent of what classics and history did for the education of 19th and early 20th century elites and would-be elites in public and organizational affairs": Warren Ilchman, "Social Sciences and the Universities in Southeast Asia," mimeographed (New York: Ford Foundation, 1978).

33. Republic of Kenya, *Report of the Training Review Committee*, The Wamalwa Commission (Nairobi: Government Printer, 1973); Republic of Tanzania, *Report of the Management Training Study* (Dar es Salaam: Ministry of Cooperatives, 1975).

34. International Labour Office, *Employment Incomes and Equality: A Strategy for Increasing Productive Employment in Kenya* (Geneva: International Labour Office, 1972).

35. Institute for Development Studies, "Agenda for Academic Board Meeting 12" (16 October 1978).

36. Republic of Kenya, *Report of the National Committee on Educational Policies and Objectives* (Nairobi: Government Printer, 1976).

37. See Aprodicio and Eleanor Laquian, "Social Science Journals in East Africa," mimeographed (Nairobi: International Development Research Centre, 1978).

38. Anyang, "The Teaching of the Social Sciences in East Africa," p. 15.

39. Yashpal Tandon, "Status Report on the Third Year Faculty Course: East African Societies and Environment," mimeographed (Uni-

versity of Dar es Salaam, Faculty of Arts and Social Science, 1974), p. 2.

40. Mazrui, *Political Values and the Educated Class in Africa*, p. 241.

41. Some of these are described in David Court, "East African Higher Education from the Community Standpoint," *Higher Education* 6, no. 3 (1977), pp. 45–66.

42. An assessment of the early experience of the new admission policy is contained in Geoffrey R.V. Mmari, "Implementation of the Musoma Resolutions: The University of Dar es Salaam Admissions Experience," *Papers in Education*, no. 3 (University of Dar es Salaam, Department of Education, 1976), pp. 15–51.

43. See, for example, Kabwegyere, "What Kind of Social Science in Africa?"; and Anyang, "Teaching of Social Sciences in East Africa."

44. Peter Anyang-Nyongor, "Academic Freedom and Political Power in Africa," Department of History, *Staff Seminar Paper No. 8* (Nairobi: University of Nairobi, 1979).

45. Justinian Rweyemamu, "Reorganization of the Faculty of Arts and Social Science," *Taamuli* 2, no. 1 (December 1971), pp. 36–38.

46. For a succinct summary of this approach see B.L. Hall, "Participatory Research: An Approach for Change," *Convergence* 7, no. 2 (October 1975), pp. 24–32.

47. Faculty of Arts, "Report of the Special Committee of the Board of the Faculty of Arts on the University Crisis, October 1974" (Nairobi: University of Nairobi, 1974).

48. The Economic Development Research Project involved a full-time research group of expatriate and East African economists who in the period 1963–67 pursued individual studies organised within a common framework.

49. Professor Kenneth Prewitt, Personal communication, 16 November 1972.

50. Republic of Kenya, *Economic Survey 1978* (Nairobi: Government Printer, 1978), p. 170. Kenya spends approximately 33 per cent. of its total annual budget on education. The actual amount allocated to higher education was approximately nine million Kenyan pounds (£K0·75 = £1 sterling).

51. University of Nairobi, Department of Economics, mimeographed report (1972).

52. B. Lewis, "Evaluation of the B.Phil. Programme," mimeographed (New York: Ford Foundation, 1972), p. 1.

53. Rweyemamu, "Reorganization of the Faculty of Arts and Social Science," p. 38.

54. Institute for Development Studies, *Second Overall Evaluation of the Special Rural Development Programme* (Nairobi: University of Nairobi, 1975).

55. See James S. Coleman, "Academic Freedom in African Universities" (Paper); and idem, "The Academic Freedom and Responsibilities of Foreign Scholars in African Universities," *Issue* 7, no. 2 (Spring 1977), pp. 14–32.

56. Edward Shils, "The Academic Profession in India," *Minerva* 7, no. 2 (Spring 1969), p. 364.

57. University of Dar es Salaam, "List of External Grants to the University, 1978," mimeographed (Dar es Salaam, 1979).

58. A good example from Kenya involves work which is described in Anthony Somerset, "Socio-Economic Influences on Primary School Performance: The Possibilities and Limits of Change" (Paper presented at the Conference on Social Science Research and Educational Effectiveness, Bellagio, Italy, 25–29 July 1977); and B.M. Makau and Anthony Somerset, "Primary School Leaving Examinations: Basic Intellectual Skills and Equity: Some Evidence from Kenya," mimeographed (Nairobi: Ministry of Education, 1978).

59. Clifford Geertz, "Social Science Policy in a New State: A Programme for the Stimulation of the Social Sciences in Indonesia," *Minerva* 12, no. 3 (July 1974), p. 381.

60. Court, "Scholarships and University Development."

61. Hyden, *Political Development in Rural Tanzania.*

7 Profile of the Social Sciences in West Africa

Akin L. Mabogunje

The proximity of West Africa to Europe meant that it was the scene of some of the most intensive rivalries among European powers during the nineteenth century. As a consequence, it came to be characterized by extreme political fragmentation. Today, there are fifteen states in the region, nine of which were former French colonies, four former British colonies, one a former Portuguese colony, and the last a territory established for former slaves from the United States, with whom it has continued to maintain strong social and economic ties. West Africa's colonial past is important for any assessment of the current state of the social sciences in the region.

This chapter is divided into six parts. The first examines the colonial roots of social sciences in West Africa; the second studies the effects of colonialism on both institutional development and the training of social scientists; the third considers the trends and problems of research activities in the social sciences in the region; the fourth reviews the impact of the social sciences on public-policy formation; the fifth assesses how far the region has progressed in indigenizing both the personnel and the enterprise of the social sciences. A concluding section discusses the prospects for the social sciences, both in terms of their continued development and their utilization in public policy. Although the chapter deals with all of West Africa, there is a special emphasis on Nigeria, the country for which data are most readily available to the author.

The Colonial Roots of the Social Sciences

The history of the social sciences in West Africa dates to the period between the two world wars, when the major colonial powers were concerned with consolidating administrative control over their respective colonies. The immediate objective was to learn more about the culture, social organization, and way of life of numerous ethnic groups whose territories had by then become part of the colony of one European power or another. Within the British colonial territories, for example, the development of the social sciences occurred in four fairly distinct phases:

The first can be described as the period of the free-lancers. It extends from the early days of African exploration right up to the time during the colonial administration when funds were made available to British colonial officers to publish studies of African customs.

The second phase involved the commissioning of special studies, either by experts or by committees, to facilitate important aspects of colonial administration. Thus, in 1908 the administration of Southern Nigeria, faced with the difficulty of transplanting to its area of jurisdiction a system of administration that had been instituted in 1900 in the north of the country, appointed an anthropologist as government ethnologist.[1] Similarly, in 1920 the government of the Gold Coast (now Ghana) created a post of government anthropologist to which it appointed R.S. Rattray, an administrative officer whose researches into Ashanti customs subsequently had an important influence on the official policy of the territory.[2] The anthropological studies of ethnic groups in Nigeria by C.K. Meek and P. Talbot provided a valuable preface to the 1921 census of the country.[3] Perhaps the most notable of the committees was the West African Lands Committee, established in 1912 to inquire into the land-tenure situation in the four British colonies. Owing to differences of opinion, the committee did not issue a report, but its minutes provided valuable material for the study of traditional land rights in West Africa.

The third phase in the development of social sciences was marked by the establishment of specialized institutions in the metropolitan country for the study of social and cultural conditions in the colonies. One such institution was the International African Institute, established in 1926 with the objective of promoting cultural as well as linguistic studies of African peoples. The institute received financial support not only from the British government but also from a number of other foreign governments and donor agencies—notably The Rockefeller Foundation and the Carnegie Corporation in the United States. One of its most significant achievements was the comprehensive ethnographic survey of Africa inaugurated in 1944.

Another important institution established during this phase was the Colonial Social Science Research Council. Inaugurated in 1944, the council was expected to deal with problems of social research arising in the British colonies. Under its auspices, financial support was provided—from funds made available by the Colonial Development and Welfare Acts—to a number of research projects, including the ethnographic survey of Africa already mentioned.

The fourth phase involved the establishment in the colonies themselves of institutions for social-science research and training. The Colonial Social Science Research Council helped to secure funds for the foundation of the West African Institute of Social and Economic Research at about the same time it was sponsoring the creation of a similar institute in East Africa. The West African institute began to operate in 1951, in very close collaboration with the new University College opened in Ibadan in 1948. One of its immediate tasks was to study the economic and social organization of farmers in the cocoa-producing area of Yorubaland in western Nigeria. This fourth phase dovetailed into the postindependence period, when many more institutions were established by African governments within newly self-governing territorial units.

The situation in the French colonies paralleled that described for the British. Initially, the French government relied on social studies by administrative officers for information concerning the culture and social life of peoples in its territories.[4] Such research did not have the same compelling purpose as in the British colonial territories, where the administration was trying to experiment with a system of ruling through native authorities. The French colonial policy of assimilation, and their direct-rule system, initially made social studies largely of academic and antiquarian interest. Later, when the French government came to pay some attention to the welfare and development of the colonial territories, they established institutions for social research and came to depend heavily on them.

This new phase began, as in the British case, with the establishment in metropolitan France, of the Conseil supérieur de la recherche scientifique et technique d'outre-mer to serve as an advisory body to the Ministère de la France d'outre-mer in coordinating overseas research. Well in advance of the British, the council encouraged the establishment of a research center in the French colonies as early as 1938—the Institut Français d'Afrique Noire (IFAN), with headquarters in Dakar and a branch in each of the territories of French West Africa. IFAN devoted most of its initial activity to the study of problems arising in the field of the physical sciences or in economic development. Later, it established a section dealing with ethnology and other social sciences. This section organized research on urbanization in Dakar, St. Louis, and Cotonou, on migrant labor in the Mossi region of Upper Volta, on the development of modern cults in the Ivory Coast and in northern Dahomey, and on the problems arising from the relations between the nomadic Fulani and the sedentary peoples through whose country they move.[5]

For most of the colonial period, the social science of most interest to the administrations was social anthropology: it offered information and ideas about the customary laws and activities of their dependent populations. The need for social anthropology became more compelling as strains and stresses arose from the imposition on these societies of European economic and political institutions. Even the French—who because of their policy of assimilation had not found such studies imperative—had to admit that *"on n'agit pas utilement sur des hommes que l'on ignore."*[6]

For much the same reason, human geography—along with its physical complement—had been of some interest in the colonial period, especially in France. Indeed, as early as 1872 a chair of colonial geography was created at the Sorbonne. In 1946 similar chairs were instituted at Strasbourg, Bordeaux, and Aix-en-Provence. The journal *Cahiers d'outre-mer* was published by the Institut de géographie de Bordeaux, and in Dakar, IFAN had from the beginning employed geographers on its staff. Indeed, as Lord Hailey noted, some of the most active social research carried out in French Africa had been undertaken by geographers attached to the various research institutes.[7] The British had nothing comparable, although contributions to the study of African geography had been made by a number of distinguished British scholars, and the British association had established a Committee on the Human Geography of Inter-Tropical Africa in the 1940s.

Little effort was made to train local Africans to become the scientific observers of their own societies. A few individuals who got their post-secondary educations in the metropolitan countries did enroll for degrees in one or another of the social sciences, but the number was very small. This state of affairs was to change radically after the end of World War II, particularly in the British colonial territories. The primary cause of the change was the establishment of universities in many of the territories in the period after 1948: the difference between the British and French colonial territories with regard to the social sciences lay in the degree to which regulations, conventions, and practices in universities in the metropolitan country dictated standards in these new institutions.

Institutional Development and Training in the Social Sciences

The social sciences have been described as

> the complex of disciplines concerned with the behaviour of man in society and of social institutions. They include sociology, psychology, economics, political science, demography, social anthropology, the social aspects of legal, historical and geographical studies. Each of these disciplines is distinct in specialization and character, and each has its intellectual and methodological approach to problems. All, however, make use of mathematical and statistical tools, and different types of model-building.[8]

Training in these disciplines within West Africa can be said to date from 1948, when university colleges were established in both Ibadan (Nigeria) and Legon (Ghana). This is not to imply that there were no institutions of higher learning in the region before these two, nor that no training in the methodology of the social sciences had been undertaken in other types of institutions. The Fourah Bay College in Sierra Leone, for instance, had been founded by the Church Missionary Society of London in 1827 to train Africans as schoolmasters and clergymen. It was affiliated with the University of Durham in 1876 to allow for the admission of other students. But if the social sciences were taught here before the 1950s, it was certainly in the form of no more than "the social aspects of geographical studies." The same was true of the two colleges in Liberia—Liberia College, founded in 1862, and Cuttington College, founded in 1889. On the other hand, although the French had no venerable, locally based university, they had always regarded the training of *chercheurs*—researchers—as part of the activities of the Office de la recherche scientifique d'outre-mer (ORSOM) and IFAN.

After 1948, university institutions became the major centers for training in the social sciences. Apart from the two colleges in Nigeria and Ghana and the older establishments in Sierra Leone and Liberia, there was in the French-speaking territories the Institut des hautes études in Dakar, founded in 1950 and transformed in 1957 to the University of Dakar. The years immediately following the political independence of most West African countries in the 1960s saw the evolution of university colleges and similar centers of higher learning into full-fledged universities. By 1969 there were eleven universities in West Africa—five in Nigeria, two in Ghana, and one each in Liberia, Sierra Leone, Senegal, and the Ivory Coast. In the 1970s, during a second wave of university foundation within the region, thirteen other universities were established. Eight of these were in Nigeria, and one each in Ghana, Benin, Upper Volta, Niger, and Togo. By the end of the decade, all of the five English-speaking territories, with the exception of Gambia, and six of the nine French-speaking territories (the exceptions being Guinea, Mali, and Mauritania) had at least one university. (The three French-speaking exceptions, however, had institutions of higher studies, particularly in administration.)

The growth of university institutions in West Africa should not imply extensive training in the social sciences. Indeed, in the colonial period there appears to have been some resistance to introducing in these institutions training in the core social sciences of economics, political science, psychology, and sociology. In the University College, Ibadan, for example, although it was intended as early as 1948 that training in these subjects would begin, it was not until 1957 that economics began to be taught, with the other social sciences being introduced much later. Within the British and American university tradition, however, the social sciences have legitimacy as independent fields of academic endeavor. Consequently, virtually all universities in the English-speaking territories have faculties of the social sciences or teach the social sciences within the Faculty of Arts. There may be differences in emphasis, but most faculties include economics, sociology, and political science (some universities emphasize public administration rather than politics per se).

The situation in the French-speaking territories has been very different and generally reflects the situation in the metropolitan country. Here, the centralized educational system and its major emphasis on the training of teachers within the "licence-aggregation" curriculum meant that the social sciences had a difficult and checkered career. Because of the need to justify the founding of new disciplines in terms of the *lycée* curriculum, differentiation of the social sciences from existing subjects was curtailed within the French system.[9] Nevertheless, in recent years geography has gradually become differentiated from history, though it remained within the faculty of letters (arts); psychology, sociology, and ethnology have emerged from philosophy in the faculty of philosophy; and economics, political science, and statistics have been differentiated from law in the faculty of law.

In the universities in French-speaking West Africa, this evolution has progressed rather unevenly. There is no faculty of the social sciences. Economics is taught within the faculty of law, except in the Ivory Coast, where it is now established as a faculty in its own right. Geography remains closely tied to history within the faculty of letters, which in the Ivory Coast and Senegal is referred to as the faculty of letters and the human sciences. Under the latter rubric Senegal offers, in addition to geography, courses in psychology and sociology, while the Ivory Coast offers a master's degree in the social sciences and in geography and a doctorate in geography and in ethnosociology. Moreover, except in Benin and Upper Volta, the French-speaking countries with universities also have schools of administration, where training is undertaken in some of the social sciences.

Table 7−1 shows the enrollment at institutions in English-speaking and French-speaking West African countries for the period of 1965−1973. Even

Table 7−1
West Africa: University Enrollment in the Social Sciences, 1965−1973

	1965	1970	1973
English-speaking Countries			
Total population (in thousands)	60,187	68,234	73,820
Total university enrollment	15,173	24,116	34,050
Enrollment in the social sciences	2,589	4,098	5,007
Social sciences as % of total	17.1	17.0	14.7
Graduate enrollment in the social sciences	—	—	277
French-speaking Countries			
Total population (in thousands)	25,276	28,371	34,500
Total university enrollment	4,523	10,723	17,050
Enrollment in the social sciences	284	1,278	2,291
Social sciences as % of total	6.3	11.9	13.4
Graduate enrollment in the social sciences	—	—	82

SOURCE: Compiled from statistics in UNESCO, *Statistical Yearbook, 1976* (Paris, 1977).
— = not available.

at the later date, the number of university students in the region as a whole was just over 50,000, a figure less than that of Belgium (population 9.74 million) or Israel (population 3.21 million) at the same time. Of this number, fewer than 8,000—some 14.3 percent—were enrolled in the social sciences. There was a slight decline in the relative importance of the social sciences—while enrollment in the universities was increasing at the very high annual rate of 12.64 percent, that in the social sciences was increasing at 12.36 percent.

While the relative position of the social sciences in the English-speaking countries was declining, it was rising in the French-speaking countries. However, even at its highest in 1973, the percentage of students enrolled in the social sciences in French-speaking West African countries was lower than that in the English-speaking. It is worth noting that UNESCO, which is the source for this table, defines the social sciences as embracing "banking, commerce, diplomacy, economics, ethnology, geography, home economics, international relations, journalism, political science, public administration, social welfare, sociology, statistics, and similar subjects." Some of these disciplines are often assigned to faculties other than the social sciences.

Of special significance is the graduate enrollment in the social sciences. For the whole region, the figure in 1973 was about 350, less than 5 percent of undergraduate enrollment. The availability of the figure for only one year makes it difficult to talk about trends. However, given that the 1970s saw another major wave of university foundation in the region, it is not unlikely that undergraduate enrollment increased considerably. At the same time, as programs in the older, and some of the newer, universities mature, graduate studies will receive a considerable boost and the number of graduate students can be expected to rise significantly.

In Nigeria, and most likely in other West African countries as well, there has been diminished social prestige attached to the academic life, along with increased attractiveness for young graduates of commercial and industrial activities in the private sector. This situation has had the effect of enticing away from graduate studies and research programs a sizable proportion of qualified students.

The actual structure of training does not vary substantially from that received from the metropolitan country. Undergraduate courses are oriented toward specialization in one of the social sciences over a three-year period, although in the first and second years the students are encouraged to take courses in other related disciplines. At the end of their undergraduate courses, students in most West African universities are already professionals in particular social sciences. The content of the programs is also similar to that in the metropolitan country, especially with regard to courses that are theoretical or methodological in orientation. English-speaking countries tend toward greater concern with quantitative techniques than do French-speaking countries. The former also show a stronger trend toward courses concerned specifically with African and West African problems.

A problem persists concerning the availability of suitable textbooks. The conference on the teaching of economics in Africa held in Dar es Salaam in 1969 called attention to the critical importance of Africanizing the undergraduate program. It noted that to do this requires "firstly, revising existing textbooks, introducing in them as much African data, material and example as possible, and secondly producing new textbooks based on the African situation and experience."[10] Although there has been some progress in this general direction—in some subjects more than in others—the overall situation in West Africa with regard to textbooks is still far from satisfactory. One reason for this is related to the European legacy of what is regarded as real scholarship—books are produced on topics and at levels of sophistication acceptable to colleagues throughout the academic world rather than relevant to the needs of young undergraduates in the few universities in West Africa. The other, equally pertinent, reason is the high cost and low profitability of producing books for the comparatively small market of West African or even African students.

Graduate education has been less successful in the region than undergraduate training. Where graduate programs exist, they involve one or two years for a master's and two to three years for a doctorate. The inherited tradition from Europe is to leave the student to grapple on his own with acquiring the methodological and conceptual tools needed to write a thesis, under the general supervision of a member of the faculty. However, with the increasing contact with American practice, many social-science departments—especially in English-speaking West African countries—now offer formal courses for graduate students preparatory to their field work. There is general acceptance of quantitative methodology and an increasing use of high-speed electronic computers in research activities. Less satisfactory with regard to graduate education is the rather restricted outlet for making the findings of doctoral and master's theses more widely known, a problem further compounded by the dual-language situation in the region. The lack of adequate dissemination operates as a barrier to the recognition of comparable experiences and the enrichment of inductive generalizations with examples from somewhat different political systems.

Research in the Social Sciences

Much of the research in the social sciences in West Africa has been done by foreigners, partly because of the continued importance of colonial links (particularly in the French-speaking countries), and partly because of the inchoate research organization in most countries in the region. Even during the colonial period, the French had established local research centers in their various territories as branches of the Institut français d'Afrique noire. At independence, each branch became autonomous and changed its name to l'Institut fondamental d'Afrique noire; some countries later changed the name again. The French then formally established local offices for the Office de la recherche scientifique et technique outre-mer (ORSTOM), where French scholars and scientists continued to be funded by their government to engage in research on conditions in each of the territories.

Apart from these vestiges of colonialism, new research institutes have been established in a few countries, notably the Ivory Coast. These institutes are usually based within universities. In the Ivory Coast, two of the better known are the Institute of Ethno-Sociology and the Institute of Tropical Geography.

In the English-speaking countries, the West African Institute of Social and Economic Research did not last long enough to become West African in scope. It was essentially a Nigerian institution, and not much was lost when in January 1957 it became the Nigerian Institute of Social and Economic Research (NISER). The new institute remained a department of the government, although it was based within the University of Ibadan. In recent years, its relation to the government has tended increasingly to be emphasized, both in its definition of research problems and the conditions of service of its staff.

With the exception of NISER, in English-speaking West Africa research institutes in the social sciences have usually developed within universities. Thus, in Ghana, the Institute of African Studies, the Institute of Statistical, Social and Economic Research, and the Regional Institute of Population Studies are all part of the University of Ghana in Legon. This trend has significant implications for funding. As part of the universities, the research institutes lack independent visibility and have to compete for finances with departments and faculties whose claims on university resources are usually viewed as more urgent, if not more justified. As a result, most research institutes have tended to depend for funding on external donor agencies, which often make grants for research in fields of interest to them. Sometimes the grants are tied to scholars from the country of the donor, so that the institutes serve as no more than field stations for foreign researchers.

In most West African countries there is no national coordinating body for social-science research. Where one does exist, it is relatively ineffective. In Ghana, for example, an Academy of Arts and Sciences has existed since 1959; it contains a humanities section with which many academic associations in the social sciences are affiliated. The academy has not coordinated or given direction to social-science research in the country, but it has given grants for individual research projects. It has also provided subsidies for the publication of journals such as the *Ghana Sociological Journal* and the *Journal of the Ghana Historical Society;* and it has provided support for conferences. However, the worsening economic situation of the country has made such gestures increasingly difficult. In Nigeria, efforts are under way to establish a Council for the Humanities and the Social Sciences and to determine its relationship to the existing Academy of Science, which serves the natural and physical sciences. The academy itself has had a checkered career: the hope is that the recent establishment of a government Ministry of Science and Technology to which the academy can directly relate—especially for purposes of funding—should help it to have a greater impact on research activities in general.

A few countries in the region—like the Ivory Coast—already have ministries of science and technology, which help to maintain a relationship with the government and coordinate research activities in the country. Such ministries should help to better define national priorities in social-science research and ensure more-adequate financial support from internal governmental sources. This is already happening in the areas of agricultural and industrial research; there is hope that when the social sciences are organized, they can call on the same sources.

In the meantime, most research activities in the social sciences continue to reflect individual preferences and judgment as to the most pressing national or regional problems. Invariably, most of these problems relate to issues of development, emphasizing in the 1960s the role of industrialization, and in the 1970s the problems of rural development. They also include concern with the growth and movements of populations, particularly the massive influx of young people from rural areas into the cities; the continuing problems of ethnicity and political instability; issues of political leadership and administrative effectiveness; and the changing international relations of most West African countries.[11] In recent years, most social sciences in the region have begun to grapple with problems likely to arise from the move toward increasing regional cooperation within the framework of the Economic Community of West African States (ECOWAS).

Nonetheless, in all these activities the social sciences have operated largely through individually defined research projects. The conceptualization of such projects often reflects the approach of a particular scholar to the new Marxian philosophical and analytical system of thought. Such research finds outlets either through journals—most of which are published abroad—or occasionally through conferences, which are strictly national in scope and attendance. There have been a number of attempts to establish national journals in various fields of the social sciences. The most successful in the region include the *Nigerian Journal of Economics and Social Studies* and the *Nigerian Geographical Journal.* The former, though giving preference to economic articles, provides an outlet for all the social sciences. In recent years researchers in sociology and anthropology have tried without success to establish their own separate journals. On the other hand, the *Quarterly Journal of Administration*, published at the University of Ife, is already making its mark on the academic and professional scene.

Outside Nigeria, the situation in English-speaking African countries is not promising. Both the Economic Society and the Geographical Society of Ghana have published bulletins only irregularly. The semiannual *Sierra Leone Studies* has been experiencing serious difficulties in recent years. Most French-speaking West African countries have retained the earlier publications of the IFAN. Thus, the Republic of Benin has the *Études dahoméennes,* Niger the *Études nigeriennes,* Togo the *Études togolaises,* Guinea the *Recherches africaines,* and Upper Volta the *Notes et documents voltaiques.* Senegal maintains the full list of IFAN publications, which for the social sciences includes *Serie B—Sciences humaines, Notes africaines, Memoires de l'IFAN,* and *Initiations et études africaines.* In most of the smaller countries these publications are now coming out irregularly or not at all.

Particularly in the English-speaking countries, academic journals in the social sciences are the organs of learned societies and professional associations of scholars. Many of the papers published have previously been read at the annual conferences of the societies. There is no indication of the existence of such societies or associations in French-speaking West African countries outside the framework of such officially sponsored organizations as the Centre des sciences humaines in the Ivory Coast and the Institut Fondamental d'Afrique noire in Senegal. However, in emulation of the successful regional organizations of the medical and physical/natural sciences, the Nigerian Economic Society in 1979 helped launch a West African Economic Association to include all the countries in the region. The association has already held one succcesful conference in Lagos, but an outlet for publishing papers aimed at such a regional audience of social scientists remains to be found. The headquarters of ECOWAS (the Economic Community of West African States) are also in Lagos, a fact that may increase the chances for favorable decisions concerning such a publication outlet. There has also been an effort to establish a West African Research Council on Population and Development, which is currently awaiting the decision of the Council of Ministers of the West African Multinational Programming and Operational Centre (MULPOC—one of the regional groupings into which the United Nations Economic Commission for Africa has divided the continent for greater operational effectiveness).

Few research institutions or organizations in the social sciences in West Africa are largely policy-oriented in their activities. One is the Nigerian Institute of Social and Economic Research, which since 1970 has maintained strong working relations with government ministries. The result has been the establishment within the institute of five major divisions: Agricultural and Rural Development, Economic Development and Planning, Physical Planning and Development, Social Development, and Business and Industrial Consultancy. The first four divisions undertake both short- and long-term research on economic, social, and environmental aspects of life in Nigeria. They respond also to the specific research demands of various government ministries and offer consultancy services—especially feasibility studies for industrial projects—for the federal Ministry of Industries.[12]

There is some indication that because they are able continually to recruit high-level manpower under one form or another of technical-assistance programs, the various territorial branches of the Office de la recherche scientifique et technique outre-mer perform similar functions for those French-speaking West African countries where they exist. For the region as a whole, however, the United Nations African Institute for Economic Development and Planning (IDEP), based in Dakar, Senegal, retains a primary role. In addition to training specialists and officials of African governments responsible for economic development and planning, this institute conducts research on aspects of development of regional or continental interest. There has, however, been some criticism that in terms of research on matters of continental interest, the institute has not lived up to expectations. Another continental organization with regional interest is the Council for the Development of Economic and Social Research in Africa (CODESRIA), also based in Dakar. The council has undertaken the preparation of directories of social-science institutions on the continent, as well as an inventory of research projects conducted there.[13] Again, inadequate financial support and weak leadership have impaired the effectiveness of the council. Recently the council has sought funding from external donor agencies to enable it to commission or undertake research within the various social sciences.

These aspects of the nascent institutional and organizational framework are not the only problems affecting social-science research in West Africa. Perhaps even more serious are the inadequacy of the data base and the relatively weak organization for the collection of data. In many countries, the collection of social statistics remains a primary responsibility of the national office of statistics. Many of these offices date from the colonial period and the main focus of their data collection has been concerned with external trade and internal population growth. Although in many offices Africans have replaced the European personnel, there has been little evidence of a new and imaginative concept of the range and type of data necessary to provide some indication of the changing social and economic conditions over large areas of each country. Social surveys, other than demographic ones, are encouraged hardly anywhere in the region. Social scientists are often forced to be their own major data source, and the effectiveness of their efforts depends largely on the availability to them of financial resources. As a result, undue importance tends to accrue to researches funded by external donor agencies or undertaken by foreign scholars financed from their own countries.

These conditions do not reflect a social climate antipathetic to research; rather, in most West African countries, the climate can be described as one of indulgent indifference. Except for the rare occasions when an individual in power may be apprehensive of the likely political impact of the results of a social-science research project, social scientists are allowed to go about their work without help or hindrance. Foreigners are encouraged to seek affiliation with a local institution that can guarantee them to be bona fide research workers.

One reason for the indulgence and indifference is, of course, the attitude of many government officials and the general public toward academic research as an arcane activity. As Akiwowo observed, the social scientist in most Third World countries is caught in a duality resulting from the existence of two types of audiences (central and peripheral) to which he has to relate.[14] The central audience comprises professional social scientists throughout the world, while the peripheral audience is made up of policymakers, the general public, and the potential public in his own country or region. Most of these scientists tend to address their research to their central audience, for reasons deriving from what Akiwowo calls "academic colonialism." For example, he writes, "hardly any Nigerian social scientist . . . can be elevated by his University authorities to the level of either an associate professor or full professor without reference to a host of unseen assessors of the Inter-University Council" of Great Britian, which "controls in essence the direction, the rate and the number of contributors" to the development of the social sciences in Nigeria.[15]

Impact of the Social Sciences on Public-Policy Formulation

The preoccupation of much current social-science research in West Africa with its central audience is perhaps one reason why its influence on policy formulation has not been as strong as might be expected. Yet, it would be unrealistic to assume that such influence is nonexistent. From the early years of independence of most West African countries, the preeminence given to the issue of economic development has meant that professional economists, particularly foreigners, have been important in drawing up national-development plans and determining major lines of economic and social policies. A number of countries now make less use of foreign economists and place greater reliance on local ones. Despite the change in skin color of the professionals concerned, however, the definition of problems and the proffered solutions have changed hardly at all, mainly because of the continued strength of academic ties to the metropolitan country. The numerous failures of these solutions and the growing perception of their basic inappropriateness provide a unique opportunity for reappraisal and for generation of novel, homegrown theories.

Apart from their role in the production of development plans, social scientists have had some influence on policy formulation through serving on special government commissions, committees, boards, or panels. Especially where such bodies have come out with clear sets of recommendations their implementation for better or for worse has given some clout if not to the social sciences in general, then certainly to individual social scientists. In Nigeria, a large number of social scientists were canvassed and their views clearly reflected in the final set of recommendations on local-government reforms, which were implemented.

A new means through which the social sciences may come to exert greater influence on public-policy formulation is the growing use of consultancy services by various arms of government. This development has achieved considerable momentum, in Nigeria more than elsewhere in West Africa, but it is already affecting many other countries in the region. Besides the Nigerian Institute of Social and Economic Research, which has a Business and Consultancy Division that provides advisory and consultancy services to various ministries, in the past few years the number of private Nigerian consultancy firms, staffed largely by former university faculty members and government officials, has grown steadily. Most of these firms operate mainly in the economic sector; their role in the social and political fields has been minimal. As a result, one of the most interesting developments in Nigeria in recent years is the public acceptance of university consultancy organizations—both the public and private sector can make use of the considerable expertise within their walls. Much of this expertise at Ahmadu Bello University and the University of Ife has been placed at the service of local governments on a consultancy basis paid for by the state and the federal government.

The presidential form of government adopted in most West African countries in recent years has also provided the social sciences with some direct access to power. In Nigeria, for example, this system of government has meant the appointment of special advisors on social and economic issues to the president and state governors. It has also meant the possibility of direct access to the legislative bodies through senate or house committees set up to keep certain social and economic issues under continuous surveillance. It will not be long before social scientists find themselves in an advocacy role, acting before such committees on behalf of groups of concerned citizens.

The opening of so many channels of influence in recent years, reassuring as it may seem, simply underscores the immense potential of the social sciences in any society for good or ill. It also calls attention to the need to examine how far the social-science enterprise within West Africa has succeeded in helping to illuminate and identify critical societal problems and in indicating alternative policies for their amelioration. Realization of the potential of the social sciences in West Africa, and the possibility of their having real impact on policy and society, can occur only as the product of a dialectical process. This process must begin with a greater openness in the social sciences themselves, so that ideological assumptions, value systems, and theoretical formulations become matters for both professional and public discussions.

Such discussions go back to the issue of audiences, and the need for social science in West Africa deliberately to engage its peripheral audience. In West African countries where newspapers are sophisticated (Nigeria, Ghana, the Ivory Coast), a number of social scientists have used this medium to comment on various important current issues. Where there are other media such as television and radio, the voices of social scientists have been loud and clear. However, although such occasions may provide opportunity for the views of some social scientists to influence, however tangentially, policies and events, the ephemeral nature of these media undoubtedly limits their effectiveness to the shorter term. Moreover, for real intellectual exchanges, radio, television and newspapers do not provide an appropriate forum for substantive discourses of the type likely to launch and sustain the dialectical process.

Clearly, what is needed is something between the specialized disciplinary journals and the fugitive media outlets currently available. How to make such a venture commercially sustainable, if not profitable, is beyond the concern of this chapter. There can, however, be no doubt that there is a need for such an intermediary structure to allow West African social scientists to reach out more appropriately to their own society. Indeed, Akiwowo suggests that such efforts must go beyond engaging that segment of the audience that is literate and educated in one of the European languages in which most scholarly works are currently produced. He argues for translation into the vernacular and refers to the recent achievements in this respect of the Institute of Ethno-Sociology of the University of Abidjan, which has translated more than two dozen studies undertaken by its staff.[16]

Clearly, one of the most important factors limiting the influence of the social sciences on both government policies and the society for which those policies are designed is inadequate communication between the profession and its large, local, currently peripheral, audience. This lack of communication is reflected in the public demand for greater social relevance in training and research in various institutions. The need to communicate, apart from any other goal, must have the salutary effect of forcing social scientists to identify and define problems and issues of significance to their own society. Such a vital constraint, if successful, must result in concepts and hypotheses that are locally and culturally specific and that eventually should lead to a certain indigenization of the West African social-science enterprise. The next section discusses West Africa's progress in indigenizing social science and the special problems likely to confront any determined efforts in that process.

Indigenization of the Social-Science Enterprise

The social sciences in West Africa are little more than two decades old in terms of developing a coterie of local practitioners. Although the number of people trained in the various fields has been growing rapidly, the proportion who remain in the universities to do graduate work and acquire the necessary skills and competence for research remains small. In addition, attrition occurs in the ranks of senior social scientists, who are enticed to more powerful positions in government and the private sector, or are lost to the region through the brain drain to developed countries. The result today is an enterprise largely of front-line managers, with very few established and senior colleagues to provide direction and guidance.

This weakness at the top is made more serious by the high degree of political fragmentation in the region. It has been difficult for social scientists to attain the critical numbers necessary for the type of innovative interaction that is a precondition for successful indigenization of the theories and methodologies of the various fields. The problem of the small size of the countries is further compounded by the English-French dichotomy, as well as by the large number of ethnic groups within each territory. All these factors contrast sharply with the situation in Latin America, where, despite political fragmentation, the use of a common language—Spanish (even Brazilian social scientists can read Spanish)—helps to consolidate the necessary exchange of information among countries. There can be little doubt that the early emergence of virile regional organizations will be crucial for the speed and thoroughness with which indigenization proceeds in West Africa.

One aspect of the problems of indigenization has to do with the impact of external circumstances on regional consciousness of the need for such a process. To date, the predominant social concern in many West African countries has been with development. Most political leaders and the public at large see the whole societal effort as directed toward this particular goal. Nevertheless, it is now generally agreed that the model of development endorsed by the leaders of these countries has been far from appropriate.[17]

It has tended to stress the need for capital investment and foreign assistance rather than the importance of mobilizing the people to engage actively in their own development. As such, the so-called development process has been conceived with little regard for the population itself.

In such a situation, there is no serious tension between traditional norms of organizations and institutions on the one hand and on the other emergent systems necessitated by the modernization process. Rather, emphasis is on mindless imitations and borrowings from abroad of a type that makes the crucial process of modernization nothing more than an out-and-out effort at Westernization. The result is that development in these countries has been accompanied by the disintegration of the cultural and social environment, rather than by the generation of a lively tension in the process of adapting traditional institutions, ideas, and value systems to the demands of changing circumstances and social objectives.

To some extent, then, it is possible to maintain that the social sciences have not been seriously challenged to find new theories and methodologies, because the major societal processes operating within West Africa have ignored the people themselves. Of course, it can be argued that the investigation of the pattern and effects of such alienation should have constituted the grist of social-science research in the region. But this growing realization is itself a matter of hindsight. Most social scientists in the 1960s and early 1970s acceded wholeheartedly to the imperatives of the prevailing paradigm of development. Furthermore, it is doubtful whether any funding agencies would at the time have been willing to sponsor research investigations along these lines. National governments would have frowned on such research, ostensibly on the ground that it would have been a waste of scarce resources, but really because it would have undermined their rather precarious legitimacy.

One can therefore hope that the growing concern with self-reliant development can be seen as constituting perhaps the most auspicious opportunity for the social sciences in West Africa. Self-reliance can mean nothing other than how a people use their resources of social organizations, cultural institutions, beliefs, and value systems to improve their general conditions and standard of living. The social sciences have the challenging tasks of researching the strengths and weaknesses of these traditional social resources and hypothesizing circumstances in which they can be a crucial factor for various forms of mobilization and action. Such an orientation is sure to engage virtually all the social sciences and to force them to greater historical specificity. Indeed, part of the difficulty of indigenization of the social sciences to date is the dearth of explanations rooted in the historical reality with which their societies are familiar.

Although research into institutional and organizational history is essential, concern with the mechanics of conceptual and theoretical formulation is equally vital to the indigenization of the social sciences in West Africa. It is easy to assume that individuals who have acquired doctorate degrees from some of the best universities in the world should have no difficulty in identifying and spelling out generalizations in a way that would permit eventual evaluation of their theoretical efficiency. But years of experience within West Africa show that this is far from the case. The relative isolation in which most scientists work in the region is no doubt one reason for this state of affairs. There is also lack of opportunity of the type provided, for example, by the National Science Foundation in the United States, for workshops, postdoctoral, and midcareer training that emphasize continuous upgrading of the methodological skills of the academic staff of universities and research centers. Such workshops, seminars, and training devoted specially to methodological issues may well be crucial to producing the kind of scientists who can effect indigenization of the social sciences in West Africa.

All these efforts will have more of an impact if they are aimed at groups of scientists rather than at individuals, however talented. The challenge of organizing group research activities is quite different from that of sponsoring individual scientists: it is more expensive, and it puts a premium on organizational and leadership talents. As such, it is less attractive, particularly for external funding agencies, which generally have inadequate knowledge of possible leaders and organizers in the region. It is crucial first to accept the legitimacy of the idea as a working hypothesis. How to make it a viable basis for promoting social-science research in West Africa can be left till later.

Certainly, some effort has been made to indigenize the social-science community, particularly in English-speaking West African countries. But many oustanding and promising individuals have left the community, and consequently a replacement effort is called for. This enterprise has been successfully launched in most of the countries, but contributions to making it grow as a robust, indigenous organism have been individualistic, disparate, and not as yet strongly successful. The future looks more propitious, especially if governments in the region move toward a more self-reliant model of development, and if their efforts at regional grouping facilitate communication and interaction among members of the social-science community.

Conclusion

What, then, can be done to speed this process on its way? Effort is needed to further the development of the social sciences within the region and to induce greater use of them in formulating public policy. First, a more effective organization of the social sciences must be encouraged within each country and within the region. The existence of ministries of science and technology or academies of arts and sciences will surely facilitate the process, but it will be necessary to ensure that they have a social-science section. Where no such ministry or academy exists—or even where it does—a national social science research council is a vital necessity. Membership of such a council should include not only scientists, but also seasoned bureaucrats, who may have strong and valuable views on problem areas requiring research. In any event, in many underdeveloped countries the presence of such individuals is another way of reaching the peripheral audience of the social sciences. The role of these organizations is not only to make local financial support for research more available, but also to help identify and define vital research areas and through financial allocations to reflect some order of priority.

Second, the competence of members of the social-science community should be improved, particularly with a view to enhancing their ability to indigenize the field. In the 1960s, and to a lesser extent the 1970s, many external donor agencies were concerned with staff development in West African universities. This concern often involved sending young and promising scholars abroad for a year or more to universities in either Great Britain or the United States. Given the number of new universities recently established, there is likely to be a continuing need for this type of assistance. However, effort should increasingly turn toward locally based enhancement of expertise through workshops, seminars, and summer schools. The emphasis of such meetings should be to devise curricula, write suitable textbooks, or explore areas of methodological development relevant to problems in the region. These activities need not exclude foreign scholars, especially those with a real empathy for the region and its problems. But their role must be clearly one of assisting, not directing, the endeavor.

Third, communicating not just with colleagues but with the larger peripheral audience is a crucial aspect of the indigenization process. It requires that the social-science community be able to relate to the general public and policy makers at an appropriate level of communication. The problem is essentially not one for the scientists themselves, but for a corps of parasocial scientists who will take an intermediary role. This does not mean that some social scientists are not versatile enough to fill this role themselves, but other skills, such as those of journalists, social writers, and journal publishers, will be necessary. It is essential to set up publications that are not highly specialized but that contain serious discussions of issues. This requires funding and management. The history of many such journals begun within universities provides adequate lessons of what to do and what not to do.[18]

West Africa as a region can be said to be about to enter a most interesting phase in its development. The gradual realization of the terms of the various articles of the Treaty for the Economic Community of West

African States is changing the environment in which the social sciences in the region must evolve. The establishment of numerous universities in the last decade and the lack of hostility to social-science research are vital to the growth of the enterprise. It is hoped that, with suitable and adequate assistance of various types, the small band of workers in the region can seize this opportunity to enhance the regard in which the social sciences are held there and increase their influence on and contribution to policies directed at improving the quality and standard of life of the local population.

Notes

1. Lord Hailey, *An African Survey*, rev. ed. (London: Oxford University Press, 1957), p. 54.

2. See R.S. Rattray, *Religion and Art in Ashanti* (London: Oxford University Press, 1927); *Ashanti Law and Constitution* (London: Oxford University Press, 1929); and *The Tribes of the Ashanti Hinterland* (London: Oxford University Press, 1932).

3. See C.K. Meek, *The Northern Tribes of Nigeria*, 4 vols. (London: Oxford University Press, 1925); and P. Talbot, *The Peoples of Southern Nigeria*, 4 vols. (London: Oxford University Press, 1926).

4. See, for example, M. Delafosse, *Haut-Sénégal-Niger* (Paris: Larose, 1912); L. Geismar, *Recueil des coutumes civils des races au Sénégal* (Saint-Louis: Imprimerie du gouvernement, 1933); and H. Labouret, *Les Manding et leur langue* (Paris: Larose, 1934).

5. See Office de la recherche scientifique d'outre-mer, *Exposé, 1948–50*, p. 25; and *Courrier des chercheurs*, no. 5 (1952); see also Lord Hailey, *An African Survey*, p. 65.

6. Office de la recherche scientifique d'outre-mer, *Courrier des chercheurs*, no. 4 (1951), p. 61.

7. Lord Hailey, *An African Survey*, p. 23.

8. Organization for Economic Cooperation and Development (OECD), *The Social Sciences and the Policies of Government* (Paris, 1966), p. 21.

9. T.N. Clark, *Prophets and Patrons: The French University and the Emergence of the Social Sciences* (Cambridge: Harvard University Press, 1973), p. 245.

10. I. Livingstone, G. Routh, J.F. Rweyemamu, and K.E. Svendson, eds., *The Teaching of Economics in Africa* (London: Chatto & Windus, 1973), p. 43.

11. Not much has changed in the research agenda of social scientists in West Africa from that provided by Dharam Ghai, "Social Science Research on Development and Research Institutes in Africa" in *Proceedings of the*

Conference on the Social Sciences and Development (Bellagio, 1974), pp. 61–64.

12. See Nigerian Institute of Social and Economic Research, *1977/78 Annual Report* (Ibadan, 1979).

13. See CODESRIA, *Basic Information of Corresponding Social Science Institutions in Africa* (Dakar, 1973); and *Inventory of Research Projects in African Research Institutes, 1970,* (Dakar, 1971).

14. R. Perrotta Bengolea and A. Akiwowow, "Problems in Peripheral Regions," in the special issue of *International Social Science Journal* 26, no. 3 (1974), p. 412, dealing with communicating and diffusing social science.

15. Ibid., p. 413.

16. Ibid., p. 423.

17. United Nations Economic Commission for Africa, *Africa's Strategy for Development in the 1970s*, E/CN. 14/RES/218X (Addis Abada, 1971).

18. *The Nigerian Opinion* and the *New Nationalist,* formerly published by social scientists at the University of Ibadan and once widely read by policy makers, are now moribund because of inadequate management and financial insolvency.

8 The Economic Sciences in Latin America

Eduardo Venezian

Introduction

This chapter provides an overview of the development and current state of the economic sciences in Latin America. The focus is on university-level teaching and research and on application to public-policy issues. Given that there are many countries in the region, with marked differences in their pattern and level of educational development—particularly in the social sciences—this review attempts to identify main trends, features, and preeminent institutions in the field of economics. Special attention is given to efforts leading to the modernization and upgrading of economics education in the continent.

The term *economic sciences* is used in a generic sense to refer to the core of the discipline (micro- and macroeconomic theory, trade, money, econometrics) and to applied fields such as agricultural economics, urban economics, and economic demography. These applied fields, especially agricultural economics, have developed somewhat independently of general economics, have separate institutional bases, and draw scholars and professionals from areas other than the social sciences; hence, specific references are made to them in the text. On the other hand, business administration is not discussed specifically, although it is often closely knit with economics in Latin American universities. When this is so, the discussion of economics will subsume business administration; when the latter has grown independently and with little bearing on the science of economics, it will not be discussed.

Because of the breadth and complexity of the subject and the usual limitations of time and space, this chapter is necessarily somewhat impressionistic. Published information and data on the major centers of education and research in economics in Latin America are scanty and hard to obtain. Current evaluations of programs and institutions are confined mostly to internal documents of assistance agencies. Perhaps the best assessments remain in the minds of a few outstanding economists well acquainted with the region. A thorough analysis would require a systematic review of the published professional work of the various economics centers and firsthand visits in the field—two approaches that were beyond the means available for preparing this chapter. There may, therefore, be errors of appraisal or omission in this discussion, but on the whole the picture provided should be an accurate representation of where the economic sciences stand in Latin America today, how they got there, and what is needed to keep them moving forward.

Intellectual Roots of the Economic Sciences

The social sciences, and economics in particular as a specialized profession based on scientific analysis, started developing in Latin America only in the last forty or fifty years, beginning in the major and at the time relatively richer countries of the region: Argentina, Brazil, Chile, and Mexico. The formal teaching of modern economic sciences and empirical research, however, date only from the mid-1950s.

Prior to these dates, the study of economics was in the nature of "political economy" and came mostly within the province of historians, lawyers, public officials, politicians, or simply of cultured persons who were self-taught through reading the classical European texts. Concern with economic problems was limited to practical questions of policy, and usually economic issues were treated in a holistic manner along with social, political, historical, religious, and other considerations.

When greater technical capacity was required (such as on matters of money and banking, or taxation), expert economists were brought in from Great Britain, France, West Germany, the United States. These economists were influential in stimulating local interest in economics and in introducing the economic doctrines then in vogue, but they did not create schools of economics in the region.

Thus, there was no possibility nor effort at producing indigenous economic theories or well-reasoned strategies for Latin American economic development. A curious exception to this was the original statement (which remained ignored) by the Chilean historian Encina, in 1911, of what later was labeled the "demonstration effect" in development economics.[1] In the area of rural economics, early contributions were produced in Mexico in connection with the vast land reform of the 1920s. These contributions established a tradition for the study of agrarian economics that has continued to have a pervasive influence in that country.

The teaching of economics at universities prior to the 1950s was limited to certain subjects (primarily economic history, political economy, and economic thought) within the curricula of the faculties of law, commerce and accounting, and a few others. There were no faculties or schools of economics as such until about that decade, with the probable exception of the National University of Mexico.

Since Latin American universities were molded in the continental European tradition, the offering of economic subjects followed the same pattern, emphasizing the classical (and Marxian) study of the whole economy, rather than the more piecemeal analytical approach of neoclassical economics. It is probably correct to say that, in general, the teaching of economics was very descriptive, and that learning current economic theories and writings was required for the sake of general knowledge, rather than for their value as analytical tools for problem solving and policy purposes.

For the same reasons, economic research in Latin America was limited to descriptive (with little statistical or quantitative content until the 1930s), historical, or doctrinaire writings, usually cast in a broad sociopolitical framework, and was typically produced by independent intellectuals. The universities were not set up to conduct research, and there were no social-science research centers or institutes like those currently found in the region. The more strictly economic reports originated from the central banks (or their equivalents) as these institutions were created and became operational around the 1920s, or otherwise were done by foreign companies and governments, external advisory missions, or visiting scholars.

Given the limited availability of professional books and journals in Spanish and the proverbial poverty of university libraries in Latin America, the study of the social sciences and economics was confined to a small intellectual class and to those who had a command of foreign languages (English, French, and German). A significant change in this regard occurred with the arrival of Spanish refugees from the civil war in the late thirties, especially to Mexico City and Buenos Aires. Important publishing houses were established in these cities that substantially increased the availability of social-science literature in Spanish, thus permitting a large body of scholars, students, and practicing economists to become better instructed in economic science and methodology.

The Catholic church, despite its enormous influence in all phases of life in Latin America and in education particularly, including at the university level, has had remarkably little to do with the evolution of the economic sciences. The church has doctrinaire positions in regard to social policy, but these have not been carried into the curricula of economics faculties, and much less into theoretical developments. Thus, Latin American economics as a pure science, as well as at the applied level, has virtually no roots in Catholic doctrine.

Introduction of Modern Economic Science

Early history aside, Latin America emerged from World War II with almost no indigenous capacity for training, research, and policymaking and management in modern economics. The first significant change in this situation came about with the creation of the United Nations Economic Commission for Latin America (ECLA) in 1948, with headquarters in Santiago, Chile. ECLA formed a body of the better-trained Latin American economists, complemented by foreign experts, and provided a base for analysis, discussion, and technical assistance on economic problems of the region.

The ECLA approach to economic development has been based on what may be called an organic theory or doctrine, built around the center-periphery model emphasizing the conflict between the primary-goods-exporting economies of Latin America and the developed world. Incorporated in this doctrine are both substantial Keynesian concepts and original ideas of ECLA economists. ECLA's intellectual impact on the economic sciences in the region has been strong, particularly in the areas of economic planning, the role of the state in the economy, structural reform, and income distribution.

Although ECLA did not become directly involved in university education and research, it had a broad influence through its in-service training of vast cadres of practicing economists throughout the region. ECLA's substantive production of economic publications and its development of indigeneous socioeconomic views, doctrines, and policies for Latin America have also had a marked impact. In fact, ECLA generated a school or body of thinking known as the *escuela cepaliana*, still influential in Latin America. Whether ECLA economics is good or bad, and despite the fact that much of it does not appear to be surviving well, ECLA's work has undeniably been a powerful stimulus to and influence on the development of the economic sciences in Latin America.

The real takeoff in the development of the economic sciences, however, came in the mid-1950s with the massive influx of U.S. foreign aid, which included upgrading the economics profession as a major component of assistance programs. Because this period constitutes the birth of modern economic science in Latin America, a few reflections on the epoch seem in order.

The evolution of the social and economic sciences is conditioned by a constant dialectic among three major elements: the domestic political and social environment and the policymaking induced by it; the training and research centers that constitute the intellectual bases for analysis and formulation of policy alternatives; and the international environment and attitudes of foreign agents. Until the 1950s, governments in a majority of countries were not precisely representative of the masses, and hence were limited in their responsiveness to social needs and pressures; and, as noted earlier, the second element was traditionally very weak or nonexistent in Latin America. The international environment, on the other hand, did not become concerned with the underdeveloped nations until the late 1940s. It is not surprising, then, that economics as a science should not have received much public attention in Latin America prior to those dates. It remained the interest of a few selected intellectuals and scholars.

The radical change in world environment after the war and the prominent role assumed by the United States was soon felt in Latin America. Progress among the underdeveloped countries became a central theme in the world. Under the then predominant concept of development, economic growth was regarded as a key to social and political advancement. The prevailing view was optimistic: with sufficient investment and application of technical and managerial know-how, steady progress would be achieved. In this mood, the United States embarked on its broad program of international assistance, which included among its priorities the generation of indigenous analytical and managerial capacity in economics. In Latin America, attitudes toward these programs were generally receptive.

During the 1950s, USAID (then ICA) and The Rockefeller Foundation played the major roles in upgrading Latin American economics as a profession. Assistance was focused on selected universities, whose old schools of economics, commerce, and accounting were strengthened or transformed so as to provide solid training in economic theory and related subjects. The standard neo-classical economics taught in the United States was introduced into the Latin American schools. This meant changing curricula, content of courses, methods of teaching, systems of evaluation, and introducing research and the intensive use of libraries as essential ingredients of the learning process. In fact, the transformation of these schools and their parent universities was even more fundamental, arising from introduction of the concepts of full-time staff, academic careers, and the system of credits and semester courses. Thus, the old European-style universities were progressively converted to the American system, and over the past three decades the latter has become almost universal in Latin America.

The three basic components in the strategy for upgrading economics were fellowships for staff development through graduate training at U.S. universities, the loan of visiting professors from the United States, and provision of funds and services for introducing academic and administrative changes. Frequently, these elements were combined with a medium- to long-term contractual arrangement with a North American university, whereby it took the responsibility to carry out the assistance program. Notable among these early programs for their lasting success were the contracts between the University of Chicago and the Catholic University of Chile, and between Vanderbilt University and the University of São Paulo in Brazil. In Mexico, support at the University of Nuevo León made its School of Economics the best training center in that country for at least a decade; and support for economics at the University of Chile gave this institution an important role even at the regional level for graduate training until recently.

From the beginning, a specific effort was made to develop agricultural economics as a strong applied field. This responded to the large role played by agriculture in the economy of the Latin American countries and the need to complement the assistance programs in the agricultural sciences and technology also under way.

The launching of the Alliance for Progress in the early 1960s meant an increase in U.S. assistance for Latin America. A significant feature of the alliance was its requirement of national economic plans as a basis for assigning aid. This prerequisite induced the creation of national planning offices and an expansion of demand for economic research and professional economists. In addition, during the 1960s and up to the 1970s, the Ford Foundation was a major factor affecting the evolution of the economic sciences in the region. This foundation assigned millions of dollars annually for improvement and development of the social sciences, with almost exclusive emphasis initially on economics and management sciences and agricultural economics. Virtually all the major economics schools and research centers in the principal countries received some program support from Ford, and large numbers of fellowships for graduate training in the United States (and occasionally in Europe) were assigned to candidates at large.

Support by USAID and the foundations for the development of economics during this period extended also to application of the science in planning and policymaking. The Harvard Advisory Services were active in Colombia; the Massachusetts Institute of Technology assisted Chile in economic planning; Iowa State University similarly collaborated with the Peruvian government in planning; several U.S. university programs in agricultural economics worked with government research units in Brazil, Peru, Colombia, and other countries.

This sustained effort over two decades, which reached its height in the early 1970s, was on the whole strikingly successful. National interest and support rose steadily, so that most of the new training and research programs have become fully institutionalized and nationally funded. A new generation of well-trained professional economists was formed who now staff university faculties, research institutes, government agencies, banks, and other organizations. Many have occupied top government and political positions, thus affecting national development policies. The multiplier effect of the foreign-assisted economics programs has been large. Also, as the new centers were consolidated and the number of professional economists increased (including the number of foreign scholars, who now found attractive academic environments in the region), the output of local research and publications increased, enriching university curricula with topics and readings of national relevance.

Since the mid-1970s, USAID and the foundations have drastically reduced their programs in Latin America. What support remains for economics is usually narrowly focused on specific institutions or subfields of the science (such as economic demography and natural-resource economics). Among the many reasons for the reduction in support, a major one is that the job of establishing economics as a respectable and useful science in Latin America has been essentially accomplished.

Thus, North American influence on the development of modern economics in Latin America has been preponderant. However, a small number of visiting professors came also from European universities (mainly the United Kingdom), and many Latin Americans went for graduate studies to the United Kingdom, France, Belgium, West Germany, and other counries. This European contact, however, has not had a visible influence in terms of forming economic schools of thought in the region, or even clusters of economists at given institutions that would thus impart a different academic flavor. Perhaps one exception is El Colegio de México, where British-trained economists are in the majority. Another exception might be the people trained at Louvain, who at times have clustered in certain institutions (including a private research center known as DESAL) and provided an orientation to economics associated with the social doctrine of the Catholic church.

As the introduction of modern (neoclassical and monetarist) economics continued, a portion of the profession and universities remained outside the trend and developed along Marxian lines, without ostensible foreign assistance. Noteworthy are the undergraduate schools of economics at some of the national universities, including Mexico, Venezuela, and Colombia; and some research centers. Aside from their philosophical orientation, a distinguishing characteristic of these institutions is their approach to economics as political economy, merging the subject with other social sciences. Although such a broad view makes this approach to economics intellectually appealing and apparently more relevant for developing countries, it also results in poor training in economics. Latin American economists with this orientation, though perhaps brilliant as social theorists, lack command of operational theories and techniques in economics, and therefore their professional role qua economists is negligible, or even negative. Their failure as economic technicians when called to perform (for example, in Cuba, Chile, Peru) tends to confirm the deficiency of Marxian-oriented economics in Latin America. Consequently, practically no economics institutions adhering to this line of thinking are of the first rank in Latin America.

Finally, international agencies have played a considerable role in the development of economics in the region. As mentioned earlier, ECLA and its training arm, the Instituto Latinoamericano de Planificación Económica y Social (ILPES), had a deep influence on research in economic development, training of civil servants, and policymaking in the region, especially up to the mid-1960s. Other agencies have also had an impact by demanding the services of economists, mainly the Interamerican Development Bank, the World Bank, and the International Monetary Fund. The increased national support for economics training and research (especially in the areas of monetary economics, project evaluation, and international-trade policy) certainly was stimulated by loan requirements imposed by these agencies. In the field of agricultural economics, the United Nations Food and Agricultural Organization (FAO) and the Inter-American Institute of Agricultural Sciences stimulated the demand for applied economists and gave some assistance for the development of national capacity through fellowships, provision of foreign experts, in-service training, and the like.

The various dynamics of the development institutions and forces operating in Latin America since the 1950s resulted in the economic sciences and professional economists taking a leading role in society, policymaking, and government. In fact, the post-1950 period can be characterized as "the decades of the economists." Other professionals, particularly lawyers and civil engineers, have clearly been displaced from positions of leadership in economic matters in the region.

Institutions for Economics

The general historical evolution of economics in Latin America, the socioeconomic disparity among nations in the region, and political vicissitudes in specific countries have resulted in a complex pattern of institutions concerned with the economic sciences. The availability of professional resources is not only uneven among countries and institutions but also unstable over time. Hence, what may be a strong or a weak position in one year may be quite the opposite a few years later. Furthermore, the lack of complete and current statistics on the economics profession makes it impossible to give an accurate, objective description of the situation. Conceptual problems in definitions and quality of resources compound the difficulty.[2]

The institutions that engage in economic research and training may be grouped in the following six categories: university faculties, centers, and institutes; autonomous institutes, centers, and foundations; national government agencies; regional institutes and centers of international organizations; studies departments of private business corporations; and other institutions. Some institutions do not fall neatly into any of these categories, and so will be placed in the one that fits best according to the type of activity performed.

University Faculties, Centers, and Institutes

There must be approximately 200 university faculties, centers, and institutes in Latin America, since the schools of economics and business administration alone numbered over 120 a few years ago.[3] To these should be added economic-research centers, departments of agricultural economics, departments of industrial and engineering economics, and so on. In this category are included national, state, and private schools. Some are mass institutions, like the National Autonomous University of Mexico, which enrolls thousands of students annually in economics. Others are quite small, with as few as twenty or thirty students in any year, like the Economics Center of El Colegio. The great majority offer only undergraduate education and do not engage in research. The variability in other characteristics (infrastructure, staffing, degree of modernization of curricula, and quality of output) is just as great.

Beyond this generalization, a more useful appraisal requires applying criteria that would permit identifying the stronger professional university centers. A rough standard of evaluation could be devised on the basis of the curricula offered, the number of highly qualified full-time staff members (say, trained to the Ph.D. level), the offering of graduate programs, the volume and quality of research and academic publications, the quality of graduates, the stability or sustained strength over several years, and other such characteristics of the academic institutions under consideration. Knowledgeable observers of Latin America would agree that, according to such a standard, there are relatively few institutions in a few countries that qualify as reasonably well-developed centers of economics. These are briefly discussed below.

In Brazil, the outstanding centers are the Institut de Pesquisas Econ-ômicas (IPE) of the University of São Paulo and the Graduate Economics School of the Getulio Vargas Foundation.[4] Both offer doctoral-level training in economics, the only schools in Latin America to do so. Another nine or ten universities in Brazil offer graduate programs at the master's level. Of these, the Center for Regional Economics (CEDEPLAR) at the Federal University of Minas Gerais deserves mention because of its specialization in the fields of economic demography and national-resource economics. The Faculty of Economics of the Federal University of Brasilia was developing quite well during the 1970s but appears to have lost ground lately. Some of its best staff are now at the Catholic University of Rio de Janeiro, which has brought its economics faculty to a prominent position in recent years.

With respect to agricultural economics, Brazil has developed four master of science–level programs with the long-term support of USAID and the Ford Foundation. The one at the Institute of Rural Economics of the Federal University of Vicosa, established in 1962 and ably backstopped by Purdue University, stands out because it is the oldest such program in Latin America, and it has produced a large output of well-trained graduates and good research reports. It also offers a Ph.D. program in agricultural economics.

In Argentina, the serious political instability of the last two decades has deeply affected university life, so that the condition of the economics schools is weak. The outstanding school appears to be the one at the University of

Tucuman, followed by the University of Cordoba. As will be seen below, the weakness of universities as centers for the growth of economic science in Argentina has shifted the weight of the profession to other kinds of institutions.

It is paradoxical that the richest agricultural country of Latin America should not have a single school for training and research in agricultural economics. An excellent graduate school (at the master's level) functioned for a few years under the aegis of the National Agricultural Research Institute at Castelar, but was disbanded in 1976 at the fall of the Peronist government.

In Chile, the School of Economics of the Catholic University has long been the center of excellence, even beyond the country's borders. It has derived its strength from a long-term and extremely successful association with the University of Chicago, whose approach to economics it follows closely. The School of Economics of the University of Chile in Santiago is also relatively strong, although it is now less so than during the 1960s, when it offered, among other things, a good master's program of regional scope (Escolatina).

In the applied areas, Chile has a good graduate center for agricultural economics at the Catholic University, which has regularly offered a master's program since 1967. This program is important not only because it stands up to the criteria indicated earlier, but also because it is one of two such programs that have become firmly established in Spanish America (the other one being in Mexico). It thus serves a valuable role for advanced training on a regionwide basis.

In Colombia, the single outstanding university institution in economics is the faculty at the University of the Andes (CEDE). The university's relative insulation from the constant political turmoil that has hampered other universities has permitted it to attract substantial foreign assistance. Consequently, it has been able to introduce a modern curriculum, maintain a full-time staff that includes several Ph.D.−level professors, and conduct significant research.

In Mexico, the best-known institution in economics is the Center of Economics and Demography (CEED), at El Colegio de México, established in 1962. Although El Colegio has the status of an autonomous university, it is peculiar in that it almost exclusively offers graduate training, and it emphasizes research as a major activity. El Colegio has long been a primary recipient of foreign assistance (largely because of the xenophobic attitude of the National and other major state universities in Mexico). The CEED offers a master's program with electives in economics, demography, and urban studies. A majority of the economists on its staff were trained in England, in contrast with the staffs of all the other centers throughout Latin America, most of whom were trained in the United States.

El Colegio's reputation as the leading center of economics in Mexico may eventually be challenged by the Undergraduate School of Economics of the Instituto Tecnológico Autónomo de México (ITAM), which over the past five or six years has emerged as another strong institution.

Mexico has the longest tradition in Latin America in the field of agricultural economics, both in training and research. However, modern analytical economics did not play a role until the creation of the Agricultural Economics Center at the Postgraduate School of the National School of Agriculture (Chapingo), in 1965. That center remains the strongest base in this field in the country, although it has to function in an educational environment that is strongly inclined toward "agrarian revolutionary" and Marxian tendencies antagonistic to neoclassical, analytical, and quantitative economics.

Finally, a note must be made of an institution in Venezuela, the Center for Development Studies (CENDES) of the Central University in Caracas. CENDES was an outstanding social-science institution devoted to postgraduate training and research until the early 1970s. At that time, as has frequently happened in so many countries in Latin America, political intervention in the university brought about the demise of CENDES. There has been no comparable institution to take its place since, at least in regard to economic sciences.

Autonomous Institutes, Centers, and Foundations

The many shortcomings of universities as centers for intellectual pursuits in the social sciences in Latin America have led to the formation of independent nonprofit academic centers. Universities have encountered not only political but also organizational and financial obstacles, resulting in constant instability and periodic radical changes in working conditions. The autonomous centers have sought to provide institutional environments that are insulated from these difficulties and in which individuals are freer to critically investigate problems of the national societies and to propose policy alternatives. Because of their objectives, frequently these centers are set up as, or soon become, interdisciplinary.

In Argentina, the Di Tella Foundation has been for many years the most important intellectual center for the social sciences. Its Center for Economic Research (CIE), which maintains a core of eight to ten well-trained economists, serves as an in-service training base for younger staff, and produces a significant research output. The foundation is unique in that it systematically includes research in economic theory. Despite suffering its share of political and financial vicissitudes, it remains a stable, strong, and productive institution in Argentina.

The Centro de Estudios Macroeconómicos Argentinos (CEMA), formed in the late 1970s, is currently considered the strongest professional group in economics not only in Argentina but in all of Latin America. This judgment is based on the fact that CEMA has brought together seven or eight of the top Argentinian economists, drawing them from academic positions in the best U.S. universities, the IMF, the World Bank, and elsewhere. It remains to be seen whether this center will survive, and how it will make its talent influence training and public policy in the country and region.

In Brazil, the Centro Brasileiro de Análise e Planejamento (CEBRAP), formed in the late 1960s by senior academic refugees from political shake-ups at the universities, is a social-science institution of hemispheric significance. Economics, however, is the weakest segment of the institution, largely because of the preponderant orientation toward Marxian economics. CEBRAP has been funded mostly by the Ford Foundation and is supported through other private contributions, grants, research contracts, and its own income.

In Chile, the Corporación de Investigaciones Económicas para Latino-america (CIEPLAN) is an autonomous center formed in 1975 by a group of professors who dissented from the academic orientation and policies pre-vailing at the Catholic University. CIEPLAN has a full-time staff of a dozen economists, most with doctorates from top U.S. universities. Its research output has been voluminous and strongly oriented to social-policy issues. It does some in-service training of students through research. CIEPLAN draws its resources largely from foreign grants and research contracts.

In Colombia, the principal autonomous center for economics is the Fundación para la Educación Superior y el Desarrollo (FEDESARROL-LO), created in 1971 and funded through private business contributions, foreign grants, and research contracts. It brought together a number of highly qualified economists who had held high positions in government, a feature that has continued to characterize FEDESARROLLO in subse-quent years. The emphasis of this institution is on public-policy analysis, but it also promotes economics education and publishes a widely circulated quarterly journal, *Coyuntura económica*.

National Government Agencies

Economic research in Latin America was initiated by the studies depart-ments formed by central banks. These departments remain important in this activity, though they are more significant in countries where universities and autonomous centers are weak or nonexistent. Central banks have often also played a key role in promoting and aiding the development of sound eco-nomics teaching and research at universities.

In Mexico, the Banco de México has traditionally been the strongest group for general macroeconomic research. In Colombia, the Banco de la República, along with the University of the Andes and FEDESARROLLO, does most of the economic research for the country. In Chile as well as other countries, the central banks have conducted or supported research primarily on money and monetary policy.

The other principal agencies in economics are the national planning offices, which usually have special research units. In Brazil, the Institute of Economic Research (IPEAS), dependent from the Ministry of Planning, is one of the most important and productive research centers. In Mexico, the studies group at the Secretariat of the Presidency (equivalent to a planning office) has done valuable research on economic planning; in collaboration with the World Bank, it has prepared some large quantitative models. In the smaller Central American and Caribbean countries, the planning offices usually constitute the principal source of economic research and policy analysis.

In some countries, development banks or corporations also provide important research services. Notable among these is the Superintendencia para o Desenvolvimento do Nordeste (SUDENE) in Brazil, which has both conducted and supported most of the research on the country's impoverished northeastern region. There are several similar agencies in Brazil that influence the development of economics in their respective regions. The Development Corporation of Chile (CORFO) was at one time responsible for the national accounts and in this capacity played a role in the use and development of economic science there.

Although agencies such as those named above do sometimes engage in basic and long-term economic analysis, the majority of research done by central banks and planning offices consists in preparing descriptive studies, which mainly entails gathering statistical data, and evaluating alternatives for short-term economic policies.[5] These agencies fulfill a particular need in the area of application of economic science, which complements the work done by universities and other centers.

Regional Institutes and Centers of International Organizations

Several international and regional organizations have established offices in Latin America that frequently function in an economics-research capacity. Among these, the United Nations Economic Commission for Latin America (ECLA) has been by far the most important and influential, as discussed earlier. Other international institutions include the Latin American Free Trade Association (ALALC), based in Uruguay and recently renamed; the Central American Common Market, based in Guatemala; the Institute for Latin American Economic Integration (INTAL), sponsored by the Interamerican Development Bank and located in Buenos Aires; and the Andean Free Trade Association, originally formed by five countries and based in

Lima. All of these have been concerned with regional integration and trade, fields in which they have done (or contracted) considerable applied research. They are also important as users of the services of Latin American economists and as such have provided a stimulus to the profession.

The Center for Latin American Monetary Studies (CEMLA), located in Mexico City, is a specialized training and research institution formed by the central banks of Latin America in the 1950s. It maintains a small staff of six to ten highly qualified economists. It is a unique institution that has had an appreciable impact on the region's central and development banks over the past twenty years. Its research output on monetary and fiscal matters is large, and increasingly focused on regional versus national problems.

The Economics Secretariat of the Organization of American States and the Interamerican Development Bank, though located in Washington, D.C., are two regional agencies that have produced many economic publications and have had considerable influence on the development of economics in the region. In addition to their own research work (most of it descriptive and macroeconomic), they have supported various national training and research programs, provided graduate fellowships, and generated a significant demand for well-trained Latin American economists.

In regard to agricultural economics, ECLA has operated in conjunction with the regional FAO office, and together they have been responsible for many economic studies in this field, for policies adopted by countries on various aspects of agriculture, and for training of technicians and bureaucrats in agricultural planning, economic analysis, and statistics. The role of FAO in improving the data base for research, especially through the agricultural censuses, is particularly noteworthy. The Inter-American Institute of Agricultural Sciences (IICA) has been important in supporting graduate training in agricultural economics, through both sponsoring national programs (such as at Castelar in Argentina and at the Catholic University in Chile) and regional training seminars and providing graduate fellowships.

In economic demography, the Centro Latinoamericano de Demografía (CELADE), based mainly in Santiago, has been a key institution in the region, even though the thrust of its work is on demography. It has cooperated with El Colegio de México and CEDEPLAR in Brazil, the two principal national institutions that excel in this field.

In labor economics, the Regional Program for Employment in Latin America and the Caribbean (PREALC), dependent from the International Labour Office of the United Nations and located in Santiago, is the most significant specialized institution. It has done important research on employment and labor economics generally, and it provides assistance to national governments on policy matters in this area.

Because the headquarters and a majority of the staff economists of several of the international agencies named are located in Santiago, the impact of these agencies on training and research in economics has been greater in Chile than elsewhere. This, among other reasons, may explain the relatively earlier and stronger development of economics in Chile, which is not one of the larger or richer nations of Latin America.

In the politically unstable environment that has typically existed in Latin America, one in which economists (and other social scientists) become frequent casualties in the employment market, the international agencies have had a stabilizing role in the profession. They are able to hire people more or less independently of their political affiliations, and thereby retain professional expertise in the region. The experience gained by economists while at the international centers also represents a useful form of high-level training.

Studies Departments of Private Corporations

This brief survey of institutional resources for the economic sciences would be incomplete without a reference to the studies departments of some large business corporations (private and public) in Latin America. Most notable among these corporations are commercial banks, many of which employ small groups of highly qualified economists, who engage primarily in short-term analysis of the national economies. Such research reports are occasionally made public; some provide valuable information for policymaking purposes and some constitute top reading material for university courses.

Large corporations in specialized fields and public utilities (including electric power, construction, and mining) also frequently maintain economic-research departments, which produce studies and reports of significance in their areas of concern.

Other Institutions

Among other institutions that have promoted the development of economic science in Latin America, two deserve specific mention. First, the Programa de Estudios Conjuntos Sobre Integración Económica Latinoamericana (ECIEL), formed in 1963, has been especially important for its encouragement and execution of collaborative research projects on problems of economic development and integration. ECIEL is an association of twenty-five to thirty economic-research centers, both university-affiliated and autonomous (most of those discussed above are members), that share common interests and see an advantage in working cooperatively at the regional level. For about ten years, the Brookings Insititution in Washington served as secretariat for the group; since 1974, headquarters have been located in

Rio de Janeiro, where a small economics staff is based. ECIEL's work centers around selected major topics, or research projects: prices and economic policy; employment; composition and determinants of consumption; income distribution; economics of education. Members determine what projects they will participate in and carry out their share of research. ECIEL provides partial support and sponsors seminars twice a year in different places to discuss approaches, methodologies, and so forth. Funding for ECIEL has come from the Ford and Rockefeller foundations, the Interamerican Development Bank, UNDP, USAID, the World Bank, and others. ECIEL is widely acknowledged in the Latin American economics community for having effectively increased the exchange and cooperation among institutions from different countries, for its initiative and encouragement to investigate difficult but relevant subjects, and for having helped to retain scholars in the academic environment.

The other entity is the Consejo Latinoamericano de Ciencias Sociales (CLACSO), an association of social-science centers established in 1967 with Ford Foundation support, and which is reminiscent of the Social Science Research Council in the United States. It includes among its members many of the same centers that form ECIEL, except that typically the economics staffs participate in the ECIEL projects and meetings, while those associated with CLACSO tend to be mainly sociologists, political scientists, and historians.

CLACSO, which has its secretariat in Buenos Aires, performs two basic functions: it allocates research funds (received mainly from the Ford Foundation) to projects submitted by its member institutions, and it sponsors meetings and seminars for its associates. Although CLACSO is interdisciplinary, in practice it has been more valuable for the noneconomic social sciences. It has served as a stimulant to increased communication and cooperation among research centers, including some devoted to economics. Lately, it has turned some attention to rural development, approaching it in an interdisciplinary fashion rather than just as an agricultural economic problem.

Human Resources for Economics

The foregoing discussion of economic institutions suggests how difficult it is to quantify and categorize the human resources available in the economic sciences in Latin America. However, it is clear that at present, well-qualified economists (with Ph.D. and M.A. or M.S. training, recent graduates of the best economics schools, and experienced professionals) number in the hundreds. To have been included above, an institution must have more than five or six such staff members. More important, however, is the fact that the academic bases have been laid to produce a permanent flow of the new brand of professional economists. Not only have many of the undergraduate schools been significantly improved, but there have been several graduate programs (M.S. and Ph.D.) set up in various Latin American countries—the majority of them in Brazil.

In addition, the number of economics students doing graduate work abroad, mostly at North American universities, has probably grown, despite the reduction of foreign assistance in the last years. National institutions and governments are increasingly funding the costs of training abroad, which is a clear recognition of the value attached to such training. Of course, the presence of many foreign-trained economists in high decision-making positions has something to do with this trend.

Two general observations that still seem valid in Latin America are that a majority of research economists have had graduate training abroad and that, on the average, the staff of research institutes is relatively young. The same is true of the better training programs, both undergraduate and graduate.

Finally, note must be made of the high rotation of personnel experienced by most academic and research institutions. The principal cause is not politics, but economics—that is, the high salaries being commanded by good economists everywhere in Latin America, in business and other nonacademic jobs. The brain drain of the 1950s and 1960s, when economists went to international agencies and developed countries, is now more intraregional, with economists moving from one Latin American country to another. Thus, many good Argentinian economists, for example, are working in Brazil, Chile, and elsewhere. Furthermore, in several countries of the region there has recently been a noticeable reversal of this brain drain, with economists returning to their home countries after extended periods abroad.

State of the Art in Training and Research in Economics

There is obvious variability in the approaches to and quality of economics training and research in Latin America, given the pattern of development of the science and the many institutions involved in its practice. It remains valid to distinguish three main strains of economics in the region: Marxian, modern neoclassical, and the indigenous ECLA school that falls in between these two.

In regard to university training, institutions can roughly be classified under these general types, depending on the degree to which their curricula includes or emphasizes certain subjects, although they all have a large set of courses in common. Perhaps the extreme difference is that the institutions with a Marxian bent give only a cursory treatment of marginal theory, and then make little use of it in the rest of the courses, and emphasize Marxian analysis of the economy; while the institutions following the neoclassical approach ignore altogether any reference to Marxian analysis, are heavy in monetary economics, and tend to have few or no courses in "development."

Methodologically, the Marxian-oriented institutions emphasize literal or nonquantitative approaches in theoretical and applied subjects; even planning courses are generally of an accounting nature and do not apply more-sophisticated mathematical programming. In contrast, the modern economics institutions have introduced substantial requirements in mathematics and statistics, the teaching of theory is heavily mathematical, and econometrics and quantitative methods are standard courses. These methodological differences are apparent in undergraduate theses, in the institutions that require a thesis for graduation.

Most of the undergraduate schools of economics, however, follow an intermediate course: neoclassical theory forms the core of the curriculum, but in a less quantitative form; some courses on Marxian economics are included; and substantial emphasis is placed on "development" subjects, in which the ECLA doctrines and descriptive studies play an important role. These doctrines essentially are the "falling terms of trade," from which the prescriptions for domestic industrialization and trade protection follow; and the "structuralist" explanation of inflation and underdevelopment, from which another series of prescriptions in fiscal policy, land reform, and state intervention follow. The originality and specificity to Latin American countries of the ECLA economic ideas has naturally made them appealing to many of the schools in the region that look for nationalistic ideologies and (apparent) greater relevance in what they teach their students.

At the graduate level, practically all the existing centers (about fourteen in Brazil, including agricultural economics programs, and about ten in Spanish America) are in the neoclassical category, although at this level there is a progressive tendency to pay greater attention to other theoretical approaches and policy concerns. Thus, one may find courses devoted to the Cambridge controversy, or to the theory of economic planning, or to income distribution, and so forth.

In research, the output of fair to good professional work has expanded so much in the last two decades that it becomes impossible to make any reasonable generalizations. Practically any imaginable topic and analytical technique has been, or is being, covered. Perhaps only the four characteristics noted below apply to all spheres.

1. As research centers have become consolidated and the profession has matured, there is less tendency to copy from abroad or to extend the Ph.D. dissertations done for U.S. universities; instead, researchers have turned their attention to national and regional problems. The resultant numerous studies on inflation, employment, income distribution, trade, and land reform reflect a greater concern for local relevance and for using modern

analytical techniques to understand better the Latin American economies, and frequently research seeks policy results.

2. Research studies by the younger, better-trained economists tend to be subject-specific and empirical. Comparatively narrow topics are defined and hypotheses about them are tested in applied contexts, in contrast to the broad conceptual or theoretical research of earlier years.

3. The paucity of data and statistics is a severe limitation for quantitative research in Latin America. Nevertheless, a growing number of econometric studies and mathematical programming models are being developed. These efforts are in turn inducing an improvement in national economic statistics. The use of computers has become a mandatory feature at all the better research centers.

4. There has been a large and important contribution to research by foreign scholars. In addition to the research on Latin America conducted at U.S. or European institutions, a considerable amount is done in collaboration with, and in residence at, Latin American centers. Besides the intrinsic value of this work, the training it has provided and its stimulating effect on national researchers are extremely valuable. Unfortunately, the reduction in foreign-assistance programs and funds is making this collaboration less frequent at a time when it would likely be more productive, given the greater number of qualified young Latin American economists that could participate in joint research.

The diffusion of research results is still limited, but it has improved markedly. There are several scholarly economic journals that have been issued regularly for many years. The oldest is *Trimestre económico*, published in Mexico; there are several in Brazil, notably those put out by IPE/São Paulo and by IPEA; *Cuadernos de economía* of the Catholic University of Chile; *Desarrollo económico*, published by the Instituto de Desarrollo Económico y Social in Argentina; *Coyuntura económica* of FEDESARROLLO, Colombia; and others. In addition, there are economic journals of a less academic nature, such as those published by central banks and other government agencies.

Each research institution also publishes its studies in many different forms (predominantly mimeographed), which have a more restricted circulation. Books remain rather rare, mainly because of the high costs of publication. They are usually limited to broad topics of national or regional significance, which are likely to have a larger market.

Limitations and Prospects of the Economic Sciences

Progress of the economic sciences in teaching, research, and application to public policy has been enormous in Latin America over the last twenty-five years. Progress has been uneven, however, so that some countries are at present in a stronger professional and institutional position than others. Similarly, the national institutional (particularly university) scene is often fragile; the number of well-qualified scholars is still relatively small, and they are easily shifted to other activities. It will take some years before a sufficient number of centers become firmly enough consolidated in each country to achieve overall stability. In this respect, Brazil appears clearly to be ahead of other countries. Within this general picture, there are important limitations that suggest areas where further outside assistance would be most productive.

1. Many countries continue to lack a single good center of training and research in economics. There ought to be a minimum domestic capacity (however defined) in this field, among other reasons because its absence prevents greater regional cooperation in research and the utilization of training facilities in neighboring countries. Support for selected institutions in countries such as Peru, Bolivia, Guatemala, in a fashion similar to that applied elsewhere, seems called for. The greater availability of human, institutional, and Spanish-language resources should make the task easier now than it was in the past.

2. Research in the advanced centers is being funded almost exclusively through contracts with government and other agencies. Unfortunately, there has not yet developed in the region a tradition of funding research through the regular budgets of universities or research centers, and local philanthropic foundations are few and generally small. This situation greatly limits the kinds of research that can be undertaken: basic or theoretical work is virtually impossible, most studies must be short-run (usually of less than a year's duration), and there are obvious restrictions on the degree of freedom to choose topics and to perform critical analyses. Selected outside funding for research is thus essential to broaden opportunities and experience. Indeed, recognition of this situation has led the foundations, and lately the IDRC of Canada, to provide selective support for specific research projects; but the needs are much greater than the funds currently available.

3. To increase the limited opportunities for conducting critical research, the role of the economics centers should include objectively assessing important national problems and searching for alternative solutions. Under the political conditions prevalent in much of Latin America, the environment and forms of funding research are not conducive to performing this task effectively. Very skillfully managed foreign assistance is needed to promote this role of the science so that it does not become politically subversive. The record on this score has not been impressive over the last few years.

4. The national professional communities are still largely unorganized. This limits the possibility of peer review, academic competition, and group

stimulation, which are essential for the continued strengthening and growth of economic science. Except for Brazil, which has a reasonably good organization in its National Association of Economics Centers (ANPEC) and its Society of Agricultural Economics (SOBER), there are no well-functioning national associations of economists. This is another prime area where some outside support could have high payoff. Given the fact that most countries in Latin America use Spanish, a regional association should have a good chance to become operational. In fact, ECIEL and CLACSO have to some degree acted as professional associations, though they are not designed as such.

5. A great deal more needs to be done to publish the results of research and to make them widely available to all countries. Similarly, a much greater effort should be made to publish basic textbooks in Spanish and Portuguese designed for use in specific countries, with illustrations of principles and theory referenced to the local economies. A relatively small amount of outside assistance would have a large impact throughout the region.

6. Institutions and scholars can rapidly fall behind in the science if they do not maintain close contact with the leading economics centers in the world, which means mainly certain North American universities. Reading the journals is probably not enough, especially if the local libraries are not well supplied. Thus, a broad program of sabbaticals, attendance at seminars, faculty exchanges, joint research, and the like, involving selected institutions from outside the region, is essential. Although some of these activities now occur through various funding schemes, on the whole they are extremely limited and are becoming increasingly difficult to implement since the traditional international assistance agencies have cut back their support in Latin America. A much greater effort is needed in this area, which could be conveniently coordinated with support for professional associations.

7. Finally, there is a need to broaden economics to make it more interdisciplinary. A move in this direction would probably be disastrous, however, if the economics curricula and research were to be so transformed. Analytical rigor and sharpness are what have given economics the strength and prestige it now enjoys in Latin America; they should not be diluted and weakened. Multidisciplinarity must come through cooperation among well-trained social scientists, each highly competent in his own discipline. The necessary broadening of economics at this higher level suggests supporting multidisciplinary research in the most advanced centers. International funding for these kinds of projects would be welcome, but such support should be carefully conceived and monitored.

In sum, there is much room for improvement of economics in Latin America, and many opportunities exist for outside assistance in achieving further progress. The economic sciences are exerting a strong influence on national policies in all countries of the region, although they may sometimes fail the practical tests of social and political betterment. To help make them more relevant and successful in these respects should be a priority of the immediate future.

Notes

1. Francisco Encina, *Nuestra inferioridad económica*, 3d ed. (Santiago: Editorial Universitaria, 1972).

2. For a discussion of this topic, see Rolf Luders, "Investigación en ciencias sociales en América Latina" (Washington, D.C.: Organization of American States, 1975).

3. See Luders, "Investigación en ciencias sociales."

4. The Vargas Foundation, though not strictly a university, engages in substantial training and research in economics, administration, statistics, agricultural economics, and related fields in ways that make it more akin to a university than any other category of institution.

5. See Luders, "Investigacíon en ciencias sociales."

9

Social Sciences in the Periphery: Perspectives on the Latin American Case

Jorge Balán

Introduction

Latin America has a special status as the most westernized region within the periphery of the modern world. This is largely the result of a continuous Western presence for almost five centuries, in a relationship that includes conquest and colonization, immigration, military and political intervention, foreign investment and imported technology, markets for regional exports, institutional and ideological diffusion, and the display of positive and negative models of development. By the end of the sixteenth century most of today's populated areas in Latin America had been charted, the main cities founded, and the broad delineation of political units established by Europeans. But the special status of Latin America also derives in part from its relatively early and prolonged independence: The Caribbean excepted, the countries in the region became independent during the first half of the nineteenth century. Only occasionally have they felt the military presence of foreign powers during the last 100 years, with the exception of U.S. intervention in Central America and the Caribbean from the Spanish-American War (1898) to the present. There is considerable cultural continuity within and among these countries. In each country there is only one official language, and in the whole continent only two—Spanish and Portuguese. Indigenous languages have a subnational importance in Peru and Bolivia, where Quechua and Aymara are spoken, and a local importance in Guatemala and Mexico. There is one major religion, Catholicism, and one predominant family type, monogamous and nuclear. Cultural continuities throughout Latin America are a result of Western influence and not of indigenous development. Nations, however, are an indigenous creation arising from long and continuous independent rule. Indo-American and Afro-American cultures became parts of these nations, though only in the last three decades in Peru, Bolivia, and Guatemala.

After independence—the basic cultural traits had already been established under Iberian influence—the predominant Western influence came from countries at the center of the capitalist world system. In the nineteenth century, Latin America formed strong economic ties with Britain, France, Germany, and the Low Countries. The United States became important in Mexico, Central America, and the Caribbean after the American Civil War, and elsewhere after World War I. But Western settlers were mainly from the Mediterranean—Spain, Portugal, and Italy—although in some areas central and eastern Europeans, including Germans, had some influence.

Until World War II, Latin America was seldom at the center of world politics. The Monroe Doctrine often led the United States into inter-American conflict, but until 1941 the challenge to U.S. hegemony in the region was seldom strong enough to demand a very active policy on the part of the United States.

Western thought has played a major role in Latin America. The "long" nineteenth century (1780–1930) was largely dominated by France. Napoleonic ideals regarding the role of the state vis-à-vis the church and civil society influenced liberals in the region, resulting in centralist administrations, which often failed, and an attempt—also quite unsuccessful—to introduce the Napoleonic university as a means of spreading public education down to the primary level. Utilitarianism, then evolutionism, and, above all, Comtean positivism were the most fashionable trends among liberals: all were opposed by conservative Catholic thinkers. As the century ended, faith in science and progress, represented by the university, was widespread.

The social sciences are a cultural product of the West, developed in Britain, France, Germany, and the United States, then growing and spreading through Western-influenced countries worldwide. The social sciences have availed themselves of heterogeneous mechanisms of transmission and have encountered widely divergent local conditions. Within the social sciences developmentally there have been many phases or cycles of diffusion. In Latin America, the most important cycle is fairly recent, marked by the implantation of disciplines and styles of work originating in the United States. Beginning soon after the end of World War II, it can be considered complete.

Several characteristics of this cycle can be identified. It was led by those disciplines that, following in the steps of economics, had gained influence in U.S. academic circles as well as in broader society and government: first sociology, then political science. Quantification and the use of sample surveys were already the methodological trademarks of the new disciplines when the cycle began, while structural functionalism was becoming the predominant theoretical framework. Within U.S. sociology, interest in other Western and non-Western societies was very limited, and the claim for universality of theory and methods overshadowed a substantive focus on comparative issues. Comparative politics had a more central role within that discipline, but the influence of behavioralism prevented the application of sociological methodology to other political systems. The stimuli and opportunities created by the government, various foundations, and university expansion were essential in directing attention to the developing world. The diffusion of the model, by and large, was not a consequence of inner-directed developments in those disciplines. It was first fostered by receptivity in the peripheral countries and later by the opportunities opened up by area-studies programs in the United States.

This chapter deals with the social sciences other than economics, which I have discussed elsewhere. Sociology, anthropology, and political science, together with social and economic history, form the disciplinary nucleus of the social sciences in Latin America; geography and psychology are marginal. The five countries that have the largest social-science communities—Argentina, Brazil, Chile, Mexico, and Peru—will be the focus of discussion. In addition, I will touch on the transplantation of the social sciences to Latin America as a historical process. My view of the latter does not assume continuous progress within a unilineal evolutionary model, against which particular developments are evaluated. Although the temporal dimension is latent throughout, I do not attempt a strict periodization, or even a chronology for the whole region.

In the first section, I consider the local innovators at the time when the social sciences first came to national attention, and activities were expanded impressively in the 1950s and 1960s. Because I want to discuss those innovators' roots as well as their views of the scene they were so radically changing, I then move back in time to discuss the immediate antecedents associated with the social sciences in their university setting. The second section focuses on the external agents—mainly foreign social scientists—their institutional support, and their relation to local social scientists and institutions. Although external assistance has increased tremendously in the past two decades, I prefer to look at it in a longer-term perspective, beginning with the 1920s and 1930s but focusing more closely on the recent period and the important shifts within it. Then I deal with variations from one country to another, mainly in the present, focusing on the relationship between the social-science community and the state, classified into three categories. The final section deals with the region as a whole, for which I attempt to indicate major research interests and describe the social-science network. I also indicate what seem to be relatively stable characteristics of social science in Latin America and important emergent trends.

The Local Innovators and Their Antecedents

Social-science teaching and research programs in Latin American universities are essentially a post–World War II phenomenon. They were initiated locally in several countries, including Brazil, Argentina, Mexico, and Chile. International agencies within the United Nations network, technical-assistance programs from the United States and other countries, private foundations and foreign universities, as well as local governments, universities, and individual scholars of different origins and affiliations—all played a role in the initial and in later stages. These roles, of course, varied from country to country. The section below presents a simplified picture of the local participants who in the 1950s led institutional developments in several countries, the political and intellectual scene in which they moved, and the main antecedents found in the university traditions for the development of the social sciences.

In the 1950s, hopes for social and political reform were growing in Latin America. The major countries had experienced rapid industrialization and urbanization, but it was generally felt that social and political changes had lagged behind. The end of the war and the reorganization of international trade were posing new challenges to the newly industrialized countries. Reformist hopes were partially focused on the educational system, which had to be revamped and improved to meet new demands. A renewal of the university system, the strengthening of research in the sciences, including the social sciences, and a technical orientation were essential. New jobs in areas such as economic and social planning and the administration of welfare services demanded professionals who would be able to depart from the traditional model of the liberal professions. Training in the new social sciences was thus part of a broader renewal of the educational system and of reformist goals in society.

The word *desarrollismo* ("developmentalism") would catch the spirit of the time quite correctly, were it not for the fact that it also became a label for an important intellectual and political force, later challenged by both the conservative right and the revolutionary left. *Desarrollismo* in its many versions implied a need for the formation of new professional and intellectual cadres, to be supplied only by universities, who would play a key role in national development. Planning and the social sciences, however, soon became suspect in countries like Argentina and Chile as a new form of centralism, *étatisme* in the French fashion, or, even worse, in the view of the conservative right, socialism. In Mexico, on the contrary, the predominant revolutionary imagery was more conducive to their acceptance. The leftist view, slower in developing, was that planning meant reformism, that it would effectively discourage revolutions, that it was an instrument not of change but of renewal within an oligarchic system. The local version of Keynesianism and of welfare-state policies, as much as the growth of the social sciences as a new profession, thus became identified with *desarrollismo* in an intensive ideological debate about development.[1]

At a regional level, the main intellectual promoter of *desarrollismo* was—from its inception in 1948—the U.N.'s Economic Commission for Latin America (ECLA, or CEPAL), based in Santiago, Chile. Beyond its significance in guiding ideologies of economic development in Latin America, the role of ECLA in legitimizing social and economic planning within the state apparatus, and the new professions associated with it, was enormous—particularly in South America. ECLA's position was important for the noneconomic social sciences in at least two major points. First, Raúl Prebisch's thesis on the deterioration of terms of trade against peripheral countries paid explicit attention to social and political forces, such as labor unions and large corporations in the central countries. Second, ECLA's analyses of developmental problems in Latin America always referred to the internal power structure (land-tenure systems and highly unequal income distribution) and its negative effects upon economic growth. Thus, ECLA's hypotheses promoted economic as well as social and political analyses of development issues. Furthermore, they stressed the need to develop local capacities for dealing with these issues, and for assisting local governments regarding social and economic policies.

Although in the 1950s other agencies began to assist governments in this way—most notably U.S. technical-assistance programs in countries like Chile, Bolivia, and the Central American nations—they tended to assume a considerably narrower and more technical viewpoint. It was not unusual for such agencies to collaborate with ECLA, as in the case of the advisory team sent to Bolivia after the 1952 revolution, but it became clear that they represented contrasting schools of economic thought and practice as well as overall views of development. For instance, the joint Chicago–Catholic University program established in Chile in the 1950s was explicitly designed to provide an alternative to ECLA's position.[2] Whatever the merits of each school, it is obvious that ECLA gave much greater weight to the noneconomic social sciences. Thus, its influence under the reformist governments in Chile in the 1950s and 1960s, in Argentina before the 1966 military coup, in Brazil from Kubitschek to Goulart (1955–1964), and in Mexico under Lopez Mateos (1958–1964) resulted among other things in greater support for the development of the social sciences. This trend, however, would be reversed by the authoritarian regimes that followed those governments.

At a national level, the link between *desarrollismo*, university and other structural reforms, and the role of the social sciences was evident almost everywhere, but assumed particular clarity in the Brazilian case, which illustrates the spirit of the times in the entire region.

The renewal of social thought in Brazil took place in institutions specifically founded to focus on developmental issues, like the Instituto Superior de Estudos Brasileiros (ISEB), while both the ideology and practice of the new economic planning centered around state agencies like the recently created Superintendency for the Development of the Northeast (SUDENE). The strongest push for social research, however, came in attempts to reform the educational system. Universities were seen as unresponsive to the new needs of society. Social scientists involved in educational reform suddenly gained the visible position in Brazilian society that economists were achieving in regional and national economic planning.[3] In 1952, when Anisio Teixeira became head of the National Institute of Pedagogical Studies (INEP), a wide program of research on education began. It diagnosed the university system as elitist, ineffective, and wasteful. The old literary education, verbalistic and ornamental, had to give way if the very poor educational levels of primary and secondary school systems were to be upgraded. The research program at INEP (with the help of a UNESCO-sponsored program in Rio) housed the work of social scientists like Roberto Moreira and Darcy Ribeiro, who were joined by foreign experts such as Robert Havighurst and Bertram Hutchinson. Other social scientists, among them Fernando de Azevedo in São Paulo and Gilberto Freyre in Recife, also became involved.

In 1957, INEP was charged with the design of the public educational system, including the university, for the new capital, Brasilia. Under Darcy Ribeiro, a well-known anthropologist, it became the model for a new university. Established as a private foundation with its own endowment, it gained autonomy from the state. The university was to dispense with the old system based on professional schools and dominated by the *catedras* ("chairs"). The core of the educational program was to be a basic three-year course, preceding professional training. Faculty would be organized in departments, within the basic *institutos*. Technology and science were to receive priority, but the social sciences would also find a hospitable environment.

A similar link between *desarrollismo,* university reform, and the social sciences developed under very different circumstances, but with less success, in Argentina and Chile. In Argentina, favorable political conditions in the mid-1950s allowed a reformist movement at the University of Buenos Aires, the largest and most influential among the six national universities. Under the leadership of social historian José Luis Romero, the old goals of the university-reform movement initiated in Cordoba in 1918, which pushed for autonomy, student participation, and the like, blended with the new trends oriented to a research orientation, a full-time faculty, departments formed by discipline, and so on. Basic changes included differentiation among and strengthening of the social sciences, which for the first time became a focus of university attention. Highly influential in Latin America but with an institutionally uncertain existence in the country itself, Argentine sociology in the 1950s and early 1960s became a symbol of the new, empirically oriented, "Americanized" discipline, with a strong teaching and research program at the University of Buenos Aires as well as at the recently created Catholic University.

In Chile in the 1950s, both the national and Catholic universities were receptive to change. Cooperative university programs were started, with an emphasis on economics in the social sciences. The most crucial development affecting the noneconomic disciplines was the launching of the Latin American School of Social Sciences (FLACSO), which began operation as a UNESCO-supported program in Santiago in 1957. It was the first graduate training program of the new variety, involving two years of intensive course work, the equivalent of an M.A. thesis, and a small group of full-time students recruited from all over the region. The program was directed initially by a group of foreign experts, mainly Europeans, with a subsequent increase in the role of Latin Americans trained outside the region, all sharing the new, quantitative, and professional orientation to the discipline. The setting, however, was as important as the formal content of the training program. A small group of full-time students and teachers (both mainly foreign) worked in a training and research institution that was isolated from the local university and from university politics. This created a special atmosphere, and the first group of graduates had a great influence on the programs in their own countries.

The new social-science paradigm entered Latin America in the form of sociology programs, mainly in Argentina, Brazil, and Chile, and somewhat later in Mexico, where anthropology retained its leading role. Local training was the rule at first, although it was handled by foreign scholars and locals trained abroad or locally (including some with little formal training in the social sciences). These programs expanded considerably and spread to most other countries in the region during the 1960s. Fellowships for studies abroad became available in greater numbers, with Ph.D. programs in sociology and political science at North American universities the favorite choices.

The enterprise launched in the 1950s and 1960s had roots in the national and regional prevalence of reformist policies and academic freedom. Local experiences differed widely, however, in the degree to which new trends in the social sciences elsewhere in the world were absorbed, and in the continuities and discontinuities established with the local intellectual traditions. Certainly many of the innovators saw the new model not only as antithetical to old styles, but also as a necessary sign of progress. The Rostovian metaphor of stages of development, including the notion of a takeoff, was used implicitly or explicitly for both social science and society. The reviews of political science and sociology on, and in, Latin America, presented in a 1963 conference, made this clear. For Merle Kling, what had been done until then were traditional studies of politics, but there were signs of a transition toward modernized research: "Political research on Latin America resembles the area which is the object of study. It retains underdeveloped and traditional features; it is under both internal and external pressures to modernize."[4] Rex Hopper's adaptation of Gino Germani's description of the stages of sociological development, in the same seminar, explicitly accepted the idea of a progression from the presociological period, through the institutionalization of sociology in the universities, to the beginnings of scientific sociology.[5] For some of the critics, this view of the field restricted alternatives, equating the adoption of the North American model of social science with progress.[6] But like the broader Rostovian model, the real problem was how poorly it fitted reality, and how the notion of innovation was simplified and subsumed under a necessary, always repeatable, takeoff stage. In fact, it soon would suffer its own crises and demonstrate increasing multilinearity, as well as some very traditional revivals.

An opposition between modern and traditional styles of work developed in the 1960s. The introduction of American models of the new hegemonic disciplines, sociology and political science, brought about a notion of discontinuity with past activities in the social sciences and with the predominant university traditions in some countries. In Brazil, for example, political science in the 1960s was largely a new discipline introduced through the training of a generation of social scientists at FLACSO and at U.S. universities. Discontinuities between generations and between disciplines were widened by the choice of new institutional settings, outside the major traditional centers of activity, and by the very active presence of foreign sources of support.[7] FLACSO itself, as a regional school established in Chile, developed an image of discontinuity with past activities early in the 1960s. FLACSO, the sociology department at the University of Buenos Aires, and the exponents of the new anthropology in Mexico were often seen as belonging to a heavily Americanized, "empiricist" school of thought, unaware of the intellectual problems on which Latin American debate had focused for decades.

The opposition between styles of work was indeed a reality, in research and even more markedly in training, in those universities where reformers actively sought a discontinuity with the past. In research, although empirical (or empiricist) versus nonempirical styles were the nominal, conceptual opponents, the practical distinction introduced by the new disciplines was the development of large-scale research projects (sample surveys being the ideal type), often demanding extensive fieldwork, relatively large teams, and plentiful resources. This was opposed to craft styles, which at best coordinated the efforts of one master and several disciples, each working on an independent piece with limited resources. Sample-survey technology, after all, sounds today very much like an assembly plant, with the innovative thinking limited to the designer's desk.

Yet, my impression is that the opposition was clearer in terms of the organizational setting, which involved the nature of research, links with teaching and the universities, and the professional identity of the participants. The innovators were reacting against the figure of the *catedrático*, or chairholder, who dominated social science in the professional schools.[8]

Normally a generalist with no disciplinary training, whose writings were more often *about* sociology than *in* sociology, the *catedrático* did not encourage research and had to maintain some distance from current social and political issues, about which the allegedly apolitical universities were supposed to be neutral. By training lawyers, philosophers, and to a smaller extent historians, these chairholders of sociology or political science in schools of philosophy and law were seen largely as a conservative drag on the growth of a professionally oriented discipline. In some countries like Argentina—where antipositivism in the 1920s and 1930s had generated an extreme distrust of observation, experimentation, and quantification in the study of society and culture—the social sciences as practiced in universities stood in many ways in opposition to the intellectual model the innovators wanted to establish. Elsewhere, as in Mexico or Brazil, nationalism became an issue dividing the new, U.S.-trained or -inspired social scientists from the established groups in the universities.

The attempted innovations implied that there was little in the past practice of Latin American social science that was relevant to the training of new social scientists. Also, formal instruction about local society and politics, past and present, came far behind training in abstract tools of theory and methods. There was no assurance that such knowledge would be transmitted elsewhere, outside the formal curriculum. Thus, in an almost innocently perverse way, these new programs tended to instill a new scholasticism as isolated from social and political issues as that of the traditional *catedrático*. In both cases, heavy political involvement and hot political debate outside the classroom counterbalanced this trend, but at the same time created a divided world of science and politics.

The confrontations among the various styles of work are considerably less heated today, although they have by no means ceased. It is of some interest here to review, even briefly, the traditional styles of work and their relationship to the university settings, since the problems they faced are not so foreign to the experience of the younger generations of social scientists: then, as now, the most influential social and political thinking in most Latin American countries was essentially done outside the universities.

As in France, national politics in Latin America has dominated the universities, in contrast to the Anglo-American model, with universities under private or decentralized state control until modern times, or to the German model, where universities won considerable autonomy from the state in the early nineteenth century.[9] In Latin America, the idea of a university was almost always based on the Napoleonic model, just as the nineteenth-century beliefs in science and progress were borrowed from French positivism. Acceptance of the model, of course, was highly uneven. The first successful attempt to renew the medieval Spanish tradition of higher learning, that of Andres Bello in Chile in 1842, was made possible largely because of the early establishment of an integrating, unified oligar-chic rule in that country, after a relatively short period of postindependence turmoil.[10] Other Spanish American countries could not establish a central-ized, Napoleonic university until order and stability were achieved. Mexico, with its protracted nineteenth-century turmoil, is a case in point. Brazil did not suffer from the same problem, but the central authority was severely limited in administrative capacity, and a national university was not estab-lished until the 1920s. In sum, the idea of a university was that of an instrument of centralization of the educational system, an instrument to be used by the state to build a modern nation, but one that could exist only as a consequence of political hegemony. National politics were thus expressed in the overall purpose of the university enterprise, as well as in recruitment and curriculum. The fight for autonomy has been chronic, and the difficulties encountered in establishing the social sciences have been symptomatic of this lack of autonomy.

Since 1918, the university-reform movement in Latin America has consistently demanded greater political autonomy so that the universities could address themselves to national issues. The state, on the other hand, has seen the problem more often as one of keeping the universities out of national politics, rather than one of keeping politics out of the university operation. The emergence and development of a problem-oriented social science within the university, whether in the traditional approach or in the modern research-oriented one, has been hindered until today by the dilem-mas of autonomy and the dependence of universities on the state.

At the turn of the century, the most influential social and political thinking in Spanish American countries was being done outside the universi-ties, and this continued to be the case even after the social sciences were established within the universities.[11] The so-called *pensadores* ("thinkers"), whose work has been reappraised recently, were political men or profes-sionals in the natural sciences, medicine, or engineering, trained for obser-vation in other fields, who nonetheless had done original research on social or political problems.[12] In Brazil, social thinkers such as Oliveira Vianna or Azevedo Amaral did not participate in the institutionalization of the social sciences in that country, which proceeded rapidly in the 1930s. They were politicians and members of the higher echelons of the much-respected Brazilian bureaucracy who, if anything, were linked to the law schools, those prestigious settings for the training of political leaders and bureau-crats.[13] The work of generations of social and political philosophers, though certainly not highly original from an epistemological viewpoint, was very influential in the societies where they lived, since they provided the first diagnoses of social problems and discussed the directions of social and political change. Their essays, too, often contained a number of empirical observations and analyses that offered important clues to researchers in areas such as rural-urban relations and the role of cities, immigration and ethnic problems, land-tenure systems, regional disparities, family structure and social class, and local and national political systems and power structures.[14]

In addition to the essays and descriptive studies of the *pensadores* and commentators, more-carefully-controlled empirical research was conducted almost entirely outside the universities, until the postwar innovations. The most impressive case is that of anthropological research, especially in Mexico, where museums and governmental departments charged with Indian populations provided the most coherent settings for its growth.[15] From early efforts at building a research operation in archaeology and anthropology within the National Museum, which had been established in 1911, and the creation of a Department of Anthropology under the ministry of education in 1917, the growth of a research tradition in Mexican anthropology was linked with *indigenismo* on the one hand and the Mexican bureaucracy on the other. The issues were always relevant politically, because educational, social, and economic policies regarding the large Indian population were at stake. Debates and confrontations, some of them violent, were carried out in national forums. Yet, the universities provided little of the institutional setting for either research or discussion, and even training in anthropology tended to take place within relatively autonomous departments or schools in the university. The 1910s and 1920s, a period of consolidation of the Mexican state, allowed little room for social research within the universities, despite considerable institutional reform.[16]

Before the 1950s, the most impressive development within the social sciences in a university setting took place in São Paulo. Interestingly enough, of all the major countries in the region, Brazil had the weakest university tradition. Isolated professional schools, the most prestigious being law schools, had dominated higher education in that country, with the federal government unable to establish a national university until the 1920s. The state of São Paulo, the focus of economic as well as intellectual turmoil in the 1920s and 1930s, availed itself of the prevailing regional autonomy to establish a strong university in 1934, consolidating previously separate schools of law, medicine, and engineering. The main innovation was the founding of a School of Philosophy, Letters, and Science, which was supposed to provide preparatory, preprofessional training while serving to train teachers for the secondary system. The French model is evident, and French professors were hired for key positions. A *licencia* ("teacher's certificate") in the social sciences was established, and therefore chairs in sociology, anthropology, and political science were created. A research program slowly but surely took shape, with anthropologists and sociologists concentrating on Indians and race relations respectively. At the same time, private groups in São Paulo founded the Free School of Sociology and Politics. The school, unlike the faculty at the state university, had no role in training secondary teachers, and it was supposed to be oriented more toward practical problems and applied research, although the differences were at times blurred.

In sum, the universities had seldom been the bases for either highly influential social and political thinking or for the development of empirical social research before the innovations attempted in the 1950s. Dominated by the state and strongly influenced by frequent national political struggles, universities could not or would not allow the development of a critical social science; a literary and scholastic tradition tended to preclude an empirical orientation. Thus, the social sciences as institutionalized within the university system produced little that would be of interest to social scientists of the new, modern style in the 1960s.

The Shaping of Latin American Social Science: External Influences

The rapid growth of activities in the social sciences has been marked since the 1950s by the presence of massive foreign assistance, and since the 1960s by the large-scale training of young scholars in foreign universities. Although many at the time saw it as an unusual, perhaps unique, period in Latin American intellectual and institutional history, that was clearly not the case. The local innovators who had been responsible for launching new programs in the 1950s were themselves products of a previous generation that, in a different way, had also reflected the permanent intellectual links of Latin America with Europe and the United States.

Consider, for example, three of the most influential sociologists of the 1950s and 1960s: Medina Echavarria, Gino Germani, and Florestan Fernandes. The first two were actually immigrants themselves, or rather, political exiles. Echavarria and his generation of Spanish scholars, trained in England and Germany in the 1920s and early 1930s, had a solid background in philosophy, political studies, and economics in the European tradition. Their exile after the civil war had a pervasive influence in Mexico, Argentina, and throughout Spanish America. They translated much of the best that had been produced in the European tradition by the 1920s, and they would later incorporate contributions by the North Americans. The Fondo de Cultura Económica, with branches in Mexico City and Buenos Aires, became the vehicle for introducing this literature to the region. These scholars also wrote influential books of their own, such as Echavarria's *Sociología: Teoria y técnica,* and they were institutional innovators, as in the case of the creation of El Colegio de México and ECLA (where Echavarria worked for decades).

Gino Germani was exiled from Mussolini's Italy, where he had trained first in economics, later studying philosophy in Argentina. As a young scholar during the war years, he injected the new American sociology into the recently created sociology journal of the University of Buenos Aires. An empirically oriented sociology was then absent, effectively rejected by the predominantly antipositivist school of philosophy, which in Argentina included sociology. Germani would introduce it in the 1950s, when there was a change in the political climate.

Florestan Fernandes was the product of early university reform in the state of São Paulo, under strong European influence and direct French assistance. His work on Indians, in the line of British functionalism, as well as the projects on ethnic relations in São Paulo, were directly influenced by the presence of French scholars such as Claude Lévi-Strauss and Roger Bastide.

These developments took place in the 1930s and 1940s, when the region supposedly was more self-absorbed than ever. In fact, the writings of Europeans and North Americans always have found their way into the libraries of Latin American intellectuals. Works written in English and French, and, to a lesser extent, in German, are widely read, and European "classics" are often translated into Spanish before they appear in English. But it is not the broad topic of Western influences in general that I want to discuss here, but the presence in the Latin American social sciences of foreign-born scholars and their links with home (Europe or North America) as well as with local institutions. To put the recent cycle into perspective so as to evaluate it comparatively requires an impressionistic approach, for despite the publication of many works on the history and sociology of social science in Latin America,[17] there are few documented case studies on the development of social sciences and the external influences that shaped them.

Before World War II, foreign scholars tended to be in the region as individuals, rather than as part of a program or large-scale project, although a large number of anthropologists, archaeologists, and historians received support from the Carnegie Institution of Washington. They often stayed for long periods: a large number were actually immigrants or exiles. These scholars often became influential through their involvement in research with local assistants and colleagues within a craft type of environment. This was true particularly of anthropologists and archaeologists, due to their long fieldwork experience, their need for close local contacts, and their style of work. Although German naturalists in the nineteenth-century tradition, like Curt Nimuendaju, who settled in Brazil and had a crucial role in the development of anthropology in that country, and French scholars like Paul Rivet and Lévi-Strauss were important, the Americans were more numerous and their influence more pervasive.[18]

Anthropologists became more important in countries with archaeological interests, which were also those with large Indian populations. Mexico and Peru are the prime examples, although there was also an important development in the ethnography of lowland South American Indians. The North American anthropological and archaeological enterprise of that time was not linked to any particular official interest in the region; other consid-erations prevailed in drawing the interest, of say, the Carnegie Institution, as well as individual scholars like Robert Redfield and Sol Tax to the area. Unlike Africa or Polynesia under European colonial administrations, these were independent countries, and the U.S. government had little interest in their administration or internal policies: at the time, Latin America was of little political importance to any of the world powers.

But the interest of local scholars—historians, archaeologists, and ethnog-raphers—was as much political, and increasingly "policy oriented," as it was scientific. The Indian population had long been a subject of political preoc-cupation; the national states had inherited the interest from colonial admin-istrations and as a result had instituted specific legislation and administrative controls. Almost every generation of social thinkers had addressed the Indian question. In the 1920s and 1930s, important *indigenista* movements sprang up everywhere, especially in Mexico and the Andean countries. The work of the new brand of scholars would have an important influence on and would be stimulated by political developments. The particular relationship between local and foreign scholars evolved within this context.

Mexico was the scene of the most activity in this area during the period, and must be considered a very special case because of its proximity to and involvement with the United States.[19] Interest in pre-Columbian cultures was on the rise before the 1910 revolution, and Franz Boas and other American social scientists were involved in promoting—among enlightened officials like Genaro Garcia—within the National Museum what was to become the institutional setting for the expansion of anthropology in Mexi-co. Manuel Gamio, usually recognized as the key figure in the discipline at the time, studied under Boas at Columbia and had an important role in the more academically oriented museum. Gamio was also the first head of the Department of Anthropology under the ministry of agriculture and wrote the first important modern study of cultures in the valley of Teotihuacán.

Both archaeology and anthropology in Mexico developed considerably, and government funding was generous. Applied interests, however, tended to prevail over academic ones in both areas, and site reconstruction was important in efforts to revivify the national heritage, which played a key role in the new nationalism. Ethnography was expected to guide educational policies as well as administrative and economic ones. Anthropology in Mexico, in the words of one of its better-known practitioners, "was born and grew under the random support of public administration and, from its beginnings, it acquired the status of an official science."[20]

Close and intensive interaction among local and foreign scholars, much of it in the field, was crucial for the early training of anthropologists in Mexico, Peru, and elsewhere. In Mexico, the interaction was massive and sometimes conflictive; since official interest was evident, issues were highly politicized, and the local community of scholars was large and politically influential. It should be pointed out that foreign scholarly influence was at that time most important at a technical level: Americans were more academically and theoretically oriented than Mexicans, who developed an applied anthropology.[21] The broader, nontechnical issues were closely related to politics, from which Americans maintained some distance, not just as foreigners respectful of local autonomy but also for the sake of scientific neutrality. Moreover, given this academic and apolitical orientation, some of the most influential anthropological studies of the period avoided crucial determinants of the Indian communities being studied. The foremost example, of course, is Redfield's work on the village Tepoztlán, which emerged in the book wholly free from its actual involvement in the revolutionary peasant movement and its broad political and economic links with Mexico City, only some sixty miles away. Technical, methodological, and theoretical issues are not easily differentiated, and thus the pervading influence of American scholarship at the time implied a trained avoidance of the problems leading to speculation and political debate, which only much later would be incorporated in anthropological research.

In the 1930s and 1940s, American anthropologists working in Latin America moved from the study of Indian groups to that of *mestizo* communities and even of entire societies like Puerto Rico. In those decades, anthropologists in the region conducted some of the most influential studies of sociocultural change and acculturation (Redfield's *Tepoztlán*, Sol Tax's *Penny Capitalism*, Julian Steward's *The People of Puerto Rico*). Rural sociologists like Carl Zimmerman, T. Lynn Smith, and Lowry Nelson joined this undertaking during the 1940s and further advanced the study of rural communities in transition. This spurt of community studies, unlike the work on Indian groups and archaeological explorations in earlier years, was partly supported by a growing official interest on the part of the U.S. government. The Good Neighbor Policy and World War II led the United States to seek enlightened assistance in formulating Latin American policies, for the first time since the building of the Panama Canal.[22] The academic community of Latin Americanists was called on to collaborate; it consisted largely of language and literature specialists, historians, geographers, and anthropologists, of which only the last two groups had firsthand experience of fieldwork. In 1942 the Joint Committee on Latin American Studies was founded, and the Institute of Social Anthropology was created within the Smithsonian Institution, resulting in a new series of monographs under the direction of Julian Steward in 1944. This burst of research activity and training had a very influential role in American anthropology. The names of people like Gillin, Beals, Foster, Holmberg, Eresmus, and Adams are associated with the institute, while Steward's Puerto Rican study, started in 1947, launched the professional careers of Americans like Eric Wolf and Sidney Mintz, as well as Puerto Ricans Eduardo Seda and Elena Padilla.[23]

Under direct U.S. government support, and often based at the local American embassy, a number of rural sociologists were commissioned to review the rural scene and agricultural production during the war. The outcome was a set of important descriptive monographs at a national level. The well-known books by Taylor on Argentina, T. Lynn Smith on Brazil, Nelson on Cuba, and Whetten on Mexico resulted from this enterprise. Taylor's work, for example, produced careful descriptions of the variety of rural environments and agricultural production in a country that actually knew very little about itself—despite the fact that regional disparities had been at the center of attention for many years and recently had been discussed extensively by influential authors such as Juan Alvarez and Alejandro Bunge. It is important to note that Taylor's work had no enduring impact on Argentine social science. His excellent book was not translated into Spanish and thus was largely unavailable to the public.

In sum, from the 1920s to the 1940s the work of North American social scientists on Latin America became more important, had increasing official support from the U.S. government, and tended to shift its interests to contemporary issues related to social and cultural change. The local impact was greater in Mexico than in any other country, but it was felt also in Brazil, Peru, Puerto Rico, and elsewhere. The importance of Indian cultures, on the one hand, and international politics, on the other, largely determined the choice of countries. A significant legacy of this work, in those instances when the collaboration of local researchers was sought and found, was the establishment of a tradition of empirical, craft-type work, and the training of investigators to conduct descriptive studies. This legacy was stronger where visiting scholars remained longer and had a local institutional affiliation. The case of São Paulo, both at the university and at the Escola Livre de Sociologia e Política, is illustrative.

The relevance of such studies for theory or policy locally was less obvious. First, it should be clear that policy relevance was not a usual motivation for researchers at the time, and when it became important during the war, the issue was relevance for U.S. policy exclusively. Theoretical relevance, on the other hand, became increasingly important, but there was little or no interaction at that level with local scholars, who did not constitute an audience for this debate. This was not the result of lack of theoretical concerns among the latter, but rather of a difference in focus. Theory tended to have a much greater normative connotation, as a guide for action rather than a generalization from facts; the focuses of debate in Latin America were the political issues of the Indian question, agrarian reform, popular building.

The ascendance of sociology in the United States, followed somewhat later by that of political science, was accelerated by the war. Both proved useful and were becoming methodologically more sophisticated, following the lead established by economics. The greater weight assumed by these disciplines vis-à-vis the general public, private enterprise, and the public sector came together with the paradigmatic hegemony of quantitative analysis. Although the expansionistic characteristics of these disciplines over "traditional" social sciences, as well as beyond the national borders, was clear, their influence within Latin America was accomplished only rarely by the presence of more Latin Americanists within those fields. In fact, there were very few of the latter before the war (rural sociologists were the main exception), and they were not attracted to the region in greater numbers for some time. Sociology was not oriented to comparative research or interested in foreign lands or cultures, as were anthropology or political science. Thus, sociology would become influential almost in spite of its lack of interest in the region per se. The case of political science was somewhat different, for it blended the traditional interest in comparative government (now comparative political systems and comparative politics) with the growth of the behavioralist model. Cross-cultural and cross-societal studies became important. Funds, however, were more plentiful where U.S. policy interests were at stake: in Eastern Europe, Asia, the Middle East, and Africa.

In the 1950s the external influence most responsible for the spread of the new gospel of the social sciences was that of agencies within the United Nations network, especially UNESCO, which reflected the spirit of application of the social sciences corresponding to the *desarrollista* movement in Latin America. European experts participated in many of the important intellectual enterprises of the decade—for example, the Center for Educational Research and the Latin American Center for Social Research, both in Rio, and FLACSO in Santiago.

The presence of North American sociology and political science in Latin America in the 1950s was still quite limited in comparison with the boom of the 1960s. The relative importance of applied areas (health, nutrition, agriculture, education) in the activities of U.S. government-assistance programs, as well as the orientation of private foundations like Rockefeller and of cooperative university programs, implied a preeminence of economists over other social scientists and a limited interest in social-science institutional development per se. Where such interest existed, as was the case in economics in Chile, it was clearly linked to providing a basis for applied work that would be free of Marxist perspectives and those of ECLA.[24] Nationalism in countries like Mexico and Argentina at times limited seriously the presence of foreign scholars in the university setting, or isolated those involved in technical assistance programs from the main intellectual debates. The appearance on the scene of economists, sociologists, and political scientists with policy concerns that had been absent in the previous generations of Latin Americanists led to new strains in relations with local scholars.

The Cuban revolution in 1959 and the Alliance for Progress under Kennedy started a new era in Latin American studies in the United States, giving momentum to the continuing diffusion of the North American model of social science in the region, until then in the hands of locals and Europeans. For the first time, these disciplines (as well as economics) became the center of attention. The effort was assisted from the late 1950s on by the U.S. government, both within the United States and in Latin America: the establishment of National Defense Education Act language and area centers and research and scholarship programs funded by USAID and other agencies are the prime examples. The international programs of American universities rapidly expanded the amount and range of contacts with Latin American institutions. Private foundations—primarily the Ford Foundation, in the case of social sciences—channeled funds to area-studies programs and institution building within Latin America.

The effects of these new programs on Latin American area studies within the United States have been documented through a series of careful reports.[25] The effects on the Latin American social sciences, though much debated, are more difficult to assess, but are, of course, directly relevant here. The effort was so massive that it is impossible to disentangle the effect of the presence of North American scholars, including doctoral candidates, from that of the institutional presence of foundations, universities, and governmental agencies, or from that of the sheer number of Latin Americans studying in the United States or Europe.

Three distinct styles of work and forms of collaboration can be distinguished within the last two decades. The first goes from the late 1950s to the scandals surrounding Projects Camelot and Simpático in 1965, U.S. government-supported research projects that were to provide the bases for policies to prevent subversion in the region. The second phase, from 1965 to the mid-1970s, was a period of sustained interest but one that had a different direction. The last phase begins with the sharp decline in financial support that has continued to the present, with Latin Americanists in the United States in search of a new role.[26]

The first obvious point is that North Americans had started coming to Latin America in very large numbers. A good indicator can be obtained through a study of doctoral dissertations on Peru presented to North American universities, a small number of which were written by Peruvians.[27] Between 1869 and 1976, some 553 dissertations were approved; three out of four of them were completed within the last fifteen years, and the largest number in the social sciences. Younger and less established scholars now had access and opportunity within the field, which meant that many more promising scholars were recruited, but that the overall selectivity (among junior and senior scholars) was lower and they had, on average, a shorter acquaintance with the region.

Collaborative programs and joint projects became common, but there was also an increasing number of projects, large and small, with very limited local participation. Foreign scholars and their institutions and supporting agencies could define topics and approaches and carry out their work themselves, needing assistance only at the level of data collection. That, of course, was not new, but there was a difference in styles of research. The contrast between the extensive fieldwork and the search for bits and pieces of information in objects, written material, oral statements, and public life that characterize traditional anthropology, on the one hand, and the rigorous sample surveys required by modern sociologists, on the other, serves to highlight the difference. Traditional anthropology permits much greater involvement with locals at all levels. In fact, a debate in the 1960s about styles of work of Latin American and North American scholars stereotyped the former as "taxi professors," jumping from one job to another (an indication of limited time as well as low professionalism), and the latter as "researchers by cable."[28]

Obviously, there were too many scholars and too many institutional arrangements and personal styles to allow for generalization. But new phenomena were, besides large numbers, large-scale projects often involving complex technology, extensive rather than intensive fieldwork, a division of labor whereby the top researchers did not need to spend much time in the field, and a growing community of increasingly confident local scholars. Collaboration was still largely defined by the visiting team, who had access to funds and scholarly prestige. This prestige, unfortunately, often implied a more "scientific" status attached to a newer style of work than to the older styles as practiced in the region, or, for that matter, as practiced by previous generations of Latin Americanists, whatever their geographic origin. The scandal arising from Project Camelot challenged all elements in this model:[29] first and foremost, the right of visiting researchers (with or without U.S. government support) to do research on any topic without advance notice and without prior disclosure to local social scientists; second, the "scientific" neutrality of the project, since in this case it was explicitly absent in the design; and third, the collaborative arrangements involving local junior trainees as data collectors.

As a result, foundations and other agencies learned some lessons and gained a better understanding of the need for local institution building. Until then, such "construction" operations had focused on strengthening "resource bases" in American universities and had channeled funds to local Latin American institutions only for fellowships abroad and visiting professors. But new pressures resulting from politicization, combined with the strengthening of local groups, allowed a new policy vis-à-vis local institutions and also led to considerable restrictions against North American grantees. The foundations started a trend that universities and government followed, at least on the latter point.

The second phase was characterized by the growing importance of foreign assistance directly channeled to training, research, and network construction within Latin America, contributing to a more equal relationship between local and visiting scholars. The participation of local scholars in evaluation and peer review, as well as that of regional associations like CLACSO (the Latin American Council for Social Research) in the administration of programs often supported from outside the region and involving both local and visiting scholars, was certainly important in establishing a more balanced relationship. But more than anything else, the maturation of the new generation of largely foreign-trained social scientists and their effective blending within local communities and institutions increased the chances of collaboration between foreign and local scholars. Of course, receptivity to foreign assistance has varied by country since its rapid growth in the early 1960s, so that this picture is truer for Chile, Peru, and Brazil than for Mexico or Argentina.

The third phase is characterized both by increased contact and mutual influence between foreign Latin Americanists and local social scientists, and by the search for a new role for U.S. area studies in the face of rapid decline in resources. As expressed in a conference report in 1975, "Latin American studies in the United States must find new roles in the seventies under the handicap of rather severe constraints, constraints which are having decided effects on its present shape and future direction."[30] (The main constraint, of course, was a decline in resources after what some saw as an overexpansion of Latin American studies in the 1960s.)

The new dialogue was not just a result of maturation of the social sciences in Latin America. Social sciences in the United States also had experienced important changes. Area studies were marked by the breakdown of the modernization paradigm, as well as by increasing relativism in the social values underlying it—that is, the image of a developed, modern society as a good society. But more generally, the disciplines (even sociology) became more pluralistic. As has been noted recently, the deviationists of the 1960s, from ethnomethodologists to Marxists, became institutionalized within American academia, with their own departments, journals, meetings, and participation in the profession. The old compartments of theory and research are no longer so neat and congruent, and very traditional styles of work, like the essay, are being reappraised.[31] Old-timers, of course, do not necessarily accept these facts, and clearly these are not quantitatively dominant trends. What exists is simply a pluralism of approach.

This is important in the dialogue, since social science in its Latin American version can claim to contribute to the more general enterprise at the same time that it remains occupied with "local" issues. The old issue of "national" sociology versus a universal discipline is not raised here in the same form. Rather, the argument is that the new pluralism is ready to accept the idea that universal conceptual frameworks created on the basis of the historical experience of some societies are likely to seem less valid when other historical experiences are taken into consideration.[32] A sociology "of Latin America" thus involves an effort at theory building as much as the accumulation of data relevant to the region.

The Social Science Community in Latin America Today

The focus of this section is on the relationship between the social-science communities and the national states and societies in various Latin American countries today. I will discuss the institutional setting, with less attention to human resources and training. Although the public sector, in Latin America as elsewhere, plays a crucial role in the support of social-science institutions, the unique characteristic of Latin American social science (including economics) today is the qualitative importance of nongovernmental research and training institutions. These include strictly private, nonprofit research centers; private universities, depending in varying degrees upon public-sector funding; and relatively autonomous centers established by international or intergovernmental agencies.

In Latin America, social-science policy is part of higher educational policy. This is the most crucial source of cross-national variation in the relationship between social-science communities and the state, for the latter has the primary responsibility for higher education everywhere. Therefore, I will focus on the universities and nongovernmental research centers.

Three types of countries should be distinguished: the first includes those where higher education has expanded and consolidated with considerable participation by the social sciences, which thus have achieved a high degree of legitimacy. The two major examples are also those where the social science community is largest: Brazil and Mexico. The second comprises countries where higher education has become involuted, and where the social sciences have been among the major targets of political control within the higher educational system. Chile and Argentina will be discussed. The third category includes cases of breakdowns in which the change from supportive to restrictive policies has not been so sharp, and where the system of higher education, more recently established, is not viewed with such suspicion. Peru is the example I will discuss in this category, although Colombia probably also belongs here.

Brazil and Mexico have contrasting intellectual traditions and patterns of development in the social sciences. Mexico is a much more centralized country politically. The national state, since the 1910–17 revolution, has consistently enlarged its spheres of influence. Since their inception, the social sciences have found a place, partly in the universities, but even more so within the administrative apparatus. The "official" character might not be noticed upon first glance at the university scene, which is characterized by a very vocal political opposition.[33] But beyond the surface of student mobilization, participation in and control by the state apparatus has been extensive, for the state provides jobs. Social scientists, like other intellectuals in Mexico, have enjoyed the benefits of full-time jobs in the universities, governmental agencies, or government-supported programs in private institutions. Thus, social scientists have developed a close, though not always comfortable, relationship to the state.

In Brazil, until recently, this has not been the case. The Brazilian government has always had a place for lawyers but not necessarily for social scientists. The new role of the federal state evolved in the 1950s, with planning and the expansion of welfare agencies, but the relationship with social-science intellectuals was strained. Regional autonomy allowed for some distance between universities and the national state, as in São Paulo. After the 1964 military coup, there was open conflict, with the state banning the social sciences in some universities and labeling the noneconomic disciplines as outcasts. This trend, however, was reversed in the 1970s, bringing Brazil closer to Mexico in the actual functioning of the social sciences within the national scene.

The critical issue in the recent growth and institutionalization of the social-science community in Brazil, and to a lesser extent in Mexico, has been the rapid expansion of graduate programs, linked to university enrollment. Total enrollment in higher education in Brazil increased more than fivefold between 1964 and 1975. The rise was particularly impressive between 1968 and 1973, when annual rates of growth always surpassed 20 percent. Moreover, enrollment in the basic courses, normally housed in the faculties and institutes where the social sciences are taught, increased even more. These areas comprised 28 percent of the so-called professional cycle in 1964, and 42.4 percent in 1974.[34] In 1968, a new university law was passed that introduced a number of reforms, including new requirements of postgraduate degrees for university professors and the establishment of nationally uniform criteria for their careers. Employment opportunities thus increased, along with the demand for postgraduate courses in all the disciplines.

The growth in postgraduate education was only partially a consequence of these policies, which stimulated demand. It is clear that the state was developing two approaches. With regard to undergraduate education, it was allowing for growth in enrollment without a comparable increase in financial support. Private universities and schools (the so-called isolated institutes not belonging formally to a university) and the less expensive humanities and social sciences grew more rapidly than public universities and the hard sciences. Access to university education was seen by the new middle classes as a means of social mobility; and granting that access was mainly a political move. The expansion of postgraduate education, however, was part of those policies favoring scientific and technological development, a genuine interest developed within policymaking circles in Brazil.

My impression is that the growth of noneconomic social-science activities in graduate programs, with the concomitant growth in research support, was largely a consequence of policies whose main goals were primarily the development of hard science and technological studies. The first spurt of social-science training and research programs took place with very little involvement with the national educational ministry, and at times in spite of it. Social scientists alienated from official policies (and often banned from any official position), as well as the Ford Foundation, gave the initial impetus to those programs. These were based either outside universities or within university settings segregated from undergraduate education, where politicization had been seen as a challenge by the administration. Yet, in the 1970s new policies at the graduate and postgraduate levels were fostering the social sciences within the universities. By the late 1970s several doctoral programs were established—in anthropology, sociology, and political science—and over twenty research-oriented M.A. programs existed throughout the country.[35] Teaching and research are closely related within them, although the separation from undergraduate curricula tends to remain. Social scientists participate in scientific policymaking agencies, which provide an essential means of supporting academic social-science research. A thriving association of postgraduate and research centers was established a few years ago, and professional associations in the disciplines were founded or given new life. Both serve to establish standards and evaluation criteria, and thus increase autonomy from the state. External support from private foundations and other agencies, crucial under repressive circumstances, are of less importance today.

This scenario also applies to Mexico, despite a different historical pattern. In Mexico, more than in Brazil, state policies vis-à-vis postgraduate education and advanced research have been the crucial factors. An important difference is the much greater initial involvement and demand by the Mexican public sector. The Mexican state has required more from university teachers in terms of research output under a variety of contract mechanisms that make research an implicit element in the position of a full-time professor in the social sciences. The state has also employed great numbers of such academics at the federal, state, and municipal levels: social-science advisors and researchers have become an integral part of the operation of many agencies. In the more technically oriented programs, this trend has been a major source of early attrition in postgraduate programs, attracting students before their course work or dissertation is completed.

Basic research in the noneconomic social sciences in Mexico today is carried out mainly in semiautonomous, government-supported institutes and in private universities. Both are relatively isolated from massive undergraduate teaching and therefore from both the more pervasive everyday political pressures and the administrative power of the state apparatus. Some of the major examples include El Colegio de México, a private, nonprofit organization whose budget comes largely from the ministry of education. It combines research in problem-oriented, as well as discipline-oriented, centers with several postgraduate training programs. Also, the Centro de Investigaciones Superiores of the National Institute of Anthropology and History, a public institution with considerable autonomy, is the site of a research and training program in social anthropology. Finally, the Instituto de Investigaciones Sociales at the National University of Mexico (UNAM) is a large research center within the largest university, with projects in all noneconomic social sciences, especially sociology and politics. It has no formal responsibility for the teaching carried out within the schools at the same university.

These three institutions are, by Latin American standards, relatively old (four or more decades) and have tended to develop a solid position within the governmental budget, thus remaining somewhat protected from political shifts. Stability of staff is also impressive by Latin American standards. Finally, all are located in Mexico City; this concentration is a source of concern, and recent policies have suggested a reversal of the trend.

In Brazil the picture is more complicated. Some of the most influential research groups are housed in private institutions with little or no governmental support—for example, the Centro Brasileiro de Analise e Planejamento in São Paulo, which has no training programs, and the Instituto Universitário de Pesquisas do Rio de Janeiro, only formally part of a private university but with graduate programs in sociology and political science at the M.A. and Ph.D. levels. Federal and state universities also house important research groups, in separate institutes or in fully integrated departments of new universities such as Brasilia and Campinas. The mechanism of a state-supported foundation exists to give relative autonomy to universities, like Brasilia, or university-like centers, like Fundacão Getulio Vargas. Finally, private universities have grown considerably, but have not, with the exception of IUPERJ, created powerful and autonomous research operations.

This diversity can be perceived within a single discipline, anthropology. Research is carried out in three settings: (1) museums within universities that also have graduate training programs; (2) university departments with graduate programs; and (3) isolated museums or research institutes with no training programs. There are at least two examples of each of these categories today, located in six different cities: São Paulo, Campinas, Brasilia, Rio de Janeiro, Recife, and Belém.[36] Interestingly, the national and state universities provide greater stability of employment (with purges, like that of 1968, notorious because they are exceptional) but also witness more attempts at political control. In contrast with Mexico, research is considerably more decentralized, even if the Rio—São Paulo axis is taken as a single unit.

In sum, through university-expansion and research policies, the social-science communities in both Mexico and Brazil have grown larger and become more solidly established within the broadly defined contours of the state apparatus, with greater incorporation in Mexico, where nongovernmental centers are less important. Although the legitimacy of the enterprise is not seriously challenged, the degree of professional autonomy and the uses of social sciences and their products are not clearly defined. Furthermore, the universities cyclically become important forums for political discussion, with social-science faculty and students taking a very active role. Political repression also moves cyclically, and when it is at a peak it unavoidably affects a disproportionate number of social scientists and students.

This situation demonstrates considerable stress and strain in the relationship between social-science professionals and the state. Common complaints among the former include the lack of real participation in policy-making, even in areas that demand advice and research; the ever-changing and opportunistic directions adopted by science policymakers and by agencies employing social scientists; and the sense of powerlessness and dependence when professional associations and the media offer little to counterbalance the might of the state. In Brazil, it seems clear that the growth in opportunities has already reached a peak, and with increasing economic and political difficulties the delicate equilibrium in the relationship between social scientists and the state may become destabilized.

Countries in the second category, which includes Argentina and Chile, can be analyzed together because of the common roots of their educational systems and the equally conflictive relationships of the social sciences and the state. In Argentina and Chile, the legitimacy of the social-science enterprise is challenged by the military regimes. Both countries are characterized by the relatively early and widespread modernization of the educational system at all levels. Compulsory elementary-education laws and a system of public elementary schools to implement them are well established, while secondary and university educations have been more accessible than in Brazil or Mexico. Fostered by a much more stable political system than in Argentina, Chilean higher education developed firmer traditions of autonomy and participation in national policies before 1973.

In Chile, university enrollment grew rapidly from the mid-1960s, under Christian Democratic and socialist administrations, until 1973.[37] The social-science community, much enlarged due to the presence of U.N.-related agencies in Santiago, increased and diversified. In newly created universities, as well as in the older ones, which underwent important reforms, social scientists played a leading role and found support for teaching and research. The development of welfare-state and planning agencies made use of many social scientists, primarily but not exclusively economists.

After 1973 the universities, planning agencies, and many other state activities changed radically and became targets of repression and financial cuts. Enrollment between 1975 and 1977 declined 5.6 percent a year; first-year openings decreased 19 percent between 1974 and 1978. The goal was to deactivate and demobilize, as well as to limit students' access to higher education. Financial cuts at the national university were the largest. In addition to purges, a considerable brain drain took place. The traditional institutional strength of the public universities (mainly the University of Chile) and the Catholic church's open confrontation with the government acted as moderating influences, even under the rule of the military *rectores*. But the noneconomic social sciences (and non-Chicago economics) have been the most vulnerable portions of the university system. The return to a "professional" university and part-time faculty left little room for the social sciences, already weakened by purges and severely limited in academic freedom. Pure research also suffered greatly (in contrast with the professional schools, applied research, and technical training). The same pattern obtains in Argentina, extending to other periods of university-state confrontations as well. Selectivity in recruitment, on the one hand, and dependence on the state, on the other, are possible reasons for the common fate of social scientists and pure researchers in the natural sciences under authoritarian regimes.

In Argentina political instability has been much greater and the universities have suffered more. The 1966 military coup dealt a serious blow to the social sciences. During the following years, the number of universities with social-science undergraduate-degree programs and the number of students enrolled in such programs increased, but there were no graduate programs or research centers within the universities, and there was an obvious decline in academic standards. Heavy politicization and the spread of irrationalistic tendencies in the social sciences, in both leftist and rightist forms, became the leading trends. This turbulence was already declining when the 1976 military coup put a stop to the ferment and mobilization of the previous decade. The coup was geared to bringing order and discipline and very little else. Argentina's higher-educational policies since then demonstrate few deviations from the Chilean pattern. Restriction of admissions, purges, financial cuts, return to part-time (and grossly underpaid) faculty, and ideological control—all are similar devices. The traditional, but considerably less vigorous, professional university—the university of lawyers, physicians, and engineers—is back in operation. Argentine policy has less direction and greater inertia than the Chilean, with less effort devoted to building an alternative to the inherited university model.[38] In Chile, the strength of the

Catholic church and its influence on Catholic universities, as well as the permanence of academic networks built over the previous decades, have maintained a degree of intellectual life and academic freedom. In Argentina these have been eroded by irrationalism and obscurantist policies since 1966.

The social sciences that are based within the university systems of these two countries are marginal, both quantitatively and qualitatively. Of Argentina's fifty-one universities, about half of them public, only four now offer an undergraduate degree in sociology, compared with ten in 1970.[39] In anthropology only three of six programs survived. In at least one university it has been reported that very little social anthropology, sociology, or psychology is taught, and that physical anthropology and archaeology, which complement routine courses in the humanities, seem outdated.[40] The closing down of undergraduate programs in sociology was supposed to lead to a shift toward graduate programs, the rationale being that the discipline is more appropriate for mature students. However, graduate programs exist only nominally in two private universities and have not been popular in public ones. A research orientation is found in only one private university, and very little research is actually conducted within university settings. Full-time positions in the social sciences do remain, with support of the national agency for scientific research, but they do not form any core university-related group. Some nonuniversity centers benefit partially from this support.

Social-science research in both Argentina and Chile survives largely outside the universities, and as basic research at best, neglected and obstructed by the state apparatus. The prevailing model is the private, nonprofit research center, specializing by problem area rather than by discipline, with limited research-training programs. These centers tend to be small, interdisciplinary groups. The largest number of centers (about ten) is found in Buenos Aires. Only one, the Instituto Di Tella, has some stable source of local, nongovernmental funding and, after twenty years, is old enough to have some visibility. All centers have a professional, full-time staff with the requisite academic credentials, including in most cases a Ph.D. degree earned abroad (there never have been doctoral programs in Argentina) and considerable professional recognition at a regional and international level. Sociologists and political scientists predominate, but disciplinary differentiation is not stressed. Foreign assistance and international research contracts have played a major role in the life of centers of this type in both countries, since governmental contracts in recent years are almost nonexistent.

Voluntarism and self-management characterize the efforts of these centers, which display considerable institutional strength in spite of powerful threats. The Instituto de Desarrollo Económico (IDES) in Buenos Aires, for example, though a professional association supported largely by its members, has published a major social-science journal *(Desarrollo econó-mico)* for over twenty years and houses the best-attended postgraduate courses in the social sciences in Argentina. In Chile the church has provided an important institutional link, while in Argentina informal networks, built over a longer period of time, are more important. Researchers in these centers are very active in regional associations, mainly the Latin American Council for the Social Sciences.

Although this is the prevailing model, other research activities with little visibility and of uncertain quality are still conducted in governmental agencies and at some universities. Inertia has played a role, at least in Argentina, and some research activities initiated during the two previous decades are still being carried out. At the provincial and municipal level, as well as in odd corners of the national administration, one finds some applied research being done by social scientists. But it is clear that the model of society toward which the current regimes of Argentina and Chile are striving allows social scientists no significant role, and coherence is not achieved. The decline in social welfare and planning are explicit goals, but some professional interests remain entrenched in the bureaucracy and defend those activities, perhaps relying on simple inefficiency within the regime for their survival.

Finally, the situation in Peru provides a useful contrast. Although Peruvian social science has important antecedents, mainly in social anthropology but also in social and political thought, institutionalization within the universities did not begin until the 1960s. Perhaps more than anywhere else in the region, the development of social sciences in modern times was seen as a tool for the social and economic transformation of society. Official support and pressure to turn attention to concrete problems increased with the military coup of 1968 and lasted a decade. Centers multiplied as rapidly as university-related programs. State agencies, often run by professionals with social-science training, employed an increasing number of social scientists. Political and ideological debate was very active and permeated all social-science activities. In two decades of rapid social change, marked mainly by the incorporation into the nation for the first time of various ethnic groups, strata, and regions, the social sciences experienced a similarly dramatic cycle, achieving an expanded presence in the national society. The result has been, by the end of the 1970s, a highly heterogeneous and uneven institutional setting, fostered by both state demands and external support, in which the social sciences faced a critical phase when the entire Peruvian economy fell into its worst recession of modern times.

A local observer of Peru has called the early 1970s a period of *sociologización*, referring to that presence in its national life.[41] A base for it, as in Brazil and Mexico, was found in university expansion, with enrollment tripling within a decade. The number of social-science departments in Peruvian universities jumped from seven in 1960 to fifty-four in 1977, while the number of students enrolled in them went from around 500 to more than 32,000, over half in economics. In 1977, in sociology alone, there were thirteen programs, plus one graduate program, and almost 6,000 students. Moreover, in the same year there were twenty-four centers outside the universities, a majority of them involved in action and applied research but employing mainly social scientists. Five were founded in the 1960s and the rest in the 1970s. All but three were in Lima, the national capital.[42] Most of them, however, seem to have had a very shaky institutional base.

Sheer numbers do not indicate the heterogeneity of this enterprise. In fact, two university programs had a clear advantage in quality and prestige. The program at the Catholic University has been the most influential, with a graduate training program, considerable research, and support from international agencies. Its graduates have had a great influence on other university developments, research and action-oriented centers, and public administration. The state has been the major employer of social-science graduates, mainly during the expanding cycle of the military regime. Simultaneously, outside funds for social-science research and training increased many times. An official source estimated that foreign support amounted to about $2.2 million in 1977, coming from European (28 percent) and U.S. and Canadian (37 percent) foundations and governmental agencies, and from U.N. agencies (29 percent). Economic and noneconomic social sciences each received approximately half of these funds, and university programs and independent centers were the largest beneficiaries.

During the economic crisis of the late 1970s, it became clear that the structure of the social sciences could no longer be solidly based on either state employment or foreign assistance, and expansion ceased. Unlike the situation in Argentina and Chile, it does not appear that drastic government policy changes have caused a shift in the relation between the state and the social sciences. Rather, all Peruvian society seems to have been affected by the recession and contraction of government spending.

The Intellectual Scene: Recent Trends

It has often been noted that Latin American sociology, like the other social sciences, is concerned mainly with development,[43] whereas in the United States and other developed countries the sociology of development is only a specialty, and a relatively minor one at that. The Latin American focus on development reflects the long-standing centrality in these countries of developmental issues. Theoretical and political debate on those issues is of general concern to a majority of social scientists, and very often they pose guidelines for approaching particular research problems or providing a rationale for their relevance. From the days of the *pensadores* to the present, a concern about the direction of social and political change, with an implicit or explicit comparison with other Western models, has been at the core of the enterprise.

One consequence of this concern with development is that it has provided the main forum for paradigmatic debates about modernization theory, CEPAL *desarrollismo*, Marxian approaches, or dependency theory. Debates between and within paradigms gain in salience at times and attract a broad social-science public, mainly when important new formulations are offered. My impression, however, is that their importance has been magnified as the teaching of the social sciences has become widespread. The actual practice of research is not so clearly affected by them. Another consequence of a very different nature is the importance of debate on national or Latin American "realities." Brazilians, for example, talk about *a reliadade brasileira* as a focus of concern, an area in which research results and analyses are tested for relevance. This evaluation of policy relevance contrasts with the concrete uses that private enterprise or policymakers make of research results, an approach usually negatively labeled as technocratic.

The strengthening of the network of Latin American social scientists and institutions in recent years has been rooted in this orientation toward development. The Latin American Council for Social Research has sponsored a number of research groups in various problem areas that implicitly find a core concern in developmental issues. These research groups function as forums to discuss theoretical formulations, research strategies, and research results; they have had a distinct influence on the diffusion of theories about social development. In a similar fashion, the doctoral programs within CLACSO's network, although they were ultimately organized within specific institutions, to some extent shared a common philosophy. The points on which there seemed to be a consensus were, first, that postgraduate programs should emphasize problems relevant to Latin American society; second, that they should contribute to the production and diffusion of an awareness about social problems of development in their societies; and, third, that training in the social sciences should not be oriented toward the technocratic approach, nor toward purely disciplinary concerns unrelated to broad social and political problems.[44]

The pervasive influence of national developmental concerns can be seen even in research areas where theoretical problems are not derived immediately from a comprehensive development paradigm. A good example was offered recently in a discussion with Brazilian anthropologists about research on kinship and social organization among some Indian tribes in that country.[45] The theoretical problem was posed several decades ago when early ethnographic studies showed the inadequacy of concepts regarding social organization that had been developed on the basis of classical ancient societies or contemporary African and Polynesian groups. But the growing interest today is clearly linked with material and ideological aspects of the "Brazilian miracle" and its crisis. On the one hand, the expansion of settlement in the Amazon frontier and the ecological changes it poses directly affect Indian territories and lives; concern about Indians in the Amazon is related to concern about a style of development from the point of view of resource use. On the other hand, the way the incorporation of these Indians (a very small minority in Brazil today) into the national society proceeds reveals something about Brazilian society in general and the broad definition of citizenship. Thus, Indian anthropology is no longer an exotic field, nor is it a field justified only in terms of advising governmental agencies in their dealings with the Indian population.

The centrality of developmental issues and their impact upon research is also evident in the Latin Americans' expectation of challenging the "universality principle" in the social sciences. This concept—that theories and methods are not bound to the time and place of specific societies—has until recently been a major impediment to the creation of new concepts and frameworks useful in capturing the specific aspects of Latin American (or other) realities; the Latin American experience was allegedly only an instance of a general course of events already studied elsewhere in the history of the developed countries.[46] The rejection of this principle, however, does not necessarily lead to the Balkanization of social sciences into a large number of national or regional versions, each dealing with aspects or patterns of development in particular societies. Rather, it specifies the nature of theory building in the area of development by indicating a need to identify types and to elaborate comparative frameworks. Latin American social scientists are striving, not for a romantic defense of the uniqueness of their own societies, but for more circumscribed kinds of theories.

What are the more significant current trends in research within this traditional study of developmental issues? In what areas is the research on Latin America by Latin Americans and others becoming relevant for broader theoretical discussion? Two major focuses of recent research warrant discussion.

The first, a pervasive interest in the nature of agrarian capitalism, reflects a marked shift from the urban emphasis of the 1950s and 1960s, when the cities were the major loci of research. Capitalism and industrialization in the periphery; urbanization and the nature of the urban middle classes, the industrial working class, and the marginal population; populist movements and mobilization—these are some of the urban-oriented problems that received much attention. In the 1970s, however, a radical reconsideration of agrarian social structure occurred, stimulated by both historical research then being completed on haciendas and plantations, and by new anthropological and sociological studies of peasant economies. Going beyond the older question of the nature of feudalism and capitalism in agrarian social structure in various countries in the region, the new emphasis focused largely upon the links between urban-centered, capitalist development and agrarian structure, both today and in the past. The most notable innovation, therefore, was not a change in focus from urban to rural, or a "rediscovery" of rural problems that had been the area of most extensive empirical research before the 1950s. Rather, the rural-urban nexus became crucial in research on many discrete issues, including the transformation of the peasant economy, the role of provincial cities, variation in migration patterns, and the urban "informal" sector.

This research trend, though led by anthropologists and historians, has had a widespread influence on sociology and political science, making traditional disciplinary boundaries less relevant. The distinction between a rural-oriented anthropology and a sociology of urban processes lost validity when an emphasis on the rural-urban nexus caused their subject matter to be linked intrinsically.

This new focus requires lasting revision of notions of development as they relate to Latin America. The urban bias referred to above implicitly responded to the notion of duality, of a transition to industrial, capitalist societies that suggested transactions between an urban-centered, "Western" society, and a rural-centered, non-Western, traditional, noncapitalist one. However, given that Amerindian societies have been profoundly influenced by commercial capitalism since the Conquest, in contemporary Latin America these two sectors—rural and urban—are viewed as reflections of two moments of Western, capitalist development in the present. In recent years, social and economic history of rural society has emphasized the cyclical nature of those interactions: during boom periods urban markets grow and technology—and often labor—flows into rural areas; bust periods are characterized by decline, involution, and outmigration. These cycles seldom repeat themselves exactly, however, for they reflect the effects of different historical contexts. Thus, past and contemporary interactions between an urban-dominated capitalist economy and a rural society that has a dynamic of its own cannot be ignored in analyses of development.

The second important trend is in the area of political studies. Several observers in the mid-1960s were dissatisfied with the status of political studies on Latin America. The common approaches of that time were characterized by either a formalist, legalistic conception of the role of the state, or a reductionist conception whereby its nature and changes were largely a consequence of the social and economic structure.[47] Furthermore, until then, research on Latin American politics had barely scratched the surface of the major issues arising from the failure to establish stable democracies in the region. In the last fifteen years, however, approaches and research styles have changed drastically. The intellectual stimuli from theoretical developments elsewhere are undoubtedly important: the renewal of Marxist thought in France, under the influence of Althusser and Poulantzas, in Italy in the Gramscian tradition, and in Britain, had a lasting influence in Latin America. Furthermore, the breakdown of the modernization paradigm in American comparative politics and in the behavioralist assumptions of political science in general occurred while many Latin American graduate students were in the United States, and their return to the region made a significant difference in research capabilities and orientations. Finally, there were clear internal stimuli for study to be found in the new forms of nondemocratic regimes that have flourished in the region during the past fifteen years.

This maturation of political studies in the region focused on the nature of nondemocratic capitalism. This implied, first, a search for continuities and discontinuities with older forms of nondemocratic politics. This trend to historical revisionism required a new look at political history in many cases, and at the political theory elaborated locally. The classics of the region were reread for clues about the ideological origins and foundations of state domination, as much for their intrinsic value as for their interpretations of historical events. Second, this focus suggested more careful consideration of some of the key actors in the new nondemocratic regimes. The revision started with the role of the military, but increasingly focused on civilian groups, traditional political parties, and new technocrats, and on the relation between the bureaucratic professionals in the state apparatus and the civil society.

This reappraisal of the role of the state and the wave of studies in politics had a radical influence in the region upon the social sciences in general, including economics. As with the renaissance of rural studies and the reconsideration of agrarian capitalism, the boom in political studies carried with it important revisions in the broader concepts of development. It also brought increased attention to phenomena until then largely disregarded, such as ideologies and mass communications.

Finally, there has been a change in research styles. To the extent that it is legitimate to generalize across countries, disciplines, and problem areas, perhaps what is most impressive about recent trends in Latin America today is the growth of small-scale, intensive, and qualitative studies. This is in part a reaction against the bureaucratized and expensive large-scale, sample surveys. It also reflects the predominant heterodoxy; there is no research procedure that is not used effectively by someone. And it is not unrelated to funding and organizational problems: government agencies excepted, there are fewer and fewer cases where research institutions can carry or have access to results of large-scale data bases. Finally, research grants for academic purposes are usually tailored today for smaller-scale studies.

There is also another rationale for this style of work: the importance attached to the human document. Small-scale qualitative studies, based on interviews and/or observation of urban households, workers in factories, peasants, street vendors, temporary migrants, and other "common" people, are justified for two related reasons. First, certain topics for which these techniques are more applicable have gained considerable currency. These always include what can be termed broadly "the actor's perspective." Thus, problems of meaning and ideology become crucial. In this sense, there is a rediscovery of "culture," but not necessarily within a culturalist perspective (one that would isolate cultural products from relations of production). The second reason relates to the conception of social science and its role in society. Documenting the perceptions and discourse of those low on the economic scale allows seldom-heard voices to become part of the social record.

Social historians of these strata have faced difficulties regarding their sources that political and economic historians have not. The "archaeology" of sentiments and ideologies has to be based upon flimsy interpretations of preserved statements or the writings of untrained observers. Documentation gathered in small-scale studies, while incorporating meanings attached to certain actions or situations, broadens the interpretation of larger problems because it gives this perspective. Neither of these reasons, however, implies a return to subjectivist approaches, and the concept of *verstehen* is being revived, not in opposition, but in addition, to other approaches. This revival is a symptom of greater pluralism in social research and in its definition as an instrument for knowledge.

Notes

1. Jorge Graciarena and Rolando Franco, "Social Formations and Power Structures in Latin America," *Current Sociology* 26, no. 1 (1978).

2. Richard N. Adams and Charles C. Cumberland, *United States University Cooperation in Latin America: A Study Based on Selected Programs in Bolivia, Chile, Peru and Mexico* (East Lansing, Mich.: Institute of Research on Overseas Programs, 1960).

3. Charles O'Neil, "Problems of Innovation in Higher Education: The University of Brasilia, 1961–1964," *Journal of Inter-American Studies and World Affairs* 15, no. 4 (1973).

4. Merle Kling, "The State of Research on Latin America," in *Social Science Research in Latin America,* ed. Charles Wagley (New York: Columbia University Press, 1964), p. 168.

5. Rex Hopper, "Research on Latin America in Sociology," in ibid.

6. José Nun, "Notes on Political Science and Latin America," in *Social Science in Latin America,* ed. Manuel Diégues, Jr., and Bryce Wood (New York: Columbia University Press, 1967).

7. Jorge Balán, "Notas sobre los programas nuevos de posgraduación en ciencias sociales en el Brasil," mimeographed (Rio de Janeiro: Ford Foundation, 1973).

8. Gino Germani, *La sociología en la América Latina* (Buenos Aires: Editorial Universitaria, 1964); and idem, "The Professor and the Catedra," in *The Latin American University,* ed. Joseph Maier and Richard W. Weatherhead (Albuquerque: University of New Mexico Press, 1979).

9. Hanns-Albert Steger, *Las universidades en el desarrollo social de la América Latina* (Mexico: Fondo de Cultura Económica, 1974); and idem, "The European Background," in *The Latin American University,* ed. Maier and Weatherhead. See also Richard R. Renner, ed., *Universities in Transition: The United States Presence in Latin American Higher Education* (Gainesville: University of Florida, Center for Latin American Studies, 1973).

10. Kalman H. Silvert and Leonard Reissman, *Education, Class and Nation: The Experience of Chile and Venezuela* (New York: Elsevier, 1976).

11. William R. Crawford, *A Century of Latin American Thought,* rev. ed. (Cambridge: Harvard University Press, 1961).

12. See, for example, Aldo Solari et al., *Teoría, acción social y desarrollo en América Latina* (Mexico: Siglo XXI, 1976).

13. Wanderley G. dos Santos, "A imaginacão político-social brasileira," *Dados* 2, no. 3 (1967), pp. 182–193; and Henry J. Steiner, "Legal Education and Social Change: Brazilian Perspectives," *American Journal of Comparative Law* 18 (1971).

14. Solari et al., *Teoría, acción social y desarrollo.*

15. Ralph L. Beals, "Anthropology in Contemporary Mexico," in *Contemporary Mexico: Papers of the IV International Congress of Mexican History,* ed. James W. Wilkie et al. (Berkeley: University of California Press; Mexico: El Colegio de México, 1976).

16. Michael E. Burke, "The University of Mexico and the Revolution, 1910–1940," *The Americas* 34, no. 2 (1977), pp. 252–273.

17. Graciarena and Franco list 121 works in their bibliography to "Social Formations and Power Structures in Latin America."

18. Charles Wagley, ed. *Social Science Research in Latin America* (New York: Columbia University Press, 1964); and Diégues and Wood, *Social Science in Latin America.*

19. Beals, "Anthropology in Contemporary Mexico."

20. Gonzalo Aguirre Beltrán, *El proceso de aculturación* (Mexico City: Universidad Nacional Autónoma de México, 1957).

21. Beals, "Anthropology in Contemporary Mexico."

22. Wagley, *Social Science Research in Latin America.*

23. Ronald J. Duncan, ed., *The Anthropology of the People of Puerto Rico* (San German: Inter American University of Puerto Rico, 1981).

24. Adams and Cumberland, *United States University Cooperation in Latin America.*

25. Richard O. Lambert, *Language and Area Studies Review,* American Academy of Political and Social Science, Monograph no. 17 (Philadelphia, 1973).

26. Institute for International Education, *Latin American Studies: New Roles, New Constraints,* IIE Report no. 7 (1975); and Alejandro Portes, "Trends in International Research Cooperation: The Latin American Case," *American Sociologist* 10 (1975): 131–140.

27. Hector Maletta, "Cuatrocientas tesis doctorales norteamericanas sobre el Perú (1869–1976)," *Estudios andinos* 8, no. 15 (1979), pp. 57–134.

28. Jorge Graciarena, "Algunas consideraciones sobre la cooperación internacional y el desarrollo reciente de la investigación sociológica," *Revista latinoamericana de sociología* 1, no. 2 (1965), pp. 231–242; and Johann Galtung, "Los factores socioculturales y el desarrollo de la sociología en América Latina, *Revista latinoamericana de sociología* 1, no. 1 (1965), pp. 72–102.

29. The scandal erupted first in Chile in 1965, but spread rapidly throughout Latin America. A good collection of materials about the project and its aftermath can be found in Irving L. Horowitz, ed., *The Rise and Fall of Project Camelot: Studies in the Relationship between Social Science and Practical Politics*, rev. ed. (Cambridge: MIT press, 1974).

30. Institute for International Education, *Latin American Studies,* p. 6.

31. Bennett M. Berger, Review of Edward Shils' *The Calling of Sociology and Other Essays on the Pursuit of Learning, Society* 18, no. 2 (1981), pp. 84–87.

32. Glaucio A.D. Soares, "Latin American Studies in the United States: A Critique and a Proposal," *Latin American Research Review* 11, no. 2 (1976), pp. 51–69.

33. Daniel Levy, *University and Government in Mexico* (New York: Praeger, 1978).

34. Jerry Haar, *The Politics of Higher Education in Brazil* (New York: Praeger, 1976).

35. David O. Hansen et al., "Rural Sociology in Brazil: Institutional Growth (1965–1977)," *International Review of Modern Sociology* 9 (1979): 31–48.

36. Julio Cezar Melatti, "Situacão e problemática da antropología no Brasil," *América indígena* 40, no. 2 (1980), pp. 225–279.

37. Daniel Levy, "Higher Education Policies in Authoritarian Regimes: Comparative Perspectives on the Chilean Case," mimeographed (New Haven: Yale University, Institute for Social and Policy Studies, 1980).

38. Ibid.

39. Carlota Jackisch, "Situación de las ciencias sociales en la Argentina" (Buenos Aires: CLACSO, 1980).

40. Leopoldo J. Bartolomé, "La antropología en la Argentina: problemas y perspectivas," *América indígena* 40, no. 2 (1980), pp. 207–215.

41. Enrique Bernales, "Estado y problemas actuales de las ciencias sociales en el Perú" (Buenos Aires: CLACSO, 1979).

42. Ibid.

43. Portes, "Trends in International Research Cooperation"; and Solari et al., *Teoría, acción social y desarrollo.*

44. Jorge Graciarena, "Algunos problemas en la orientación de los programas de posgrado en ciencias sociales en América Latina," *Revista paraguaya de sociología* 10, no. 26 (1973), pp. 7–24.

45. David Maybury-Lewis, ed., *Dialectical Societies: The Gê and Bororó of Central Brazil* (Cambridge: Harvard University Press, 1979); and Anthony Seeger, *Os indios e nós: Estudos sobre sociedades tribais brasileiras* (Rio de Janeiro: Editora Campus, 1980).

46. Soares, "Latin American Studies in the United States."

47. Nun, "Notes on Political Science and Latin America."

Part III
Social Sciences and Public Policy: Problems in Application

10 Application of the Social Sciences to Public Policies: Producers, Consumers, and Mechanisms of Mediation

Edgardo Boeninger

Any attempt to analyze the existing relation between social-science research and public policies, however preliminary and tentative, requires an initial definition of purpose and perspective. In a discussion about strengthening the social sciences in developing regions, the central focus obviously must be the social sciences rather than public policies; one must, however, also keep in mind the nature of the latter and the factors that affect them. On the other hand, the subject may also be treated purely descriptively and limited to an attempt to present events, their causes, and possible outcomes. In the last case, the view of the future must not be a simple prediction or extrapolation of tendencies, but should present several hypotheses about what is considered necessary and desirable.

This chapter attempts to combine both focuses. Because it is primarily a personal interpretation based on the author's familiarity with Latin America, and with one country in particular, Chile, the lack of empirical study plainly limits the validity of the descriptive panorama presented here. The attempted glance into the future, in turn, is conditioned by the premise that in terms of their application to public policies, the social sciences must be evaluated in light of their ability to contribute to the resolution of the most compelling problems of the developing world. Finally, the critical judgments made in this chapter are inspired by a deep commitment to democratic values.

General Considerations Concerning the Social Sciences

In an analysis of the social sciences' influence on or utility in public policy, the question immediately arises whether research and scientific knowledge or the evolution of ideas exerts greater influence.

Without a doubt, the primary systematic expression of thought concerning the broad field of social factors found in Latin America is the essay. Authors of this genre have been thinkers, intellectuals who interpreted the

251

social reality confronting them and frequently wished to transform it. The essay "is more commentary than information, more interpretation than fact, more reflection than hard evidence about the topic, more creation than erudition, more [postulation] than demonstration, more opinion than dogmatic affirmation."[1] The thinker pretends, above all, to persuade the reader of the truth or merit of his ideas; he explores the unknown, searching for ways to overcome his ignorance and proposing ways of changing the status quo. Because the essayist does not attempt to give conclusive proof of a hypothesis, we are not exactly in the realm of science. It must be recognized, however, that ideas presented in essays have been the driving forces in a number of social sciences and have exercised a strong influence on the actual development of Latin American countries.

This observation necessarily leads us to consider the relations among social science, ideology, and social philosophy. What is the role of the social sciences in the progress of society? Should they concern themselves with the definition and formulation of social objectives and their translation into policy—that is, into proposals of social action? The answers to these questions are linked to the problem of whether it is possible for the social sciences to be neutral in terms of values (the permanent aspiration of every science) or whether, on the contrary, they are inevitably contaminated by value judgments and by the controversies and conflicts of each historical moment.

This is not the appropriate place to look into the "unresolved opposition between objective explanation and normative prescription, that is to say between knowledge and doctrine."[2] It is sufficient to indicate that, in ways and degrees that differ from one discipline to another, social scientists roughly regard this matter in one of four ways. The choice they make defines and strongly influences the orientation of their studies.

1. The *militant option* is that of a social science committed to a specific conception of society. This posture is usually critical and always to some degree radical with respect to reality, which it aspires to transform. Thus understood, social science operates tightly linked to ideologies, supporting and strengthening their influence or contributing to their modification. In the militant option, both research and development of social thought do tend to be strictly contained within existing ideology. On the other hand, they can also be critical or perhaps create new ideology. Finally, the militant approach can introduce new shades or variations resulting in a departure from the original rigid framework, thus producing ideological evolution. In any case, colleagues who share this militancy consider the promotion of the ideology and its proposals for social transformation the essential point of reference and principal task. Committed social science, then, deliberately ideologizes social analysis and research, however latent the tendency may be in some social disciplines or fields of knowledge.

From this perspective, the influence of social thought or of social research upon public policies is exercised through ideologies and their concrete political expressions.

2. A *critical option* seeks to explain and judge social facts and the content of the social sciences through explicitly identifying values and other subjective premises to which diverse theories, analyses, or propositions all conform. Adherents of this approach would like scientific activity to start from a theoretical viewpoint that defines assumptions of analysis as well as moral orientations, priorities, and legitimate means. As in the militant position, there is a bias, the differences being that in the critical option this bias is openly accepted as value judgment and not as science, and that it may or may not be tied to a specific ideology. Its militancy is possible but not necessary, because the value judgments involved are specific to each case and have no inevitable universality. The humanist approaches seem to adhere to this conception.

3. The rigorously *scientific option* endeavors to be absolutely objective and neutral with respect to values. Because it seeks to describe and explain social processes and phenomena accurately, its aim is to formulate precise orientations for practical conduct. From one point of view, this aim translates into the concept of a technical optimum, in the sense that, confronted with a certain problem or social fact, science supposedly can deliver a response that identifies the "best" solution. This approach highlights the operative significance of the social sciences: it aspires to offer a set of ever more nearly perfect instruments by means of continuous improvement.

4. An *explicative and interpretative option* does not concern itself with the relation between theory and praxis, for it does not try to formulate predictions or offer solutions of strict scientific precision. Its main purpose is to understand social phenomena that have actually taken place. Historically oriented social science can affect policies only through its influence on social thought and ideologies.

However, relations between the militant or critical option and the scientific or technocratic position in the social sciences do not in practice conform to the simple schema just presented. In the first place, it is necessary to recognize that "ideology surrounds social science on all sides, but is never confused with it."[3] In the social sciences, ideological motivation and scientific purpose frequently coexist in any undertaking, and "a wish to serve that can only be sustained by ideological assumptions is necessarily found in the final limits of that task."[4]

At the same time, all the options have in common an aspiration for scientific objectivity and truth. It is, in fact, possible to acknowledge the role of values in social knowledge while maintaining the ideal of impartiality without which science is impossible.

With respect to this controversial subject, a noted author has indicated that

> although the laws of logic and the prerequisites for recognizing something
> as true are universal, the concepts, models, premises, assumptions, para-
> digms, theories or questions put forward by the social sciences are in a great
> measure peculiar. Although it wouldn't make sense to speak of an African
> truth, it is pertinent on the other hand, to affirm that there is an African
> economy which differs from the European economy.[5]

It is possible to reduce biases and errors through rigorous analysis, by accumulation of evidence, and by making value assumptions explicit. However, there will always be an ideological residue.

For present purposes, inspired social thought loaded with value judgments is considered to be as important as scientific knowledge. At the same time, together with research, essays, and other forms of intellectual production, learning from reality—that is, the accumulation of experience that arises from concrete social processes—is also an important source of judgment for the implementation of public policy.

Finally, in reality things tend to be different. For example, the most militant positions of social thought, such as the diverse currents of Marxism, have the sharpest pretense of scientific rigor (on which the force of that ideology partly depends). Meanwhile, formulations that appear to be more scientific and technocratic, such as those of the Chicago School of Economics, undoubtedly possess ideological traits and are based on value-laden assumptions about human attitudes and behavior.

The ambiguous connection between appearance and reality, and the unclear perception of existing limits between science and ideology, are elements of great importance for any analysis of the impact of social sciences on public policies. The spectacular progress of scientific knowledge in the contemporary world has made it not only an increasingly indispensable and efficient instrument for solving problems, but also a source of power of increasingly decisive strength. The power that scientific knowledge confers on the individual possessing it is certainly a stimulus for the social sciences and their application to problems of development. However, it also generates the temptation to manipulate. The social sciences cannot escape the risk of corruption that always accompanies power. Apart from its moral implications, this fact leads us to explore relationships between social science and public policy other than those stemming from theoretical or formal considerations. In short, we must conclude that the social sciences have not yet achieved an objective status as sciences strong enough to avoid constant tension between the concepts of committed and neutral science.

The fact that the social sciences concern themselves to a greater or lesser extent with the conflicting problems of society makes them strongly polemic and makes more visible the decisive components of their value-laden roots. In this respect the social sciences differ radically from the natural and exact sciences. Unlike the latter, the social sciences can genuinely flourish only in an atmosphere of freedom. The USSR, for example, has achieved spectacular scientific progress, but no Soviet social science exists beyond the techniques and instruments developed to operate within the specific framework of government-enforced political, economic, and social methods. It follows that under authoritarian regimes, the contribution social sciences can make to public policy is severely reduced or at least distorted by the monopoly usually enjoyed by studies, essays, or proposals that coincide with the ideology or political beliefs of the government.

Moreover, in nondemocratic situations, the political importance of social thought and knowledge fosters among those who hold power a permanent and nearly irresistible temptation to keep that thought and knowledge under tight control. As a noted American sociologist has indicated, social scientists are always salient candidates for political purges whenever the opportunity presents itself.

General Considerations Concerning Public Policies

Public policies are a fundamental expression of the instruments of action available to the state to achieve its economic, social, and political goals.

> Public policies are options aimed at solving problems. They form part of a broader political process of which they are partial and visible definitions, and [they operate] in a certain social ambit with the participation of agents which adopt certain positions with regard to them. They consist of state actions and omissions reflecting a certain predominant orientation and are the result of the interplay of support, opposition, and negotiations that characterize the evolution of any community.[6]

Objective knowledge, values, interests, and prejudice combine in varying proportions. Reason is thus allowed to flourish, but passions also flow intensely, and moral or ideological considerations often become decisive.

The influence of scientific research in shaping and implementing public policies obviously depends on the nature of the latter. On the one hand, there are policies at the global and national level—such as a development plan or strategy, or the political project of government; on the other hand are specific regional or sectorial policies that operate within a more limited arena and may or may not be linked with global policy. Researchers, then, are confronted with macro or micro policies whose relative autonomy with respect to the political process is variable, as are the pattern and intensity of its relation with thought, research, and knowledge generated by social science.

In almost any public policy there exists a degree of tension between political and technical factors. The latter may have an important, even decisive, weight, particularly when researchers have demonstrated substantial, cumulative progress with regard to their ability to draw up proposals and carry out actions of varying nature based on the growing body of available knowledge. Most public decisions, however, are ultimately political, in the sense that they favor the preferences of some groups of society more than those of others.

The foregoing remark is not applicable to policies meant to achieve goals already defined by a previous decision (which may have been political in nature). In this case, policies deal with finding efficient means for given ends, and operative or instrumental aspects come to be of greatest significance. Even in these cases, however, a distinction can be established between legitimate and illegitimate means. Therefore, the distinction is not as radical as it seems and really involves no more than a change in the relative weight, for policy purposes, of normative factors and neutral knowledge.

On the other hand, not all valid problem-solving knowledge comes from thought or social science. In most cases, the complex nature of public-policy problems requires the simultaneous application of lessons derived from such fields as the biological sciences, engineering, and management, as well as from social knowledge. In other words, social technologies understood as instruments for coping with social problems (assuming that the long-term plan, the immediate political program, and the specific ends desired have been previously defined) have a marked interdisciplinary character that does not belong exclusively (and at times not even mainly) to the field of social science. The multiple issues tied to the process of urbanization, to public health programs, or to the eradication of extreme poverty are examples.

From another perspective, the extent to which the social sciences can affect public policies depends on adopted development strategy and, more precisely, on the role of the state. If the state plays a minor role, the application of social-science findings is accordingly limited, mostly within the bounds of specific policies, although at an ideological level they may have played a significant part in the selection of the development strategy itself. In such cases, social researchers are faced with public policies, often implicit, that consist more in omissions than in deliberate action.

Some regimes, then, resort more extensively than others to public policies, and these governmental orientations undoubtedly generate demands and exert pressure on the social sciences. In Latin America, however, the idea of making systematic use of social knowledge to solve concrete social problems has not yet been fully incorporated into prevalent culture, despite the fact that the weight of political thought or social philosophy is unanimously acknowledged.

Other factors determining the degrees and ways in which social knowledge may be used to formulate and execute public policy are the operating capacity and level of technical sophistication of the state. Systematic response to accumulated knowledge is possible only if the public-sector bureaucracy has adequately developed its institutions, its human resources, and its decision-making mechanisms. This fact holds true at both the global level and the various levels of state administration. It is difficult to imagine, for example, adequate utilization of political science without a nucleus of political scientists on the presidential advisory staff. Likewise, proper use of economic efficiency criteria on educational subjects is unlikely if no economists work for the decision-making body of the corresponding governmental branch.

Diversity of Disciplines, Types of Research, and Public Policies

There is no doubt that the various social disciplines have reached different levels of development or maturity, that they enjoy unequal recognition or scientific legitimacy, and, consequently, that they exert varying degrees of influence. These differences, however, do not apply equally at the macropolitical level and at the level of more-specific policies.

Economics is normally considered the most scientific of social sciences because it possesses the largest body of generally accepted knowledge. The discipline has developed an impressive number of instruments and techniques for its everyday application. Although the instruments used in market economics and those applied in the central planning of economic development differ perceptibly, a substantial array is available to each. Moreover, the two fields share a body of common knowledge. In empirical research, accumulation and interpretation of data, hypothesis formulation, and the application of this information to a wide range of social problems, the superior progress achieved in economics is beyond question. Thus, even though economics has not yet divested itself of polemics and the ideological roots of the major schools of economic thought remain important considerations, economics has acquired a scientific respectability much greater than, say, sociology or political science. This status is closely related to the claim of many of its disciples that it is already an exact science.

The concern of sociology and political science with global—often conflictual—problems and the fact thay they have not developed instruments and techniques to the same extent as economics have limited their contributions to public policy despite achievements in specific fields such as the sociology of organizations, public opinion studies, bureaucratic theory, and industrial relations.

At the macrostate level, however, this scientific hierarchy does not appear to be valid. In setting global political goals, development strategies, and major social, political, or economic reforms, social thought, be it of sociological, political, or historical origin, can exert as much influence as economics, or more. It is here that we enter the domain of social theory and philosophy and frequently touch upon ideology and values, overstepping the bounds of exclusively scientific elaboration. Thus, at the global level, the current trend of sophisticated marginal analysis and the refined measurement techniques that are prevalent in economics often do not carry as much weight as economists are prone to believe.

Thus, research and social analysis (about ownership of land and agricultural production, for example) carried out in the United Nations Economic Commission for Latin America (CEPAL) and other Latin American research institutions contributed decisively to the development, in the early 1960s, of proposals for structural reforms, especially agrarian reform. Such reforms figured prominently in the political platforms and governmental commitments of many nations in the region and became high-priority goals of the Alliance for Progress.

Similarly, with respect to the viability of democracy in developing countries, the work of Samuel P. Huntington (who noted the tendency toward "praetorianism" producd by a chronic imbalance between political participation and political institutionalization) may well have influenced the recent development of authoritarian concepts in Latin America. Nor can we disregard the impact of dependency theory, supported mainly by Latin American sociologists, in relation to foreign affairs and to attitudes toward foreign investment and multinational corporations. Thus, whatever the scientific validity of these various theories, the fact remains that the social science–public policy relationship has varying features depending upon the level of analysis, and differs from case to case according to the relative weight of one or another social discipline.

History is a special case. Exploring the past for answers to troubling problems has a long tradition; historical work was well developed long before the twentieth century. Nevertheless, a direct relation does not exist between history and public policy. Mere accounts of events seem to have no broader significance. Even historical studies of a more interpretative nature do not at first appear to have any perceptible influence on present or future social processes; but such appearances may be misleading.

With regard to three Chilean historians of the nineteenth century, a contemporary Chilean historian notes that "the contribution of these historians is marked by . . . positivism as a scientific conception and liberalism as an ideological position."[7] If the work of these historians is accepted as historical truth, the influence thus exerted on society is ideologically biased, because lessons drawn from this particular interpretation of the past will carry the stamp of positivism and liberal ideology. More specifically, though in a very different sense, the work of three other national historians is a central point of reference for the most noteworthy ideologues of the current Chilean regime in their attempt to justify authoritarian politics. These historians—and the ideologues—subscribe to a historical interpretation that places the peak of national greatness during the years of what is known as the Conservative Republic (1831–1861).

A significant percentage of social-science research has been historically focused, and although such research may have little relation to specific public policy, it may nevertheless exert very significant influence at the level of overall strategy and broad social goals, which in turn may directly affect specific policies. The same applies also to work in theoretical fields, thesis studies, and all kinds of interpretative research. One should keep in mind that we are dealing here with a type of scientific activity that, while having the influence already indicated, is destined for self-consumption by the scientific or intellectual community. Its impact—as in the case of dependency theory—normally originates from numerous studies conducted by a sizable number of persons over a significant period.

More directly useful for purposes of specific public policies are studies devoted to the collection and systematic processing of data, to empirical generalization, or to the design of social indicators, as well as the development of technical instruments and of methodology for social research. The development of sampling techniques, for example, has helped governments to gather much valuable information concerning attitudes, behavior, and social aspirations. Improvement of methodologies has enabled governments to set up particular policies, as well as to determine or amend sectorial programs, or even broad outlines of general policy. In turn, studies that contribute to the correction of official statistics usually bring about changes in diagnosis and therefore in related policies.

Thematic studies centered on problems of varying degrees of generality constitute another field directly linking social science to public policy. Clearly, this is true of the analysis of strategies or broad problems of development, as well as of research on more specific topics such as the behavior of wages or prices, policy decision-making mechanisms, or the distribution of wealth and income.

In these areas, economics has without doubt had a prevailing and even excessive influence, notwithstanding the increasing importance of other contributions through social indicators, public opinion studies, and the like. The predominance of economics remains uncontested, however, in the area of technical tools. The variety of instruments at the disposal of the economist in such fields as monetary policy, taxation, financial markets, exports, incentives for regional and sectorial development, and planning techniques is a matter of great importance to the operation of the modern state.

In the other social sciences, techniques are less well developed. The problem is more acute in Latin America because of the greater imbalance in the relative levels of development achieved by the different disciplines. In Europe, for example, considerable progress has been made in devising methods to induce stable political majorities in parliamentary systems and to enhance government continuity; the "constructive veto" provided for in the German constitution is a case in point. There has been no parallel evolution of this kind in Latin America.

This being the case, a policy for strengthening the social sciences in Latin America should attend first to the needs of disciplines that are relatively less developed, such as sociology and political science. Further, priority should be given to comparative studies, a type of research that allows social scientists to take creative advantage of progress achieved in other countries. Comparative studies should include not only investigations of the intraregional context but also comparisons with more developed countries, concentrating on cases with relevant similarities.

Interdisciplinary work should also be encouraged as a means of addressing the complex problems facing contemporary society, and particularly the Third World. These problems are related to a sharp imbalance between social aspirations and the existing cultural and material reality—a volatile situation tending toward bitter conflict. Although this is in no way a new idea, attempts at interdisciplinarity have not yet been really successful. To improve the chances of obtaining better interdisciplinary results, a more solid development of the individual disciplines is required. Moreeover, within each particular science, a better understanding of the limitations of the particular field is needed, along with a minimal mastery of the language and concepts of the other sciences most directly related to the main interests of the researcher.

The Production of Social Knowledge

Social scientists, whose specific activity is research (notwithstanding the fact that research can also lead to production of social thought), are usually clustered in institutions of a permanent nature, including university departments; private research institutes; research departments of public organizations (such as central banks and departments of housing, health, or education); national, regional, or sectorial planning offices; and international organizations (including the Economic Commission for Latin America [CEPAL], Latin American Institute for Economic and Social Planning [ILPES], Centro Latinoamericano de Demografía [CELADE], United Nations Food and Agricultural Organization [FAO], Organization of American States [OEA], Facultad Latinoamericana de Ciencias Sociales

[FLACSO], and Consejo Latinoamericano de Ciencias Sociales [CLACSO]). To a lesser degree, individual research and thesis writing are conducted independently with scholarship funds from American or European foundations, or with funds from national committees of scientific research. Universities have traditionally been considered the leading institutions in this field; in the majority of Latin American countries they house the greatest number of social scientists. Nevertheless, recent trends point to a decrease in the universities' share in the overall production of social-science research and in their influence on public policy. This appears particularly true when universities are compared with autonomous and specialized research institutes.

One reason for the universities' decreased share in research may be that the number of university students has grown very rapidly in recent decades. The increased teaching load of professors leaves them with less time for research. In addition, demands on university faculty have multiplied and become more exacting. Professors can no longer rely on a small number of foreign textbooks; students and university authorities alike recognize the need to develop additional teaching material based on indigenous realities. Moreover, the content of research related to professional duties is essentially determined by the requirements of teaching and does not often appear to be of interest to policymakers.

On the other hand, universities have increasingly fallen prey to the political conflicts and instability so common in Latin American countries. Not only have they encountered recurrent student activism; in many cases, the universities have also become the "refuge of dissident intellectuals," an event to be expected considering that such persons may find it difficult to get a job in the public sector, may not want to work for the state for ideological reasons, and usually have no interest in nonintellectual private activities of any kind. This disruptive presence is sometimes encouraged by governments eager to exhibit their universities as proof of the existence of democratic pluralism in their countries. This, in turn, leads to confrontation between the state and the university, or at least to chronic isolation of the university from public activity. When the latter occurs, communication between social scientists and government is blocked. In extreme cases the entire university adopts a militant stance, and intellectual production moves away from subjects that bear any relation to specific public policies, concentrating instead on radical criticism of society.

The example of Cuba proves once again that social science cannot flourish without a minimum of political and intellectual liberty, even when the state provides heavy support for the development of so-called social techniques and tools. Research in Cuba can take place only within the framework of "scientific socialism." In a more general sense, although there are militant social scientists of great merit, it is difficult to imagine a militant social science, if by this is meant commitment or obedience to a particular political regime. An individual's value system or ideological ties certainly do not prevent serious intellectual work.

Of far greater significance in Latin America is the problem currently posed to universities and the social sciences by authoritarian military regimes. As a rule, these regimes have shown great intolerance for research of a critical nature. This attitude has often unleashed repressive processes that tend to be particularly severe in the universities, due to the institutional power of the universities themselves and to the desire of the government to avoid "contamination" of university students. At times, economics can partially escape these restrictions. Perhaps more important, many autonomous research institutes have been able to survive and even enjoy a degree of freedom (including the Instituto Torcuato di Tella and Centro de Estudios de Estado y Sociedad [CEDES] in Argentina, Centro Brasileiro de Analise e Planejamento [CEBRAP] and the Getulio Vargas Foundation in Brazil, and the Corporación de Investigaciones Económicas para America Latina [CIEPLAN] in Chile). In Chile there have also arisen centers of academic activity in the social sciences sponsored by the Catholic church (the Instituto Latinoamericano para el Desarrollo [ILADES], Academy of Christian Humanism, and, recently, FLACSO).

The political factor is not, however, the only, and perhaps not even the main, factor that has stimulated the development of social-science research centers separate from the university. Increased teaching duties, the progressively acute budgetary problems faced by universities in this period of accelerated expansion, the suffocating effects of the university bureaucracy resulting from institutional growth, and the other problems mentioned previously have resulted in the establishment of a network of specialized research institutes. These institutes today produce an increasingly significant portion of high-level studies. Moreover, because of their thematic concentration, they are particularly apt counterparts for individuals or institutions in search of social knowledge needed for application to or influence on the macro or micro policies of the state.

This situation is a mixed blessing. Universities, as the main suppliers of higher education, are sorely in need of an adequate atmosphere for high-quality research. At the very least, master's and doctoral programs can be conducted only in an environment in which research and scientific inquiry are a central part of everyday academic life.

Research departments of government agencies should not be underestimated. Studies produced by researchers working at the central banks or in the national planning offices are known to be of high quality in several countries. However, they suffer from serious limitations in that the chief concern of state entities usually is day-to-day action. As a result, low priorities attached to such groups restrict budgetary allocations and their ability to keep in touch with ministers, departments, or agency directors. Finally, government research departments work under the constraints imposed by the operating style of such action-oriented organizations; superiors not only select research goals and determine subjects and guidelines, but also dictate a rigid schedule for completion. All this is incompatible with serious scientific activity. Given these difficulties, there is a growing inclination to recognize the advantages of a division of labor in which scientific activity is carried out separately, outside the state bureaucracy, under conditions that guarantee the autonomy essential to research. The apparent advantage of the close relation between producer and consumer found within government agencies is counterbalanced by many limitations to the effectiveness of government research departments.

Similar conditions prevail in planning offices. These offices, however, have the peculiar quality of being simultaneously producers of knowledge, channels of intermediation, and proponents of public policy in several sectors. Moreover, they generally enjoy a relatively autonomous position within the structure of government. Their role as research bodies has been growing even while most countries in the region appear to have abandoned development plans and other instruments typical of a formal planning process. The contribution of the planning offices already exceeds the accumulation of facts and routine information gathered by the national accounting offices. Because the planning offices tend to deal more with prediction and with increasing state coherence and unity of action as well as proposing solutions to specific social problems, they may also play an important role in the application of social knowledge to public policy. Their mastery of available knowledge—either of their own creation or obtained from outside sources—may finally endow them with a degree of power they would never have been able to attain through the planning function itself.

Institutions whose main concern is the study of long-term problems are in a better position than others to demand and induce pertinent research work. What is more, such institutions can fulfill their functions adequately only if their work program explicitly includes an important research component. A good example is the case of the Junta del Acuerdo of Cartagena, the secretarial branch of the Andean Pact. In the first years of its existence, this group had enough time at its disposal to reinforce its proposals through serious research undertaken by itself or contracted to others. Because of the junta's later involvement in negotiations among member countries, the studies had considerable influence on the policies for industrial and technological development approved under the terms of the Andean Pact.

Of the agencies producing social knowledge in Latin America, the Economic Commission for Latin America (CEPAL) illustrates the diverse ways in which the social sciences can influence public policies. CEPAL has never been a research center as such. In Latin America, however, there is no other institution comparable to CEPAL. Its ideas have often been an interpretation of and reaction to events; at other times it has been anticipatory and highly creative. For decades it has been a significant force in the development of the region.

CEPAL's ideas came to be an ideology of Latin American development. Its views on terms of trade, industrialization through import substitution, and the need for agrarian and other structural reforms have affected the development strategies of many countries. The content of the Alliance for Progress was similarly affected. With few exceptions, CEPAL's influence was not the result of the relationship between a specific study and a particular public policy, but of the weight carried by ideas carefully thought out and patiently disseminated during two decades. These ideas influenced macro state policy in many ways and at the highest levels of national decision making.

The problems of financing research, a factor which limits volume and quantity, relevance and autonomy, affect universities and autonomous research centers equally. Insofar as it creates a precarious state of financial dependence, lack of funding makes social-science research extremely vulnerable; subjects and projects that interest the clients may have no relation to those that might be considered important from the perspective of public policies, to the areas that most interest the researchers, or to fields in which the researchers enjoy comparative academic advantage. In addition, government and private business—important sources of funds—customarily frame their demands in ideological contexts and with relatively narrow political motivations, a circumstance not compatible with autonomous research. Bias thus introduced leads to loss of relevance and legitimacy, making it difficult to make use of research in public affairs.

One means of generating a more stable and increased flow of resources appears to lie in the promotion of research funds of the kind established by several national research committees and some Latin American universities. Foreign foundations could perhaps be helpful in the development of initiatives of this type. Their willingness to participate in a consortium with Latin American institutions, provided that autonomous management of resources is assured, might be a powerful catalyst and safeguard. At the current stage of Latin American development, major financial contributions to such a fund would probably have to be provided mainly by governments and international institutions. However, foundations could exercise a decisive promotional role and press for autonomous management—that is, for freedom from political censorship or interference. Toward this end, it would be necessary to establish boards of administration composed of persons of high scientific status.

This mechanism would allow emphasis to be placed on thematic areas or problems by allocating a certain percentage of the funds for such purposes, without limiting the researchers' freedom or imposing upon them a precise area of study. This approach could generate an important incentive for research in, say, applied social science.

An alternative to annual distribution of available resources is the creation of one or more endowment funds at national or regional levels. Initial capital would consist of contributions from governments, private sources, and international donors, and the endowments could operate as suggested in the preceding paragraphs.

The Consumers of Social Knowledge

Distinguishing between national public policies and those of a more limited nature can help identify relevant users of social research (including both expressions of social thought in the sense previously indicated and scientific knowledge). Focus on public policy excludes academic "self-consumption," but implies considering all social actors that in one way or another influence the formulation of public policy. It is unnecessary here to make the distinction, however valid, between conscious users and inadvertent consumers of social-science products; what matters is whether they participate in the process of making public decisions. So defined, relevant actors may have a significant role that can be either direct and immediate, indirect (through influence), or remote.

Accordingly, the consumers may be classified as follows: (1) government institutions, including the executive authority of the state as well as entities of the public sector (ministries, central banks, regional and national planning offices, autonomous sectorial institutions, and public corporations); (2) the legislative authority—that is, the parliament in countries with legitimate democratic regimes or whoever performs the legislative function if no congress exists; (3) political parties; (4) the armed forces; (5) religious bodies; and (6) unions, private business, and other social organizations that exert influence on public policy.

The significance of any one group, at either a global level or the level of individual policies, depends on its proximity to the problem or to decision making, on its political or bureaucratic weight or power, on its capacity to absorb social knowledge and thought, and on its degree of access and receptivity to such knowledge.

If knowledge is a source of power, its influence is multiplied—whether in the form of an objective contribution or a value formulation—when it is generated or wielded by a social actor of greater relative importance. From the perspective of the formal operation of the state, the weight of actors differs according to whether the political regime is a representative democracy or some form of authoritarianism or dictatorship. In the former, the parliament and political parties are salient agents in normal decision making, whereas in an authoritarian regime the process is distorted and perhaps the armed forces, together with certain technocrats and, at times, certain economic interest groups, tend to play the most decisive role. Moreover, in an authoritarian regime, some potential consumers are exposed to deformation, while others stay in hiding or are eliminated. Typically, in situations of this kind in Latin America, the Catholic church exerts an important influence. Functioning as a reactive element or moral judge, the church possesses considerable capacity for exerting pressure because of its enormous social base of believers.

The armed forces have not usually been consumers of social-science research. Only recently have they created structures conceived as explicit mechanisms for absorbing such kinds of knowledge (such as the military academies for postgraduate study or national-security academies). Moreover, the nature, values, and even cultural identity of institutions as specialized in orientation as the armed forces or the church constitute a kind of filter that, through distillation, leads to new and different interpretations of social-science production. These consumers normally have had no close relationship with social scientists, whose work fails adequately to consider the concerns that motivate the military or the church (though this situation may be due for swift change). These circumstances may have contributed to the ideological conquest of the armed forces that seems to have taken place in more than one Latin American country. They may also help to explain the lack of communication that often exists between economists and the clergy.

The bureaucracy of the state is an ever-present factor whose relative weight in public-policy formulation changes according to the characteristics and presence of other groups (such as political parties or the military). But the bureaucracy's power is closely correlated to its ability to absorb knowledge. Customarily, the public bureaucracy is the main direct consumer of the objective facts, indicators, and instruments contributed by social science and applicable to specific problems. On the other hand, social thought, global critique of society, and ideological constructs are best received by political parties, the armed forces, social organizations, or the church.

The consumers already cited differ in nature and in their reasons for placing demands upon the social sciences. One consumer may be seeking a more or less radical transformation of society. Another may simply be trying to take advantage of the eventual legitimizing capacity of scientific or intellectual proposals. A third may require only better availability of the tools necessary to achieve a particular purpose or goal. From another viewpoint, it is possible to distinguish effective and legitimate demands from those that are only apparent or destined for manipulation of the product. In this respect, the effective influence of the social sciences on public policy has no necessary correlation with the reliability of knowledge or the intellectual quality of the essays or studies undertaken.

A final consideration is whether the decisions as to which issues to study, for what purpose, and from which analytical perspective lie with social scientists or whether the preferences of contractors prevail. In this respect, the work of thinkers or essayists, such as historical interpretation or theoretical elaboration, tends to be free of external influence; it usually is an autonomous intellectual decision notwithstanding the cultural factors, ideology, intellectual environment, or international and local situations that may influence the individual's behavior. It appears that only research that deals with specific subjects and gathers and classifies data, elaborates or improves instruments, or is directly concerned with problem solving is prone to influence by the contractor. This influence takes effect either through outright payment of salary or by way of incentive mechanisms, such as research funds that establish thematic or disciplinary priorities.

In another type of situation, research is undertaken with funds made available by sources that neither use social knowledge nor act as formal channels of intermediation. The great American foundations are the most noteworthy examples of this type of source; in this case, the priorities of these foundations can become important determinants of the kind of research produced, which may in turn be applied to state policy. This is without doubt an important factor in countries where the degree of academic and cultural development is low. Such a relationship involves a certain degree of tension due to differences in perspective, goals, and cultural and political atmosphere between the sponsoring foundation and home-country scientists.

These facts have had a significant influence on the relative development of the various social disciplines in Latin America as well as on the theoretical outlook and methodological approach prevalent in a particular field. External donors have so far favored economics over sociology, political science, or history, mainly because the former is less controversial and therefore involves less risk for foreign foundations. As a result, economics has become dominant in the region and has come to be perceived as a mature social science. On the other hand, the support of foundations has led to greater emphasis on empirical research related to qualitative work on social theory. This has doubtless contributed to the rise of serious scientific work, but it may also have retarded creative thought related to values and ideology. Curiously, comparative studies, which could be of great utility in the international transfer of knowledge and of socially valid experiments, do not seem to have received high-priority treatment from the foundations.

The Relevance of Social Sciences for Public Policies: Kinds of Contribution

In considering social-science contributions to public policy, it is necessary to make a preliminary distinction between logical or formal contributions and effective influence. An objective judgment of relevance does not necessarily coincide with actual impact, for a variety of reasons involving power, culture, degree of institutionalization achieved by the social disciplines, the ability of the state or of political parties to digest knowledge, channels of intermediation available, and so on.

In order to illustrate this point, it may be noted that social ideas or social knowledge can be used simultaneously as information, as propaganda, and as a vehicle for criticizing the establishment. For example, a few years ago, the Catholic University of Chile conducted an important study known as "The Map of Extreme Poverty." In this project, valuable background data were presented on the scale, location, and characteristics of areas of critical poverty in the country. The research was done with great objectivity and conducted without any apparent political motive. It has been extensively used by Chile's national planning office and other public institutions as an information base for the elaboration of policies directed at fighting poverty. This in turn has led the military government to promise that the eradication of poverty is its top priority in the socioeconomic field. The study thus became a source of government legitimacy. At the same time, the regime has used it as a political weapon for blaming the existence of poverty in Chile on previous governments. In which way did the study achieve the greatest real impact—technically or through government use for self-serving political purposes?

A similar situation has developed with respect to some recent research by a Chilean sociologist, entitled "The Map of Extreme Wealth." This work provides background information about the apparent concentration of wealth in the country in recent years. So far, this study has served only the outlawed political opposition as a weapon against the government's economic policy. In turn, the government has attempted to ignore or refute the report's conclusions. It is obvious, however, that if a change of regime occurred, this study would have great influence on public policies; it would in effect be utilized to justify redistributive policies. Moreover, it is likely that if social and political actors were able to exert more pressure than they are now allowed to, this research would already have had some modifying effect on existing policy, even under the present regime.

It is obvious, then, that although relevant objective judgments may confirm the validity of a particular study, the effective impact of social-science research is related to a number of other factors that may or may not be present in a particular case. Stated differently, other things being equal, scientific production will have less influence when its objective relevance is questioned. A research project may be judged by the new knowledge it produces or on the basis of inputs for public policy that can be derived from it either on technical or political grounds.

In this connection, it may be pointed out that a number of examples of declared institutional goals point to the fact that social scientists, even in empirical, objective, fact-finding work, are increasingly committed to the cause of the world's underdogs. Survey work in rural areas, measurement of aspects of the quality of life, and concern for unemployment are examples of this promising trend.

From a broader perspective, it is not only research defined *stricto senso* that can generate relevant contributions to public policies; the evolution of ideas has also played an important role. The record of CEPAL supports this assertion. Through its contributions to development ideology and the establishment of social goals (economic growth and social development), definition of strategy (import substitution), suggestions for policies in certain fields (such as agrarian reform), and the search for more-efficient instruments (planning techniques), CEPAL has influenced Latin American development in many ways.

The activity of social scientists and intellectuals, then, gives rise to varied types and forms of contribution to and influence on public policies. These can be summarized as follows:

1. Stimulation of rational reflection—that is, "making people think."
2. Further development of theory and ideology; this should help broaden the perspective of social models and eventually increase rationality in the process of producing global political programs.
3. Diversification of options and development of new criteria for selecting alternatives.
4. Improvement of understanding in broad subject areas or in relation to specific topics.
5. Incorporation of present-day conditions, causal explanation, or interpretations of facts as elements to consider in decisions at both the macro-policy and lesser levels.
6. Development of useful criteria for the evaluation of past policies.
7. Development of instruments and techniques for the analysis of state policies or their more effective implementation.
8. Provision of quantitative and qualitative instruments and indicators for measurement.

By itself, this list does not mandate any conclusions. The list does, however, demonstrate the complexity of social-science contributions and indicates that valid contribution and actual influence are produced not only through empirical work and specific research projects, but in a multiplicity of ways, including value-based intellectual production linked to the general evolution of ideas and social thought. Therefore, any action intended to strengthen the social sciences should consider the value of creative capacity at various levels and take into account the corresponding requirements. These requirements are not identical for all levels. For example, the valu-

able contribution of the Catholic University of Chile in the area of investment project evaluation recognizes the fundamental need for rigorous scientific training, including not only the use of mathematical instruments but
also an adequate understanding of factors that determine social costs and
benefits. On the other hand, the blossoming of critical thought that is
capable of generating new approaches to the future of society or development strategies better suited to ideals of justice and peace will be possible
only under conditions of political freedom, an element that does not appear
to weigh heavily in the field of project evaluation.

The Channels for Transfer in the Application of Social Sciences to Public Policies

It was previously indicated that objective relevance and real influence are
frequently different things. To study both relevance and impact, an analysis
of the transfer mechanisms that link social sciences with public policies must
necessarily refer to the processes that actually produce influence.

The mechanisms of intermediation that these processes involve are
varied and defy simple classification. They can be either direct or indirect,
narrowly or broadly focused, of immediate or long-term effect. The formal
destination of a message is frequently not the area in which it exerts the
greatest influence. It is also true that the transmission of values, and even of
empirical knowledge, does not occur in a well-defined, logical sequence,
and that the absorption and legitimization of ideas take place via routes that
are for the most part impossible to delineate. Time horizons for processes of
this kind also remain unclear. Nevertheless, in general it appears safe to
assume that ties between a particular research topic and the public policies
to which it might be applied are probably established in accordance with
more direct and precise channels, and are transmitted more rapidly than
abstract ideas or broad concepts.

In some cases it also is possible to detect irrelevance or lack of adequate
absorptive capacity in the potential consumers. For example, if, as seems to
occur in several Latin American countries, the results of educational research are usually ignored in determining educational policy, the situation
probably reflects either inadequate orientation of research (at least from the
perspective of applied science), weakness in the educational bureaucracy,
lack of communication, or a combination of these three factors. In this
respect, a program intending to increase the application of social sciences to
public policy should begin by identifying situations of this type and attempting to resolve them in a positive manner.

From a different perspective, the ready acceptance given to certain
trends of social thought at one particular time may not be due to any of the

transfer mechanisms, but to a specific set of circumstances that determines an entirely different pattern of influence. For instance, the at-this-time-unchallenged hegemony of the Chicago School of Economics in the southern cone of Latin America was made possible by the fact that a phalanx of indigenous economists was trained in Chicago and became deeply committed to the theories prevalent in that particular school. Due to a complex set of political factors, the leaders of various military coups adopted that model and then proceeded to impose these policies by force.

In general terms, the mechanisms of intermediation between producers and consumers of social-science products take the following forms: (1) teaching, (2) technocratic groups in the public sector, (3) ideological channels, (4) intellectuals, (5) publications, and (6) shaping of opinion.

Teaching

Teaching is obviously the primary channel for the transfer of scientific knowledge, as well as of values and ideology. These aspects can be analytically separated, but are transferred in a package, making it difficult for the recipient to distinguish its components. Education generally attempts to enable the student to exercise independent evaluation and to employ various analytical techniques. With the exception of some high-quality theses or some specialized courses in specific fields, teaching cannot be expected to disseminate specific research work.

In this respect, a notorious imbalance exists in Latin America between progress recorded in economics and relative backwardness in systematic high-level training in sociology and political science. Without doubt, this is partly the result of political instability and the rise of authoritarian regimes in a number of countries. It is also a consequence of the impaired communication between foreign foundations and the countries in which they work; the foundations fear involvement in conflicts and the loss of confidence of governments regarding the foundations' intentions or ideological biases. Finally, Latin American universities have given low priority to the establishment of high-level programs in these disciplines and to the development of infrastructure sciences—such as philosophy and history—that are indispensable for serious social thought.

This disciplinary weakness adversely affects the impact on public policy: it feeds a tendency toward a superficial, pamphletarian social science that has a negative influence on rational political debate and on the process of public policy formulation. As a result, there are few public institutions or cases of decision making in which social scientists have been given the opportunity to participate, and centers for decision making in the public sector have to rely on an administration that has developed a pronounced economics bias. In short, there is little room in the bureaucracy for sociologists, political scientists, or historians, while well-trained economists are being recruited at a satisfactory pace.

Public Technocracy

This pattern suggests that the social sciences influence public policy through specific actors. Among these actors, what has come to be known as the public technocracy (advisory groups, research departments, expert committees, individual or institutional advisory agencies including international organizations) stands out as particularly significant. A finely knit network of this sort, including broadly defined interdisciplinary teams and close links with levels of political decision making, enhances the influence of public technocrats. It is clear that Latin America is witnessing the emergence of an increasingly technocratic state that has filled its bureaucracies with engineers and economists and largely ignored specialists from other social sciences. The growing power of knowledge has endowed these technocrats with a political role of increasing importance in the formulation of global and sectorial public policies; indeed, certain ministerial groups are composed primarily of economists.

Given that public responsibilities at the decision-making level are by definition political in character, the importance of ideologicopolitical intermediation between the social sciences and public policy is paramount. For example, it is easy to identify in several countries of the region research centers whose entire staff—or at least a significant portion of it—are widely considered to be the technocracy that would fill government posts should political power change hands. Their work, academic excellence notwithstanding, therefore has a political connotation. For that very reason, however, their work may also be influential in shaping the decisions of sensitive governments. On the other hand, in countries where authoritarian regimes impose censorship, such research centers may be subjected to rigorous repression.

Latin America has not yet witnessed a significant development of technocratic groups in support of political parties or the parliament. Other social actors that exert a truly strong influence on public policy, such as the armed forces or the Catholic church, likewise lack sufficient systematic support of this kind. It has not yet been clearly perceived that the progressive weakening of the parliamentary role in public decisions is largely the consequence of its inferior technical position.

Political parties face a similar challenge, which can be successfully overcome only through a systematic effort to organize, rationalize, and surmount the artificial barrier that in Latin America typically separates the political and technical spheres. One of the obstacles is the persistence of an attitude still prevalent in the region that ignores or underestimates the contribution that systematic thought and social knowledge can make to social problems.

Ideological Channels

The perception of belonging to the same community of shared ideology, basic values, or religion generates a trust that facilitates transfer of the products of social science from producers to users. To the degree that this mechanism of intermediation is strengthened, the behavior of such consumers will tend to become more rational, and debate in decision-making centers will be facilitated. The social sciences would thus have a more systematic influence on public policy.

With regard to the armed forces or the church, the strengthening of the intermediation mechanisms could be particularly important in cases in which the existence of authoritarian political regimes distorts the normal patterns of social influence by eliminating or tightly controlling social actors that play important roles in an open society.

Intellectuals

A closely related phenomenon is the relatively great influence of intellectuals in many Latin American countries. They enjoy high social status, which adds weight to their opinions. Their intermediation considerably shortens the lengthy process from invention to innovation; thus, as Albert Hirschman has noted, the ideas or theories of influential intellectuals quickly become attempts at social engineering. In this context, the power of social thought in Latin America is considerable, and therefore, in the definition of public policy, intellectuals face a particularly serious responsibility. As thinkers increasingly advocate objective scientific knowledge, the influence of social science in state policy will grow.

Intellectuals and scientists in Latin America frequently play a dual role. There is no well-defined separation between public and academic functions, such as exists in the United States and Europe. With certain exceptions, the social scientist in developed countries rarely leaves his academic career, though there is considerable communication between the public and the intellectual realms. Latin American social scientists have greater opportunity and inclination to work in the public sector. Consequently, a great number alternate between academic jobs at the universities and jobs in the public sector. This interrelation of roles is not only sequential; normally a permanent tie exists between the social scientist and public problems, especially political ones. In this way, many social scientists fulfill an important role as advisers and even as active members of political parties. These relations are probably of greater intensity among those inclined to a leftist ideology. They occur more frequently in some countries than in others, but to some degree they are present throughout Latin America.

Publications

Intellectual production has traditionally been disseminated through specialized books and journals, complemented by a growing number of meetings, workshops, seminars, and various kinds of national or international conferences. Latin American social scientists generally agree, however, that the principal channels for dissemination of their writings are extremely weak or insufficient, and that as a consequence, studies that are published in the region reach only a small number of readers and have a limited impact, either within the region or in other developing areas. To develop a more systematic and expeditious method of distribution of social-science literature on a larger scale, it might be advisable to create several specialized regional editorials for the humanities and social sciences as well as adequate distribution channels. They should be independent of government and combine efficient business management with high-level technical competence so as to guarantee pluralism and nondiscrimination. Similarly, a scientific information service could be created and linked to well-run journalistic networks. It could function somewhere in between scholarly scientific journals and nonspecialized newspapers. Finally, the publication of a social-science journal jointly sponsored by a large number of Latin American research centers could be attempted once again.

Shaping of Opinion

A less systematic intermediation mechanism is that of shaping opinion. The fact that it is less systematic does not lessen its significance for public policies. In the first place, the process of gaining acceptance for certain ideas, theories, or even objective facts is usually lengthy and painful. It is, however, necessary if the social sciences are to have an effective influence on public policy. A series of studies persistently centered on a certain subject or a group of researchers distributed among a variety of centers but dealing with some topic of common disciplinary or ideological interest are examples of this type of accumulation. The influence of dependency theory should once again be recalled in order not to underestimate this method of disseminating the products of social science.

The personal prestige of an individual intellectual has also sometimes been a factor of great importance. The strong and charismatic personality of Raúl Prebisch no doubt contributed decisively to the influence of CEPAL. Public polemics on specific problems or positions can also exert influence on public policy, either directly or through political channels.

Of great current and future importance is the role of the mass communications media, particularly television. The role of the traditional methods for spreading knowledge, which have been already mentioned, is no longer decisive. Television, some newspapers, and certain radio broadcasts are increasingly influential in the definition of public policy. Journalistic messages—especially those on television—have a powerful effect in molding the opinion of large numbers of citizens. Because journalistic reports, especially those on television (inevitably brief and synthetic), tend to manipulate information and seldom deliver it in full, the mass media are coveted by power seekers. It follows that the mass-media industry has a special responsibility to ensure that journalists and commentators have an adequate command of social knowledge indispensable to their professional role in rationalizing and balancing the media's impact.

In general, social researchers must explicitly seek a more productive relationship between producers and users of social-science knowledge. Producers and consumers of research require direct and routine contact so that social science may become an efficient instrument for the formulation and implementation of public policies. Social science must not confine itself to using indirect channels of communication, where risk of distortion is great. The influence of serious intellectual and scientific work would probably be greater if social scientists clearly perceived the concerns, problems, attitudes, hopes, prejudices, and fears that confront the social actors who in one way or another influence public policy. In other words, a more systematic demand for the production of social sciences must be developed.

It is clear that the social sciences play an important role in the definition of public policy and that their influence originates indistinctly in both scientific knowledge and social thought. The nature of existing relations varies according to whether they involve macro state policy or specific public policies of lesser scope. Considering the problems of the developing world, the importance of democratic values, and the usefulness of high-quality social-science research, the various distortions and limitations encountered in the transmission of social-science knowledge to public policy decision makers ought to be the focus of attention in future efforts to strengthen the social sciences in the Third World.

Notes

1. A. Solari, R. Franco, and J. Juikowitz, *Teoria, acción social y desarrollo en America Latina* (Mexico: Siglo XXI, 1976), p. 26.
2. Ibid., p. 35.
3. Ibid., p. 46.
4. Ibid.
5. Paul Streeten, "Social Science Research on Development: Some Problems in the Use and Transfer of an Intellectual Technology," *Journal of Economic Literature* 12, no. 4 (1974), pp. 1293−94.
6. A. Solari, E. Boeninger, R. Franco, and E. Palma, *El proceso de planificación en America Latina: Escenarios, problemas, y perspectivas* (CEPAL-ILPES: United Nations, 1977), p. 69.
7. Sergio Villalobos, *Historia del Pueblo Chileno*, vol. 1 (Talleres Gráficos Corporación, 1980).

11 Social-Science Research and Public Policy in India

Myron Weiner

Social science research is a major growth industry in India. India has a large cadre of social scientists and a network of research institutions that would be the envy of many. Substantial sums of money have been allocated to the University Grants Commission (UGC) and to the Indian Council of Social Science Research (ICSSR) to nurture social science research in universities and autonomous research institutions. A number of central government ministries and state government departments give out research grants and contracts and employ their own social science research staffs. How much is actually spent for social science research in India and who is doing the funding? What kinds of research are taking place? What is the relationship between funding agencies and research institutions? How are research findings actually used and by whom? What needs are being served by the research? And to what extent do social scientists serve as consultants to government departments, ministries, commissions, and as political advisers? These are questions that have received little attention.

There is a variety of reasons for expanding research in the social sciences, not the least of which is its promise to contribute to the country's development, either in the broad sense of increasing understanding of the social, economic, political, and cultural order within which Indians live, or in the more focused sense of providing specialized knowledge on which more intelligent choices among alternative policies and programs can be made.

Social Science Research Centers

There are four types of social science research institutions in India: research institutions (sometimes called councils, institutes, organizations, bureaus, units, or directorates) located within central government ministries or state government departments or directly under their jurisdiction; government-funded but legally autonomous research institutions; degree-granting educational institutions whose faculties engage in social science research within a department or research center located within the college or university; and private consultancy firms that conduct research under contract from private- or public-sector firms and government departments and ministries. To these four types can be added a fifth: the scientific and engineering institutions that have social science cells or departments.

Government Research Institutions

Probably the largest number of social scientists, economists, and social statisticians are employed by government research institutions. These institutions were created to provide government with basic quantitative and descriptive information. Among these are the bureaus of economics and statistics located in the planning departments of the state governments, the state institutes of educational training and research in the education departments, the tribal research institutes under the departments of tribal affairs, a variety of research units attached to the departments of agriculture, labor, commerce, and industry, and, among the older organizations, the Anthropological Survey of India and the Registrar General of the Census, both under the central government. Some of these institutions are quite old—the census began in 1871—but others have been more recently established. Some are essentially data-collecting units, but increasingly, these units have responded to the growing demands of central ministries and state departments for research. A research unit in the Planning Commission or in a state planning department may initiate a feasibility study involving assessments of investment costs, resource and manpower requirements and availability, marketing, and the like, to support a project proposal. Some of these research units will also monitor and evaluate government projects. The research unit within a state planning department, for example, may evaluate the projects of other departments and use the research findings to determine whether a given program should be expanded, maintained at existing levels, modified, or terminated.

A heavy reliance on public rather than private investment and on government rather than on market determination of prices requires that government engage in research that elsewhere might be conducted by private firms or would be handled without research through decisions in the marketplace. An example of the latter is government policy on food procurement. The Agricultural Prices Commission maintains a research staff to study the costs of agricultural inputs by specific commodities, by locality, and by size of landholding to provide it with the technical information it requires to set procurement prices—though it is well understood that the ultimate decision will be heavily weighted by political considerations.

How a ministry satisfies its need for an adequate data base for development planning is illustrated by the use of research institutes associated with the Ministry of Home Affairs. Since the ministry has primary responsibility for planning for tribal areas and must work with the state governments, it has funded 11 tribal research institutes affiliated to the state governments but which provide research for the Home Ministry. Dozens of studies have been conducted in the areas of tribal education, land use, employment, and other areas intended to facilitate block-level and area-wise planning under the guidance of the Home Ministry.

There is a variety of institutional arrangements between each of these government research units and the particular ministry or department under which it works. Some units are virtually sections of the ministry under the control of a deputy secretary, while others are permitted somewhat more autonomy, may have an academically inclined government officer in charge, and may be physically distant from the ministry. In some instances, "research" is narrowly defined to mean data collection and analysis, while in other instances, the research may be more academic and less geared to meet the specific, immediate needs of policy makers and administrators. An example of the latter is the work of the Anthropological Survey of India, which employs the largest number of anthropologists and does comparatively little policy-oriented research, though its ethnographic studies of tribal India are seen by members of the Planning Commission and the Home Ministry as another kind of "data base" for policy.

Autonomous Research Institutions

In the early 1950s, the central government began to fund research institutions located outside government departments and ministries. Among the most important ones were the Indian Institute of Public Administration (IIPA), which was mandated to set up training programs for government officials as well as to conduct research; the National Council of Educational Research and Training (NCERT), with similar functions; and the National Council of Applied Economic Research (NCAER) and the Institute of Applied Manpower Research, which were created to bring academic expertise to bear on applied economics and manpower problems.

After 1968, the ICSSR actively encouraged the creation of new research centers that would differ somewhat from the first generation of research centers. These new institutions were to give more attention to "basic" social science research, along with applied or policy-oriented research; they were to be more multidisciplinary and were to incorporate social scientists other than economists; and some of them were to be more regionally oriented, located outside of Delhi, and linked financially (through a matching grant arrangement) with the state governments. Out of this initiative there emerged research institutes in Bangalore (Institute for Social and Economic Change), Trivandrum (Centre for Development Studies), Madras (Madras Institute of Development Studies), Patna (A.N. Sinha Institute of Social Studies), Varanasi (Gandhi Institute), Calcutta (Centre for Studies in Social Sciences), Ahmedabad (Sardar Patel Institute of Economics and Social Research), Hyderabad (Public Enterprise Institute), and Lucknow (Giri Institute of Social Sciences). Several older well-established research institutions also receive support from the ICSSR, including the Tata Institute of Social Sciences in Bombay, the Gokhale Institute of Politics and Economics in Poona, and the recently revived Indian Institute of Education in Poona.

The willingness of state governments to provide support demonstrated a recognition on the part of some state officials (typically in the planning and finance departments) that existing research facilities were not adequate to meet their growing needs for project planning and evaluation. Since state government project proposals must often be evaluated by central government ministries and sometimes by international agencies like the United Nations and the World Bank, which employ high-quality professional staffs, the state governments needed to increase their own research capabilities. Many state government officials recognized that autonomous research institutions with central government funding (through ICSSR), often enhanced by international funding (from the Ford Foundation, for example), could hire talented economists and other social scientists more effectively than could the state government. Moreover, some state officials recognized that a regional research center with internationally known economists could itself attract financial resources to the state. As one high official in Trivandrum noted, the Centre for Development Studies brought in many times more funds from the World Bank, the United Nations, the Planning Commission, and other agencies through the reports and proposals of its five distinguished economists than what has been provided by the state government to support the center.

Which states were given funds to create social science research institutes was determined by whether local scholars or public figures took the initiative to create a center, and whether they had support within the Union Ministry of Education and/or the state government. Some of the initiative came from scholars in public life. Three research centers in South India were initiated by former vice-chancellors, and one of these vice-chancellors is the founder of three such institutions. The minister of education was particularly sympathetic to proposals from some of his political associates in Calcutta and Lucknow, while one public figure associated with the Gandhian movement played an important role in obtaining government support for a research institute in Varanasi.

It is easy to become cynical about the process by which some of the research institutes were founded, and it is true that some were badly planned, hastily constructed, and without competent leadership; but it is also the case that some attracted able scholars who preferred to be in research institutes rather than in the universities.

For scholars who have research interests, the advantages of the research institutes over universities are too well known to need recounting here at any length. Suffice it to say that many of the universities have not provided an environment conducive to research: student demonstrations and violence, factional struggles among the faculty and administration, the involvement of political parties in university affairs, and the domination of some universities by one or another ideological or political group have made many colleges and universities inhospitable places for research. Moreover, some faculties and administrators continue to be influenced by the older traditions of universities as centers for the transmission rather than the production of knowledge, in spite of the efforts of the University Grants Commission to stimulate research. It is interesting to note that faculty members cannot ordinarily "buy" themselves time for research with UGC or ICSSR research grants, nor is it an easy matter for them to take research leave. Many scholars also complain that university procedures for spending research funds are cumbersome and unduly restrictive: in some instances, faculty members cannot hire their own graduate students as research assistants but must hire through the local employment exchange; often, universitywide committees rather than the principal investigator have the primary responsibility for hiring for research projects; and there are long waits for obtaining sanctions for the expenditure of research funds for computer time, travel, or purchasing books and supplies.

The result is that a number of able senior research scholars have gravitated to the research centers and many younger scholars have preferred to remain in these centers. It may be that the presence of the research centers has discouraged the growth of research at the universities, but more likely the centers have provided opportunities and an environment for research that were not available at most of the universities.

Educational Institutions

As we have already indicated, a great deal of social science research has shifted to nonteaching, non-degree-granting research centers. This is not to suggest that social science research is dormant at the universities; a glance at the list of institutions that have received research grants from the ICSSR shows that university departments are still the largest recipients. But it is generally argued that much of the quality research, and certainly the policy-relevant research, has moved away from the universities. The few university departments I visited did not lead me to believe that this impression was incorrect.

The Indian Institutes of Management (IIM) in Bangalore, Ahmedabad, and Calcutta, however, have emerged as major centers where there are both research and teaching. The faculty at the IIMs is generally of high quality, and the close ties of these institutes to private firms and government, their "professional" atmosphere, the high self-esteem on the part of the faculty (who know they can readily move into business and government), the freedom of these institutes from control by the state governments, their effective leadership and management, and the encouragement given to faculty members to engage in consultancy research (which supplements their income) have resulted in an atmosphere more conducive to research than can be found in any of the universities.

It should also be noted that the IIMs have broadened their scope considerably and do teaching and research in areas not normally found in management institutions abroad. The Bangalore IIM is primarily a center for research in economics and management, but it contains a demographic unit concerned with the study of primary health-care centers. Moreover, the economics research is defined broadly to include work on rural development and employment: one major study under a grant from the Planning Commission involves block-level research and planning. The IIM in Ahmedabad is a major center for agricultural research. Its interdisciplinary public systems group is also conducting research on health and family planning, education, energy, transportation, and rural development. The Institute of Management in Calcutta has a sociological unit conducting research over a wide range of subjects, including studies of the hill areas of northern Bengal, while an interdisciplinary team has prepared a report on the Second West Bengal, an attempt to project demographic trends for the state and their implications for development.

Though the Administrative Staff College in Hyderabad is not a degree-granting institution, it should be included here as an institution that combines teaching and research activities. A large part of its funding comes from its teaching contracts: it provides training to state and central government employees, and to both public- and private-sector managerial personnel. Its faculty also engage in a wide range of research that includes studies in rural development for the Western Ghats region, the management of the educational system in Andhra, the administrative organization of Command Area Development Programme (CADP)—which integrates irrigation, power, transport, and rural development in various areas of the country, the problems of food storage in industry, and public health and hospital administration.

It is interesting to note that as many of India's policy problems have become defined as problems in management and administration—that is, in the implementation of policy—the scope of research taking place within the various management institutes has broadened.

Private Consultancy Firms

Though most of India's private consultancy firms are in engineering and management consulting, a few conduct social science research. The two largest are the Operations Research Group in Baroda and Tata Economic Consultancy Services in Bombay. Tata primarily does consultancy work for private firms, but in recent years, it has provided consultants to a number of state governments. The research is entirely in economics, though the staff is encouraged to take a "broad" approach to problems. Tata generally does not do all-India studies, nor does it do much policy (as opposed to project) research; but it did prepare five studies for the Second India series focusing on the state of the Indian economy when India doubles its population.

The Operations Research Group (ORG) is the largest broad-based social science private consultancy organization. Originally created to conduct marketing studies for the Sarabhai enterprises, ORG expanded to conduct marketing studies for other firms, then used its market research facilities to conduct public opinion surveys on a wide range of attitudes and practices, including studies of fertility. Today, ORG has a staff of sociologists, survey researchers, and regional planners, as well as economists. Among its largest projects at present is a research and monitoring unit working with the Madras Metropolitan Development Authority.

The Systems Research Institute (SRI) in Poona might be mentioned here, though it is not strictly speaking a private consultancy firm. Its founder and director chose instead to make SRI a nonprofit research organization committed to the application of systems research to the public sector. It is funded by the ICSSR and has a supplementary grant from the Ford Foundation. But in its professional style of operation—consultancy research, close management of research by its director, and a concern with how its research will be used—SRI has some of the qualities of the private consultancy firms.

The ability of the private consultancy firms and of the consultancy units within the Institutes of Management and the Administrative Staff College to obtain research contracts is indicative of the kind of research sought by many government departments and ministries, and of the availability of public funds for certain types of economics, management, and social science research.

Science and Technology Institutions

In addition to the four types of social science research institutions described above, note should also be taken of the growing importance of social science research within scientific and technical institutions. The Institute of Science in Bangalore, for example, has a unit called Appropriate Science and

Technology for Rural Action (ASTRA); the National Institute of Nutrition in Hyderabad has a social science unit concerned with a wide range of nutrition issues (determinants of infant mortality, effect of food supplement programs, etc.) that require social science expertise; and in Ahmedabad, the Ahmedabad Textile Industry's Research Association, the country's leading research center on the textile industry, conducts research on problems of management and industrial relations, as well as on design and technology. It is worth noting that these technical and scientific institutions conduct research linking the social sciences and technology, while none of the social science institutes in India—with the notable exception of the Institute for Defence Studies and Analysis in New Delhi—brings technical and social science expertise together on matters of public policy.

Regional Distribution of Research Institutions

Until relatively recently, there was an overwhelming concentration of policy-oriented social science research institutions in the capital, New Delhi. Many government agencies, especially those engaged in economic planning, have their own research units. The Planning Commission, the Department of Economic Affairs, and the Agricultural Prices Commission, for example, combine economics research with policy planning. Various quasi-governmental research institutions are closely linked to specific ministries, though they have a degree of autonomy: the Institute for Defence Studies and Analysis, the National Council of Educational Research and Training, and the Indian Council of Agricultural Research are examples. Other institutions, though also funded by one or more ministries, are still more autonomous. These include the Indian Council of World Affairs, the Indian Law Institute, the Indian Institute of World Affairs, the Indian Institute of Public Administration, the Institute of Applied Manpower Research, the Institute for Constitutional and Parliamentary Affairs, the National Council of Applied Economic Research, and the Family Planning Foundation. Among those that receive support from the ICSSR are the Centre for Policy Research, the Council for Social Development, the Institute of Economic Growth, and the Centre for the Study of Developing Societies.

In an effort to reduce the overconcentration of research activities in the capital city, the UGC and the ICSSR have actively funded research activities in various parts of the country. The ICSSR in particular has played a singular role in sponsoring the development of a number of regional institutes. State governments have also expanded their own in-house research, as well as provided support to some of the ICSSR-sponsored institutes. In the small city of Trivandrum, to take one example, there are at least three research institutions located within the government: the Bureau of Economics and Statistics, which does much of the research for the Planning Board; the Kerala Institute for Labour and Employment under the Department of Labour and Employment; and the Institute of Educational Research and Training in the Department of Education. Located within the University of Kerala, but virtually independent of it, is the Communications Action Research Centre, a demographic research unit financed directly by the Ministry of Health and Family Welfare. Trivandrum also has the Indian School of Social Science, which runs training programs for trade unionists and leftist party workers, conducts Marxist-oriented research, and publishes *Social Scientist,* a journal that is widely read in Marxist circles. Finally, Trivandrum has the well-known, widely regarded Centre for Development Studies, which is jointly funded by the state government and by the ICSSR.

Nor is Trivandrum unusual. Bangalore has one ICSSR center, the Institute for Social and Economic Change (ISEC), and there is social science research in the Indian Institute of Management, the Indian Population Programme (IPP) (A World Bank–financed research center), the state Educational Research and Training Institute in the Department of Education, and a large research unit in the Planning Department. Madras has an Institute for Techno-Economic Studies, the ICSSR-financed Madras Institute of Development Studies, a regional office of the National Productivity Council, a Research Centre for Non-formal Education, and a large Evaluation and Applied Research Unit within the Department of Finance. There are also two private consultancy firms engaged in social science research: Arjay Management Centre and a regional office of the Operations Research Group (from Baroda), which is conducting a research and training program for the Madras Metropolitan District Authority.

Similarly, there are a substantial number of social science research institutions in Bombay, Poona, Calcutta, Ahmedabad, and Hyderabad. In general, social research facilities are less developed in the Hindi-speaking states and in Orissa and Assam, though the development of the A.N. Sinha Institute of Social Studies in Patna, the Giri Institute of Social Sciences in Lucknow, and the Gandhian Institute in Varanasi represent significant additions to research facilities in Bihar and Uttar Pradesh.

Types of Policy Research

What kind of policy-related research is conducted by these social science research institutions? In what ways do Indian social scientists contribute—if at all—to the generation of knowledge for the making, implementation, and critical evaluation of public policy? In each of the research centers I visited, I asked the directors and researchers to indicate which of their research projects they felt were most policy-relevant, irrespective of whether the findings had been used by policymakers. What follows is a list and brief summary of these studies. Some are completed and some are still under way. Some became part of the policy process—though their recommendations were not necessarily followed. Almost all were circulated within the government; and a few—very few—had a wide public dissemination. In some instances, the studies were not released for circulation because of objections from the funding agencies.

By way of introduction to this list, several observations may be helpful. First, many of the studies conducted by research organizations (particularly but not exclusively by government research institutions) are not social science studies, but are intended to provide the data base for policy. They do not make general formulations and systematically test hypotheses. Data on contraceptive use, for example, are collected by the demographic research units under the Ministry of Health and Family Welfare. Various labor institutes collect and report data on employment by industry, firm size, region, and the like. The Census Office publishes vast amounts of data, some of which are assembled in special reports dealing with, for example, urban growth. These findings are often useful to scholars conducting social science research on population policy, employment, and urban development, but they do not in themselves constitute social science research.

Second, a large number of the research studies conducted in these institutions focus on individual development projects. These may be feasibility studies; they may evaluate a project for its overall impact; an assessment may be made of how the benefits of a project are distributed; or the project may be examined with a specific objective (e.g., employment) in mind. On the basis of the findings from these studies, the project may be revised, terminated, extended, or enlarged. Many of the research studies cited as contributions to policy are studies of this kind, though they are not policy analyses in the broader sense.

Third, it should be noted that most policy-oriented studies are still conducted by economists, not by other social scientists. The proportion may not be apparent from the list below, since I particularly pressed the directors and researchers at these research centers to give me descriptions of projects not in the field of economics. This list, therefore, tends to overweigh the work conducted in other disciplines. In some instances, it should also be noted, the noneconomics research was also conducted by economists.

Fourth, though the reader will get some sense of the wide range of policy-relevant research going on, no conclusions should be made as to how much research goes on in a particular problem area since the list is far too selective.

Finally, it should be noted that none of the studies cited here is comparative. The studies do not draw upon research done in other countries that is relevant to the specific policy areas being studied. Some studies have indirect allusions to what is taking place elsewhere. Studies of India's new Community Health Service program may indirectly allude to the barefoot doctor program in China, and papers on the National Adult Education Programme may refer to the Cuban adult literacy efforts, but nowhere did I find systematic comparisons with policies pursued by other underdeveloped and developing countries and how these might relate to India's policy choices. Nor were there comparisons with either the contemporary or historic experiences of more developed countries.

This list of policy-oriented research projects is in no sense necessarily representative of the hundreds of research projects currently under way or recently completed. These are studies cited by researchers and directors of research institutes as their most important policy-oriented studies, or were reported as examples of projects that had an effect on policymakers or administrators, or simply caught my attention as an interesting piece of policy research. In one or two instances, I have also included some projects that have been proposed but have not yet been initiated. Wherever information was available, I have also indicated whether and how the research findings have been utilized and by whom.

1. The Sardar Patel Institute of Economics and Social Research in Ahmedabad has completed a study of the impact of prohibition on consumption patterns of a sample of residents in Ahmedabad. The study, done under contract with the Department of Prohibition of the government of Gujarat, was intended to ascertain whether a decline in alcohol consumption was accompanied by a rise in food consumption, especially among the low-income groups. Contrary to what was expected, the study found that food consumption was not affected by a decline in alcohol consumption; instead, there was a rise in gambling. The government of Gujarat refused to give permission to the Sardar Patel Institute to release the study, presumably, according to the researchers, because the findings challenged the fundamental assumption on which the government's prohibition policy rested.

2. The National Council of Applied Economic Research in New Delhi has conducted an assessment of the impact of tractor use on employment under a grant from the Ministry of Agriculture. A detailed study of a single district led the researchers to conclude that tractor mechanization reduces the use of agricultural laborers but generates secondary employment, with the result that the *characteristics* of the labor force change, though there is no *net* displacement of labor. This study is one of several financed by the ministry on the relationship between rural mechanization and employment and intended to help the government of India formulate policies toward agricultural mechanization.

3. The Indian Institute of Management in Ahmedabad conducted a study of the utilization of expenditures for rural development in a predominantly tribal district of Gujarat. A central question was why there had been

so little development in the district in spite of the presence of a substantial number of district and departmental officials and an annual expenditure of millions of rupees. The study reported that government funds were used primarily to support the 800 functionaries in the district, of whom 250 were schoolteachers and the remainder in administration. In all, 80 percent of the total expenditures in the district was for the salaries of these functionaries, and only 20 percent was actually used for development projects. The Department of Rural Development of the government of Gujarat, which funded the study, took issue with the findings, and has refused to release the study for publication.

4. The Institute of Applied Manpower Research in New Delhi has conducted a study matching estimated national needs for engineers with the project output of existing engineering colleges, and has concluded that anticipated output more than matches expected needs. According to officials of the institute, the government of India has decided to halt the expansion of engineering colleges at this time on the basis of the institute's research findings.

5. In another study conducted by the Institute of Applied Manpower Research on employment potential in selected tribal areas, the institute found that there was actually a manpower shortage in some skilled categories in industries located in the tribal areas, but that tribals did not qualify for these positions. The result was that migrants were attracted to these areas in spite of a high unemployment rate among the local tribals. The study noted that local technical training facilities were inadequate in most of the tribal areas, so that local tribals were not being prepared for the new jobs that were being created. Officials of the institute reported that the Home Ministry, which financed the study, denied them permission to publish the results since, they were informed, the findings were "sensitive."

6. The Operations Research Group in Baroda is conducting a study of the distribution and use of electricity in rural India under contract with the Rural Electrification Board in New Delhi. A survey of a sample of villages in selected states revealed that many villages considered by the government as "electrified" had no connections from nearby power lines and transformers into the village itself. Through extensive interviews of villagers, the ORG team found that many villagers considered the procedures for obtaining permission to make electrical connections so cumbersome, time-consuming, and costly that they were unwilling to go to the trouble. The team found that in most states, the state electricity boards had the same procedures (and forms) for making electrical connections in rural areas as in urban areas, which meant that villagers had to go to a number of geographically dispersed government officers in distant towns to complete the procedures. Similarly, arrangements for the payment of bills were considered unsatisfactory to cultivators who had fluctuating monthly incomes. The study revealed that state electricity boards were primarily oriented toward the production of

electric power but paid little attention to its promotion and distribution. Finally, the ORG team noted that procedures for obtaining electrical connections varied substantially from state to state, and that these differences accounted for much of the statistical variance in the actual use of electricity in rural areas.

7. The Indian Institute of Nutrition in Hyderabad has completed a study of the government's supplementary school feeding program in an effort to see whether it actually benefited low-income children. A survey of caloric intake of children revealed that the program had no significant effect since parents viewed the food provided children at school as a replacement, not a supplement, for food provided at home. Evidently, mothers have a family-centered rather than child-centered view of food distribution, which leads them to view an increase in food for any single member of the family as an increment to the total food supply available to the entire family. The institute concluded, therefore, that the program should be viewed not as a food supplement program for children, but as an income supplement for the family, and they suggested that the program should be compared with other programs to increase rural income. The joint secretary of the Social Welfare Ministry told the director of the institute that irrespective of research findings, the supplementary food program had to be continued since politically there is no way of terminating a program with so much support among politicians and low-income villagers.

8. Another study conducted by the Indian Institute of Nutrition on the allocation of food within the family revealed that small children under the age of three were likely to be fed more frequently when feeding was administered by adults rather than by older siblings, though the overall daily quantity of food remained the same. The study noted that the frequent feedings make a substantial difference in a small child's daily protein and caloric absorption rate. The study found that older children tended to feed smaller children when they themselves ate—that is, twice a day—while adults were likely to feed smaller children more frequently. These findings have led the institute to impress upon health officials the need to educate older children with responsibility for the care of small children in the necessity of giving feedings more frequently, and to include older children (generally young girls) in educational programs on the care and feeding of small children.

9. The director of the Indian Institute of Economics in Hyderabad sought funds from the Department of Irrigation to study the reasons for the underutilization of existing irrigation schemes in Andhra. The state's minister of irrigation informed the director that the study should not be done since his ministry was seeking central government funding for a new irrigation facility and he did not want any study that showed existing facilities were underutilized. The study was not conducted.

10. The State Planning Institute, a research unit of the Planning De-

partment of the government of Uttar Pradesh, has done a number of studies of state-run enterprises. In one instance, a government-run firm was closed down because of its evaluation report. Several other departmental "schemes" were reportedly terminated because of the institute's evaluation studies.

11. Under a grant from the Bihar Department of Industries, the A.N. Sinha Institute of Social Studies in Patna is currently studying several Bihar state government undertakings in an effort to find out why 48 of the 50 state-run enterprises are losing money.

12. The A.N. Sinha Institute is also evaluating the markets recently created by the Bihar Marketing Board with a loan from the World Bank. The board has created its own warehouses, weighing stations, sheds, and banking and credit facilities for use by local farmers. The institute has conducted benchmark studies of several markets and is monitoring the performance of these markets to see whether smaller cultivators are benefiting. On the basis of these findings, the Marketing Board and the World Bank will determine whether these markets (50 have thus far been created) should be expanded.

13. After the government of India nationalized the country's private insurance companies, the Administrative Staff College in Hyderabad was asked to prepare a study of how these 108 nationalized companies could be integrated into a single public-sector firm. After surveying the operations and marketing of the existing firms, the report recommended that four regional insurance centers be created, with the smaller insurance companies integrated into four of the larger original firms, and that a General Insurance Corporation be created to manage overall central policy. The study and its recommendations were accepted and implemented.

14. The dean of the National Council of Educational Research and Training (NCERT) reports that the council's studies of textbooks and other educational materials, educational technology, teacher training, vocational education, and nonformal education have been widely used by government educational planners. More specifically, studies by NCERT on the relationship between primary school dropout rates and failures led the government to create ungraded schools in Rajasthan and Chandigarh, with some success in reducing the dropout rate. Similarly, it was reported that research on the primary school dropout rate among girls has led to the creation of more all-girl schools, the greater use of women teachers, and a number of local campaigns by social workers to persuade parents to keep their daughters in school.

15. In an exercise in operational research, the Giri Institute of Development Studies in Lucknow is presently working with the district planning committees in four blocks in Uttar Pradesh, assisting them in the drafting of block development plans that might serve as a model for district planning authorities elsewhere in the state.

16. Two studies conducted under the auspices of the A.N. Sinha Institute in Patna on the Kosi Command area of northern Bihar provide alternative explanations for the underutilization of irrigation facilities. A Marxist-oriented study conducted by an economist at the institute concludes that the "semi-feudal" land system of northern Bihar, under which sharecroppers and tenants cultivate land for landlords who take half or more of the crop though they pay for none of the costs of the inputs, discourages the use of irrigation. Without a major transformation in the land system, the study concludes, there is little prospect for agricultural development in the region.

A second study, conducted by a political scientist at the institute, focuses on administrative lacunae in the irrigation system: the inadequate management of canal waters, the problem of siltage in the Kosi, the system of water rates, the inefficiency and neglect by irrigation officials, and many other features of the administrative system. This study notes that variations in the utilization of irrigation from one locality to another in spite of similarities in the land system are related to administrative performance. The study concludes that what is required in north Bihar is not a restructuring of the land system, but a restructuring of the irrigation department and other agencies concerned with the delivery of surface water.

17. The A.N. Sinha Institute was asked by the Bihar State Electricity Board to work out a rationale for tariff charges for electricity under which smaller farmers would have lower rates than bigger consumers. The detailed proposed rate structure submitted by the institute to the board was not implemented, it was reported, because of political opposition from members of the state legislative assembly who represent the interests of the larger farmers.

18. A study conducted by one of the tribal research institutes for the Home Ministry revealed that in the tribal region under investigation, landholdings were comparatively large, population density low, and that tribals lacked the resources to shift to intensive cultivation. On the basis of these findings, the Home Ministry prepared a development plan for this region which emphasized horticultural development. Another study by one of the tribal institutions led the Home Ministry to reject a state government proposal for developing irrigation projects in an area where the bulk of the tribals did not own land and would, therefore, benefit only marginally from the proposed schemes.

19. A study of the utilization of Primary Health Centres (PHCs) in rural areas, conducted by the Indian Institute of Nutrition in Hyderabad, revealed that in many localities, not more than 20 percent of the community made use of the PHCs, largely because transportation in some localities was so poor that villagers were unable to go more than two kilometers each way to a PHC. In Kerala, the study found, where transportation to health centers is readily available, children can be brought to a medical center within 20 minutes, with the result that the PHCs are extensively used. The study

concluded that improvement in transportation in India's remote areas was critical for facilitating greater use of health facilities. The director of the institute believes that an improvement in rural transportation would also increase utilization of nutrition, family planning, and educational services.

20. A closely related study by the Indian Institute of Nutrition on infant mortality rates surprisingly revealed that protein and caloric intake for children was actually lower in Kerala than in Uttar Pradesh, though the latter had a far higher infant mortality rate. The institute is currently preparing to undertake a national study to assess which factors (water supply, accessibility of medical services, education of mothers, etc.) are related to infant mortality rates. By identifying these factors in some order of priority, using multivariate analysis of field data collected from selected areas within the two states (and possibly a third), the institute hopes to determine which policy interventions are most likely to have an impact on infant mortality rates.

21. A study of tribal children in primary schools, undertaken by the director of the State Institute of Education (located within the Department of Education) in Maharashtra, found that tribal children learned more rapidly and their dropout rate declined when teaching in the early grades was in the tribal language rather than in Marathi, the regional language. Following queries in the state assembly as to whether the state government was reversing its language policy in the primary schools, the chief minister abruptly terminated the research. Though the director brought materials (and tapes) to the chief minister to demonstrate that children learned more rapidly when their mother tongue was used, and that thereafter they were able to learn Marathi more rapidly, the chief minister insisted that the project remain terminated because it was "creating misunderstanding."

22. According to a study conducted by the Gokhale Institute of Politics and Economics in Poona on the utilization of an 800 crore rupee investment in irrigation in the state of Maharashtra, 60 percent of the available waters have been utilized by sugarcane producers, with the result that comparatively little water has been available to farmers utilizing the new high-yielding variety of grains. The state government, which financed the study, has thus far refused to allow the findings to be made public.

23. A preliminary field study by a sociologist on the staff of the Giri Institute in Lucknow on the recruitment and training of community health workers, and their relationship to the villagers on the one hand and governmental medical officers on the other, found that the first "round" of workers recruited came from lower income families than the second "round," that the workers were giving more attention to medical treatment than to preventive medicine, that many were attempting to "upgrade" themselves to the status of village doctors, and that many of the medical officers in the primary health centers were sufficiently hostile to the idea of paramedical health workers that they were not playing their expected role in training and supervision.

24. The Operations Research Group (ORG) is conducting a study for the Madras Metropolitan District Authority monitoring the MMDA's $120 million World Bank—financed urban development program looking into, among other things, how the benefits from investment in slum improvement, public housing, transportation, and other areas are distributed.

25. On the basis of a study by the state Planning Department of irrigation use in Karnataka, who the beneficiaries were, and what the returns were on the use of irrigation, state government raised the water-use rates. Another study conducted by the Planning Department on medical manpower requirements in the state was used by the state Department of Education to plan future investment in medical educational facilities for the state.

26. The International Population Project in Bangalore, in a study of the management of health and family planning programs in Karnataka, found that inordinate delays in the approval of expenditures by local community health officers and medical officers had a serious impact on the performance of the program. The report recommended that local personnel be authorized to purchase drugs and be given the authority to readjust budgets from one line item to another to permit flexibility in meeting local needs. The state administration rejected the proposal on the grounds that the decentralization of the power of expenditure could not be made for one department alone without modifying the rules for all state government departments.

27. A proposal by the government of Maharashtra to impose compulsory sterilization on all males in the state with three or more children was studied by the acting director of the International Institute of Population Studies in Bombay. By assessing the demographic effects of sterilization if it took place on adults with three, four, or five children, and estimating the number of parents whose three children were female, he concluded that the proposal was likely to be an unpopular one, and that a modified scheme of compulsory sterilization of those with five or six children would be more acceptable, would affect fewer parents without male children, and would also strengthen the voluntary family planning programs. Shortly after his recommendations were submitted to the Health and Family Planning Department, the acting director was dismissed from the advisory board to the department and he was subsequently informed, though earlier he had been assured otherwise by the governing board of his institute, that he would not be made the permanent director of the IIPS.

28. The Centre for Development Studies (CDS) in Trivandrum did several studies for the Kerala Commodity Tax Commission, whose chairman was a professor at the CDS. On the basis of these studies, the state government increased the sales tax on commodities, with the result that annual income from this tax rose from Rs 80 crores to an estimated Rs 130 crores.

On the basis of this highly selective list, it would be unwise to draw any definitive conclusions as to the kind of policy-oriented research that is or is not conducted in India's research centers and universities. A more comprehensive survey would most likely reveal types of research not included in this list. Nonetheless, it may be useful to review briefly what are the kinds of research that seem to be emphasized, and those that are not.

The largest number of studies included here focus on the delivery and distribution of public services. These studies are concerned with the quantity and/or quality of public services delivered, how and to whom they are (or are not) distributed, and who does (or does not) benefit from them. On the list are studies examining the delivery of services to tribal areas (project 3); the delivery of electricity to rural areas (project 6); the benefits or lack of benefits of supplementary school feeding programs (project 7); the delivery and utilization of irrigation (projects 6, 9, 22, and 25); the provision of marketing facilities (project 12), public health facilities (projects 19 and 23), and family planning services (project 26); and the delivery of a variety of urban facilities (project 24).

These studies reflect a growing concern with the question of why services that have been funded are often not delivered to the targeted population. For explanations, researchers have looked both at the characteristics of the targeted population and at the delivery system itself. Research in this field is in a preliminary phase. Studies remain scattered and generally unrelated to one another, lack a theoretical focus, and are not as yet cumulative.

A second group of studies deals with the relationship between a particular policy or proposed policy and a policy objective or set of objectives. Among the projects in this group are those that consider the relationship between prohibition and food consumption (project 1), rural technology and rural unemployment (project 2), engineering education and employment (project 4), and the medium of instruction and school dropout rates among tribal minorities (project 21). Several of the behavioral studies dealing with food distribution in the family (projects 7 and 8) and a project study of infant mortality (project 20) are potentially significant contributions to policies dealing with nutrition, health, and child care. There are also studies, not cited above, in the fields of communications behavior and demographic behavior that are intended to link behavioral studies with policy analysis.

Particularly welcomed by government officials are those applied studies that assist government in coping with immediate program or project needs. Among these are a study to assist in the structuring of the nationalized insurance companies (project 13), a study to provide base line data for project development (project 18), and project evaluations (project 10 and others). A more comprehensive research list would provide a larger number of examples. Though many of these are conducted by autonomous research institutions, an even larger number are carried out by research units within government.

Public policy is made within a political process and implemented by bureaucrats within an administrative framework that has its own political process, partly independent of but also partly interacting with the broader political process. How does research by professional social scientists enter these processes? How can this particular kind of knowledge by utilized? Can social scientists themselves play a role in these processes? In short, can policy-oriented social science make a difference, and if so, in what way?

Potential Benefits of Social Science Research

Many people in and out of government are uncertain as to what constitutes *research,* much less what constitutes *social science* research. To some, research implies "academic" work unrelated to policy. To others, it simply means the collection of data by government departments for their annual reports. Still others view research as the technical work required for feasibility studies and cost evaluations for specific government projects.

Few appreciate the ways in which social science research can generate knowledge to bear upon the choice of policy alternatives or an assessment of the effects of policies. Although there is considerable disagreement among social scientists as to what constitutes the "scientific" dimensions of social science research (or, indeed, whether their work should be called "scientific"), there is a broad agreement that social science research involves the systematic collection of evidence, that general formulations are made on the basis of studying a range of specific situations, and that hypotheses are tested in accordance with established and accepted procedures which permit replication, verification, and refutation.

Among both policymakers and social scientists in India, there is considerable appreciation of the contribution that economists can make to policy, but great uncertainty as to the contribution, if any, that could be made by other social scientists. For one thing, since the bulk of policy-relevant social science research in India is still conducted by economists, policymakers are generally not familiar with how noneconomists can contribute to policy analysis. They regularly use the findings of economists to make judgments concerning budgetary allocations, capital investments, plant locations, the feasibility of projects, commodity prices, and a host of other economic decisions. There is also an awareness on the part of a few policymakers that, in the broadest sense, research that contributes to an understanding of how a society, economy, polity, and culture operate can be useful to those who propose to use government powers and resources to modify existing arrangements. Thus, there is some appreciation of the value of research in areas such as tribal ethnography, rural land systems, or the structure of the family that can be useful to policymakers, even when the research is not explicitly directed at policy questions. What is not generally recognized, either among policymakers or social science researchers, is how research can contribute explicitly to the policy process. It may be useful to indicate some of the contributions that can be made by policy-oriented social science research.

1. Social science can alert policymakers to new issues by pointing to changes taking place that may result in future needs or conflicts. Demographic studies of population growth rates, changes in the characteristics of population, changes in the direction and rate of migration, and so on, can help anticipate needs in employment, housing, health, and urban infrastructures. Similarly, studies of changing attitudes and values can be important for anticipating changing relations within and between castes, tribes, religious groups, and linguistic communities. Since assessing future needs is essential for all policy and planning, the systematic analysis of the future can be an important contribution by social scientists.

Social scientists have sometimes created issues for policymakers. Studies of blood policy in Great Britain, for example, generated a concern with similar policies in the United States. And studies of the family in the United States have served to generate public discussions of family policies, and of the way in which existing public policies are affecting American family life. In India, one could imagine a number of studies that considered the indirect and unintended consequences of a variety of government programs that might very well generate new policy discussions.

2. Social science can help to define alternatives. It can do this (a) by specifying the causes of specific needs that policymakers are seeking to remedy; (b) by looking at the relationship between particular policy instruments and policy objectives; (c) by calling attention to the kinds of policies that have been attempted elsewhere or at other times to deal with similar objectives; and (d) by studying the attitudes of those who may be affected by alternative policies.

Policy analysts can often dispel the notion that there is a single best policy, or that problems can be solved merely by greater expenditures on existing programs; they can use research findings to explore the costs and benefits of alternative projects and policies. For example, an examination of differences between one region of the country and another can help point to alternative approaches. A study proposed by the National Institute of Nutrition in Hyderabad to find out why infant mortality rates are lower in Kerala than in Uttar Pradesh despite recent findings that there are no significant differences in caloric or protein intake may clarify the role of education and health delivery services versus food supplement programs as alternative ways of trying to reduce infant mortality. Similarly, studies of contrasting regions with high and low school dropout rates may help state governments define alternative programs for the achievement of universal primary school education.

Comparative policy research is of particular importance in illuminating alternatives. The policy experiences of countries with similar problems can suggest both the possibilities and the limits of alternative policies; indeed, government officials often "borrow" policies from others without having the advantages of research studies that point to the conditions under which specific policies have been adopted, their costs, and their consequences.

3. Social science research can help evaluate policies. Governments regularly issue reports containing statistics on services delivered: how many schools have been built, health centers and family planning clinics opened, villages electrified, acreage irrigated, and so on; but official reports rarely tell us how individuals have been affected. How have the benefits of a particular program been distributed? Who has benefited and who has not? Are recipients pleased or dissatisfied with the way in which services have been provided? Have their attitudes and practices changed? Do they, in fact, make use of the services? In the last few years, there has been a growing number of studies in India on the impact of programs. Social science research is particularly well qualified for these kinds of systematic evaluations.

4. Social science research can contribute to the quality of the debate over public policies. The choice of most policies is largely a political matter, as organized groups attempt to influence the outcomes and politicians assess the political costs and benefits of one policy and program against another. In a democracy, much of the debate will take place in legislative bodies, in the media, and within the bureaucracy. Since the benefits of most policies are rarely as great as their advocates anticipate—or the problems as bad as their opponents warn—research findings can often create more realistic expectations and perhaps thereby dissipate some of the tensions generated in the debate.

Among the issues that arouse strong sentiments in public discussions in India is the relationship between technology and employment. Should peasant proprietors be permitted by government to import agricultural machinery? Will machinery displace agricultural labor? Will it actually reduce costs and increase productivity? Will it generate alternative needs (e.g., servicing agricultural machinery, or new marketing facilities) that will lead to new employment? Though much of the debate on these issues is heavily ideological, the substantial amount of research that has taken place in India has had a significant impact on the quality of the debate.

Similarly, there is an intense debate in India concerning the efficacy of preferential policies for scheduled castes and scheduled tribes, not only over the question of whether such policies have discriminated against those who do not receive benefits, but over the question of how these preferences have been distributed within these communities. Among the tribals, for example, there has been conflict between Christian and non-Christian tribals over the question of whether the former have received a disproportionate share of benefits, and there have been similar conflicts among the scheduled castes. Critics of preferential policies have also argued that many of the benefits have been given to those whose incomes are already equal to the forward castes who do not receive benefits, and that economic criteria should therefore replace caste and tribal criteria for social benefits. Social science research on these questions will not eliminate claims and counterclaims, but it can put the debate on a sounder factual footing.

5. Social science can help politicians and administrators make more informed assessments of the public response to policies and programs. Politicians often have a "feel" for how specific publics will react on the basis of their discussions with constituents and fellow politicians and their reading of newspapers. In developed countries, public opinion surveys have been a useful way for politicians to obtain a better appreciation of the distribution of opinions, the depth of sentiment, and the attitudes toward specific programs and policies. There are relatively few such surveys in India. One can readily see how politicians and policymakers could find surveys of considerable use. For example, politicians must decide whether family planning programs are a political liability or not, and whether variations in the population programs would find support among various groups. Similarly, the political reaction of various groups to preferential policies is often a matter of guesswork: public reactions proved to be mild in Uttar Pradesh but intense and violent in neighboring Bihar. A recent survey conducted among a small sample of landless laborers in Uttar Pradesh showed that many of the landless were more eager to acquire independent sources of income through the ownership of cattle or small business than to acquire land or factory employment, a finding which (if true) could have considerable policy implications.

How representative are the demands of vociferous groups? At present, the answer is a matter of guesswork. Do demonstrations by students, for example, command wide support? How much support is there for striking workers? For those who make secessionist demands? Policymakers generally take into account what they think their constituents want and what people will consider tolerable behavior by government; social science surveys can often make such judgments more reliable.

6. Finally, social science research can be important for justifying programs and policies. State government officials often need to sell their proposals to the central government when funding is required. Both the central and state governments may need to justify their proposals to international funding agencies. Policies need to be justified to audiences outside of government, especially to those who think they may not benefit or may even be hurt by a set of policies.

The test of how effective social science research is, is not whether policymakers follow the advice of social scientists. Knowledge is, after all, only one dimension of policy: values, political judgments, and political pressures are likely to be more important than the findings of scholars. Such knowledge can be—and in a democracy often is—an important element in the decision process, but it is as naive for social scientists to expect policymakers to do their bidding as it is for policymakers to assume that social science research will solve their policy problems.

More modestly, to recapitulate our argument, one might hope that in a democracy, social science research might anticipate new public needs, increase knowledge on which politically relevant publics and politicians, as well as bureaucrats, can make informed policy decisions, increase awareness of alternative policy choices and their costs and benefits for different groups, increase understanding of the consequences of policies and programs, contribute to the quality of debate over public policies, provide both politicians and bureaucrats with greater knowledge concerning public reactions to policies and programs, and win support for new policies and programs—in short, demonstrate that knowledge systematically acquired through social science research can be an important input to the process of policy and project formation, implementation, evaluation, revision, and termination.

Interaction of Researchers and Bureaucrats

The near-universal complaint of directors and researchers in India's social science research institutes is that their studies are rarely utilized by policymakers—even when the studies are directed at specific policy issues or the evaluation of particular programs and projects and are done under contract with government.

One complaint is that the government officers who have requested the study have often been transferred by the time the study has been completed and their successors no longer share an interest in the problem. In other instances, there is no evidence that the research reports delivered to the contracting departments are read, much less utilized, by policymakers. As the director of one research institute put it, "Only when the government takes objection to what we have written do we ever know that they have read the report." But some researchers are convinced that administrators do not want to see reports that are critical of the government. The director of another research organization summed up a widely shared view: "The government system is so vast, so complex, so immobile that any kind of change and innovation is difficult. The basic attitude of the administration is not helpful. Sometimes a few individuals in the government are open-minded and responsive to research, but the bureaucratic system as a whole is not. It is not responsive to innovation. So how can it be responsive to research?"

Officials reply to these criticisms in a variety of ways. Some state government officials believe that they know what needs to be done and that what they lack is not additional knowledge but additional funding. Experience is seen as preferable to social science research. The secretary of a state government department involved in a slum clearance and improvement program and in the construction of low-income housing justified the lack of research in his department as follows: "We know these slum dwellers well, so there is no need for research. We only need to develop programs for them." He seemed to be unaware of the criticism by local fishermen of the housing that had recently been constructed for them or that some of the new housing had already degenerated into slums.

Similarly, the secretary of a state educational department reported that no research was required for their major new program to achieve universalization of primary education since they already knew that the reason for the high school dropout rate was simply that "the parents remove the children from school and send them to work." He went on to explain that government could not force poor parents to send their children to school when the parents needed the income of their children. He was not familiar with the data that revealed poverty alone could not account for the state-to-state variations in India's school dropout rates or with the various studies that pointed to a variety of other determinants.

Some officials justified their indifference to research on the grounds that academics lacked the experience that might make their findings useful to administrators. An official in the social welfare department of one state government noted that research findings on social problems all said the same thing: "We get reports that tell us we have a beggar problem, or prostitution, or abandoned children. They tell us we should start new programs or spend more money. Our social problems are so colossal that research cannot help. Research can help only when you can expand your program to meet the needs of people you want to help." Evidently, none of the research studies submitted to him suggested how one might choose among alternative programs and projects when resources are scarce.

In defense of the government's reluctance to use outside research, a government official in Bihar said that though "there is no tradition of research within the government of Bihar and no sense that research could be useful, there is also a problem with the researchers. Their work is too academic, too removed from social reality."

While it is not clear that experience within government would necessarily make the research of academics closer to "social reality," it is true that researchers have few opportunities to work within government. A few ministries, especially the planning and economic ministries, use economists. The education ministry makes use of educationists, but these are rarely research scholars. Sociologists, political scientists, psychologists, public administrators, geographers, urban planners, demographers, and other social scientists rarely have government experience. The few social scientists and economists who enter government do so late in their careers and in an advisory capacity, rarely in line positions that would provide them with practical experience. Lateral appointments into government ministries—again with the exception of economists—are almost unknown. The result is that the research institutions do not have scholars with a feel for policy issues who can give realistic attention to the organizational problems associated with the implementation of public policies and programs or be a resource for other members of the staff who have not worked in government.

Government officers tend to have little regard for academics, including those who are conducting research on policy-related matters. An official of the Planning Board in Kerala, who has himself played an important role in trying to stimulate policy-oriented research in his state and in bringing academics and researchers together, explained:

> You have to understand that universities and government in India operate in watertight compartments. The universities are traditionally concerned with producing manpower for the bureaucracies. Bureaucrats see themselves as superior to the academics, by training and above all by their exercise of power. There are a few senior officials who are academically oriented, but they are exceptions. And the ministers are no different. This generation of political leaders—you might call it our second generation since Independence—accepts the leadership of the bureaucracy. They may oppose the bureaucrats when they are out of power, but they depend upon them once they are in power. The ministers turn to the bureaucrats for advice, not to the academics. In fact, academic research never reaches the politicians. If researchers have any impact it is on some of the bureaucrats. And if the academics have anything to say that might be useful, they never lobby for their views. I believe that the producers of ideas ought to be salesmen for their ideas. Besides, bureaucrats think the academics are not practical. There is just no interchange between the university and the bureaucracy. Maybe it would be better if people moved from one to the other.

An official of the Department of Administrative Reforms in New Delhi explained why interaction between administrators and academics was difficult:

> There is a lot of distrust between administrators and researchers that makes it difficult for them to interact. Perhaps administrators could take leave from government to work in research institutes and universities, but it would be difficult to bring researchers into government. There are so many difficulties. Who would go into government? Who would decide? What salaries would they have? Would a man from the university be willing to go back to the university once he entered the administration? Then there are also problems in administrators taking time off for research. Our administrators are not experts. They change positions from one ministry to another in accordance with seniority. So we develop no expertise. What would an administrator do in a research institute? What would be our research speciality? And even if we developed some speciality, we would soon be transferred to another department.

But, he went on to say, the problems were not merely practical ones, but also a question of the attitudes of administrators toward academics. "When I was in the university, the best graduates went into administration, and those who failed went into the universities. So what ranking government officer would like to go to a university or work in a research institute?"

Nonetheless, in spite of the attitudes of many administrators toward academics, administrators—or at least some of them—do turn to the research institutes. Two reasons were given: first, there is a growing need for research by policy planners, and second, some of the best talent for research is outside of government. Two interviews, one with the director of the state planning board in Uttar Pradesh, and the other with the secretary of planning in Andhra, illustrate these arguments:

> Some governments come to us to help prepare project reports since they know that the projects will have to be reviewed by a professional group in the ministry in New Delhi or by a professional group in the World Bank. But sometimes the department needs a more substantial project report than we can provide so we use outside consultants. We go to the NCAER [National Council of Applied Economic Research], the Administrative Staff College, Tata Consultancies, the Systems Research Institute, and so on. But mostly we go to them for technical consultancies rather than social science research.

And:

> I persuaded the chief minister to fund the Institute of Economics by telling him that we would otherwise have to set up a monitoring unit within the Department of Industries and Commerce. I told him that the state government could not hire economists and other social scientists of the caliber that could be hired by an independent research institute since many able people would prefer to be in the research institutes than in the bureaucracy.

Government Control Over the Dissemination of Research

The picture is clearly a mixed one. Officials in departments with substantial research needs (planning, especially) need and have respect for the work of social scientists outside of government, but most of the operating departments rely upon their own personnel, seek a data base rather than social science research for project formulation and monitoring, and prefer the experience of their staff to research by outsiders as a source of knowledge.

Though some government officials turn to social science research institutes for assistance in project planning and evaluations, many government officials are fearful that research might be too critical, that findings may undermine existing departments, policies, and programs, and that research results might be used by outsiders to criticize government officials. This ambivalence is another element leading many government officials to prefer research from units within government rather than research conducted outside.

In order to reduce the "political risks" of research, government-contracted research is under government rules which require researchers to obtain permission from the funding agency before their results can be released. Such rules do not apply to grants from ICSSR or the UGC, but do apply when research grants are given by state government departments, central government ministries, metropolitan development authorities, and other government and quasi-governmental agencies.

The government's position is that government-sponsored contract research is government property that should not be published if it runs counter to official policy or contains material that might prove embarrassing to government. This view was clearly stated by an official of the Bombay Metropolitan Development Authority, an agency that funds a considerable amount of research in and on Bombay:

> We have given contracts to Tata Economic Research Consultancies, the Tata Institute of the Social Sciences, the Gokhale Institute and many other research groups. Since the government commissions these reports, the government owns them. It is the same whether a study is done by a consultancy firm, a research institute or the university. The reason is that many of these studies deal with confidential matters, such as evaluating our programmes, so we wouldn't want them to be released. Some of the reports deal with very sensitive matters and are even critical of the government. Naturally we would not permit these to be published.

An officer of the Home Ministry in New Delhi explained why research conducted by the tribal research institutes funded by his department could not automatically be made public:

> We want the tribal research institutes to give us a correct picture of what is happening. When we get a correct picture of the implementation of our programmes, we can take steps to remedy their defects. Our problems would become more complicated if these research findings were published. If I give out a research contract I am interested in getting the correct picture. The researcher is more likely to be correct if he knows that the research is for me. But if the researcher has an eye on the press, then he will write differently. His writings will become political. In fact, there are some researchers who would not want to get into controversy and who would prefer that what they write only be for the government. And if they say something critical then they may be hauled up by government officers for what they write. When government commissions research it is for our administrative decisions. Let the ICSSR or the UGC give grants to researchers for public research. That is not our business.

In a similar vein, an official in the Andhra government explained that his department gave out research contracts on a confidential basis because "we often want a particular department's project evaluated, or a market study conducted for a public-sector enterprise—work that has to be kept confidential." "Would it be feasible and desirable," I asked, "to distinguish between consultancy where confidentiality was required, and research that was intended to provide a knowledge base for policy or sought to evaluate policies where the results could be publicly shared?" He thought so. But an official in one of the central government ministries saw no reason for sharing with the public any of the research funded by his ministry: "Public knowledge?" he bluntly asserted, "What is that? It's nothing much. It's the government that makes these policies, not the public. The important thing is that the government has the information base and the research is likely to be more correct if the researcher knows that it is being done only for us."

Funding of Research

There are three major ways in which a research project can be funded. First, the research institute conducts a study using its own finances, drawing from its recurring grant from the ICSSR, the state government, and, in the case of some institutes, a grant from the Ford Foundation. Under present procedures, the ICSSR provides an annual recurring grant to an institute on the condition that matching funds, also in the form of a recurring grant, be made available by the state. (An exception is made in the case of the Institute of Economic Growth and the Centre for the Study of Developing Societies in New Delhi.) Under the present procedures, the matching grant must be in the form of a recurring grant from the state government; project funds are not considered for matching purposes. These grants cover the capital expenditures and the basic operating budgets of the institute, including the library and the salaries of the permanent staff. Some of the ICSSR-funded institutes have sufficiently large recurring grants so that they could function without sponsored research, though it would be difficult to do any large-scale studies without additional funding.

Second, the institutes receive project grants from the ICSSR. The ICSSR invites applications for research grants for specified policy areas— e.g., poverty and unemployment, rural development, women's studies. The grants are generally below Rs 50,000. Some institutes complain that the ICSSR grants are too small for major studies (there is a proposal to raise the ceiling), that the ICSSR takes an inordinately long time to process grants, and that pay scales permitted by the ICSSR are sometimes below the salaries paid by research institutes. However, ICSSR funding does permit research institutes to take on projects that are of special interest to their own staff, and it gives them the freedom of inquiry and publishing lacking with some other funding sources.

Third, the institutes obtain research grants directly from operating government departments, ministries, commissions, boards, and public-sector firms. While some research institutes work closely and almost exclusively with one or two government departments, others work with a wide range of government sponsors. Research grants are generally more forthcoming from central government ministries than from state departments, though in recent years, state funding has been increasing.

The director of a research institute may approach a government official with a proposal for a project that he or a member of his staff wishes to conduct and which he thinks might be of interest to the government. In other instances, the government will approach a research institute directly to solicit a proposal for a specific project. In these instances, the government official has a specific research need and he chooses an institute he thinks has the requisite expertise and a good "track record" of completing quality research on schedule. It is not the practice of government to solicit tenders for research and to choose institutions on a competitive basis. The sponsors generally know what they want done, and who they want to do it. A number of institutes are favored for such sponsored research. On many lists are the two largest private consultancy firms, the Operations Research Group and Tata Economic Consultancies, plus the Institutes of Management, the Administrative Staff College in Hyderabad, and, for work on information systems, the Systems Research Institute in Poona. Many of the research institutes located in the capital, especially the National Council of Applied Economic Research, are on the list. A few of the regional institutes have national standing, especially ISEC in Bangalore and CDS in Trivandrum. All the regional institutes are used by the state governments and they also receive research contracts from central ministries for research within the state. Only rarely do government departments consider awarding contracts to research units within universities. ("Why hadn't you considered giving a contract to some university research group?" I asked the director of the Madras Metropolitan Development Authority after he listed the various organizations he had considered for a research contract, and had not listed a single university-based research group. "We didn't think of turning to the universities," he quickly replied, "because we wanted professionals.")

Research contracts may be for specific consultancy studies intended to help the government prepare a feasibility report, evaluate a project, reorganize a department, or improve the management of a public-sector firm. Other studies may be of a broader character: to assist the government in formulating a new tax policy, to find ways to facilitate the greater utilization of electricity or irrigation, or to formulate more effective measures for delivering health and family planning services.

It is not the practice of either the state or central government to determine in advance whether a study is intended for the exclusive and confidential use by government, or whether a study should be publicly available. The official position, as we have noted, is that government-funded research is the property of government, and only after a study is completed can a decision be made as to whether a study should be released. Generally, most studies are released, though some after modifications are made and most after a waiting period while the report is cleared by the appropriate committees and government officers. Some studies are never cleared because they are "sensitive" or because they run counter to government policy. To what extent researchers and research institutions are cautious in the choice or treatment of topics as a result of these restrictions on publication is unclear. Scholars I interviewed denied that this system of prior review inhibited either their choice of research topics or their research. The director of one institute, however, did indicate that as a result of one negative experience with a government department, his institute no longer accepted contracts that required prior review of research results before publication. Other directors considered the procedure irritating, but did not protest when studies conducted in their centers were withheld from publication. Surprisingly, none of them "leaked" findings to the press or suggested to a member of the legislative assembly that he ask the government why a report was being withheld. In the main, the directors felt it necessary to maintain good relations with funding departments and ministries even if it meant that from time to time a particular study could not be published.

Research institutes tend, moreover, to steer clear of topics that are politically too controversial. During Emergency, as one might expect, research institutes avoided conducting studies that might reveal the unpopularity of government programs. None of the demographic research centers, for example, conducted studies of public responses to the government's massive sterilization program. The director of the Indian Population Project in Lucknow explained that during Emergency, his research group decided not to collect data on public attitudes toward the sterilization program.

The Emergency aside, social science researchers have avoided researching politically sensitive issues. With a few notable exceptions (several studies by the Gandhian Institute of Studies in Varanasi), ethnic conflicts and policies resulting from (or causing) ethnic tensions are not heavily researched. None of the research centers I visited is currently engaged in studies of relations between scheduled castes and caste Hindus, though conflicts between these groups have been a major political issue; nor has the controversial issue of preferential policies received a great deal of attention in social science research.

Fortunately, however, there are exceptions. The list of current research presented earlier in this article is ample testimony to the willingness of some social scientists to write critically, even when it irritates their sponsors. The Sardar Patel Institute study of prohibition in Gujarat, the IIM Ahmedabad study of the utilization of rural development funds for administrative personnel in a tribal district, the Gokhale Institute study of who has access to irrigation in Maharashtra, a tribal research institute study of educational facilities in tribal localities with large public-sector investments, and a study by the State Institute of Education in Maharashtra of language and education among tribals—each of these studies illustrates on the one hand the willingness of some scholars to tread into areas without regard to the "vested" interests of their sponsors, and on the other the readiness and capacity of sponsoring agencies to prevent the dissemination of studies that are critical of what government has or has not done.

The impact of government policies on the restriction of publication in government-funded social science research cannot be easily measured for the simple reason that, like censorship of the press, the policy works best when government does not need to restrict publication because researchers avoid writing anything their sponsors would disapprove. The impact of this policy on the quality of social science research cannot, therefore, be measured by the number of studies that government does not release for publication. The effects are on the topics chosen for research, the self-imposed caution on the way a problem is defined and data collected, the reluctance of researchers to draw conclusions from their data that might be critical of government, and the bland way in which findings are presented.

A few scholars and institutions will not do government-sponsored contract research unless there is a prior understanding over publication. But the problem will not be resolved by individual action. Nor will the problem disappear because research funds will come from the ICSSR, the University Grants Commission, or other agencies that do not impose restrictions on publication. On the contrary, there is reason to believe—though hard data will not be available until the ICSSR completes a study currently under way of government funding of research—that research institutes will become even more dependent upon government departments and ministries for contract research, largely because of dwindling ICSSR resources in relation to the growing needs of an increasingly large number of research institutes, but also because policy-oriented research institutes will want to work for government in order to gain the access to sources that government-funded research provides.

The restriction on public access to government-sponsored research findings, except with the permission of the government funding agency, is more than merely a restriction on academic researchers. It means that elected representatives as well as the general public are denied unrestricted access to studies funded with taxpayers' money. The argument that "sensitive" studies can be misunderstood or misused is often a screen for protecting government departments and government officials against public criticism.

Social Scientists and Policy Process

While it is difficult to ascertain to what extent government officials make use of social science research studies, it is apparent that government has made use of social scientists in a variety of advisory capacities. Economists, of course, have long since served as consultants to India's planners, and there is hardly a government-appointed commission concerned with taxation, finances, wages, prices, and investment that does not contain professional economists, not simply on the staff, but as members. Men like V.K.R.V. Rao, D.R. Gadgil, K.N. Raj, Raj Krishna—the list could be a long one—have been influential either in directly shaping policy and programs or in influencing debates over economic policies. It is also clear that these men have held their positions not because of their political standing but because of their expertise.

Though other social scientists have not achieved the policy eminence of the economists, they have begun to play an influential role as friends and advisers to public figures. Several of the Delhi social scientists are "well connected" in officialdom, the Janata party, and the cabinet, and some of the directors and senior staff of the regional social science institutes are similarly well placed in relation to state secretaries of finance, planning, industries, and agriculture, and with state politicians. Whether these informal relations are translated into policy influence is not clear. One can only note that, as in the case of economists, their views enter the policy process, and they are heard not because of their political clout but because of their professional expertise.

There has been a more formal use of social scientists on a variety of government commissions—most recently, the policy commission and the Ashok Mehta commission on local government and decentralization. Members of the Tata Institute of Social Sciences, for example, are often asked to serve on commissions and advisory committees concerned with social welfare, labor welfare, labor safety, and industrial relations. Some of the most prominent social scientists—M.N. Srinivas, M.S. Gore, Pai Panandikar, and Rajni Kothari, among others—have served on commissions or as advisers to ministries.

As advisers and commission members, social scientists may bring into the policy process their own judgments as informed by social science research. But rarely do the commissions have time to contract for social science research; the time frame for the commissions is too short and the time needed to complete a research study is generally too long for new research to be useful for informing their work. Nor is there much opportunity for social scientists to do research for legislators. Politicians do not commission policy papers, and there are no legislative committees with research staffs and research budgets, as in the United States Congress.

Opportunities for making a direct input in the policy process in India are largely through the administrative process and, to some extent, through access to a broader political public.

Policy-related research, however, even when it is not restricted by government sponsors, is poorly disseminated. Studies are sometimes distributed only to the sponsors, while some studies are circulated to an academic audience with little effort to highlight policy relevance. Only a handful of scholars write for journals read by a wider reading public and only rarely do research institutes inform the press of interesting research findings that might be relevant in current policy debates.

One example comes to mind. The Indian government recently announced its determination to take steps to achieve universalization of primary education through the allocation of more funds to the states. Having interviewed education officials in a half-dozen states, however, I found no evidence that any policy-related research was being utilized on how best to allocate these resources. Yet, a number of studies would appear to be relevant. There are studies that show that dropout rates from primary schools are high when children spend a long time traveling to school—a finding that suggests it would be more effective to increase the number and dispersal of schools than to increase their size, or that educational funds should be used to transport some children to school. Other studies show that tribal children are more likely to remain in school and to acquire the regional language if their tribal mother tongue is used in the early grades by teachers and in the texts—in short, that bilingual education may decrease dropout rates. Still other studies suggest that nine- and ten-year-old girls are withdrawn from school to take care of their younger siblings, which suggests that community-run programs for preschool children might keep older children, especially girls, in school. Still another study indicates that dropout rates in the lower grades are reduced in ungraded schools where children are not failed. But almost none of these studies appears to have been read by officials, politicians, educators, or parents. Instead, current policy is made in a near vacuum. The government of Bihar, for example, is planning a free lunch program to reduce the dropout rate in primary school, though there is no evidence that such a program would increase school attendance, while a National Institute of Nutrition study suggests that the supplementary food program has no impact on the nutritional well-being of children.

There is a tendency to assume that if government is committed to a goal, enough resources are allocated, and officials work hard enough, the goal will be achieved. What is lacking in educational planning—and in other policy areas as well—is an awareness of how research findings can be utilized to maximize the benefits of alternative uses of limited government resources.

One could cite many other examples where existing research studies relevant to policy have not been an input into the policymaking and program development process. Of the many studies discussed earlier, few have been reported even in *Economic and Political Weekly*. Most remain in the form of technical reports and several have not been released because of government restrictions.

While a few scholars, especially in Delhi, consciously reach out for a larger audience by writing for *Seminar, Economic and Political Weekly,* or the editorial page of the English dailies, social scientists in the regional institutes often make little effort to reach larger audiences. Their studies are often not available in local bookstores; reports on policy-related research findings are not disseminated to the press or even to members of the state legislative assemblies; nor is there any systematic effort by the ICSSR or any of the research institutes to pull together summaries of research findings relevant to current policy debates—for example, the debate over mechanization of agriculture and rural employment, preferential policies and reservations for backward castes, or how to achieve universalization of primary education.

The role played by Indian social scientists in the policy process is partly shaped by the institutional structures within which they operate. The high turnover of government administrators, the absence of a system of lateral entry of academics and other outsiders into the bureaucracy, the preference by administrators for in-house sources of information, the status relationships between administrators and scholars, and the restrictions imposed by government on the publication of contract research all tend to limit the role of Indian social scientists in the policy process. Compared with the American political process, the Indian policymaking process does not easily lend itself to the extensive use of experts drawn from outside government. Members of the Indian parliament, unlike members of the United States Congress, do not ordinarily draft legislation; they do not have their own staffs who can work with outside consultants on legislative matters, and they are not organized into legislative committees that draft legislation, employ their own staff, hold public hearings, and commission policy studies. Some of these activities are carried out by government commissions, but their tenure is generally brief and only recently have they begun to make substantial use of social science research.

Nor have government departments developed their own internal mechanisms for the evaluation and utilization of research findings. At best, research reports are used for reviewing specific projects, rarely for the assessment of policies. If the linkage between research findings and policy is greatest in those ministries concerned with economic planning, it is because economists and those who make economic policy decisions are more likely to be choice-oriented. In contrast, both the ministries and the researchers concerned with education, health, population, housing, and social policy generally tend to be less oriented toward choosing among alternative policies or toward the development of appropriate methodologies that might facilitate choice making.

There is little, for example, in the way of cost-benefit analysis among noneconomists, and few outside the discipline of management are trained to do systems analysis. In spite of the effort of the ICSSR to sponsor methodology courses and to organize a documentation center for machine-readable data, there is still little quantitative research by noneconomists directed at policy issues. In fact, the availability of facilities in this field thus far exceeds the demand, according to a recent self-evaluation by the ICSSR.

Moreover, there is little systematic research evaluating the consequences of government programs: individual projects are evaluated, but not programs and policies as a whole. Nor are there studies of the policy-making or project development process that look at the politics of the process and the assumptions and knowledge underlying policy choices.

Though there has been a substantial increase in the number of social scientists engaged in policy research in recent years, the number still remains small. There are important exceptions to this overstated generalization: economists and those trained in management and public administration. Anthropology and psychology tend, as disciplines, not to be policy-oriented. Some sociologists are concerned with policy questions, but their research is rarely formulated in policy-usable ways—that is, by focusing on alternative choices, with costs, benefits, and consequences associated with each. Political scientists, with a few exceptions, have not been concerned with the output of government; nor have they conducted much research on the policy process itself.

Perhaps the most limiting element is that little policy-oriented social science research in India questions fundamentals. There are too few instances where policy failures have led analysts to question the assumptions on which policies rest. All too often, failures in policy are simply attributed to the "lack of implementation," without recognizing that policies must work within the existing administrative framework, incorporate new or revised administrative structures, or work outside the administrative system. There are also too few instances of scholars dissenting from the prevailing orthodox view in Indian intellectual circles, and there are too many sacred cows ("decentralization," "appropriate technology," "integrated rural development," "nonformal need-based education," restricting "monopoly houses" and "family enterprises," eliminating profit-making "middlemen," and ending "semifeudalism" and the "kulak class") that are not subjected to critical review. The result is that Indian researchers rarely produce counterintuitive findings that challenge widely held beliefs and question the basic approach to policy.

This is not to suggest that there are no radicals within sections of the intelligentsia who are critical of the existing social, economic, and political order. But, paradoxically, some of the unchallenged orthodoxy in India is itself the product of radical thinking that has not been adequately subjected to empirical investigations. Moreover, some of the radical orthodoxy is readily accepted by policymakers and administrators, for it often absolves them from responsibility when policies fail. Consider, for example, the question of why irrigation facilities are not adequately utilized: an explanation which points to the "semifeudal" land system relieves the department of irrigation from responsibility. Similarly, to the extent that low enrollment and high dropout rates in schools are simply the results of rural poverty, officials of the education departments are not responsible for India's enormous educational wastage, though other countries have found ways to overcome the barriers of poverty to keep children in school. And those who argue that only massive economic growth and greater equality of income can bring about a decline in fertility relieve policymakers (and themselves) of having to think about measures that are feasible within existing levels of income and equity. This is not to suggest that poverty, inequality, and exploitation are not fundamental constraints to many social policies; but constraints are, after all, merely constraints, not insurmountable obstacles. An ultimate objective of policy-oriented social science researchers is to subject existing policies to critical, empirical analysis and to generate creative alternatives. Except among economists, Indian social scientists have rarely produced policy suggestions or criticized existing policies in such a way as to stimulate serious debate within intellectual circles. In contrast, debate among Indian economists has proven to be an important element in educating administrators and politicians and in enlivening public debates. Precisely because economists differ on such questions as how to manage inflation and unemployment, whether and how technological change affects employment in agriculture, and countless other economic issues, their role in the policy process is important. There has not yet developed in India a comparable debate among social scientists on educational policies, preferential policies, health and family planning, housing, and other social policy issues, with social scientists bringing to the debate new, if conflicting, findings and perspectives.

Toward a Social Science Policy

A recent review of the work of the Indian Council of Social Science Research by a distinguished committee of social scientists headed by V.M. Dandekar concluded that "by far the most important question relates to the autonomy of the ICSSR." The review committee expressed its concern that the authority of the government to regulate the ICSSR by issuing "directives to the Council in respect to its policies and programmes" should be ended if the ICSSR is to obtain autonomy from government. The committee particularly expressed its concern at the near total dependence of the ICSSR on government for its finances, and it urged the council to seek private, public, and, if possible, foreign funds for creating an endowment fund to provide the ICSSR with some financial autonomy.

The concern for autonomy has to be seen in the context of a decade of close and, in the minds of many, excessive involvement of the Education Ministry in the affairs of the ICSSR. In the words of one social scientist, "The Emergency began in the Education Ministry before it began in the country." As long as the possibility exists that the Education Ministry can again play the role that it played in the past, and that a group of social scientists sharing the political and ideological perspective of the government can use their association to marshal the resources of the ICSSR to further their own objectives, the work of the ICSSR and its institutes will be excessively influenced by political currents.

The review committee gave no attention to the broader question of autonomy in research. Surprisingly few social scientists have questioned the principle that government-sponsored research shall be the exclusive property of government, subject to its review and permission prior to publication. The principle that government-funded research is publicly financed and therefore ought to be the property of the public has yet to be presented to government. In short, what is needed is a concerted effort by the ICSSR and leading social scientists to persuade government not only to provide more autonomy for the ICSSR, but to formulate a new set of policies toward government-sponsored social science research that will establish in advance the right of scholars to publish the results of their findings, irrespective of funding sources.

The poor dissemination of policy-related research severely limits the impact of research on the policy process. The first step toward dealing with this problem is for social scientists to become aware of the need to disseminate policy-relevant research findings to a variety of different audiences— legislators and politicians as well as administrators, and the educated public as well as fellow academics—that is, to bring their studies into policymaking and politically relevant public arenas.

There are a number of ways for improving the dissemination of research findings. A staff member of each of the research institutes might take the responsibility of writing press releases on studies of general public interest. Research relevant to current legislation might be summarized and distributed to legislators. The institutes could develop their own mailing lists, disseminate their lists of publications more widely, and make arrangements with at least one local bookstore to keep their publications available for sale. An ICSSR staff person could peruse research reports from the various institutes for materials to be circulated to the Delhi press and wire services. Some effort might be made to pull together summaries of research findings relevant to current policy debates.

A new journal on social science and public policy could be a useful instrument for disseminating the findings, particularly if the magazine were of high quality, had a mixed board of well-known administrators, academics, and public figures, and was created with sufficient fanfare to attract an initial audience. In addition to signed articles relating research findings to policy, the journal could also include a section that summarizes recent studies of policy interest.

With the possible exception of departments of economics, India's postgraduate programs in the social sciences do not provide training in policy research. India's small number of policy-oriented social scientists were mostly educated abroad, where they were exposed to policy-oriented research. The introduction of policy courses in departments of political science, sociology, and anthropology, and in the schools of management, would reduce the need for overseas training. Perhaps in the not too distant future, it would be appropriate to create one or two centers for the training of policy science researchers, but at this time, the talent for such a program is limited and it is widely dispersed in various research institutes and universities.

Overseas training can continue to play a useful role, particularly if the focus is not on the basic training of social scientists, but on providing a limited number of younger Indian-trained social scientists with an opportunity to work as postdoctoral fellows in graduate public policy centers abroad. The need for such training opportunities is greatest for noneconomist social scientists working in relatively neglected policy fields—health, communications, immigration, housing, nutrition, judicial reform, preferential policies, and the study of the policy process itself.

It is not self-evident that experience by academics in government would necessarily improve their capacity to conduct "realistic" policy-oriented research. Those who have had governmental experience are (sometimes) more aware of the political constraints on policy, the limitations of administrative as well as financial resources, and how the structure of administration and the interests of the bureaucracy affect the choice as well as the implementation of policy. But if some academics who have served in government become more sensitive to bureaucratic structures and processes and bureaucratic mentalities, others are made more cynical by the experience or are themselves absorbed by the bureaucratic outlook.

Nonetheless, many of the researchers and government officials I interviewed suggested that some kind of intern programs in central and state governments would be useful. Several governments in the West already have such programs under which a small number of academics spend a year in an advisory or line position in a government agency, often in a unit where there is an opportunity to observe or take part in project development and policy planning. Whether such a program could be worked out for India depends in the first place on the receptivity of government departments to interns, and secondly, on the kind of placement and "fit" of social scientists with the appropriate government departments.

The ICSSR has made a substantial contribution to the development of policy research by its role in the development of regional social science research institutes. Though these institutes have not yet made a conspicuous impact on public debates over policies, several have made state governments—at least some officials, if not politicians—aware of the value of research for policy and program development and for assessing the consequences of governmental interventions. And for the academic community in these states, the research institutions have provided opportunities for research not generally available in the universities. Perhaps their most important contribution to the academic community is that the institutes have become stimulants for empirical research. As compared with only a decade ago, there is now a greater willingness and capacity of academic researchers to test their arguments against some measures of objective reality. While the proclivity to engage in speculation without reference to empirical facts and to make inferences without data still remains strong in India, the approach of modern empirical social science has gone a long way toward changing the way in which many intellectuals approach problems.

There are, of course, great variations in the quality of these research centers, differences in how they organize themselves and in the kinds of research they do. Some work almost exclusively on economic problems, while others look at a wider range of policy issues; some are staffed only by economists, while others have other social scientists; some work exclusively with secondary data, while others conduct field investigations; some largely do micro studies of particular objects, firms, and localities, while others do broader policy-oriented studies; some focus on how one can implement existing policies and programs more effectively, while others give some attention to alternative policies and programs; some have a small, closely knit staff, while others are organized into departments and function like miniature universities; some prefer to do basic or more academic social science research, while others do more applied research; and some have staffs that could find a place on the faculty of major world universities, while others have comparatively unknown and unpublished scholars. In a country as large and diversified as India, there are bound to be such variations and differences. But a major task in the next few years will be to improve the quality of the weaker centers. The task is made more difficult by the Indian practice of giving tenure to appointments of all ranks.

There are several measures that the ICSSR could pursue to improve some of the weaker regional centers: (a) encourage interinstitute collaborative research involving some of the best institutions and scholars with some of the weaker centers; (b) organize research-cum-policy-oriented workshops where prescreened papers would be presented and discussed, again with a mix of established and less established scholars; (c) provide more detailed and critical feedback on research proposals from ICSSR project review panels. To these might be added two recommendations made earlier:

provide younger scholars with opportunities for postdoctoral training abroad; and create internship opportunities in government for younger researchers.

One additional measure might be taken to strengthen the regional institutes. Many of the regional institutes do not have a policy specialty, but are broadly concerned with regional development. The Institute for Social and Economic Change in Bangalore, the Madras Institute of Development Studies, the A.N. Sinha Institute in Patna, the Giri Institute in Lucknow, and the Sardar Patel Institute in Ahmedabad conduct research on a wide range of problems, and though they have some research priorities, these are often very broadly defined. In contrast, a few institutes have a functional focus: the Indian Institute of Education, the Systems Research Institute, and the Public Enterprise Institute. A few centers like the Tata Institute of Social Sciences combine a regional and functional policy focus.

Some of the regional institutes might be encouraged to strengthen their functional policy capabilities by developing a series of related research projects on a single problem. The benefits of programmatic research are cumulative experience for the research staff, cumulative contributions to policy, and recognition as a national center in a specialized policy area. Moreover, specialized policy research within a development institute is often broader in conception than similar research in a more specialized single-policy research center. Compare, for example, the more broadly conceived demographic research at the Centre for Development Studies in Trivandrum with the kind of demographic research conducted at most of the population institutes.

Research centers might choose to develop a specialty on, for example, health policy, communication policy, some aspects of educational policy, irrigation or electricity policy (including the problems of management and delivery), social forestry, the delivery of legal services to those with low income, urban housing policy, or nutrition policy. Some regional centers already have one or two scholars specializing in one of these areas. In most instances, the expansion of the staff to three or four scholars, a modest investment in developing a more specialized library collection, some seed money for research, and some external recognition by the ICSSR that a center has established a specialized policy research cell would facilitate the development of policy research competence within the regional institutes.

The review committee of the ICSSR has suggested that the research institutes should play a substantial role in promoting social science research, by training younger social scientists, holding seminars for local college teachers and younger social scientists, and the like. Which of the centers is strong enough to play this role, and whether such a role is compatible with the need to strengthen the centers' own research competence, are matters that need to be carefully considered.

The absence of a research center with a sustained capacity for survey research is a conspicuous gap in the social science research institutions in India. Several institutions—the Centre for the Study of Developing Societies immediately comes to mind—have done first-rate surveys. Some of the demographic research centers do good survey work, though of a limited kind. The Operations Research Group in Baroda has also completed good fertility surveys in addition to its market and media studies. The Indian Institute of Public Opinion has done some useful surveys of political attitudes and preference. Many of the ICSSR-sponsored institutions have conducted surveys for specific projects. But none of the social science research institutes has a permanent survey research staff and field investigators with the institutional capacity for sustained investigations. The result is that there are few longitudinal studies measuring the extent to which attitudes are changing, how, and under what influences. Most seriously for policy-oriented research, there are hardly any systematic surveys of public attitudes toward policies and programs.

It takes little imagination to see how research in this area could make a contribution to both basic research and policy studies. A few illustrations come to mind. Systematic research on why parents withdraw their children from school would help in formulating policies to achieve universalization of primary education. Studies of the attitudes of the public toward the police and of the police toward various ethnic groups and classes would be of help to the Police Commission. A survey of attitudes toward preferential policies for scheduled castes, scheduled tribes, and backward classes would help politicians formulate policy in this politically sensitive area. Better studies of factors that influence norms for family size would facilitate the development of new population policies. Information on the difficulties citizens encounter in dealing with officials at the local levels (judges, police, postal officials, rural credit officers, officials from the irrigation departments, health services, and electricity boards) might make it possible to find ways to improve the delivery of services to the rural population.

An institution that conducts surveys over an extended period of time is likely to increase its survey skills, especially if there is experimentation with new methodologies, sustained work with difficult-to-survey groups (e.g., the elderly, women in purdah, isolated communities, the migratory) and considerable effort is put into training and supervision of field staff.

Unfortunately, a national survey research unit is costly. The costs of maintaining a staff of field interviewers throughout the country, regional officers to train and supervise, and a central office to process data and do the analyses are high. Finding sponsors for costly national surveys on a sustained basis would be difficult.

If it is not feasible to create a national survey research organization at this time, perhaps it is possible to create one quality state survey research organization. Such an organization could become a place for the development of model surveys that might be used in other states. In time, survey researchers from other parts of the country could be sent there for training. Policy-relevant studies in a single state would not only help state government policymaking, but might illuminate some national policy issues as well. The contributions of a state survey research center would thus be greatest if it were located in a relatively "typical" state—that is, one with an average literacy rate, some relatively inaccessible areas, substantial cultural and linguistic heterogeneity, and diversified occupational patterns.

Still another major research lacuna is the absence of comparative public policy research that might expand a consideration of policy alternatives on the part of policymakers. Policy researchers too rarely assemble materials on the experiences of other developing countries; too little attention has been given to the systematic reporting of the policy and project experiences of other countries in health, education, family planning, housing, urban development, transportation, and rural development. Only a handful of researchers at the various research institutes or in government are familiar with the variety of policy experiments and innovative projects attempted elsewhere that might form the basis for policy experiments in India.

Merely to propose that India replicate China's barefoot doctor program, Singapore's housing program, Israel's land reclamation and afforestation program, Taiwan's family planning program, or Cuba's adult literacy program is of little value, especially when the social, economic, and political contexts—and the resources available—vary so much. But the experiences of others can lead to project experiments; through the observation and evaluation of these experiments, social scientists can play a useful role in suggesting whether and how successful projects can be replicated elsewhere.

Moreover, there are enormous opportunities for the development of a field of comparative public policy within India, using states, *zilla parishads,* and *panchaya samitis* as the units of analysis. Why do similar policies pursued by state and local governments achieve different results? Are differences in outcomes in, for example, health, nutrition, and education the result of different policies? Are variations in policy outcomes the result of differences in policy inputs in, for example, the amount of resources allocated, the quantity, quality, or structure of administration, or the procedures for distributing services? Or are differences in outcomes the result of variations in the characteristics of the target populations—their income or education or the structure of land ownership, for example? The systematic attention to these issues within India could not only contribute to policymaking but could be a significant contribution to the field of public policy analysis.

Profitable links could also be made to the burgeoning fields of economic and demographic history in India. The work of Asok Mitra and others on historical regional variations in communications, road transport, and irrigation facilities, in fertility, morbidity, mortality, and migration rates, literacy and education, violence and crime, and a variety of other social indicators raises the obvious question of how these variations are linked to differences in government policies by the princely states and the British raj, as well as by postindependence state and central governments.

Some Conclusions

India now has an impressive number of policy-oriented research institutions. In most instances, these have 15 or more staff members, ample research assistants and secretaries, reasonably good libraries and computational facilities, access to modest research support from the ICSSR and larger grants from government departments, and stable core funding from the ICSSR and the state governments. The major impediments to effective social science research in India are not financial and material. Indeed, some of the research institutes are better off than similar research institutes in the United Kingdom and the United States. This is not to say that the research centers could not be improved with more library resources, staff expansion, or improved physical facilities. Some of the smaller and newer centers are in need of more assistance, but several of the larger centers need to demonstrate that they can produce more quality research before they warrant additional resources. The mere fact that a center is large should not be sufficient grounds for additional support.

But the process of new institution building has not come to an end. The ICSSR actively nurtured the development of regional research centers that would contribute to the analysis of development issues within the states, contribute to state policymaking, and provide national planners and policymakers with a better grasp of what was happening throughout the country. Centers were developed in Karnataka, Kerala, Tamil Nadu, Uttar Pradesh, Bihar, Andhra, Gujarat, and West Bengal. Orissa, Madhya Pradesh, Assam, and Rajasthan could also use such research centers, as could some of the smaller states. However, the number of trained social scientists available for new regional centers remains small. The same constraint operates with respect to the question of whether additional research centers should be started in states that already have one center. In most states, the case for an additional center would have to be made on the grounds that trained personnel are available and that such a center has something new to offer, such as a specialized competence in an important policy area or approach (e.g., systems analysis or survey research).

It would be both difficult and unwise to create research centers in the next few years at the same pace as in the last decade. The ICSSR review committee has quite properly concluded that existing research institutes should be strengthened before new ones are established. The first objective ought to be the improvement of quality in the existing centers, but whether the ICSSR will be able to resist pressures for creating new centers remains to be seen.

In any event, the most pressing needs for the social sciences in India are elsewhere: to free government-sponsored research from its present restrictions; to facilitate the wider dissemination of policy-related research to officials, politicians, and the relevant publics; to improve the training of noneconomist social scientists in policy research; to bring comparative knowledge of policies elsewhere to bear on policy analysis; to develop a field of comparative analysis within India so as to bring the policy and project experiences of one area of the country to another; to provide some policy-oriented researchers with governmental experience; to develop policy specialties within the regional institutes; and to develop survey research facilities that would increase knowledge of public attitudes relevant to public policies.

A more effective linkage between policy-oriented social science research and the policy process is a central objective of a national science policy. But what is needed is a broad view of the policy process. It is not enough that social scientists conduct research that is responsive to the needs of officials. In democratic societies, policy-oriented research can also influence the thinking of politicians, interest groups, and the variety of publics that have an interest in or are affected by what government does. As we have suggested earlier, knowledge systematically acquired through social science research can be an important input to the process of policy and project formation, implementation, evaluation, revision, and termination. Precisely what kind of knowledge is generated, with what freedom—and creativity—social science researchers choose their research and how they pursue it, to whom the knowledge is disseminated, and how and by whom the knowledge is utilized are central issues in a country's social science policy. How India deals with these issues in the next few years may or may not have an impact on the shape of policies, but it will certainly have an impact on social science research.

12 Scholarship and Contract Research: The Ecology of Social Science in Kenya and Tanzania

David Court

Introduction: The Utilitarian Cast of East African Social Science

The community of East African social scientists came into existence during an era of strong expectations about what its role in national development ought to be. Originating in the planning needs of national governments, the desire of international agencies to assist them, and the intellectual climate of the "development decade," these expectations stressed the need for social science to serve national policy and public welfare in direct, immediate, and practical ways. Faced by urgent problems of planning, governments looked to university social-science departments for solutions, and their sizable budgetary contributions to higher education added weight to their demand that social scientists direct their attention to issues of immediate concern. Likewise, many technical assistance agencies, in a desire to be responsive to "national priorities," began to direct their resources toward the application of social-science expertise in university outreach and extension activities. The initial impossibility of an institutional division of labor meant that the burden of responding to developmental expectations, which in some areas was shared among a network of research institutes, in Kenya and Tanzania fell upon the single national university.

Although some eloquent voices cautioned against an overly narrow or functional path for universities in this development drift,[1] and an important critique of it grew up in subsequent years,[2] a highly instrumental view of university social science dominated the 1970s and presents its consequences for the 1980s.

The most dramatic consequence has been the incorporation of social science into the ambit of national planning and development assistance. In the early 1970s, social scientists recently returned from graduate training and anxious to apply their expertise to important areas of national development had a difficult task convincing their governments that they had anything to offer. Much time was spent in discussion about the need to "educate the policy makers" in the importance of research. Today, the situation is very different. Social science has been taken over by the policy process and able social scientists face many more requests for work than they can meet.

321

Their earlier general interest in addressing developmental issues has been submerged in a deluge of requests for service on commissions and consultancies and for the task of evaluation. As a result, in Kenya, for example, virtually all university social-science research that is not for a degree or thesis consists of short-term contract work applied to specific problems. In historical terms, the involvement of local social scientists in consultancy work is a very positive development and an essential step toward the reduction of dependency upon external technical assistance. Much work previously contracted out to foreign companies and individuals is now being done by national scholars and consultants. However, the strength of demand in relation to the supply of local scientists has meant that a particular style of social science—short-term contract work—has come to dominate social-science activity. Social science has come to mean the presentation of recommendations on a prescribed topic, in response to a request, and by means of an activity whose total time rarely exceeds six months, usually lasts two or three weeks, and sometimes is accomplished in a matter of days. In Kenya the nexus has become commercialized and in Tanzania nationalized, but the pattern and results in both cases have been remarkably similar.

The very important consequence is that a particular utilitarian view and result orientation have tended to preempt the role and self-concept of social science before the local profession has had a chance to establish and define itself. External faith in the practical utility of social science—whether from government, international agencies, or commercial firms—has submerged the profession's own reservations about the inherent limitations of its offering and encouraged overextension and the consequent risk of lost credibility if it cannot meet these expectations. At the same time, the problem-solving approach has assumed an exclusive intimacy of partnership with government in the promotion of "development," which has not always been helpful to the larger purpose of creating the level of high-quality research capacity upon which the development of social science ultimately depends.

This situation has been exacerbated by the fact that various characteristics of the university environment not only have not been strong enough to provide a countervailing academic incentive system to that provided by external demand, but in a number of ways have served to buttress this demand through deterrents to scholarship.

It is inappropriate and inaccurate to view external demand mainly as a perverse and unwarranted intrusion into the academic world. At the same time, it is clear that the volume of this tide and the full flood of its implications have not yet been accommodated by the universities or recognized by the external supporters of social science.

This chapter extends an earlier survey of social-science achievement in East Africa[3] (see chapter 6 of this volume) by focusing upon some of these implications arising from the pattern of demand for social science. It tries to document the extent to which social science in Kenya and Tanzania has become dominated by a result orientation, at the expense of the process of self-development; examines some of the reasons for the dominance of contract research, locating them in the pattern of external demand and the relative weakness of the countervailing academic incentives; considers some of the consequences of the trend on the quality of social-science activity; and suggests the kinds of assistance that might contribute to the development of social science in the particular context described.

Sources of Demand

Several different patterns of demand for social science collectively account for the dramatic trend toward result orientation. In each case, this trend is an outgrowth both of the centrality of projects in the countries' development strategies and of the associated pattern of development assistance they have received.

Government Contracts with Institutions and Individuals

In the first place, national governments have come to support the usefulness of social-science research for the purpose of project appraisal, monitoring, and evaluation. What was initially a tactical response to the known pre-dilections of agencies donating development funds has become at least partly a matter of conviction dominated by a view of social science as a problem-solving or at least a legitimizing technology. This is evident in the use the governments make of the applied-research institutions at the university, the importance that ministries now attach to evaluation, and the de-mands that governments make for the services of individual social scientists. In Kenya and Tanzania, social scientists have been co-opted into govern-ment committees, boards of parastatal organizations, and evaluation teams. In Tanzania, in particular, they have had a chance to influence policy at the highest levels. Teachers of economics have been plucked out of the univer-sity to serve as presidential advisers, principal secretaries, ministers, and bank directors. Sociologists have been used to plan "villagization" policies and settlement schemes, historians to direct cultural policy, and political scientists have been taken into high-level positions in the regional adminis-tration and the national party.

In Tanzania, the style of policy making has led to a heavy emphasis on evaluation.[4] This style has tended to stress the realization of ambitious social goals and the mobilization of popular energies rather than detailed forward planning, prior assessment of resources, or cost-benefit calculations of the full range of outcomes of a given policy measure. The main reason is the dearth of information on which more calculated planning can be based and the desire, in the absence of other preconditions for social transformation, to create a revolutionary spirit through political means. To the extent that policies are initiated before detailed information is available, their successful attainment depends heavily upon the accumulation of understanding and information through feedback mechanisms which can let policy makers know what is happening as implementation proceeds. Recognition of this fact has led to a stress on evaluation, evidenced, for example, in the Ministry of National Education's decision to create a Center for Research and Evaluation and to attach an evaluation unit to each of its nine sections. In both Tanzania and Kenya, ministries tend to contract directly with social-science departments and research units or with individual members of these institutions.

International Organizations

A second source of demand for social-science expertise is the various technical-assistance agencies, which while working with a particular ministry frequently require independent or collaborative assessments of the projects they are funding. Foremost among international agencies drawing on social-science talent in East Africa are the World Bank, International Labour Organization (ILO), United States Agency for International Development (USAID), Swedish International Development Agency (SIDA), Canadian International Development Agency (CIDA), International Development Research Centre (IDRC), Food and Agriculture Organization (FAO), and the various United Nations agencies, including particularly the United Nations Educational, Scientific and Cultural Organization (UNESCO), United Nations Development Program (UNDP), and United Nations Family Planning Association (UNFPA). Much more than in the past, these agencies are trying to anticipate and measure the social impact of their development projects and are seeking social-science advice to do so. USAID, for example, is obligated to include assessments of social impact and environmental impact in its projects. Until very recently, most agencies imported social-science consultants to provide the required expertise, but several as a matter of policy now seek out local social scientists as consultants for their projects.

While the various agencies draw upon local social scientists for work on specific development projects, they also fund and seek local assistance for less-bounded work on broad areas of policy interest. For example, as a result perhaps of the influential ILO study *Employment, Incomes and Equality: A Strategy for Increasing Productive Employment in Kenya*,[5] employment and income distribution has become a subject of particular fascination to a number of agencies and there have been no less than ten studies on this subject during the past two years.[6]

A common pattern of this type of demand for social science is the several-nation study, in which the project is usually subcontracted by the funding agency to a particular European or North American university.[7] It is usually led by a scholar from that institution, whose search for local collaborators is assisted by the inducement, in addition to cash, of travel funds for a conference once the work is completed or, in some cases, of training funds for project participants.

Regional Organizations

Various regional organizations, including the Economic Commission for Africa, the African Development Bank, and the Council for the Development of Economic and Social Research in Africa (CODESRIA), provide an Africa-wide source of demand for East African expertise. Their general pattern has been to explore particular issues or provide projects across a range of countries, and their distinctive contribution has been to utilize individuals as consultants throughout the continent rather than only in their own country. CODESRIA, for example, is developing state-of-the-art reviews on a number of developmental topics as a prelude to regional projects.

Religious Organizations

An important national source of demand for social science in Kenya and Tanzania is provided by nongovernmental organizations such as the Protestant National Christian Council and the Catholic Secretariat and, on a lesser scale, by the Aga Khan Foundation. The Christian organizations in both countries have a sizable network of projects on which they seek evaluations and also promote studies by local social scientists on topics of major social concern. Recent work of this type in Kenya has included studies of literacy methods, the ownership of wealth, refugees, relationships between different ethnic groups, and access to technical education. The national organizations are linked to international bodies such as the World Council of Churches and the Christian Student Fellowship, which involve some of East Africa's social scientists in their worldwide projects dealing with such major issues as urbanization, liberation movements, adult literacy, and refugees.

Consulting Companies

An increasing part of the demand for social-science work in Kenya is now channeled through private consulting companies that enter into contracts with government, the private sector, and international agencies. Most of the Kenyan companies have been registered in the last three years and several are owned by current or former university faculty members. They are an interesting political phenomenon, as they have recently formed themselves into an association for the purpose of wresting business from some of the established Nairobi-based foreign firms.[8]

Some have sizable capital outlays in terms of offices, equipment, and permanent staff, and play a substantial and regular role in linking social science expertise to development projects. Others have little more than a name and a letterhead—they came into existence in a speculative response to a specific project and have a precarious existence. All tend to draw upon university social scientists. The major advantage of the consulting companies over the university research units is that they are able to choose from a wider pool of experts in putting together a team relevant to the particular purpose for which they are submitting a tender. Although such companies are less common in Tanzania, there government co-optation of social scientists into evaluation teams has an effect similar to that of the private companies in channeling social-science research toward development projects.

Foundations

In the midst of this welter of large-scale demand for social science can be found an additional, more modest type of support, which is provided by the Rockefeller and Ford foundations in particular. The aim of this type of support is, in broad terms, to assist the development of local capacity for carrying out social-science research. It expresses itself through support for the projects of university institutions and staff members, and has a substantial interest in formal and informal training for research.

The Costs and Benefits of Contractual Demand

The existence of rather substantial demand for applied social science from outside the university and scholarly community has affected the *content* of social science and the *terms* on which it is conducted. From one standpoint, the external demand can be viewed as evidence for the success of social science in making itself valued outside its original base and in taking on a solidly practical content and national complexion. Few would wish to argue that Kenyan and Tanzanian social scientists ought to have been studying anything other than basic problems of development. When issues of content have arisen, they have centered on the extent to which pressure from policymakers for answers to particular problems has reduced attention to the provision of basic knowledge as a guide to understanding. From another standpoint, however, the very emphasis on practical content has significantly affected the terms on which social science is carried out, to the point that it may be neglecting to preserve and reinforce the normative and institutional structures needed to nourish its original base. It is important when considering the future to keep in mind the distinction between these two types of impact.

Benefits

Practical Emphasis. One benefit resulting from the strength of contract demand and the timing of its emergence is that social science has rooted itself in a concern for practical problems of East African society and multidisciplinary approaches to them rather than a narrower and more esoteric set of issues, which a different timetable and climate of opinion might have engendered. The subject matter of social science in Kenya and Tanzania during the past decade has consisted almost exclusively of those topical issues affecting agriculture, the economy, education, nutrition, and so forth, which have dominated the agendas of policy debate. Multidisciplinary research institutes have come into being and have channeled intellectual resources to the service of public policy. The forerunner was the Makerere Institute of Social Research, followed by the Institute for Development Studies (IDS) at the University of Nairobi in 1965 and the Economic Research Bureau (ERB) and Bureau of Resource Assessment and Land Use Planning (BRALUP) at the University of Dar es Salaam shortly after. The rationale for these units, as exemplified by the IDS terms of reference, was "a response to a strongly felt need for organized full-time research on urgent social and economic problems of development."[9]

At the individual level, the demand for social-science contract work—whether from ministries, private firms, or international organizations—has had the effect of directing the attention of faculty members toward immediate widely recognized problems and putting them in touch with ministries and other concerned organizations to ameliorate them. This has provided a means for faculty members to infuse their teaching with some research and practical experience. This idea was central in the rationale for the Tanzanian practice of rotating university staff members between civil service and teaching positions. Because consultancy requests to an individual have usually been stimulated by recognition of his particular knowledge or expertise, they have in many instances served to reinforce an intellectual interest rather than simply commandeer an available talent.

Productivity. The demand for contract research has also encouraged productivity. Whether the method of payment is cash for service as in Kenya or government contracts as in Tanzania, the result has been that a lot of work has been done that might otherwise not have materialized. The external incentive system has put a premium on completion, with a self-correcting mechanism in which good performance is rewarded in material terms or government approbation, and poor performance is penalized because services are not requested again. The contrast between the quality of work done for a consultancy and that done for a seminar, *by the same individual*, provides striking evidence of the power of the incentive. What is more important, government officials will find time to read a commissioned piece, while generally they disregard the stream of research papers that cross their desk simply because they are on a mailing list. Social-science work that is dismissed as at best irrelevant and at worst subversive in open-ended seminar format can become an important input when expressed in the form of a consultancy report.

The Development and Application of National Capacity. A third major benefit of the scale of demand for contract research has been to direct attention to the importance of having a pool of national professionals who can provide the required analysis and to accelerate the process of reducing dependence upon foreign companies and individuals for the provision of this expertise. Both Kenya and Tanzania can provide a variety of examples of major development projects that have foundered because they were based on plans prepared by outside consultants who were insufficiently attuned to the realities of the administrative and cultural context in which the projects were to be implemented. Reducing dependency upon foreign technical assistance is in itself a major goal of national development. One incidental effect of government and international emphasis on national participation in consultancy work has been to increase the status of social scientists in their own society.

University Retention of Talent. The existence of external incentives—the opportunity to increase one's salary or work for government without leaving the university—has enabled the universities to retain the services of talented individuals who might otherwise have sought higher rewards in other employment sectors. The University of Nairobi has just formally accepted the principle of consultancy work and secondments into the terms of service of faculty members. Until recently, faculty were viewed as being in full-time employment, although consultancy work during the vacations was tacitly accepted. Now the university has bowed to the logic of a salary structure in which university salaries are not competitive with those outside, especially in the professions. The new acceptance of consultancy is based on the rationale of enabling faculty members to put their expertise at the service of development. Having accepted the principle, the university has requested all faculties to propose possible arrangements so that consultancy does not impinge upon teaching. The university seems unlikely to move to the kind of variegated part-time contracts that are familiar in American universities. More likely are regulations governing the type of work that is viewed as acceptable—for example, putting an emphasis on the research component—and another model has already been provided by the Faculty of Engineering, which has established its own consulting unit and pays the university a proportion of its profits. The University of Dar es Salaam has also just established regulations to guide consultancy work by academic staff.

The Problematic Impact of External Demand

The expanding demand for social-science work is testimony to its positive contribution to development projects. However, the benefits to the development of university-based social science just mentioned are modified by some more questionable effects. These have posed some dilemmas for aid agencies, government, individual scholars, and university social-science departments alike.

Commercialization. The most visible consequence of the external demand structure has been the commercialization of social science. An able social scientist at the University of Nairobi can multiply his university salary through the selection of international consultancies. Projects organized by the United Nations agencies in particular have been especially influential in their impact on the overall incentive system for social-science work. The secondment of East African professionals from their university roles is facilitated by irresistible salary scales and other benefits, including duty-free importation privileges, access to foreign exchange, and the opportunity to sport diplomatic car license plates and acquire a vehicle. At the other end of the scale, typists lucky enough to be assigned to such projects can supplement their regular activity by generous piecework rates. Such rates can command the best available talent at all levels, but can also generate serious friction because of the invidious distinctions they provoke.

Neglect of Absorptive Capacity. A second consequence of external demand derives from its frequently large scale of operation. Another project in Kenya is putting $4.5 million toward researching a system for the introduction of alternative energy sources for the Kenyan poor. The project is highly relevant, massively funded, and has strong government support. However, it ran into difficulty because of its large scale and hasty preparation. It was designed in four weeks with inadequate professional involvement, little local consultation, scant regard for the social conditions and bureaucratic environment in which it would be operating, and no systematic consideration of whether existing capacity could absorb the intended scale and pace of implementation. The government participants quickly assessed the direction and probable outcome of the activity and devoted their efforts to ensuring that they acquired the material aspects of the project—Land Rovers and office equipment—before the project foundered.

Competition for Scholarly Services. The state of competition for scholarly services among providers of technical assistance, which results from excess demand, has other consequences in addition to raising the price of social-science work. It increases the importance of political as well as professional criteria in recruitment. In addition to competence, university status—such as being a dean or research director—is a marketable commodity, for the inclusion of certain names on the roster of a research proposal can strengthen the competitive posture of an agency bidding for a tender. In this context, the home background of local researchers is also important; in other words, it is an asset if it coincides with that of the main government decision maker on a project or with the site of the proposed activity. A project that was developed by the Ministry of Economic Planning with a budget of several million dollars aimed at improving arid-land agriculture and attracted bids from seven international firms. Because of the sizable social-science component, most of the firms were at pains to solicit a university social scientist into their team in order to strengthen their portfolio, with the bizarre consequence that department was pitted against department in a competition of international agencies.

Other consequences of this competition lead to some interesting anomalies. For example, several social scientists from the University of Nairobi are involved in the ownership of consulting companies, placing them in positions of potential conflict of interest. Cases of double grants for a single purpose have also been known, the most notorious occurring when a university-based project in Kenya that was funded and completed with assistance from one agency was subsequently sold as a private consultancy to another. Furthermore, the competition by particular consulting companies or individuals encourages attempts to corner parts of the market. It is also relatively common for officials awarding contracts to insist on the involvement of specified colleagues as consultants in the planned activity, with sometimes harmful consequences to quality.

The government itself, unable to compete with private firms for the services of, say, economists, is often a victim of a situation in which funding agencies compete to outbid each other. At the same time, foreign scholars seeking academic collaboration with local social scientists both contribute to and are the unwitting victims of the competition. Grant-funded academic research is typically intended to be a collaborative effort between foreign and local social scientists. On the one hand, it offers an alternative to consulting and at the same time provides the necessary funding and perhaps professional rewards to local scholars. On the other hand, such grants can rarely compete with consultancies.

These pressures and consequences are not unique, and most countries have had to devise procedures for regulating them. In East Africa, they are novel and significant because they are occurring while the social-science community is still relatively weak and before regulatory procedures have been established.

The Locus of Research Initiative. The main general effect of contract demand upon university social science has been an increase in the proportion of total work commissioned by an outside body rather than initiated by the university department or a research institute or individual scholar. Virtually all research at the Institute for Development Studies in Nairobi and the Economic Research Bureau in Dar es Salaam is now of this type.

Frequently, of course, the department or individual will be involved in the conception or design of the project and, among the East African research institutes, BRALUP in Dar es Salaam has been particularly successful in retaining the initiative to both identify new subject areas and persist with old ongoing programs. Nevertheless, even here the bureau reflects the general picture of a demand for services that exceeds resources.[10]

Individual Overextension. Just as the demand for the services of research institutes exceeds their resources, so able individual social scientists face more requests for work than they can possibly carry out. Sometimes the requests respond to recognized areas of scholarly competence, but often they simply reflect the need for someone to do a job. Most social-science faculty members at the University of Nairobi are simultaneously involved in several pieces of commissioned work, which have been entered into either on a personal contract basis or within a general contract awarded to their department or research institute. The commitments come on top of extensive community obligations that stem from educated status, family obligations, and a demanding set of academic responsibilities. A senior social scientist at Nairobi or Dar es Salaam is likely to be involved in extensive teaching, departmental administration, university committee work, coordination of several university projects, and service on various government committees—all of which puts him in the category of "the most common specie of the East African university scene: the overcommitted researcher, *Homo Overcomitecus.*"[11]

Diversification of Interest. The relatively small pool of social scientists, and the increasing demand from government and international agencies that projects make use of local as well as imported expertise, mean that East

African social scientists tend to be requested to provide advice across a wider range of topics than their counterparts elsewhere. The result is a tendency toward dispersion of interests and attachments. For example, among the writings of a former member of the government department of the University of Nairobi are papers on topics ranging from the role of women in rural development to technical education, East African poetry, and political theory. Following completion of a large-scale study of arid-land agriculture for UNESCO, this same individual left the university and—as if symbolically—moved to a career in journalism.

Faculty Attrition. A by-product of the opportunity for diversified experience within the university is a corresponding widening of scope for work outside it. Movement by social scientists out of the university into other spheres of activity has been a steady trend. For example, of the East African social scientists on the staff of the Universities of Nairobi and Dar es Salaam in 1973, 30 percent are now working outside the university. Among different types of social scientists, economists have displayed the most mobility. Of forty who obtained a Ph.D. in economics at an overseas university on a Rockefeller Foundation scholarship in the period 1963–1977,[12] a high proportion were the outstanding undergraduate economists of that period and were selected by the university as prospective members of staff. Of this highly selective group, only eight, or 20 percent, are still working in a university. The explanation lies in the scarcity value of economists, although it is interesting that the attrition rate is similar for both universities despite very different structures of alternative opportunity. In Kenya, which has a free-enterprise economy, the scarcity value of economists has enabled them to seek positions with salaries that the university cannot match. In Tanzania, where few opportunities for private employment exist and where salaries are standardized throughout the public sector, which includes the university, university economists tend to have been seconded into government planning positions.

Teaching. The effect of attrition upon teaching has been particularly strong because it has involved the first generation of East African social scientists. Of the thirteen original indigenous heads of the social-science departments and research institutes of the Universities of Nairobi and Dar es Salaam, all but one of whom were first appointed within the past decade, three remain at the university, and of the ten who moved on, eight work for international organizations. It is possible that this kind of internationalism can assist local social science by giving it a voice in the world community and contributing to what Mazrui has referred to as a process of "counterpenetration." This can happen only if the international experience is ploughed back and if a strong local social-science community already exists and can itself provide a professional satisfaction strong enough to balance the international sources.

As already mentioned, Tanzania has institutionalized the idea of rotating faculty members between university and government. Part of the rationale for this was the expectation that circulation between university and government would bring fresh ideas to government and keep faculty in touch with practical realities of development. Although some circulation has occurred, there has been a net outflow from the university. The social scientists have made important contributions in their assigned roles; however, the constant inroads into departments have disrupted the continuity, diluted the quality of teaching and research, and delayed the achievement of a self-renewing social-science community.

Relationship with Government. Two additional dangers for social science arise whenever it is perceived and justifies itself exclusively in terms of its problem-solving capability. The first danger is the risk of diminished credibility stemming from its inability to provide the developmental "answers" that may be expected. The second danger arises from the very intimacy between university and government that treats them as part of the same arena. Regimes change but universities continue. An environment in which teaching and policymaking positions are interchangeable may tend to encourage exposition rather than critical analysis and reduce the scope for those exercises of critical imagination that seem to be the lifeblood of the social sciences. At the same time, the emphasis on the nation or regions within it as the units of attention—which is one consequence of the applied and governmental framework of East African social science—risks parochialism if it cuts the community off from strong international professional sources.

Training. The pressure on departments and research institutes for research results can also set back training programs, because young scholars tend to be pressed into service on institutional projects and have too little time left for graduate study. The recent report of the BRALUP review team at the University of Dar es Salaam made the point in strong terms: "The demand for the services at BRALUP exceeds its own resources; consequently there is a tendency to stretch these to the utmost, leaving little room for attention to the crucial issue of staff development."[13]

The Curriculum. The effect of external demand upon the curriculum is evident mainly in the increasing emphasis on service courses within social-science departments which are explicitly geared to future lines of civil-service employment. Examples from Nairobi include the B.Phil. program in economics for staff of the Ministry of Finance, the social-work subdepartment in sociology, and the emphasis on development administration and management in political science. The University of Dar es Salaam has given substantial thought to new ways of organizing social-science training.[14] This has found expression in two distinct emphases. The first aims to give the curriculum a work orientation and this is evidenced by the admissions policy, which requires prior work experience, work-study programs in the long vacation, and national-service schemes. The second emphasis has been upon cross-disciplinary structures of organization and training in the search for a vocational rather than a disciplinary base to the organization of the social-science faculty; the inclusion of a common course—development studies, formerly East African societies and environment—for all students; experiments with a common interdepartmental course in research methodology; and, finally, an emphasis upon home-based graduate degrees that incorporate some work at a foreign university but minimize the amount of time spent by an individual overseas. Despite a high level of institutional imagination, these developments do not yet seem to have crystallized into a new concept of social-science training and research, but they may well contain the elements of an important future framework.

Social-Science Literature. Another curriculum-related effect of the dominance of contract work is the reduced availability of pertinent literature. Although commissioned work may be read by government officials, much of the work is restricted in circulation or is tailored to a rather narrow audience and therefore does not contribute to the stock of publicly available knowledge that is incorporated in teaching texts. Ironically, this material is often more easily available to international colleagues than it is to local scholars. The report of the BRALUP review indicates that approximately one-third of BRALUP publications have consisted of restricted consultancy reports or service papers, with the remainder of the work divided among reports, monographs, and unpublished seminar papers.[15]

Professional Norms. The contract emphasis has inevitably had an effect on the development of professional norms in social science. Contract research by definition has its source outside the university, which means that the reference group for the scholar is not his peers but the sponsors of the work, and the tendency for exclusiveness is increased when, as is frequently the case, it is labeled as confidential or restricted. The idea of research output as the principal criterion of academic productivity and professional assessment is difficult to implement in a context where service work occupies a large proportion of a scholar's time. Tanzania has attempted to take account of this reality by incorporating practical experience into the criteria of assessment for university staff. Thus, there have been several cases of academic staff members' being promoted while seconded to, and as a result of, government service.

Quality and Capacity. At a more general and more familiar level, the establishment of quality in social science is endangered by the dominance of policy research in the total research culture. The pressure to provide "answers" and recommendations that East African social scientists continually face can lead to a concentration on factors that are subject to manipulation rather than on more inaccessible institutional processes or more fundamental aspects of the social context. It is typically after-the-fact research relying on secondary sources because of the shortage of time for conducting systematic and sustained data collection. Furthermore, it produces a standing temptation to generalize beyond the claims of the data. This situation is a familiar and general feature of policy research:

> The capacity for suspending judgement is limited; they must reach conclusions on whatever evidence is available within a relatively short period of time. This inevitably affects their standards of proof; the threshold at which they become satisfied that an analysis is sustained by the evidence is necessarily lower.[16]

External Orientation. Central to the development of social science are its ability to reproduce itself through teaching, the creation of an incremental body of literature, and the institutionalization of norms of professional practice. These activities have traditionally been located in the university. Yet, a general consequence of the prevailing emphasis on contract research is the tendency it has partially created to separate social science from its university base. Research institutions aspire to autonomy within or outside the university, individual researchers seek private arrangements with funding organizations, and the organizations themselves try to avoid the necessity of dealing with the university. The desire to bypass established institutional structures is often motivated simply by the wish to avoid the bureaucratic control mechanisms that inhibit action. As a general tendency, however, it has significant implications. It can stunt the growth of the institution on which elsewhere social science has relied for self-renewal and development.

The Scholarly Environment

The earlier argument that a particular pattern of activity has come to dominate East African social science suggested that this was largely a consequence of the external demand structure and government planning needs that have grown up in the past ten years. It is equally clear that in addition to the "pull" factors of external demand, features of the academic environment itself have also contributed, as "push" factors, to determining the characteristic shape of East African social science.

These features of the academic environment tend to strengthen the result and external orientation of social science by constituting themselves as deterrents to alternative approaches. Many of them are shared by Kenya and Tanzania and seem to derive from basic commonalities of their economic, social, and academic condition, despite some major differences in educational policy. If reformative action is to be based at the university, it is important to consider the kind of incentive structure it does and might provide. How harmful are some of the conditions to local capacity for producing knowledge? What are some of their effects? Which ones are especially important? To what extent are they amenable to change?

Facilities and Resources

Perhaps the most obvious problem area is that of logistical-support facilities. Access by social scientists to computer, typing, editorial, and clerical assistance and transportation facilities is problematic in varying degrees. The absence or weakness of these facilities produces distinctive styles of operation and management that either dispense with the required resources—necessitating typing one's own paper, sending the data overseas for processing, doing the administrative task oneself—or require heroic patience, persistence, and ingenuity in actually striving to make the system work. For example, organizing a workshop that involves the usual production and dissemination of papers and the transport and accommodation of participants requires prodigious feats of energy, improvisation, and entrepreneurial talent in order to ensure adequate access to all the required resources for the specific purpose in hand.

Some of these factor shortages are simply manifestations of poverty and of an environment in which factors cannot be set aside for exclusive purposes. Thus, for example, a faculty Land Rover cannot be held for a sustained period of research because it is required to transport junior staff to their homes in the absence of any alternative transportation. A more extreme manifestation of the problem beset the University of Nairobi in 1979, when, in the face of a call for austerity but in disregard of the university constitution, the whole of the research allocation was placed in a common fund, leaving no university money at all for research that year.

The shortage of foreign exchange is having a severe effect on what can be achieved. It restricts the purchase of typewriters, paper, vehicles, the exchange of journals with overseas universities, travel by staff members, and a variety of activities or services that are taken for granted by social scientists in more wealthy contexts. Scholarly communication is further hampered by the escalating cost of travel and political and other impediments to it. Travel between the capitals of neighboring Kenya and Tanzania, formerly a one-hour flight, now may require two days while passing through a third country. The cost of the air travel necessary for communication within a large continent is now markedly restricting scholarly communications. At the same time, the high cost of printing and the limited national and regional market for scholarly publications have made local publishers leery of taking on journals or academic manuscripts and have made publication possible only by means of a subsidy or through an international publisher.

University Administrative Structure

Compounding the problems of resources and facilities is a university administrative structure with performance characteristics that inhibit the pursuit of social-science research. Because of the hierarchical quality of departmental organization, decision making tends to be centralized and to reflect the diffusion of chain-of-command civil-service norms within the institution. The most important effects are the blurring of boundaries between academic and administrative arenas and the tendency for inherently academic matters to be decided by administrative action. At the heart of the structure is the university finance office, which, with its regulatory manner and interminable procedures, is widely seen as serving more to delay than to facilitate the prosecution of research projects. Its processing of research funds—as required by university regulations—is one of the biggest single sources of frustration among researchers. Difficulties arising from an overloaded financial administration can be exacerbated by the existence of scattered power centers within the university through which the operation of personal, political, and ethnic considerations sometimes overrides the apparent authority structure defined by the university itself.

The Academic Environment

The social-science community worldwide is sustained by a set of professional norms operating within the universities that emphasize such features as promotion by merit, peer review, and the centrality of research. These principles are sought after at both East African universities, but several features of the academic environment pose obstacles to their attainment.

The most important general feature of the academic environment is the relative weakness of the incentive for research and writing. Not only is research difficult to organize and time-consuming, less rewarding financially and more demanding than consultancy work, and faced with problems of finding publication opportunities, but, in addition, it has not featured very centrally in the determination of faculty promotions. Some scholarly writing is a necessary but not sufficient condition for promotion. The University of Nairobi tends to emphasize teaching and administrative responsibilities along with seniority in recruitment and promotion, and at Dar es Salaam, practical work experience and social commitment are also relevant factors. The university-inspired pressure to write social scientists face in the United States is not echoed in East Africa. This has advantages and disadvantages. On the one hand, it leaves scope for quality rather than quantity in production, but on the other, it deprives academic departments of any sanction for the encouragement of scholarly productivity to balance the inducements of external demand. Where promotion depends only partially on research productivity and where dismissal for incompetence is rare, department chairmen and research institute directors have limited resources for encouraging productivity.

Several factors in the academic environment relate directly to the development of peer review. In the first place, peer review is necessarily difficult where social scientists form a small and intimate community concentrated in a single faculty. Second, the presence until very recently of expatriate majorities in many departments created a difficult psychological climate for peer review. Third, hierarchical styles of departmental management have tended to mitigate against collective decision making. Fourth, the university emphasis on teaching and administration has meant that research and publications have not provided the kind of tangible basis for peer review that might otherwise be available. Finally, awareness of the operation of ethnic criteria and personal influence has tended to place a high premium on formal qualifications in initial recruitment rather than leaving scope for differentiated professional judgment of an individual's qualities of mind and experience.

Government Attitude

A rather different kind of deterrent has been the effect on faculty morale of government's fluctuating attitude toward the university in general and social scientists in particular. On the one hand, social-science expertise and ideas are sought for planning purposes, and on the other, tolerance for opinions that imply criticism is limited. In the intimate and centralized political structure of which the Universities of Nairobi and Dar es Salaam are each separately a part, the line between advocacy of new ideas and strategies as part of the responsibility of social scientists and criticism perceived as tantamount to subversion has not always been easy to draw. Several events at the Universities of Nairobi and Dar es Salaam have dramatized the ambiguous and often-fragile standing of social science in the political order (see chapter 6).

This rather bleak recitation of some of the university conditions surrounding social science in East Africa deliberately leaves aside a corresponding account of achievement in order to focus attention on the infrastructure. The achievements in terms of research, scholarship, and intellectual vitality over the past ten years have been remarkable and have been documented elsewhere (see chapter 6). The point of emphasis here is that their preservation and development may now be threatened by some of the deterrents present in the university environment.

It has long been clear that many of the conditions surrounding and supporting social science outside Africa—economic resources, a favorable political context, established academic traditions, administrative infrastructure, and popular understanding—were not immediately available in Africa. It is now equally clear that their continued absence or weakness is not a transitory phase that will wither away in face of the development of social science itself. Shortages of foreign exchange, political pressures, management styles derived from resource shortages, the operation of ethnic influence, and impediments to scholarly communication are part of an interrelated set of factors that constitute a condition of underdevelopment. That condition is not going to disappear quickly. It is the environment of social science.[17]

The recent history of social science in East Africa suggests that two kinds of conditions have combined to determine the shape of social-science activity. The first is the set of givens associated with prevailing culture, traditions, and economic circumstance that forms the environment. The second kind is added by educational and social policies: the value assigned to social science, the use made of it, the concept held of it by a national government and populace. The first kind of condition is shared by Kenya and Tanzania as well as other African countries. The second can vary among nations. Although the emphasis of this chapter has been the substantial similarity in the pattern of social-science activity in Kenya and Tanzania and the suggestion that they derive from common economic conditions and historical circumstances, there are some important differences in the organization, expression, and status of social science between the two countries that derive from policy emphases. Space does not permit a review of these here, but they do illustrate that social science is not in the grip of immutable environmental conditions or an overpowering and absolute model but can be modified by policy.

Some of the surrounding conditions are amenable to planned change and conform to a stages-of-growth or mature-environment model of social-science development. It *is* possible to regulate consultancy arrangements, to devise cross-disciplinary teaching programs, to pursue new types of research and new styles of training. Other conditions such as resource constraints and government pressure are less tractable and are best seen as features of the system than as problems permitting easy solutions. The challenge is to identify the ingredients of social-science infrastructure that can be strengthened for the betterment of social science and the elements of the imported model that require modification in order to respond more adequately to the conditions presented by the East African context.

Conclusion: Strengthening Social Science in East Africa

The emergence of a vigorous indigenous social-science community—evidenced by Africanization, research output, curriculum reform, and contributions to policy—have coincided with and contributed to a powerful demand for policy relevance in all forms of education. Occurring when the social-science community was still small and fragile, this demand has tended to narrow the scope of social science to a single line of activity—commissioned work—to give it a commercial basis, and to take its point of reference outside the university. The direction taken by social science has produced much interesting work and some achievements that might otherwise not have been made, but it has also had some deleterious consequences for the long-term health of the activity. The narrow construction of policy relevance has tended to undercut the effectiveness of social science by creating inflated expectations about what it can contribute, including the illusion that social science can solve social problems. It has also eroded the autonomy necessary for the full development of social science and led to a neglect of the activities necessary for its self-renewal and maintenance.

The issue in East Africa is not the increase in policy research, which is a worldwide phenomenon and a local necessity, but the fact that a particular conception of it has taken root before the establishment of a local science independent of the contract motivation. Consequently, alternative approaches, standards, methodologies, and points of reference are limited to those dictated by the problem-solving imperative. Along with the risks of fragmentation, lack of continuity, and overextension in a research program, which can arise from an overdependence on contract research, can come the more fundamental danger that social science is allocating a disproportionate amount of its human capital to contract work and hence losing the means to renew itself. The corresponding need is for a broader conception of policy research than the one that has prevailed and a means of sustaining the kind of social science that can serve it. The first would concentrate less on the ability of social science to provide specific answers to defined policy questions than on its ability to produce knowledge that can increase understanding about policy issues. The second requires some decisions about what institutional bases and procedures can best sustain this kind of social science.

Several developments point in the direction of new goals for social science and the means for achieving them that can help restore balance to the situation described in this chapter. The broad goal is the "creation of a relevant and autonomous social science" and was reiterated most recently by the report of the UNESCO committee concerned with the future of social-science policies in Africa.[18] The particular task and rationale have been summarized thus by one of East Africa's leading social scientists:

> For it is only by trying to create a community of "home grown" researchers and scholars, capable of initiating, organizing and executing their own research, into indigenous socioeconomic issues will we also have a local reservoir of social literates from which the state can recruit its planners and the university its researchers and teachers. The need is to begin a process of self centred academic growth in terms of intellectual formation—through local graduate schools; research conception organization and execution—through native researchers and institutions; and research communication—through local journals and publishing firms.[19]

The achievement of this goal seems likely to involve social science in the pursuit of three broad themes and a variety of practical tasks during the 1980s.

First, social science is likely to find its purpose less in its ability to solve problems than in its contribution to understanding them through the provision of knowledge that can improve the quality of the debate in which policy issues arise. This contribution to policy relevance will come through building a body of knowledge and posing alternative strategies. This capacity in turn derives from the acquisition of analytical skills and understandings. The general ideal has been characterized thus:

> The function of policy research is at least as much to describe and discuss the premises and objectives of policy as it is to predict policy effects. . . . Applied research does not necessarily reduce disagreement. Instead it calls attention to the existence of conflicting positions . . . and sometimes generates new issues altogether.[20]

The change of emphasis for research institutes has been well stated with reference to Tanzania and BRALUP:

> In a developing country like Tanzania, where resources especially in high level and trained and experienced personnel are very scarce, research for the sake of research cannot easily be afforded. Everyone is expected to contribute to the national development effort. This however does not imply that research institutions should limit their aspirations and activities to consultancy services alone. To overcome the immediate problems of poverty and underdevelopment Tanzania has committed herself to a development programme requiring structural reforms and involving all Tanzanians. In such a changing situation there is a need for independent reflection and of monitoring of actual effects of reforms. Independent research with a long term perspective is also a necessary base for high-quality and relevant consultancy.[21]

Second, although in terms of its content social science in East Africa will continue to organize itself around problems of development, organizationally it needs to find a measure of independence from consultancy arrangements and the restrictions associated with them. This may require forging new kinds of links with all the institutions that now concern themselves with the application of research to public policy.

The third general theme, implied by the first two, is the strengthening of the scholarly mission of university social science: strengthening the quality of the formal infrastructure and informal processes that contribute to improvement of the quality of research and teaching.

A variety of tasks is implied by these purposes; several developments already in process provide a guide to further action.

Training

The shortage of researchers in relation to the demand for their services is at the heart of many of the problems discussed here. It can be removed only by training more of them, but it is questionable whether traditional forms of training are necessarily any longer feasible or desirable as optimum ways of meeting this need. Consideration of new forms of training in social science is overdue. In East Africa, a Ph.D. degree from an overseas university still has the greatest prestige for prospective social scientists. However, the escalating cost of overseas training, together with the enhanced ability of local departments to mount graduate programs, makes it timely to investigate the range of possible alternatives to the four- or five-year overseas Ph.D. course. More important, the now-questionable relevance of discipline-based and theory-oriented courses of study to the kinds of research and policy needs that pose themselves in East Africa suggests the usefulness of a search for new types of training programs in the social sciences organized around problem areas, emphasizing the common elements of alternative disciplines and drawing on their separate strengths. Both the East African universities and those who support social-science training have paid lip service to the idea of reducing dependence upon a single form of overseas training and to such notions as combination degrees and new cross-disciplinary programs, but there remains room for more vigorous attention to these ideas. At the same time, it must be remembered that the East African social-science community is only two generations old. The first and second generations have borne the brunt of development to the present and cannot be expected to create a new kind of social science. It is to the third and perhaps fourth generation that East African social science will look for the creation of a self-sustaining profession.

Integration of the Social Sciences

Several trends encourage the usefulness of exploring new methodologies that link different disciplines in research as well as training. The social-science research units have provided some very successful examples of teamwork involving different types of social scientists and a holistic approach to research issues. This is paralleled by interest at both universities in common research-methodology courses. The agricultural-research institutes in East Africa furnish some examples of the expanded understanding that can be attained through the incorporation of a social-science dimension into the conception, monitoring, and evaluation of agricultural projects. At the same time, consultancy companies provide some of the best examples of a broad integration of social-science knowledge into engineering or urban projects. The resurgence of history and the humanities as guides to understanding the effects and prospects of development policies is evident in both the involvement of historians in developmental research projects and the increasing attention of governments to cultural factors. These developments go beyond the time-worn call for interdisciplinarity but have not yet led to any convincing reconceptualization of the social sciences or to an integration of the strengths of different approaches.

Incentives to Scholarship and Research

The task of reconceptualization is unlikely to take place as long as contract research dominates the incentive system and research agenda. The difficulty is that the idea of professional vocation remains fragile and institutionalized social-science roles are few. Ways of strengthening the scholarly element of the social-science enterprise are a prerequisite to finding a more balanced and hence more integrated relationship with policy work. Some measures are under way. Others have yet to be tried.

The encouragement of social-science literature is perhaps the most important of the steps needed to strengthen academic incentives. Long-term subsidies to key journals and inducements to the writing of books and articles through writing sabbaticals or more direct means can provide the necessary foundation.

Two broad types of work seem to be especially important as immediate contributions to the creation of social-science knowledge and new ways of obtaining it relevant to the current state of the East African profession. Work dealing with new approaches and texts on the methodology and philosophy of social-science work would make a much-needed contribution to thinking about the development of relevant social science. Second, the

East African countries have had fifteen years of experience with development. So that the lessons of this accumulated experience are not lost to East African society, evaluations of specific projects should be supplemented by more-comprehensive assessments of the development experience. In addition, it is possible to balance short-term projects with support for other types of work such as long-term research, small-scale intensive projects, and pieces of detailed analysis of a kind not feasible within the context of a short-term, commissioned project. The direction is again described by the report on BRALUP: "a slight narrowing of focus, a deepening of research capacity and an extension of tasks requiring observation and monitoring."[22]

One further way in which East African social science can begin to assert its autonomy is to identify some new areas for research attention. Although there is an abundance of funds for research in some areas, especially those that are of particular interest to funding agencies—population and women's studies are current examples—in other areas there may be a shortage, and there is scope for vigorous local assertion of alternative priorities.

Research associations can provide important support to professional roles. Particularly where the national profession is small and the social-science work commercialized, regional associations can provide important peer support for scholarly activities. In this regard, the recent emergence of the Organization for Social Science Research in Eastern Africa (OSSREA) is likely to prove an important development for the future of East African social science. Having grown out of a small group of social scientists who met to critique each other's work, it starts with a commitment to the promotion of scholarship.

There remains a demand from social-science departments for occasional visiting social scientists. They can make a useful contribution by leading workshops—especially in such areas as methodology and computer applications—by engaging in collaborative research, and, more generally, by providing a scholarly and professional presence. One of the ironies of the historical evolution of East African social science is that in an earlier epoch of abundant funds for visiting professors, the social-science departments were in a weak position to make use of them, whereas now that departments actively seek particular scholars, funds for their recruitment have dried up. In contrast, there is no shortage of funds for external consultants, who frequently are the same individuals who in an earlier era were the visiting professors to social-science departments at the universities.

The organizations that provide much of the external demand for social-science work are slowly coming to recognize the importance of contributing to the development of research capacity, on which the long-term quality of policy work ultimately rests. The World Bank decision to increase the training component in many of its educational projects and the beginning of interest in training by the International Development Research Centre are important developments in this direction. The achievement of East African social science in the past ten years has been to establish the idea that social-science knowledge and methods have something to offer policy. The challenge for the 1980s is to strengthen the incentives of the scholarly environment, to identify the most important requirements of contract research, and to seek associations between the two that can be the basis for a worthy new relationship between social science and social change.

Notes

1. Colin Leys, "The Role of the University in an Underdeveloped Country," *Journal of Eastern African Research and Development* 1, no. 1 (1971), pp. 29–40; Peter Marris, "What Is a University For?," *Mawazo* 1, no. 1 (1968), pp. 6–11; Justinian Rweyemamu, "Reorganization of the Faculty of Arts and Social Science," *Taamuli* 2, no. 1 (1971), p. 38.

2. "Final Report of the UNESCO Experts' Meeting on the Future of the Social Science Policies in Africa South of the Sahara, October 1979."

3. "The Idea of Social Science in East Africa: An Aspect of the Development of Higher Education" originally appeared in *Minerva* 17, no. 2 (1979). Interest in comparisons with the state of science in East Africa can be found in Thomas Eisemon, "African Academics: A Study of Scientists at the Universities of Nairobi and Ibadan," *Annals of the American Academy of Political and Social Science* 448 (March 1980).

4. This characterization is developed by Göran Hyden, "We Must Run While Others Walk: Policy-Making for Socialist Development in the Tanzania-type of Politics," in *The Tanzanian Economy: Perspectives in Development*, ed. Kwan Kim, Robert Mabele, and Michael Schulteis (Nairobi: Heinemann, 1979).

5. International Labour Office, *Employment, Incomes and Equality: A Strategy for Increasing Productive Employment in Kenya* (Geneva, 1972).

6. Examples include M. Cowen and K. Kinyanjui, "Some Problems of Income Distribution in Kenya" (Institute for Development Studies, University of Nairobi, paper prepared for the Division for Socio-Economic Analysis, Sector of Social Sciences and Their Applications, UNESCO, 1977); P. Collier and D. Lal, "Poverty and Growth in Kenya" (IBRD Working Paper, January 1980); W.S. House and T. Killick, "Social Justice and Development Policy in Kenya's Rural Economy: A Survey" (Report commissioned by the ILO, July 1979); E. Grawford and E. Thorbecke, "Employment, Income Distribution, Poverty Alleviation and Basic Needs in Kenya" (Report of an ILO mission, Cornell University, 1979).

7. Examples of projects of this sort include District Development Planning Project (USAID, University of California); The Organizational

Conditions for Effective Small-Scale Self-Help Development Projects (USAID, University of Iowa); Public Sector Salary Policies in Africa and the Middle East (IDRC, Sussex University).

8. N. Mwaniki, "Development of Indigenous Consultancy Organizations in Eastern and Southern Africa" (Survey commissioned by the United Nations Economic Commission for Africa, Addis Ababa, 1979).

9. Institute for Development Studies, *Research and Publications* (University of Nairobi, 1977), p.4.

10. *BRALUP 1967–1979* (Report of the team appointed to evaluate the Bureau of Resource Assessment and Land Use Planning, University of Dar es Salaam, Dar es Salaam, 1979), p. 34.

11. Aprodicio Laquian, "The Social Sciences in Eastern Africa," mimeographed (Ottawa: International Development Research Centre, 1979).

12. David Court, "Scholarships and University Development in Kenya and Tanzania," *Higher Education* 8 (1979): 535–552.

13. *BRALUP 1967–1979*, p. 34.

14. See David Court, "The Experience of Higher Education in East Africa: The University of Dar es Salaam as a New Model?," *Comparative Education* 2, no. 3 (1975); and G.R.V. Mmari, "The Role of Higher Education for Development: Responses to Manpower Needs: The Case of the University of Dar es Salaam," in *Higher Education and Social Change*, ed. Kenneth Thompson et al. (New York: Praeger, 1976), pp. 187–214.

15. *BRALUP 1967–1979*, p. 30.

16. Paul Starr, "The Edge of Social Science," *Harvard Educational Review* 44, no. 4 (1974), p. 401.

17. The need to conceive ways of reducing the cost of higher education was a principal theme of the address by the chancellor of the University of Dar es Salaam on the occasion of the tenth anniversary of the university. See Julius K. Nyerere, *Address by the Chancellor of the University* (Dar es Salaam: Government Printer, 1980).

18. "Final Report of the UNESCO Experts' Meeting."

19. Anyang Nyongo, "The Teaching of the Social Sciences in East Africa: An Evaluation Report," *Africa Development* 3, no. 4 (1978), p. 79.

20. David Cohen and Michael Garet, "Reforming Educational Policy with Applied Social Research," *Harvard Educational Review* 45, no. 1 (1975), p. 42.

21. *BRALUP 1967–1979*, pp. 25–26.

22. Ibid., p. 49.

Social Sciences in Developing Areas: An Annotated Bibliography of Selected Periodical Literature, 1970–1980

Elizabeth J. Brooks

Introduction

Social scientists are accustomed to analyzing modern phenomena in terms of systems: political systems, economic systems, and social systems are three of the more common. A fourth system, the knowledge system, deserves equal attention because it informs and interprets the other systems. The social sciences, as part of the knowledge system, can be conceptualized in two ways: as a body of knowledge comprising theories, facts, and methods; and as a social system composed of scientists and the patterns of communication among them. In this bibliography, social sciences are considered both as a body of knowledge and as a social system.

The major focus is on Third World social sciences. The term *Third World* is used in the general and commonly accepted way to refer to the industrially less developed countries of Latin America, Africa, and Asia (excluding Japan). Social sciences include anthropology, economics, geography, political science, public administration, social psychology, and sociology, along with any variations or combinations thereof.

The works in the bibliography follow the major themes of this book:

1. *The internationalization of the social sciences.* These articles generally conceive of social science as an international social system through which social science as knowledge has been convened historically. They address such issues as the role of Third World social sciences in the international knowledge system, patterns and implications of international exchange on Third World social science, and the transferability of theories and methods from one societal context to another.

2. *Regional profiles.* Social sciences in a particular geographic area are assessed as social systems—that is, as social scientists, their activities, the institutional locus of their activities, and the nature of their activities. The profiles also address the knowledge content of social sciences—the theories, concepts, and methods used. How have social sciences developed in a particular country or region? What is their current status, and what will or should be the directions of future development?

3. *Policy utilization.* How suited are Third World social sciences to policy needs? What role have they played in public policy, and how can they be enhanced to play a greater role in the achievement of societal goals?

In all three categories, articles are chosen for their direct treatment of the themes. This is not, therefore, a bibliography about development; it is a bibliography of articles about social science—the nature of social sciences in developing countries and the utility of social sciences for understanding development issues.

Arrangement and Selection

Although a thematic arrangement of the articles according to the three topics listed above would be useful, the topics are so closely related that they do not allow mutually exclusive classification. Many of the articles treat more than one of the themes. They have, therefore, been arranged by geographic area rather than by theme. The themes addressed in each article are indicated, however, by a 1, 2, or 3 in brackets following the citation. These numbers refer to the first, second, and third themes discussed above. Works with no geographic designation or works pertaining to less developed countries in general are placed in the first, general, category. Following that are the articles on Africa, Asia, and Latin America, respectively. Within these four categories, the works are alphabetized by author.

The bibliography consists of, but is not restricted to, all articles pertaining to the three themes published between 1970 and 1980 in the following journals:

CEPAL Review

Developing Economies

Development and Change

Development Dialogue

Development Digest

Economic Development and Cultural Change

Indian Economics Review

Inter-American Economic Affairs

International Development Review

International Social Science Journal

Journal of Development Economics

Journal of Development Studies

Journal of Economic Literature

Journal of Modern African Studies

Knowledge: Creation, Diffusion, Utilization

Malay Economics Review

Minerva

Nigerian Journal of Economic and Social Studies

Pacific Affairs

Pakistan Development Review

Philippine Journal of Business and Economics

Prospects

Third World Quarterly

Third World Review

World Development

In addition to the coverage of the foregoing journals, *Sociology Abstracts* was covered for the same period.

Overview

Most of the articles included in the bibliography can be characterized as (1) descriptions of the historical development and/or the current state of social sciences in a given area, or (2) analyses and evaluations of theoretical and methodological trends. Many fit both categories. The descriptive material is most often based on the impressions and experiences of the authors, who are themselves social scientists. Some of the articles include quantitative data to support observations; in a few, the data are original data generated for the particular study, most often by means of survey research. When textual analyses are used, they are generally impressionistic, as opposed to a systematic content analyses.

The analytical studies typically treat the epistemology of social science, the relation of theory to method, the transferability of theories, and/or methods and their policy relevance. Most of these studies are general in nature. The exceptions treat specific theories, methods, or policy applications by means of case studies.

The content of the literature reveals several issues that cut across a number of theoretical perspectives and national differences. Two of these issues stand out. The first is a concern for dependence and neocolonialism in the social sciences. For the most part, the social sciences were introduced as part of colonial education systems or development assistance programs. After World War II, private foundations and governmental agencies in Europe and the United States began assistance programs to help develop social-science communities and national economies. This was the cultural equivalent of early economic-development theories, which held that socio-economic development would be achieved by the diffusion from developed to less developed societies of material goods in the form of capital invest-ment and equipment, and of cultural goods in the form of technology, institutions, theories, and values. In each of the three regions, the literature portrays the 1950s and 1960s as a period of one-way knowledge transfer, professionalization, and institution building in the social sciences.

The literature of the 1970s reflects disenchantment, distrust, and ques-tioning of these earlier efforts and the assumptions on which they were based. In Latin America, theories of *dependencia* are applied to social science. Asian and African social scientists refer to cultural neocolonialism. Although positions vary according to ideological and theoretical perspec-tive, the issue raised by positivists, structuralists, and Marxists alike is epistemological—namely, whether theories, concepts, and methods ema-nating from one social context can be transferred to a different social context. Answers to the question range from a very few unqualified "yeses," through "yes but with appropriate adaptation," to "definitely impossible." Arguments for the last two positions are the most frequent. They tend to vary according to ideological position rather than by country or region. The concern transcending all perspectives and regions, however, is for the de-velopment of "national" social sciences: sciences of, by, and for individual developing societies.

The tendency toward nationalism is closely related to the second—a political—issue raised throughout the literature: the relationship of social science to society. The relationship between state and science affects social science in its content, its activities, and its institutions. Each geographic region has examples of this impact. In Latin America during the 1960s, growth and professionalism of the social sciences occurred in the service of moderate reform governments interested in economic and social develop-ment. Social scientists were called on to use their theories and techniques to solve problems and promote national goals. This involvement in the solution of social issues led to a questioning of social science inherited from Europe and North America. The literature represents an initial questioning and then a change in concepts and approaches. Social scientists are in the process of formulating concepts to deal with developing societies. They are endeavoring to replace disciplinary approaches with interdisciplinary research programs more suited to the understanding and amelioration of socioeconomic problems of development.

The literature on Latin America also reflects changes in regime in Argentina, Chile, and Brazil: these countries moved to authoritarian military regimes, and social sciences in national universities were repressed. Even under more-moderate governments, some social scientists perceived the need to choose between the status quo and major structural change. Those who identified with the former became *técnicos*, social and natural scientists working with national governments on purely technical aspects of development without addressing issues of political control. This group had been greatly influenced by positivist and quantitative approaches imported from the United States. A second group of social scientists, who in their theories had determined the need for basic structural change in society, had to change political and intellectual identities. Their articles deal with the dilemma of having to choose between professional standards and political militancy. The resolution of the dilemma for others seems to be a third approach, which integrates social concerns and professional integrity through the development of a set of value-oriented social theories directed toward social change. This approach points to the potential of value-based social science and represents the middle way between the status quo and radical approaches. All three approaches are represented in the bibliography and are found in the works from each region.

Conditions are different in Africa and Asia, but the theme of political influence on social science runs through the literature on those regions as well. Asian and African social scientists have experienced the need for interdisciplinary problem-oriented knowledge that can be applied to social problems. Social-science institutions have received support, been tolerated, or been repressed as national governments have either seen the need for or felt a threat from social sciences. Changes in regime have influenced the content as well as institutions of social science. The most striking Asian example was China under Mao's regime, when social sciences were proscribed and often dismantled. They are currently being reinstated. In sociology, for example, a professional association was formed in 1980, an Institute of Sociology is being organized, and sociology departments are again being established in the Chinese universities. The new sociology will be based on Marxist principles and will be oriented to the solution of problems in a socialist society. In Taiwan, on the other hand, sociology is still very much in the mode of North American positivism.

Similar readjustments of institutions and theoretical approaches occasioned by political changes can be observed in the literature on Egypt and

Algeria. Elsewhere in Africa, social scientists continue their activities with the support of their government, as in Egypt, or with at least a wary tolerance, as in the authoritarian military regimes.

An analysis of the literature reviewed here reflects two basic imbalances: one is the underrepresentation of economics as a discipline vis-à-vis the other social-science disciplines; the other is the overrepresentation of Latin America vis-à-vis other regions. The strength and development of economics, which has been noted frequently in this book, is not reflected quantitatively in the number of articles in this bibliography. Indeed, there is a striking reverse imbalance: only one out of three of the articles dealing explicitly with individual disciplines concerns economics. In large measure this apparent paradox is most likely a function of the subjects defined for inclusion in the bibliography. It does not include articles reporting the substance of social-science research in the developing countries, a vast area of thousands of articles, which no doubt would have reflected the dominance of economics.

The focus in the bibliography is explicitly upon the narrower issues previously noted, namely, the internationalization of the social sciences, the state of the social sciences as disciplines in the developing world, and problems and issues in their application. With few exceptions, the professional journals in economics tend to be less concerned than those of other social sciences with epistemological and philosophical issues of North-South transferability. Economists also tend to be more fully and effectively integrated in the public-policy process. An assumption of a non-culture-bound universalism—rather than an insistence on contextual relativity—has tended to prevail in their discipline. In their primarily instrumental function they are more inclined to believe in only "one economics" than other social scientists are to believe in the oneness or universality of their specializations. The articles of economists therefore tend to concentrate on research on practical problems of development rather than on self-reflective critiques of the nature of their discipline. Such critiques have been particularly prominent among noneconomist social scientists in Latin America. This fact, along with the deeper historical roots of Latin American social science, helps to explain the disproportionately large number of articles on that region in this bibliography.

In conclusion, the literature surveyed for this bibliography shows social sciences in developing areas to be relatively new and in general suffering from scarce resources, rudimentary institutionalization, and inadequate communications mechanisms. These generalizations are more appropriate for some areas than for others. There are some outstanding exceptions, such as the Getulio Vargas Foundation and other private institutions in Brazil, the Nigerian Institute of Social and Economic Research in Ibadan, the Institute for Development Studies of the University of Nairobi, the Institute of Population Studies of Gadjah Mada University in Indonesia, and the Institute of Economic Development and Research at the University of the Philippines. There are national and regional differences in content and institutional structure, but the major differences seem to stem from the ideological position of the scientists and the relationship of the social sciences to the political and economic system in which they function.

The importance of the relationship between social sciences and the social system is observable at the international level as well as at national levels. Internationally it is expressed in terms of *dependencia* and neocolonialism, which have been applied to the social sciences as part of a broader international system. At the national level, the relationship is expressed in the nature of social-science institutions and theories, as well as their relation to the governmental structures of the particular society. In all cases, however, the literature of the 1970s represents a profound questioning of the role of social science in the international system and in national societies.

As social scientists find answers to their questions, their findings will affect the three major concerns of this bibliography. At the international level, social-science exchange and learning will either become a two-way process of mutual benefit, or it will cease, to the detriment of all social science. Nationalism in the social sciences will produce indigenous social theories and research methods that will have policy relevance whether the policies are official or oppositional. The literature under review represents growth and challenge to all social scientists.

Selected Bibliography

General

Alger, Chadwick F., and Lyons, Gene M. "Social Science as a Transnational System." *International Social Science Journal* 26, no. 1 (1974),
pp. 138–149. [1, 2]
A report on and discussion of key issues raised at a 1973 seminar
attended by social scientists from all parts of the world. These issues
include asymmetry and dependency, nationalism, ideology, pluralism,
and community in the social sciences. The authors suggest areas of
future research on international social science.

Allman, James, and Mathsson, Bertil. "Social Science Research on Family
Planning in Developing Countries." *International Social Science Journal* 27, no. 1 (1975), pp. 174–182. [3]
A brief review of the family-planning programs and an evaluation of
related social-science research. Results of two types of research (knowledge, attitudes, and practice studies; and evaluation studies) have been
disappointing. The authors suggest the use of in-depth case studies as a
means of gaining information necessary for policies designed to change
behavior.

Altbach, Philip G. "Servitude of the Mind? Education, Dependency, and
Neocolonialism." *Teachers College Record* 79, no. 2 (1977), pp. 187–
204. [1]
Using data on educational systems, book publishing, and other knowl-
edge-related activities, the author shows how existing inequalities between centers and peripheries are evident in the global intellectual
system.

Amin, Samir, et al. "New Forms of Collaboration in Development Research and Training." *International Social Science Journal* 27, no. 4
(1975), pp. 790–795. [1, 2]
Two trends exist in development research and training: self-reliance in
the Third World and new forms of collaboration between Third World
institutions and participants from developed countries. The two trends
are not mutually exclusive. Proposals for more-effective collaboration
are made by a panel established after the 1972 Belgrade Conference of
Directors of Research and Training Institutes.

Apthorpe, Raymond. "Development Studies and Social Planning." *Journal
of Development Studies* 6, no. 4 (1970), pp. 1–28. [1, 3]
Development studies are criticized for their domination by economics.
Sociology, on the other hand, is seen as too preoccupied with social
typology. Following the critique, the author looks at social planning
from an historical perspective and suggests how development studies

might be improved and how they might contribute to more effective social planning. He suggests interdisciplinary studies.

————. "The New Generalism: Four Phases in Development Studies in the First U.N. Development Decade." *Development and Change* 3, no. 1 (1971–1972), pp. 62–73. [2, 3]

A historical overview of development studies, their relation to national planning, and their deficiencies. The last stage is characterized by interdisciplinary studies for planned change. In an evaluation of this type of study, the author makes particular reference to studies by the Economic Commission for Latin America (ECLA).

Ashcraft, Norman. "Developmental Economics: Some Critical Remarks." *Journal of Developing Areas* 7, no. 1 (1972), pp. 3–10. [1]

In an "editorial comment," the author criticizes the theoretical assumptions, concepts, and methods of development economics for presenting a fractionated and distorted picture of underdevelopment.

Belshaw, Cyril S. "Anthropology." *International Social Science Journal* 24, no. 1 (1972), pp. 80–94. [1, 3]

An overview of the contributions of social anthropology to development processes. The author discusses propositions from the anthropology literature and their policy relevance in the areas of education, science and technology, and communications. He makes three recommendations to the discipline: increase the number of anthropologists from developing countries and assure their recognition; encourage anthropologists from developed countries to work toward establishing indigenous scientific communities; and train an interdisciplinary, broadly educated core of policy advisers.

Blaug, Mark. "Economics and Educational Planning in Developing Countries." *Prospects* 2, no. 4 (1972), pp. 431–441. [3]

Economics of education is a youthful field, having emerged only recently as a separate branch of economics. The author describes the current state of the field and from it derives practical guidelines for educational planners in less developed countries. One such guideline, based on cost-effectiveness analysis, is to invest in primary instead of vocational education.

Braibanti, Ralph. "The American Experience in Diffusing Administrative Technology." *Annals of the American Academy of Political and Social Science* 428 (1976): 65–76. [1, 3]

Using examples from former British colonies, the Middle East, and Latin America, the author offers an impressionistic evaluation of American efforts to influence administrative reforms. He finds efforts over the past twenty-five years moderately effective in that administrative technologies have been diffused (as opposed to transferred) and adapted to the indigenous situation.

Castro, Josué de. "The Policy That Failed." *Prospects* 2, no. 1 (1972), pp. 43–47. [1, 3]

In a general but eloquent discussion, the author analyzes the failure of the "developmental decade" and its transformation into a decade of disappointment. The major mistake was to assume that the economic-development processes of today's developed countries could or would be repeated by today's less developed countries. This was the basic assumption underlying an inappropriate transfer of economic theory, in which the local conditions of less developed countries were not taken into account. Underdevelopment is a form of undereducation, and the author calls for a new form of education that will be able to achieve an economy of development that is human and balanced.

Cherns, Albert. "Relations between Research Institutions and Users of Research." *International Social Science Journal* 22, no. 2 (1970), pp. 226–242. [3]

In an article that does not deal specifically with developing countries as such, the author offers a general description that can be applied to particular cases. He shows how needs for different kinds of research require sophisticated knowledge about the various kinds of existing research institutions. He offers a typology of institutions and suggests how to utilize them. He uses the Volta Dam project in Ghana as a successful case of administrative utilization of research institutions and their capacities.

Court, David. "The Idea of Social Science in East Africa: An Aspect of Development of Higher Education." *Minerva* 17, no. 2 (1979), pp. 244–282. [1, 2, 3]

This valuable article is reprinted in chapter 6 of this volume.

Desai, Padma. "Third World Social Scientists in Santiago." *World Development* 1, no. 9 (1973), pp. 57–65. [1]

The author reports on the conference of April 1973 in Santiago and discusses major themes. Although many ideological and theoretical orientations were expressed, all agreed that basic ideas and ideologies for the Third World must come from within and that Third World social scientists must seek institutional means to influence power centers. They were critical of UNCTAD for failing to adequately utilize Third World social scientists and drafted a resolution for an intellectual Forum of the Third World. The resolution is included.

el-Yacoubi, Hassan Hasan. "System Analysis, System Management, and Scientific Typology as Applied to Development in the Third World." *Impact of Science on Society* 26, no. 3 (1976), pp. 213–226. [3]

The author calls for a scientific paradigm and methodological technique suited to the complex reality of developing societies. He suggests systems analysis as the tool for integrating political and economic complexity with the goal of improved forecasting and planning.

Epstein, I. Scarlett. "The Ideal Marriage between the Economists' Macro-approach and the Social Anthropologist's Micro-approach to Development Studies." *Economic Development and Cultural Change* 24, no. 1 (1975), pp. 29–45. [3]

The author's education and research in India and New Guinea are used to argue for an integration of economics and social anthropology and of macro and micro studies. The proposed result would be a new model of "socioeconomic man" to replace the outmoded "rational economic man."

Freund, Wolfgang Slim. "Das Stadt-Land Problem: Agrarsoziologische Überlegungen am Beispiel Ägyptens und Tunesiens" [The urban-rural problem: Agro-sociological considerations of the examples of Egypt and Tunisia]. *Die Dritte Welt* 5, no. 1 (1977), pp. 7–26. [3]

The author proposes the unification of rural and urban concerns in an independent discipline of agrosociology. He uses descriptions of Tunis and Cairo to make his case. Had an integrated agrosociological policy been implemented, urban overpopulation and stagnation could have been avoided. The author suggests policies to reverse the direction of migration and create an outflow from urban to rural areas. He notes that such policies are not likely to come from Third World ruling elites—the masses must be politicized.

Friis, Henning. "Towards a Policy of Social Research: Introduction." *International Social Science Journal* 22, no. 2 (1970), pp. 187–194. [1, 2, 3]

The author raises several issues and follows them up with suggestions as to how social-science research can enhance policymaking in both developed and developing countries. He reviews the role of social scientists in social change, the imbalance of social research in developed versus developing countries, and how international cooperation can be used to enhance social research.

Goldstone, Leo. "Improving Social Statistics in Developing Countries." *International Social Science Journal* 29, no. 4 (1977), pp. 756–771. [3]

After a review of the typical weakness of social statistics in developing countries, the author offers suggestions for improving statistical data and collection capacities. He begins with a description of the current state and proceeds to describe an integrated approach that meets a realistic minimum. The main components are statistics on food and nutrition, housing and water, health and medical care, labor, education and training, social welfare, and major demographic elements.

Haque, Wahidul; Mehta, Nirajan; Rahman, Anisur; and Wignaraja, Ponna. "Towards a Theory of Rural Development." *Development Dialogue* 2 (1977): 11–137. [1, 2, 3]

The authors discuss their disillusionment with traditional Western theories of development. They redefine development, propose new theoretical approaches to rural development, and present current studies of rural development in several countries. The most salient part of the study is the proposal of new rural-development strategies and a clearly defined outline of the role of "action research" as an integral part of rural development. Examples of action research in evaluative field studies are provided.

Healey, Derek. "Development Policy: New Thinking about an Interpretation." *Journal of Economic Literature* 10, no. 3 (1972), pp. 757–797. [1, 3]
This article traces the evolution of conventional wisdom about economic development theory and the changes in policy that followed from shared international experience. The author then reviews the results of a particular economic policy in Brazil, India, Pakistan, Mexico, the Philippines, Taiwan, and Argentina as reported in 1970 by Little, Scitovsky, and Scott for the OECD Development Center.

Hill, Ellen B. "Introduzione: La Modernizazione al Bivio" [Introduction: The modernization controversy]. *Centro Sociale* 19 (5–13 December 1972): 106–108. [3]
A critical consideration of the concept of modernization and its value orientation to Western industrialized society. The author challenges rationality, efficiency, and the role of the social scientist in policy-making, given his or her identification with modernizing values and the status quo. Modernization as a concept and as an approach to research is found inappropriate to preindustrial societies.

Hiller, Harry H. "Universality of Science and the Question of National Sociologies." *American Sociologist* 14, no. 3 (1979), pp. 124–135. [1, 2]
A comprehensive cross-national study of the global emergence of the idea of national sociologies, in both developing and developed countries, partly as a reaction to the claims of American sociology to universality and to the Americanization of the discipline, and partly as an assertion of the need to indigenize the discipline. Under the rubric "the de-Americanization and re-nationalization process," the author examines the factors and forces contributing to the increasing emphasis on contextual relativity. An excellent bibliography is appended.

Jahoda, Gustav. "Psychology and the Developing Countries." *International Social Science Journal* 25, no. 4 (1973), pp. 461–474. [1, 3]
Noting that the profession of psychology has paid very little attention to the developing countries and that psychologists have assumed the universality of their concepts, the author concludes that psychology needs developing countries in order to test the extent to which its knowledge is generalizable. On the other hand, the author is less certain that developing countries need psychology. He supports his reservations but makes concrete suggestions as to how current psychology might be of use and

what can be done to make future psychological research useful for development purposes.

Karachi Conference communiqué (opening statement by Mahbub ul Haq). "The Third World Forum: Intellectual Self-Reliance." *International Development Review* 17, no. 1 (1975), pp. 1, 8–13. [1]
The communiqué deplores the partnership of unequals and the use of borrowed concepts in economic development, and calls for intellectual liberation and self-reliance. The forum would provide an intellectual platform for organizing socioeconomic research and exchange of views among Third World countries and work toward a new international economic order.

Kitamura, Hiroshi. "Challenges of Development Economics: Relevance of Economic Theory to Contemporary Development Problems." *Developing Economies* 13, no. 1 (1975), pp. 3–21. [3]
The author evaluates contemporary economics in terms of its utility for planning and policy in developing societies. He examines the conditions in Third World countries, the logic of planning, and the assumption underlying orthodox economic theories, and finds a lack of fit among the three.

Kumar, Krishna. "Some Reflections on Transnational Social Science Transactions." *International Journal of Comparative Sociology* 19, nos. 3–4 (1978), pp. 219–234. [1]
The author reviews the issues raised about social-science transactions between industrialized and less industrialized countries and then discusses three critical questions: Are indigenous social sciences curtailed by asymmetrical transactions? Do such transactions have spin-off effects in industrialized countries that increase the gap between the two areas? Do social science transfers contribute to ideological dependence?

Lengyel, Peter. "Social Science and the Post-Imperial." *Trans-Action* 11, no. 6 (1974), pp. 72–76. [1]
The article describes historical center-periphery relationships in the social sciences. Four major centers were Britain, France, West Germany, and the United States. The author maintains that, since the mid-1960s, the center-periphery pattern has been continued through the internationalizing efforts of international governmental and nongovernmental organizations.

Lindholm, Richard W. "A Tested Program for Third World Economic Development." *American Journal of Economics and Sociology* 36, no. 2 (1977), pp. 165–169. [1, 3]
The author attributes the failure of Western-oriented Third World countries to establish viable democratic institutions partly to policy

advice based on Keynesian theories suitable to the United States of the 1930s. Instead he recommends policies based on theories of capitalism pertaining to the United States of the nineteenth century.

Lipton, Michael. "Interdisciplinary Studies in Less Developed Countries." *Journal of Developing Studies* 7, no. 1 (1970), pp. 5–18. [2]
The author addresses three questions: Why are interdisciplinary studies more strongly indicated in less developed countries? Why are interdisciplinary studies in LDCs so sparse and of such poor quality? How can interdisciplinary studies be improved?

Mafeje, Archie. "The Problem of Anthropology in Historical Perspective: An Inquiry into the Growth of the Social Sciences." *Review canadienne des études africaines* [Canadian journal of African studies] 10, no. 2 (1976), pp. 307–333. [2]
The author takes the position that anthropology is not the only social science born of imperialism: in conditions of oppression all bourgeois social sciences with roots in positivism take the position of the oppressors. Only through a move to socialism in society will the social sciences be liberated from their identification with oppressors. In the meantime, the current anthropology is the best available.

Malkhasvan, Eduard. "Problemite ne stranite ot T. Nar. 'Treti Svyat' v rabotata na Sedmiya Svetoven Kongres po Sotsiologiya" [Problems of the countries of the 'Third World' in the work of the Seventh World Congress of Sociology]. *Sotsiologischeski Problemi* 3, no. 1 (1977), pp. 91–104. [2, 3]
The author reviews issues raised at the Seventh World Congress of Sociology, such as paths of development, national liberation movements, and neocolonialism, and discusses the role of Marxism-Leninism as the basis for social sciences in developing countries and specific problems of sociology in such countries.

Mansilla, H.C.F. "Lateinamerikanische Entwicklungsvorstellungen und die Dritte Welt" [Latin American development concepts and the Third World]. *Die Dritte Welt* 6, nos. 3–4 (1978), pp. 378–412. [1, 2, 3]
The author contrasts development concepts in Latin America with those in other Third World countries, and finds similarity among general development goals: industrialization, modernization, and state consolidation and expansion. Differences occur in the particular styles of development, where there are revivals of national traditions and ideologies. The author observes a stronger influence of Western models on Latin American development concepts than on African or Asian development models.

Moore, M.P. "The Logic of Interdisciplinary Studies." *Journal of Development Studies* 11, no. 1 (1974), pp. 98–106. [2]
A theoretical discussion of the need for and appropriateness of interdisciplinary studies in the less developed countries.

Nolan, Michael F.; Hagan, Robert A.; and Hoekstra, Mary S. "Rural Sociological Research 1966–1974: Implications for Social Policy." *Rural Sociology* 40, no. 4 (1975), pp. 435–454. [3]

A systematic review of articles published in *Rural Sociology* from 1964 through 1974 finds they have limited relevance to social-policy concerns and little to offer in terms of policy recommendations. Reasons for the inadequacies are presented through a comparison of policy research with critical theory. The two perspectives are evaluated in terms of their implications for rural sociology as a discipline.

Perrotta Bengolea, R., and Akiwowo, Akinsola. "Problems in Peripheral Regions." *International Social Science Journal* 26, no. 3 (1974), pp. 411–414. [1, 2]

The authors point out the vulnerability of Third World social-science communities to "academic colonialism," which occurs when First World institutions confer status and provide recognition for Third World social scientists, when foreign research councils and funding agencies dictate research topics, and when foreign researchers extract data from Third World countries but leave no record of their findings. The authors call for the development of Third World theories, research projects, and publications. A discussion by a panel of U.N. social scientists follows.

Pinches, Christine R. "Economic Development: The Need for an Alternative Approach." *Economic Development and Cultural Change* 26, no. 1 (1977), pp. 139–146. [1, 3]

Using Libya as an example, the author outlines the limitations of neoclassical theories of economic development and shows how policies based on the body of theory are unlikely to result in development. She offers an alternative approach, in which development is conceived as a process of self-generated, self-sustained change.

Prebisch, Raúl. "Towards a Theory of Change." *CEPAL Review* 10 (1980): 155–208. [1, 3]

The last of a series of articles in which the author presents a critical interpretation of the functioning of peripheral capitalism and shows the inability of neoclassical theory to comprehend it in depth. This article reviews the author's earlier critique and then traces the lines along which the system should be changed. He presents a synthesis of liberal and socialist theories.

Seers, Dudley. "What Are We Trying to Measure?" *Journal of Development Studies* 8, no. 3 (1972), pp. 21–36. [1, 2, 3]

The author traces the historical concerns of developed-world economics and other social sciences and how their societal context conditioned them. The resulting theories and methodological techniques are inadequate for studying underdevelopment. The author briefly discusses implications for development planning.

Srivastava, R.N. "Some Antecedent and Current Ideas of Development and Limitations of Development Theory." *Sociological Bulletin* 22, no. 2 (1973), pp. 283–296. [2]
A historical analysis of development as a theoretical theme, concluding with the limitations and irrelevance of development theory. Lacking a scientific theory of development, sociologists are nonetheless making valuable progress in research design, measurement techniques, and conceptual clarification.

van Nieuwenhuijze, C.A.O. "Development: The Elusiveness of Its Social Dimensions." *Die Dritte Welt* 6, no. 3 (1978), pp. 316–322. [1, 3]
The segmentary economistic approach of development studies is a reflection of modern Western society and as such is inappropriate to the study of developing societies. The author prescribes holistic development studies that incorporate social, cultural, and value concerns and produce policies more sensitive to human needs.

————. "Public Administration, Comparative Administration, Development Administration: Concepts and Theory for Relevance." *Development and Change* 5, no. 3 (1973–1974), pp. 1–18. [3]
A general, theoretical discussion of the conceptual bases of public-administration theory. The author relates public administration to development processes and cautions against confusing theory with reality, neglecting the degree of politicization of public policy in the Third World, and being misled by the close identity between state bureaucracy and development administration in Third World countries.

————. "Social Development and Non-Economic Factors of Development." *Die Dritte Welt* 7, no. 1 (1979), pp. 32–37. [1, 3]
The author relates the colonial distinction between advanced and backward to the later one between developed and underdeveloped. The author analyzes the inapplicability of welfare-state social policies to societies in which the need is for structural social change. He calls for a social science interested in structural change and a move of Third World policymakers away from strictly economistic prescriptions.

Whyte, William Foote. "Toward a New Strategy for Research and Development Agriculture: Helping Small Farmers in Developing Countries." *Desarrollo rural en las Americas* 9, nos. 1–2 (1977), pp. 51–61. [3]
A new model of rural development gives social scientists an important role. Social scientists work with agricultural scientists to plan integrated exploratory programs involving farmer participation beginning in the earliest stages. The author illustrates the new model with a case study.

Wolfe, Marshall. "Development: Images, Conceptions, Criteria, Agents, and Choices." *Economic Bulletin for Latin America* 18, nos. 1–2 (1974), pp. 1–12. [1, 3]

The author discusses traditional images or definitions of development and how the limited nature of these images has precluded a variety of styles of development. To fill this void, the author presents several different styles of development. The task of the social scientist and planner is to help the political leadership make more-rational choices in pursuit of a style of development that is viable and acceptable to all parties involved and the population in general. He discusses political constraints on these choices.

Ziman, John. "Three Patterns of Research in Developing Countries." *Minerva* 9, no. 1 (1971), pp. 32–37. [2, 3]
Although the author's comments are directed mainly to physical sciences, they incorporate social sciences as well. The article presents three approaches to research in developing countries, each based on a particular time criterion: short-term applied research aimed at the solution of immediate problems; medium-term research aimed at developing capabilities in a few carefully chosen areas; and long-term research aimed at establishing a scientific community. The author describes the requirements for each type of research.

Africa

Adepoju, Aderanti. "Migration and Development in Tropical Africa: Some Research Priorities." *African Affairs* 76, no. 303 (1977), pp. 210–225. [2, 3]
Migration is examined in historical perspective. Current studies of migration are found to be lacking in reliable data and based on inappropriate concepts. The author reviews existing knowledge, identifies inadequacies, and makes policy suggestions for filling in needed areas. In addition to a detailed inventory of current knowledge on migration and lacunae in such knowledge, the author lays out policy implications for national-development planning.

Akiwowo, Akinsola. "The Role of Social Scientists in Africa—Further Reflections." *International Social Science Journal* 28, no. 1 (1976), pp. 198–201. [1, 2, 3]
Essentially a commentary on suggestions made by P.E. Temu on improving social sciences in Africa. The basic problem is a too-willing acceptance of Western social science. The author seconds the suggestion of removing linguistic barriers among African nations and suggests the formation of regional social-science councils. These and other suggestions are unlikely to be realized, because African governments have a large role in the universities and are not supportive of radical change.

————. "Sociology in Africa Today." *Current Sociology* 28, no. 2 (1980), pp. 1–126. [1, 2]

This broad, thorough survey and trend report on the state of sociology as a discipline in contemporary Africa includes an analysis of the colonial traditions in the sociology of African societies, the concept of "African sociology," the status of sociology as a discipline in thirteen African countries, and problems of communication and diffusion of social-science knowledge in Africa. The article includes a comprehensive bibliography of more than 700 items, over 300 of which are substantive articles published by African social scientists in over 100 African social-science journals, plus 300 final-year-students' theses from selected African universities (in Nigeria and Ghana).

Arcand, Suzanne, and Brillon, Yves. "Comparative Criminology: Africa." *Acta Criminologica* 6 (1973): 199–217. [1, 2]

A description of crime and the efforts of the International Center for Comparative Criminology in supporting the Institute of Criminology in Abidjan, Ivory Coast. The need for a regional institute was made evident by rising juvenile delinquency in West Africa and the inadequacy of available information and data. The purpose of the Institute is to improve statistical data and increase understanding of the relationship of economic development—with its related destruction of traditional culture—to social maladjustment and crime.

Berman, Edward H. "Foundations, United States Foreign Policy, and African Education, 1945–1975." *Harvard Educational Review* 49, no. 2 (1979), pp. 145–179. [1]

The author reviews the activities of the Carnegie, Rockefeller, and Ford foundations in support of educational programs in Africa. One area of assistance was strengthening social-science capacities at the university level. The author relates these efforts to the strategic and economic objectives of the U.S. government and U.S. corporations. The article is followed by commentaries by foundation representatives.

Bongoy, Mpekesa. "Role and Status of Economics in Zaire: A Critical Survey." *International Social Science Journal* 30, no. 1 (1978), pp. 181–190. [2, 3]

The current status of economics in Zaire and its contribution to Zaire's development is critically analyzed through the use of questionnaires, statistical data, and the author's faculty and administrative experience in the economics department at the National University in Kinshasa. Economics teaching and research are found to be ill suited to the needs of the country, and specific reforms are suggested.

Bouhdiba, Abedlwahab. "La sociologie du développement africain" [The sociology of African development]. *Current Sociology* 18, no. 2 (1970), pp. 1–102. [2]

A selected bibliography of social research on Africa, accompanied by analysis of trends in the literature. The author notes that most of the research was produced in Europe and North America. Despite the recent establishment of several African studies centers in Africa, the distribution of research is still uneven. The author observes a fragmented approach to development, lists key topics, and calls for an integrated participatory approach grounded in African reality that would enable sociologists to contribute to development.

Coleman, James S. "Some Thoughts on Applied Social Research and Training in African Universities." *African Review* 2, no. 2 (1972), pp. 289–307. [2, 3]

The author surveys four interrelated problem areas regarding the applied-research and training functions: where the function should be situated—within the university, within the government, or elsewhere; the relationship of university-based social-science institutes to the rest of the university, and particularly to the disciplinary departments; the relationship of such institutes to the government; and the problems of institutionalizing an applied social-science research institute in an African university setting.

Collomb, Henri. "Social Psychology in Africa: The Psychiatrist's Point of View." *International Social Science Journal* 24, no. 1 (1972), pp. 95–110. [1, 3]

In the broader context of the applicability of transferring Western social psychology to an African context, the author describes his research experiences in Dakar, Senegal. He discusses difficulties arising from a colonial past and the need to replace manipulation with participation in a truly collaborative effort between Europeans and Africans. Only in this way can Western social psychology serve African development.

Copans, Jean. "Note critique: Dangers et difficultés de l'étude des résistances primaires" [Critical note: Dangers and difficulties of studying primary resistance movements]. *Revue canadienne des études africaines/ Canadian Journal of African Studies* 11, no. 1 (1977), pp. 97–99. [1, 2]

A short epistemological and theoretical critique of studies of resistance movements and their roots in the colonial disciplines of history and anthropology. According to the author, an adequate perspective of liberation movements cannot be obtained through data and documents produced by the colonial dominators.

———. "Pour une histoire et une sociologie des études africaines" [Toward a history and sociology of African studies]. *Cahiers d'études africaines* 11, no. 43 (1971), pp. 422–447. [1, 2]

A critical discussion of the relation between political domination of Africa by Western powers and its reflection in Western studies of Africa. Such studies have refused to develop theories that incorporate the reality of dominance. To the extent that such theories are accepted by Africans, they serve to perpetuate dominance. The author proposes that political and theoretical solutions will be found in Marxism developed by Africans themselves.

————. "Les stages de terrain en milieu rural français pour la Formation à la recherche en Afrique noire (FRAN)" [Field training courses in a rural French setting for the Training of Researchers in Black Africa (FRAN)]. *Études rurales* 66 (1977): 47–58. [2]
A description of research training techniques used in French black Africa. Field research, generally focused on communes, follows a standard general procedure developed by the organization but encourages the development of new procedures and techniques.

Dugbaza, G. Tetteh; Aidoo, T.M.; and Adjabeng, Selina. "The Role of Social Anthropology in the Sociology Syllabus of Cape Coast University." *Ghana Journal of Sociology* 8, no. 2, and 9, no. 1 (1974), pp. 24–28. [2, 3]
The study uses survey research to evaluate the utility of social anthropological studies to the development needs of Ghana. Based on questionnaire data from sociology students at Cape Coast University, the authors conclude that social anthropology has been limited by its concern for "primitive cultures" and that the designation "primitive" is highly value-based. Social anthropology in Ghana is seen as irrelevant to societal needs and offers few employment opportunities.

Dunham, H. Warren, and Lutfiyya, Abdulla. "Research Communications: I. Sociology in Egypt." *Journal of Asian and African Studies* 6, no. 2 (1971), pp. 118–126. [1, 2, 3]
A historical account of the development of sociology in Egypt that describes impediments, influences from abroad, and the relation of sociology to postrevolutionary social planning. Since the revolution, the government has supported social sciences by founding research centers and utilizing social-science knowledge in development planning.

el-Saaty, Hassan. "Sociology and Development in Contemporary Egypt." *Die Dritte Welt* 5, nos. 2–3 (1977), pp. 242–255. [2, 3]
A history of sociology in Egypt that concentrates on the role of sociology in development planning. Egyptian sociology is described as being mainly concerned with Egyptian social reality, socialistic in orientation, and interdisciplinary. Although sociologists as a group were discredited after the 1952 revolution, individual social scientists have been highly involved in policy formulation, and Egypt's national ideology calls for social change based on scientific research in the natural and social sciences.

Etienne, Bruno. "Les sciences sociales—leur impact sur le développement en Algérie" [The social sciences—Their impact on Algerian development]. *Die Dritte Welt* 5, nos. 2–3 (1977), pp. 189–227. [3]
The author describes the relationship of social sciences to the state in pre- and postrevolutionary Algeria. After the revolution, the desire was to change the social sciences so they would both reflect Algeria's Arab-

Muslim past and provide the knowledge necessary for modernization. Today the social sciences are in alliance with the state's development project and are not areas for a critical study of knowledge.

Giles, B.D. "Economists in Government: The Case of Malawi." *Journal of Development Studies* 15, no. 2 (1979), pp. 216–232. [3]
The problem of the relation between economic rationality and decision making in Africa is seen largely as a problem of communication among economists, administrators, and politicians. The author describes how economists are integrated into the machinery of government in Malawi and briefly compares it with the process in Zambia, where the Ministry of Development Planning was effectively excluded.

Hammett, Ian. "The Role of Sociologist in Local Planning." *Journal of Development Studies* 9, no. 4 (1973), pp. 493–507. [3]
Reviewing his experiences as consulting sociologist on a rural agricultural project in Swaziland, the author generalizes about the misunderstanding regarding a sociologist's role. The technologists expect sociologists to produce answers to unreal and unanswerable questions on matters such as peasant attitudes toward phenomena they had never experienced. Such misunderstandings have undesirable consequences for development research and can distort the planning team's recommendations.

Kimball, Helen. "On the Teaching of Economics in Africa." *Journal of Modern African Studies* 7, no. 4 (1969), pp. 713–741. [1]
A review article giving an account of problems encountered in teaching economics in black African universities. The author touches on weak motivation and lack of adequate mathematics training of students, cultural constraints, and overreliance on memorization, but her main focus is on the textbook problem. She points out the unsuitableness for African students of the Anglo-Saxon industrial-economy-oriented textbooks available before 1968–1969. The need for relevant teaching materials for African students was taken up at a conference at Dar es Salaam in March 1969, and some of the papers presented are discussed. Two new (1969) Africa-oriented textbooks are evaluated.

Mujaju, Akiiki B. "Political Science and Political Science Research in Africa." *African Review* 4, no. 3 (1974), pp. 339–358. [2]
Political science, once a popular field of study, has fallen out of favor in some African countries since independence. The author explores the reasons, citing among other things the connection between political science and liberalism ("value liberalism"), which arouses the suspicion of the government, and the subsequent connection between political science and authoritarian governments (with scholars focusing on "stability"), which arouses the disapproval of intellectuals. The conflict between political scientist Ali Mazrui and President A. Milton Obote of

Uganda (before 1971) and its implications for the discipline are discussed.

Murphy, Lawrence R. "Social Science Research in the Middle East: The American University in Cairo, Egypt." *Journal of the History of the Behavioral Sciences* 15, no. 2 (1979), pp. 115–127. [1, 2]

A description of changes in the American University (Cairo) Social Research Center as it has responded to social and political pressures. Founded in 1952 with U.S. university and Ford Foundation support, it has moved from mainly foreign personnel to exclusively nonforeign personnel, from research on specific topics to large interdisciplinary studies, from foreign-oriented concerns to topics of Egyptian concern. The author proposes the center as a model for other developing countries.

Obikese, D.S. "A New Approach to Social Research in Africa: The Exchange Process." *International Social Science Journal* 31, no. 4 (1979), pp. 732–740. [2, 3]

The article begins with a description of problems of social research in Africa, such as a population unaccustomed to empirical research, a social-science community divided by ideological and epistemological differences, and inadequate funding and facilities. The author's main purpose is to propose a type of research that overcomes many of the problems, is suitable to the African context, and has policy implications. The essence of exchange research is involvement of those under study in the research decision-making processes. A case study of a successful exchange-research project is described in each of its stages.

Okonjo, Chukuka. "On the Teaching of Economics in Nigeria." *Nigerian Journal of Economics and Social Studies* 5, no. 2 (1963), pp. 197–210. [3] ("Comment and Reply" by C.C. Wrigley [1964].)

The author attempts to fill the perceived lacunae in the National Development Plans for 1962–1968. These plans implicitly required trained economists but left consideration of the actual provision to universities. The author addresses issues of who and what should be taught, and how it should be taught in higher levels of education.

O'Loughlin, Carleen. "What Is the Village? The Relevance of 'Village Studies' in West African Social Research." *Ghana Social Science Journal* 2, no. 1 (1972), pp. 19–26. [1, 2]

Although village research constitutes a valid subfield of study in Europe and Asia, the author cautions against importing its concepts and methods into Ghana without considerable modification. After describing the African village and how it differs from the assumptions of village research, the author puts the research into an African context.

Onibokun, Adepoju. "Directions for Social Research on Self-Help Projects

and Programmes in Nigeria." *Community Development Journal* 11, no. 1 (1976), pp. 60–69. [3]
Recent government policies in Nigeria have shifted to strategies of local self-help. In order to inform such strategies, research was conducted on the conception, achievements, and orientations of self-help projects. This research is systematically evaluated through survey methods and literature reviews, and the results are presented.

Onoge, Omafume F. "Counterrevolutionary Tradition in African Studies: The Case of Applied Anthropology." *Nigerian Journal of Economic and Social Studies* 15, no. 3 (1973), pp. 325–345. [1, 3]
Extending the radical reevaluation of Africanist anthropology to the British school of applied anthropology, the author traces the development of the subfield in the service of colonialism, apartheid, and exploitation, criticizing the views of a number of colonialist anthropologists as irrelevant for anticolonial movements. He calls for a new "liberation anthropology," as opposed to one that places blame on African culture. Fanon has provided the guidelines for this new approach.

Owusu, Maxwell. "Ethnography of Africa: The Usefulness of the Useless." *American Anthropologist* 80, no. 2 (1978), pp. 310–334. [1, 2]
The author discusses epistemological and methodological problems in anthropological research in Africa. Referring to specific ethnographies, the author observes basic problems such as Eurocentric values, chronological misrepresentations, and inaccuracies due to use of native interpreter-informants. He calls for knowledge of relevant African languages by European ethnographers, basic research done by African researchers, and more exchange between foreign Africanists and African social scientists.

Preiswerk, A. Roy. "Neokolonialismus oder Selbstkolonisierung? Die Kulturbegegnung in den europäisch-afrikanischen Beziehungen" [Neocolonialism or self-colonialism? Culture encounter in European-African relations]. *Europa Archiv* 28, no. 24 (1973), pp. 845–853. [1, 2, 3]
The author develops the concept of self-colonialism to describe strong identification with France on the part of black elites in former French Africa. Self-colonialism differs from neocolonialism in that it is an eagerness to adopt Western ways in the effort to be "supermodern." This is particularly evident in government administration and in educational systems. The author recommends development of a psychology and sociology of decolonization.

Princy Ranaivoarivony, Guy de. "Il ruolo della sociologia nella planificazione dello sviluppo in Africa" [The role of sociology in the planning of development in Africa]. Translated by Alberto Guaraldo. *Quaderni di sociologia* 20, nos. 3–4 (1971), pp. 315–327. [3]

Italian translation of a paper presented at the Seventh World Congress of Sociology in Varna, Bulgaria, in September 1970. The author begins by rejecting the economic definition of development based on increase in gross national product. He outlines a socialist definition of development that incorporates traditional African humanism and is measured by individual, material, spiritual, and cultural improvement. He then outlines needed interventions at the global and national levels to achieve development. He prescribes a sociological approach to planning that is interdisciplinary and based on African reality.

Rimlinger, Gaston V. "Administrative Training and Modernization in Zaire." *Journal of Development Studies* 12, no. 4 (1976), pp. 364–382. [2]

A description and analysis of the rise and demise of the École nationale d'Administration (ENDA) in Kinshasa, 1961–1971. The author discusses problems such as the search for a role in national planning, attempts at recognition, conflicts with the university establishment, and the need to adapt to rapid social change.

Temu, P.E. "Reflections on the Role of Social Scientists in Africa." *International Social Science Journal* 27 (1975): 190–194. [2]

The author views African social problems in a historical context. He charges that because foreign social scientists lack an African perspective, their work has had little impact on the African scene. He suggests that African scholars need an institute that would overcome language barriers by providing training in English and French—later adding Arabic, Portuguese, and Spanish—and by promoting translations of social-science work in these languages. He also wants more programs to train African social scientists and more communication among the social scientists of different African countries.

Van Etten, G. "Towards Research on Health Development in Tanzania." *Social Science and Medicine* 6, no. 3 (1972), pp. 335–352. [3]

The author prescribes new forms of social research on health care and training services. Beginning with a detailed description of past studies and current health-care facilities of Tanzania, the author suggests that health care could be improved by social research on the political and cultural conditions of the country and an evaluation of medical care to determine how it could be integrated more effectively into the society.

van Velsen, Jaap. "Social Research and Social Relevance: Suggestions for a Research Policy and Some Research Priorities for the Institute for African Studies." *African Social Research* 17 (1974): 417–553. [2]

A description of past research on Zambia and a prescription for future research. Such research should begin from the perspective of Zambia as a modern, industrial nation comparable to other such nations. The author presents criteria for accepting contract research and for resolving the dispute between basic and applied research. Future social-science research should cover demography, labor history, urban studies, and industrialization. Additional staff will be needed by the institute to carry out all the proposed research.

Welsh, David. "Social Research in a Divided Society: The Case of South Africa." *Social Dynamics* 1, no. 1 (1975), pp. 19–30. [2]
The author describes how the social problems of the larger society are reflected in social research in South African universities. Certain topics such as race relations and social change are especially difficult to investigate. There is no funding and no likely publication of research on such sensitive topics. In addition, funding for social-science research in general is limited, public statistics are inadequate, and trained researchers are few—all due to lack of governmental and nongovernmental support.

Asia

Abdullah, Tahrunnessa A., and Zeidenstein, Sondra A. "Finding Ways to Learn about Rural Women: Experiences from a Pilot Project in Bangladesh." *Sociologia Ruralis* 18, nos. 2–3 (1978), pp. 158–176. [3]
Lack of information is considered the main cause of failure of a project designed to integrate women into rural-development processes in Bangladesh. The project is described, unavailable but necessary information identified, difficulties assessed, and a solution proposed. The solution was a program of "barefoot sociologists"—local people trained to conduct interviews in order to obtain necessary social information.

Agrawal, Binod Chaud. "Indian Models versus Western Models: Some Perspectives in the Study of Civilization." *Eastern Anthropologist* 31, no. 1 (1978), pp. 31–39. [1, 2]
The author contrasts Western-generated with Indian-generated models used in describing and analyzing Indian society. He also discusses the utility of "emic" and "etic" approaches to the study of India, using a particular research study to indicate the advantages of the "spatial emic approach."

al-Qazzaz, Ayad. "Sociology in Underdeveloped Countries—A Case Study of Iraq." *Sociological Review* 20, no. 1 (1972), pp. 93–103. [1, 2]
A description of sociology in Iraq and its historical evolution since the 1920s. The author looks at institutions and published works and concludes that only one Iraqi sociologist has consistently and systematically applied a sociological framework to Iraqi reality. The article also discusses political problems afflicting the Iraqi Sociological Association and the strong influence of North American sociology.

———. "Impressions of Sociology in Iraq." *International Social Science Journal* 27, no. 4 (1975), pp. 781–786. [2]
The author traces the historical development of sociology in Iraq and

reviews the current sociological literature by Iraqi sociologists. The development of sociology in Iraq is attributed, in part, to the return of Ph.D. students from programs in the United States and to recognition of the utility of sociology by the Iraqi government. Iraqi literature is characterized as general and theoretical rather than empirical, due to the lack of sociological works in the native language and to the expense of empirical research. Exceptions to the generalizations are noted.

Atal, Yogesh. "Professionalization of Sociologists." *Indian Journal of Social Research* 12, no. 2 (1971), pp. 137–142. [2]

Showing how Indian sociology has become increasingly professionalized, the author concentrates on the development of professional conferences. He traces trends in the discipline by looking at conference topics and papers across a number of years. He finds a marked broadening beyond the early concentration on empirical studies of Indian villagers. He discusses the role of the Indian Council for Social Science Research in the growth and professionalization of social sciences.

Atalas, Syed Hussein. "The Captive Mind and Creative Development." *International Social Science Journal* 26, no. 4 (1974), pp. 691–700. [1]

The captive mind, as it exists in Asia, is one that is unconsciously dominated by Western thought and is unable to adapt its Western learning to the national situation. Universities, including Asian universities, promote this captive mind, which tends to view purely Western phenomena as universal and accepts the assumption that phases of development in Asian countries will follow the same sequence as in the West. The author proposes the creation of university courses, books, and journals aimed at countering the imitative captive mind and producing emancipated thought.

Béteille, André. "Intellectuals and the Indian Emergency." *International Social Science Journal* 30, no. 4 (1978), pp. 944–946. [2]

A description of the impact of national political life on the social sciences during the Indian emergency of 1975–1977. Social-science research was restricted, and social scientists were discredited as playing a parasitic rather than productive role in Indian society.

———. "The Language of the Social Sciences." *International Social Science Journal* 29, no. 3 (1977), pp. 531–532. [2]

A brief analysis of the problems involved in translating ambiguous social-science terminology from one language to another. The problem is acute in India, where many regional languages are involved. Government translations are poor and result in alterations of the material. A truly comparative sociology is unlikely to evolve without standardization of terms and concepts.

Cant, R.G. "Territorial Socio-Economic Indicators in Development Plans in the Asian Region." *International Social Science Journal* 27, no. 1 (1975), pp. 53–77. [3]

A rigorous analysis of the utility of spatial planning in national development. After describing what spatial analysis can contribute, the author discusses specific research traditions such as multivariate regional studies, social indicators, and factorial ecology. More generally, the author counsels national-planning agencies to develop flexible and comprehensive data banks, to specify appropriate indicators, and to study the relationship of spatial dynamics to development processes.

Clinard, Marshall B., and Elder, Joseph W. "Sociology in India: A Study of the Sociology of Knowledge." *American Sociology Review* 30, no. 4 (1965), pp. 581–587. [2]
The authors survey the status of sociology as a discipline in India and critically examine six of its general characteristics: rejection of Western empirical sociology as too materialistic, use of historical-religious materials to understand the present, emphasis on village rather than urban studies, relative lack of emphasis on research in university activities, government pressure for action-oriented studies, and resentment of exploitation by foreign researchers in India. The authors conclude that sociology in India will continue to be modified by new pressures of time and place and by findings and issues that arise in the discipline in India and elsewhere.

David, Randolph S. "Sociologists Consider the Problems and Prospects of Societal Change." *Philippine Sociological Review* 21, nos. 3–4 (1973), pp. 287–289. [3]
The author summarizes the five main themes presented at the 1973 convention of the Philippine Sociological Society: the role of sociologists in government policymaking, the nature of agrarian reform, the problem of getting legislation for social reform, population growth and policies, and education and other means for inducing social change in the Philippines.

Davidian, Harutuin. "The Application of Some Basic Psychological Theories in the Iranian Cultural Context." *International Social Science Journal* 25, no. 4 (1973), pp. 532–546.
Although the author's comments are made from a clinical perspective, they are important for researchers as well. The author shows how theories and treatments developed in Western societies must be modified to suit the Iranian situation. He discusses the Iranian family, sex and sex education, marriage and childbirth, acquisition of social behavior, and the changing Iranian society.

Gardezi, Hassan N. "Contemporary Sociology in Pakistan." *International Journal of Contemporary Sociology* 8, nos. 3–4 (1971), pp. 342–351. [1, 2, 3]
A detailed description of sociology in Pakistan since its inception in 1955 with the first sociology department. The results of heavy North American influence are described: its narrowly empirical, nontheoretical,

ahistorical approaches to topics are not related to conditions in Pakistan. The author describes research projects fitting this description and concludes with indications of a more creative and independent discipline engaging in problem-oriented research with newly developed methods.

Geertz, Clifford. "Social Science Policy in a New State: A Programme for the Stimulation of the Social Sciences in Indonesia." *Minerva* 12, no. 3 (1974), pp. 365–381. [2]
The author outlines in detail measures that might be taken to improve the state of sociology and anthropology in Indonesia. Such efforts are needed to balance the larger attention given to physical sciences and economics. The basic element of the proposals is the establishment of a strong research-training program.

Glassburner, Bruce. "Political Economy and the Soeharto Regime." *Bulletin of Indonesian Economic Studies* 14, no. 3 (1978), pp. 24–51. [3]
The author argues against some criticisms of the policies of the Soeharto government found in recent literature. He refutes the charge that Soeharto's American-trained "technocrats" are excessively influenced by foreign (procapitalist) agencies and denies assertions that the government has been excessively monetarist or that it should have reduced foreign trade to a minimum. However, he agrees with the critics that Indonesia's promotion of import-substitution (high-capital) industries was a mistake; promoting labor-intensive exports would have been more advantageous. The article also comments on agricultural policy, corruption, and conspicuous consumption.

Gokhale, S.D. "Organisational Set Up for Planning Social Programmes in India." *Indian Journal of Social Work* 23, no. 1 (1972), pp. 1–11. [3]
The author presents two basic objectives of development planning in India: the economic goals of production and the sociological goals of distribution. The author attributes weakness in planning to lack of coordination between the sociological processes of determining goals and the administrative processes of program implementation. He calls for modification of social-planning skills and techniques and for reorganization of planning machinery. Social sciences would play a role in the former.

Heller, Mute. "Die Rolle der Sozialwissenschaften im Entwicklungsprozess: Betrachtungen zur 'Entwicklungsproblematik' im Mittleren Osten anlässlich eines Internationalen Kongresses in Kairo" [The role of the social sciences in the development process: Considerations on the 'development problems' of the Middle East occasioned by an international congress in Cairo]. *Die Dritte Welt* 5, nos. 2–3 (1977), pp. 136–158. [1, 2, 3]

Based on the European-Arab dialogue initiated at a 1975 conference in Cairo, the author discusses the relevance of traditional European-derived sociology to Middle Eastern reality. One example with broader significance is the emphasis in mainstream sociology on social control (deviance and abnormality). Third World conditions call for a sociology of coercive relationships and strategies to overcome these relationships. The author calls for further Arab-European and intra-Arab dialogue.

Heper, Metin, and Berkman, Umit. "Administrative Studies in Turkey: A General Perspective." *International Social Science Journal* 31, no. 2 (1979), pp. 305–327. [1, 2, 3]
A comprehensive study of public administration as a social-science discipline. The authors trace its history, systematically describe its current theoretical and conceptual content, present university curricula, and survey the careers and opinions of public administration graduates. They contrast public administration with other social sciences as being more disposed to accept foreign theories and methods without adapting them.

Joshi, P.C. "Reflections on Social Science Research in India." *Sociological Bulletin* 24, no. 2 (1975), pp. 139–162. [1, 2]
The author offers impressions of the shortcomings of social-science research in India. The major problem is the postcolonial retention of Western perspectives, theories, and concerns. The "haves" are studied more than the "have nots." The development of scientific values is threatened by commercialism, politicization, bureaucratization, and ideological fanaticism. The author also discusses institution building in the social sciences and makes general suggestions for the future.

Kerr, Graham B. "Strategies for Collecting Information for Development Programs and Social Research Design: A Case Study of Afghanistan." *Journal of South Asian and Middle Eastern Studies* 111, no. 2 (1979), pp. 53–69. [2, 3]
The author discusses the difficulty of carrying out social-impact studies often required by development agencies in advance of enacting a program. Grant-development plans are rendered useless by lack of information and data. The role of the social scientist is to provide necessary data. The author presents a case study of data-gathering methods used by Afghan Demographic Studies, an agency of the Afghan Planning Ministry.

Kiray, Mübeccel B. "Teaching in Developing Countries: The Case of Turkey." *International Social Science Journal* 31, no. 1 (1979), pp. 40–48. [1, 2]
In a historical description, the author talks about conservatism in both society and the universities as an early impediment to the development

of social sciences in Turkey. In the 1960s, however, the national government saw the possibilities of scientifically based disciplines and encouraged a period of professionalization and institution building. The political crisis and rise of totalitarianism in the early 1970s had negative repercussions on the newly established social sciences. By 1975, however, social scientists were reinstated. Today, research stresses basic social change, and the author believes that social scientists from Turkey and other developing countries will make major contributions to dynamic theories and methodologies.

Lakshmanna, C. "Teaching and Research in Sociology in India." *Sociological Bulletin* 23, no. 1 (1974), pp. 1–13. [2]

A historical description of sociology in India from 1917 to recent times. The role of the British and of Indian universities is discussed. Interest in sociology has recently been high, as measured by the number of people drawn into the field. Current focus is on the transitional social order of a developing country. The author prescribes the use of Indian and foreign teaching materials, continued theory building, and the teaching of sociology from the lower levels of school.

Lim, David. "The Role of the University in Development Planning in Malaysia." Appended note by Harry G. Johnson. "Observations on the Role of the University in Development Planning." *Minerva* 12, no. 1 (1974), pp. 8–38. [1, 2, 3]

The author assesses the opportunities for and limitations on academics participating significantly in development planning through teaching, research, and consultation. Limitations include uncritical adoption of Western models, inappropriate syllabi, incompatibility between the schedules and aims of universities and governments, mutual stereotyping by academics and civil servants, and institutional factors within the university constraining academic consultancies. The author recommends measures that international organizations, national governments, universities, and academics should take to expand academic participation in planning and public policy.

Lorenzo, Conrado L., Jr. "Strategies for Development." *Philippine Sociological Review* 25, nos. 1–2 (1977), pp. 13–16. [3]

Population strategies are first approached by clarifying basic concepts and defining development in terms of human well-being. The author then gives a brief description of the institutional element in Philippine population planning, the Population Center Foundation, whose purpose is to encourage private-sector involvement in population programs. Areas of involvement are research, innovative programming, and technical assistance.

Madan, T.N. "The Teaching of Sociology in India: Some Comments." *Sociological Bulletin* 23, no. 1 (1974), pp. 113–118. [2]

The poor state of sociology in Indian universities is blamed for the brain drain that leaves Indian social sciences with less than the best researchers. Specific remedies are proposed.

Mohseni, Manouchehr. "Sociological Research in Iran." *International Social Science Journal* 28, no. 2 (1976), pp. 387–390. [2, 3]

A brief historical account up to recent times of the development of sociological research in Iran. The early influences came first from France and the United States. The majority of the 163 universities in Iran have offered sociology courses, and as of 1975, 23.7 percent of Iranian students specialized in the social sciences. Support from the state has been strong as planners have recognized the need for social research.

Mukherjee, Ramkrishna. "Indian Sociology: Historical Development and Present Problems." *Sociological Bulletin* 22, no. 1 (1973), pp. 29–58. [2]

A historical description of Indian social science. Three overlapping stages are identified: pre-twentieth-century "proto sociology"; professionalization and development of descriptive and explanatory theory during the first half of this century; and the current stage, marked by a need for "diagnostic sociology." The author discusses the role of sociology in identifying potential areas of social change.

———. "The Sociologist and the Social Reality." *Sociological Bulletin* 23, no. 2 (1974), pp. 169–192. [2]

In a presidential address to the Twelfth All-India Sociological Conference in 1974, the author assesses the strengths and weaknesses of Indian sociology since 1947. Strengths are in theory formation and methodological refinements; weaknesses are in gross empiricism or dogmatic adherence to grand theory. The author ends with a discussion of the role of values in social research.

———. "Sociology and 'Developing Societies': Some Observations (with Special References to India)." *International Journal of Contemporary Sociology* 9, nos. 2–3 (1972), pp. 132–147. [2]

The author questions concepts of social development and change as they are used in contemporary Indian sociology. He proposes replacing a sequential model of social change with a more complex model that differentiates between sets of social behaviors and between groups and institutions within society. Such a model should allow for underlying social stability and no change in some variables. He proposes a series of questions that such a model might answer.

O'Hara, Albert T. "A Report on the Development of Sociology in China since Its Political Division." *Journal of the History of Behavioral Sciences* 15, no. 4 (1979), pp. 340–345. [2]

The author briefly compares the development of sociology in mainland

China and in Taiwan after 1949. In China, university-level sociology
departments were disbanded and sociology is currently taught as an
interdisciplinary subject in other departments. In Taiwan, the U.S.
model of sociology has been adopted, and according to the author the
discipline is progressing.

Papanek, Hanna. "Women in South and Southeast Asia: Issues and Research." *Signs* 1, no. 1 (1975), pp. 193−211. [1, 2]
A thorough survey of research on women carried out in South/South-
east Asia, Indonesia, Bangladesh, Pakistan, and India through 1974. A
useful selected bibliography is included. The author compares research
contexts and needs of Asian societies with those of North America and
Europe and makes specific suggestions for future research projects and
institutions.

Peele, John, and Potts, Malcolm. "The Sociology of Population Control."
Social Science and Medicine 7, no. 3 (1973), pp. 179−190. [3]
The authors examine the role of social scientists vis-à-vis population-
control problems in less developed countries. Social scientists have been
neither integrally involved in nor supportive of population programs,
which generally have emphasized clinical aspects. The authors prescribe
greater cooperation between sociologists and medical doctors in the
design of population programs that would use local social patterns to
best advantage.

Planck, Ulrich. "Die ländlische Soziologie in der Türkei" [Rural sociology
in Turkey]. *Sociologia Ruralis* 12, no. 2 (1972), pp. 181−196. [2, 3]
This history of rural sociology in Turkey since 1923 covers university
curricula, research methods, published works, and the application of
rural sociology to Turkish villages. Rural sociologists have had an
important role in government policies and in the establishment of a
Ministry for Village Affairs.

Raksasataya, Amara. "A Case of Social Science in Thailand's Higher Education." *Thai Quarterly Journal of Public Administration* 5, no. 3
(1965), pp. 440−462. [2]
Thammasat University is virtually the only institution of higher education in Thailand that offers social-science training. The author describes
the structure and growth of the university, listing and describing the
faculties, and includes tables of statistics on faculty and students. Of
special interest are the statistics attesting the large number of part-time
teachers in the older faculties and the large number of female teachers in
the newer schools.

Saksena, R.N. "Social Research and Social Welfare in India—Base for an
Interdisciplinary Approach." *Sociological Bulletin* 23, no. 2 (1974), pp.
193−201. [2]

A general discussion of the concepts of social welfare and the welfare state in India. Because the basic value in the society is the individual human being, the goal of social policy should be to promote and maintain the individual's standard of living. Social scientists can best point the way toward this goal by uniting the efforts of the separate disciplines in the study of human behavior in society.

Salcedo, Juan, Jr. "Scientists and Progress in the Philippines." *Impact of Sciences in Society* 22, nos. 1–2 (1972), pp. 175–185. [2, 3]
The discussion centers on the physical sciences, their development and institutionalization, and their role in national development. Social sciences are treated secondarily, but the author calls for a sociology of the application of science and technology.

Śarana, Gopāla. "A Note on the Urgent Need of Indian Anthropology." *Eastern Anthropologist* 24, no. 2 (1971), pp. 203–205. [2]
The author addresses the question of why Indian anthropologists have relatively low status both in anthropology and in Indian society. A partial answer is found in their lack of identity. Anthropology is traditionally defined as the study of other cultures, with self-study yet to begin. Indian anthropology is encouraged to stress the integration of sociology and anthropology and apply insights and techniques from the latter to Indian cultures.

Shukla, S. "Sociologists Adrift." *Indian Journal of Social Research* 12, no. 2 (1971), pp. 143–145. [2]
A highly critical assessment of the Tenth All-India Sociological Conference held in Hyderabad in 1970. The author attributed the pedestrian character of the conference to its main theme—the sociology of social revolution—coupled with the fact that those present knew very little about the topic.

Singh, Yogendra. "Constraints, Contradictions and Interdisciplinary Orientations: The Indian Context." *International Social Science Journal* 31, no. 1 (1979), pp. 114–122. [2]
A brief, general discussion of contradictions in Indian sociology that result from India's colonial past, regional diversity, and development needs. The author describes the innovative interdisciplinary program established in the Jawaharlal Nehru University in New Delhi and its approach to social science and social problems.

———. "The Role of Social Sciences in India: A Sociology of Knowledge." *Sociological Bulletin* 22, no. 1 (1973), pp. 14–28. [1, 2]
A thoughtful analysis of the historical development and role of social sciences in India. The author analyzes the relationship of social sciences to the societies from which they emanate. Because social-science theories and methods reflect the conditions and values of particular socie-

ties, he criticizes the use of Western social sciences in India and calls for the establishment of social sciences based on the reality and needs of Indian society.

Srinivas, M.N., and Panini, M.N. "The Development of Sociology and Social Anthropology in India." *Sociological Bulletin* 22, no. 2 (1973), pp. 179–215. [2]

A chronology of the development of sociology and social anthropology in India. The authors define three stages since the late eighteenth century and amply refer to significant individuals and works of each stage. The most recent stage is characterized by a marked increase in scientific research. Such research is important to policy planning in India. Although the disciplines have been strongly influenced by European and North American social sciences, they have maintained a recognizable Indian identity that will become much more pronounced in the future.

Stambouli, Fredj. "Remarques epistemologiques sur sciences sociales et développement" [Epistemological remarks on the social sciences and development]. *Die Dritte Welt* 5, nos. 2–3 (1977), pp. 307–311. [2]

The author calls for the reconceptualization of Western-oriented social sciences for Arab reality and needs. Prescriptions include bridging the gap between academic training and social relevance, overcoming provincialism and overdescriptiveness, critically rethinking the Arab-Islamic cultural past, and developing a new and radical social theory.

Tavassoli, Gholam Abbas. "Growth and Significance of Social Sciences in Iran." *International Review of Modern Sociology* 4, no. 2 (1974), pp. 117–128. [2]

A description of the development of social sciences in Iran since World War II. The social sciences were first introduced into university curricula shortly after the war. With UNESCO assistance, the Institute for Social Studies and Research was established at the University of Teheran in 1957. Data on education, research, and employment in the social sciences during the 1960s and 1970s indicate rapid growth in all areas and an emphasis on data collection. The author concludes that more attention should be given to conceptualization and methodology.

Varma, S.C. "Whither Change Studies?" *Eastern Anthropologist* 30, no. 4 (1977), pp. 467–470. [2]

The author reviews a study by Singh and Cohn (*Structure and Change in Modern India* [Chicago: Aldine Publishing, 1968]) to support the general critique of studies on India as being functional and nondialectical. This approach is identified with imperialism and fails to incorporate the more profound understanding of Marxist sociologists.

Wang, Kang. "One Year after the Restoration of Sociology in China." *American Sociologist* 15, no. 4 (1980), pp. 186–191. [2, 3]

The author, an officer in the Chinese Academy of Social Sciences, discusses the reinstatement of sociology in China (since its proscription in 1952). He tells of the new Chinese Sociological Research Association and its efforts to establish a discipline oriented toward the understanding and solution of China's problems within a Marxist framework.

Weiner, Myron. "Social Science Research and Public Policy in India." *Economic and Political Weekly* 14, nos. 37 and 38 (1979), pp. 1579–1587, 1622–1628. [2, 3]
A slightly revised version of this two-part article appears in chapter 11 of this volume.

Weldon, Peter D. "Teaching and Research in Sociology in Southeast Asia: A Survey." *Social Science Information/Information sur les sciences sociales* 12, no. 5 (1973), pp. 143–156. [2]
After briefly sketching the history of sociology in Southeast Asia, the author presents the findings of a questionnaire designed to assess the current level of the field and sent to all university departments in which sociology might be taught. Results, qualified by a very low response rate, indicate lack of trained personnel and funds for research, heavy teaching loads, few graduate programs, and limited employment opportunities for sociologists. The author prescribes regional rather than bilateral solutions.

Young, L.C. "Mass Sociology: The Chinese Style." *The American Sociologist* 9, no. 3 (1974), pp. 117–125. [2]
A description of sociology from before the Communists came to power, through the period of the Cultural Revolution, to the time of publication. Although sociology departments were abolished during the Cultural Revolution, sociological studies continued on a more popular basis. Based on Mao's principle of beginning from an accurate empirical base, the general public has been involved in obtaining accurate data on social problems and is capable of sophisticated sociological reasoning.

Latin America

Aguirre Beltran, Gonzalo. "Applied Anthropology in Mexico." *Human Organization* 33, no. 1 (1974), pp. 1–6. [2, 3]
The author relates Mexican social anthropology and particular anthropologists to national policy. Anthropology has traditionally been concerned with rural Indians, and its applied form has strongly influenced Mexican Indian policy. The current planning model, developed by anthropologists over the past twenty years, is described. Both anthropology and planning have shifted to concerns related to migration, urbanization, and agrarian problems.

Alvisa, Daisy Rivero. "Algunas experiencias e investigaciones sociales en la Universidad de La Habana, Cuba" [Some social experiences and research at the University of Havana, Cuba]. *Revista Mexicana de Sociología* 35, no. 1 (1973), pp. 189–196. [2, 3]
A very positive account of the social sciences and social-science research in postrevolutionary Cuba. Major research efforts have focused on underdevelopment and social change in rural areas. The research has been carried out by interdisciplinary teams of faculty and students using local records, interviews, and oral histories. In the process, theories and methods have been developed and refined. Future areas of research are outlined.

Amendola, Giandomenico. "Terzo Mondo e sociologia: Il Congresso di Caracas" [The Third World and sociology: The Congress of Caracas]. *La critica sociológica* 24 (1972–1973): 181–183. [2]
The author finds little new or useful in the papers presented at the 1972 Caracas congress. Most topics centered on political struggles in Latin America and ideological critiques of North American sociology, especially functionalism. The author believes that dependency theories failed to deal adequately with the social dialectic and therefore fail as dynamic theories capable of explaining Latin American social problems.

Argüello, Omar; Fausto, Ayrton; and Ramallo, Luis I. "Enseñanza e investigación en ciencias sociales: La experiencia de la Elas" [Instruction and research in the social sciences: The experience of the LASS (Latin American School of Sociology)]. *Revista mexicana de sociología* 35, no. 1 (1973), pp. 63–86. [2]
The authors critically assess the teaching and research efforts of the Latin American School of Sociology in Santiago, Chile (the sociology affiliate of the U.N.–related Facultad Latinoamericana de Ciencias Sociales—FLACSO). Criticism centers on the limitations of the school's theoretical framework, which derives from structural functionalism. After describing deficiencies in the school's curriculum and research efforts, the authors present the fundamental reorientation under way. Changes include the incorporation of dialectical and historical approaches and a concentration on social change in Latin America.

Babini, Dominique. "Conducta informativa de los científicos políticos argentinos" [Informational behavior of Argentine political scientists]. *Revista argentina de relaciones internacionales* 12 (1978): 56–63. [2]
By means of survey techniques, the author systematically studies the communications patterns of Argentine political scientists and the diffusion of scientific information. The author recommends the establishment of new centers for the communication and dissemination of knowledge and proposes a greater role for social science in the National Research Council.

Barak, Jim A., and Bezerra, Agamenon. "E depois do behavioralism: O quê?" [And after behavioralism: What?]. *Revista de ciências sociais* 5, no. 1 (1974), pp. 11–17. [1, 2]
Methodological eclecticism involves a high degree of partiality with respect to positivism or scientism. The authors attack the empirical/quantitative trend in the social sciences, and the application of the sociological theory of symbolic interaction to political theory and research. The history of political thought should be reincorporated into the university curriculum. Instead of quantitative analysis of the "correlates of revolutionary activity," Barrington Moore's *Social Origins of Dictatorship and Democracy* could serve as a model of social research.

Benaprés, Raúl Atria. "Notas preliminares para la investigación social del derecho en America Latina" [Preliminary notes in social science research on law in Latin America]. *Estudios sociales* 8 (June 1976): 46–58: [3]
One of the relevant areas of empirical research that should be pursued is in the area of law—namely, to what extent are laws and national legislation instrumental in dealing with problems of development and change? Benaprés challenges the validity of several models prevalent in the last decades because of their simplification and overgeneralization. Research must be geared to issues of income distribution; structure and generation of employment; distribution, growth, and composition of the population; and forms of political organization and social participation.

Benítez Zenteno, Raúl. "Desarrollo científico, el papel de las ciencias sociales y el Centro de Sociología de Oaxaca" [Scientific development, the role of the social sciences and the Sociology Center of Oaxaca]. *Revista mexicana de sociología* 37, no. 2 (1975), pp. 523–529. [2]
The sociology center in the University of Oaxaca is used as a case study of institution building in the social sciences. The purpose of the center is to provide specialists capable of making scientific and intellectual contributions to social change. The negative experiences of similar institutions are discussed, including such problems as academic dependence on foreign sources, lack of scientific communications, and national and university crises.

———. "Notas sobre la planeación de la investigación científica en la Universidad Nacional Autónoma de México" [Notes on the planning of scientific investigations at the National Autonomous University of Mexico]. *Revista mexicana de sociología* 38, no. 1 (1976), pp. 227–237. [2]
An evaluation of efforts to plan and coordinate scientific research at the National Autonomous University of Mexico with prescriptions for future research. The author suggests better training for researchers, the development of basic research, more and better resource materials, and a practical approach to Mexico's problems.

Cardoso, Fernando W. "The Originality of a Copy: CEPAL and the Idea of Development." *CEPAL Review* 2 (1977): 7–40. [1, 2, 3]
CEPAL (Comisión Económico para America Latina) has had great impact on Latin American thinking about development. The author outlines the central ideas and their relationship to other theoretical perspectives such as neoclassical theories of international trade and development, Marxist theories, and dependency. Also described are the ways in which CEPAL's ideas influence development policies.

Casas Guerrero, Rosalba. "La investigación en las ciencias sociales en México (1973–1974)" [Social-science research in Mexico (1973–1974)]. *Revista mexicana de sociología* 37, no. 1 (1975), pp. 182–215. [2]
The results of a quantitative study conducted by the Mexican National Council on Science and Technology to assess activities of research and development institutes in Mexico. Data were gathered on research disciplines; location of research projects; types and topics of research projects; distribution among basic, applied, and experimental categories; and the like.

Castano, Humberto S. "La economía en la planificación urbana" [Economics in urban planning]. *Revista interamericana planificación* 12, no. 45 (1978), pp. 127–133. [3]
The author discusses the general failure of Latin American urban planners to incorporate knowledge and methods of urban economics. The author describes each step in an experimental research-and-planning project in Colombia that utilized basic principles of urban-planning economics.

Corradi, Juan Eugenio. "Cultural Dependence and the Sociology of Knowledge: the Latin American Case." *International Journal of Contemporary Sociology* 8, no. 1 (1971), pp. 35–55. [1, 2, 3]
An analytical history of the relation between political/economic dependence and intellectual dependence. The author discusses the dilemma of Latin American social scientists, who have had to choose between the developmentalism of national governments and political opposition. The former is concerned with purely technical aspects of development and ignores issues of political control, and is closely allied with North American social science. Radical social scientists offer an alternative to either developmentalism or political militancy in the formation of a social science directed toward Latin American political priorities and social change. The author discusses the nature of emancipatory self-knowledge for Latin American social scientists.

Cross, Malcolm. "Problems and Prospects for Caribbean Social Research." *Boletín de estudios latinoamericanos y del Caribe* 22 (June 1977): 94–111. [2]
The author reviews the accomplishments of the past two decades and offers suggestions for achieving greater balance in future research. He

sees a need to relate demographic classifications to aspects of social structure and advances an explanation of the relations between the social structure and the system of productive relations (or "that governing the allocation of power").

Cuellar, Oscar, and Heisecke, Guillermo. "Ciencia política y sistemas de dominación: Notas sobre la enseñanza e investigación en America Latina" [Political science and systems of domination: Notes on teaching and research in Latin America]. *Revista mexicana de sociología* 35, no. 1 (1973), pp. 27–38. [2]
This discussion of teaching and research within the discipline of political science in Latin America begins with contributions made by empiricist and functionalist approaches and includes later efforts in historical and multidisciplinary research. The current need is for political science to focus on systems of domination—their formation, maintenance, and dissolution. The authors present a specific set of concerns for such study. Both authors were members of the Latin American School of Political Science in Santiago, Chile.

Filgueira, Carlos H. "25 años de sociología uruguaya" [Twenty-five years of sociology in Uruguay]. *Revista paraguaya de sociología* 11, no. 30 (1974), pp. 147–177. [2]
The author finds the absence of reliable social sciences in Uruguay incongruent with other progressive aspects of the society. He traces the institutional history of sociology through four chronological stages, ending with the dissolution of sociology programs through political force. He uses quantitative data to support his point that progress made during the 1960s has been reversed. The political environment is not favorable for social science.

Filho, Aluizio Alves. "Por una sociologia da coisa nossa" [A sociology for our country]. *Revista de ciências sociais* 1 (January–June 1970): 118–143. [2, 3]
The call for a Brazilian sociology reflecting Brazilian social and political reality began early in the twentieth century. The major proponent was A. Torres, and under his influence sociological studies began in 1932. The author describes the historical development and objectives of the original sociology program in Brazil. The objectives were oriented toward peaceful solution of Brazil's problems through the education of political, economic, and administrative leaders.

FLACSO. "Escuela Latinoamericana de Ciencia Política y Administración Pública FLACSO" [The FLACSO Latin American School of Political Science and Public Administration]. *Revista mexicana de sociología* 35, no. 1 (1973), pp. 87–115. [2]
A detailed description of the new (1972–1973) School for Latin American Political Science (ELACP) established under the U.N.–sponsored Latin American Faculty of Social Sciences (FLACSO) in Santiago,

Chile, giving information on entrance requirements, curriculum, and faculty. The program is designed to train political scientists and public administrators. It is based on the principles of integrated teaching and research, theoretical and methodological pluralism, interdisciplinary approaches, programmatic focus, and emphasis on Latin American concerns.

Foxley, Alejandro, and García, Eduardo. "The Role of Projections in National Planning: A Methodology for Medium-Term Projections and Their Application in Chile." *Journal of Development Planning* 4 (1972): 64–97. [3]
The article consists of three parts: a general analysis of the role of economic programming and projection techniques in development planning, with a critique of traditional techniques; a description of a medium-term projection technique developed by the authors; and a report on the application of the technique in Chile.

Franco, Rolando. "Veinticinco años de sociología latinoamericana. Un balance" [Twenty-five years of sociology in Latin America. A balance]. *Revista paraguaya de sociología* 11, no. 30 (1974), pp. 57–92. [1, 2]
The author reviews major trends in Latin American social sciences: the dominance of North American thought, the rejection of development theories by Marxist theorists, and the increasing nationalism of Latin American social science communities. He describes the fruitful efforts of UNESCO and CEPAL to expand the number of social scientists and to increase the opportunities for communications among them.

Godoy, Ricardo. "Franz Boas and His Plans for an International School of American Archaeology and Ethnology in Mexico." *Journal of the History of the Behavioral Sciences* 13, no. 3 (1977), pp. 228–242. [1]
A detailed, thoughtful account of the efforts of Franz Boas to expand and enrich American anthropology through the founding of the School of American Archaeology and Ethnology in Mexico. The mission of the school was to conduct rigorous anthropological studies in Mexico. Unfortunately, Boas was too much concerned with professionalizing the discipline and too little concerned with its sociopolitical environment. The school ended with the Mexican revolution. The reasons given by the author for the failure of attempts to reconstruct it are instructive.

Godoy Urzúa, Hernán. "El desarrollo de la sociología en Chile: Resumen crítico e interpretativo de su desenvolvimiento entre 1950 y 1973" [The development of sociology in Chile: A critical survey of its evolution between 1950 and 1973]. *Estudios sociales* 2, no. 12 (1977), pp. 33–56. [2]
The social forces and ideological trends conditioning Chilean political evolution are reflected in the development of Chilean sociology as a discipline. Five phases are discerned, coinciding roughly with the succession of five distinct political regimes. The theoretical frameworks

used to analyze Latin American development, rooted in the European tradition, should be considered as heuristic devices rather than incompatible paradigms, in order to avoid methodological reductionism.

Gonzalez Casanova, Pablo. "La sociologie du développement latino-americain" [The sociology of Latin American development]. *Current Sociology* 18, no. 1 (1970), pp. 5–31. [1, 2]
A comprehensive bibliography and report on trends in the sociological literature of Latin American development. The author identifies three historical stages and key approaches in each stage. The current stage is characterized as being increasingly empirical while at the same time returning to theoretical sociology. He illustrates how approaches to particular topics have changed under North American influence. Since its earliest stages, Latin American social thought has reflected the political and social problems of the societies under study, a point carefully made by the author.

Graciarena, Jorge. "Las ciencias sociales, la crítica intelectual y el estado tecnocrático. Una discusión del caso latinoamericano" [Social sciences, intellectual criticism, and the technocratic state. A discussion of the Latin American case]. *Revista mexicana de sociología* 37, no. 1 (1975), pp. 127–148. [2, 3]
The policies of the technocratic state have become increasingly authoritarian, legitimized by the technical and efficiency criteria of the neocapitalist, dependent model of modernization. While science and technology are used to legitimize decisions, intellectual dissent is repressed. Universities have become factories for the production of "human resources," and the professional technocrats are guided by apolitical professionalism, efficiency, and specialization. The author questions the objectivity and neutrality of the social sciences and social scientists.

———. "La crisis latinoamericana y la investigación sociológica" [The Latin American crisis and sociological research]. *Revista mexicana de sociología* 32, no. 2 (1970), pp. 195–228. [1, 2]
The author describes how social problems in Latin America are reflected in Latin American social science. He characterizes the latter as lacking an agreed-upon set of definitions and functions, divided as to ideological and methodological tendencies with little cooperation and communication among the separate factions, and institutionally unstable. He cites particularly the group of sociologists who are strongly identified with North American social science and how they threaten to make the discipline closed, formal, and removed from Latin American reality.

———. "Las funciones de la universidad en el desarrollo latinoamericano" [The function of the university in Latin American development]. *Revista paraguaya de sociología* 8, no. 22 (1971), pp. 63–92. [2, 3]
A broad and detailed analysis of the role of universities in rapidly

changing societies. Topics include the role of the university in providing human resources for development, in educating for the academic professions, and in providing science and technology for development. The author points out the need for an educational policy that concentrates scarce resources on the critical needs of society, and he presents social-science research efforts in Central America as a case in point.

————. "Notas para una discusión sobre la sociología de los intelectuales en America Latina" [Notes toward a discussion on the sociology of intellectuals in Latin America]. *America Latina* 13, nos. 2–3 (1970), pp. 63–69. [2]

A brief but thoughtful discussion of the historical relation between Latin American intellectuals and Latin American society. The quality and nature of intellectual thought are socially conditioned, and the different types of conditioning are analyzed. In the Perón era, intellectuals were alienated and polarized. Today they are called upon to participate in national development.

Grindle, Merilee S. "Power, Expertise and the 'Técnico': Suggestions from a Mexican Case Study." *Journal of Politics* 39, no. 2 (1977), pp. 399–426. [3]

The role of the *técnico* in policymaking is evaluated through interviews conducted in the Compañía Nacional de Subsistencias Populares (National Company of Public Welfare). *Técnicos,* trained in both social and natural sciences, fit the criterion of expertise but also need political understanding in order to initiate policy. Currently, *técnicos* produce background information in support of policies based on political decisions.

Guttmacher, Sally. "Social Science, Social Policy, and Public Health in Cuba." *Human Factor* 12, nos. 2–3 (1974), pp. 66–83. [3]

After a comparison of pre- and postrevolutionary health conditions and medical care, the author describes the health policies of the Castro government. They include the reorganization of health care service on a nationwide basis, the deemphasis of hierarchy among practitioners, the equalization of services, and a shift in focus from curative to preventive measures. Social-science research and practice have played a major role in the improved utilization of health facilities and in prevention programs.

Gyarmati K.G. "Social Sciences in Chile: Professionalization, Codes of Ethics and Ideological Confrontation." *International Social Science Journal* 26, no. 1 (1974), pp. 152–155. [2]

A short description of the professional ramifications of political conflict in Chile and the dilemmas faced by Chilean social scientists.

Hansen, D.O.; Scheider, I.A.; and Vicente de Paula, Vitor. "Rural Sociology in Brazil—Institutional Growth." *International Review of Modern Sociology* (India) 9, no. 1 (1979), pp. 31–48. [1, 2, 3,]

Data from a recent survey by the Brazilian Ministry of Education are used to review five graduate programs in rural sociology. The findings are discussed in the context of the role of sociology in Brazilian national development policies and programs. The paper suggests areas of potential collaboration between Brazilian and foreign sociologists and discusses scientific exchange and research collaboration.

Hodara, Joseph. "Estilos de ideologización. El caso de la sociología mexicana, 1960–1970" [Styles of Ideological Interference in Scientific Research: The Case of Mexican Sociology, 1960–1970]. *Revista mexicana de sociología* 37, no. 4 (1975), pp. 885–899. [2]
The author argues that in the context of underdevelopment and fragile institutionalization of the social sciences, it is more difficult to judge the appropriateness of ideological interferences in scientific research (for example, the degree of explicitness of premises). At times, rigorous objectivity may affect the evolution toward institutionalization of the sociological enterprise. Specific styles of ideological orientations to research do not necessarily result in cognitive distortions.

Ianni, Octavio. " Sociologie et dépendance scientifique en Amérique latine" [Sociology and scientific dependence in Latin America]. *Social Science Information* 9, no. 4 (1970), pp. 95–110. [1, 2]
An analysis of Latin American societies and the social theories used to interpret them. Social concepts generally have been imported (mainly from the United States), and because they reflect the conditions and concerns of the exporting society they are inappropriate for Latin America. The author specifically criticizes concepts of dualism and political instability, showing how they misrepresent Latin American society. He presents alternative ways of conceptualizing social problems in the region.

Ietswaart, Hellen F.P. "A Successful Development Project in Ecuador: The Institute of Economic Research." *International Social Science Journal* 31, no. 1 (1980), pp. 175–178. [2]
A report on a UNESCO-sponsored project to revive the inactive Institute of Economic Research. Goals of the modest but successful project were to provide teaching service in economic theory and methods, establish a research program, and create linkages with other research institutes, especially the Latin American Social Sciences Faculty (FLACSO). The author evaluates the project and analyzes reasons for its success.

Imaz, José Luis de. "El 'técnico' y algunos sistemas políticos latinoamericanos" [The "technologist" and some Latin American political systems]. *Revista paraguaya de sociología* 10, no. 26 (1973), pp. 49–64. [3]
A systematic examination of *técnicos*, social and natural scientists who act as members of or consultants to Latin American governments. Motivations, values, and professional characteristics are studied empir-

ically, and a systematic comparison is made between *técnicos* and intellectuals. Because they are members of governmental teams and identify with the system, *técnicos* cannot be neutral observers. The author develops propositions regarding the role of *técnicos* in authoritarian versus democratic regimes.

Kahl, Joseph A. "Some Lessons from Latin American Sociologists." *Cornell Journal of Social Relations* 11, no. 1 (1976), pp. 13–22. [2]

The works and careers of three leading sociologists are reviewed to illustrate how Latin American social scientists have responded to economic and social conditions by developing high-quality social theory. Each has approached Latin American reality in a different way: G. Germani through the scientific study of modernization, Gonzales Casanova in his concern for marginal populations, and F.H. Cardoso through political and economic structures. All three have had to confront the issues of general theory versus historical specificity and the valid use of empirical data and techniques. Their research shows the possibilities of value-based scholarship.

Kratochwil, German. "Estado actual de la sociología en Argentina" [The current state of sociology in Argentina]. *Revista latinoamericana de sociología* 6, no. 1 (1970), pp. 167–176. [2, 3]

A historical overview of social thought in Argentina that emphasizes the role of sociologist in a dependent society, the issue of theory versus praxis, and scientific neutrality versus political advocacy. The brief essay covers institutional history, intellectual trends, and the activities of Argentine social scientists in public agencies.

La Barge, Richard A., and Osborn, T. Noel. "The Status of Professional Economics Programs in Mexican Universities." *Inter-American Economic Affairs* 31, no. 1 (1977), pp. 3–24. [2]

A general description of university economics programs in Mexico in terms of numbers of students, characteristics of faculty, ideological preferences, library facilities, and career placements of graduates.

Lopes, Juares R.B. "Reflexões sôbre as ciências sociais em São Paulo" [Some reflections on the social sciences in São Paulo]. *Revista mexicana de sociología* 35, no. 1 (1973), pp. 135–149. [2]

The author provides an institutional history of social sciences in Brazil beginning in the 1930s under the influence of European and North American professors. After the military came to power in the 1960s, university social-science disciplines came under strict surveillance. Faculty members who were forced into retirement either left the country or formed private research institutes. The author describes several of these institutes and their research interests and makes general suggestions for future research.

Mancilla, H.C.F. "La actitud escéptica ante la problemática social" [The asceptic attitude toward social issues]. *Cuadernos americanos* 232, no. 36 (1977), pp. 115–126. [3]
The gap between socioscientific theory and the realities of the world's diverse political systems is rooted in the academic attitude of ascepticism, or abstention from value-laden judgements. Such an attitude ignores conflicts of ethics and social conscience by assuming a stance of cognitive relativisim. Despite its positive consequences (such as antidogmatism), Third World scientists and intellectuals should transform it into a search for a just social order.

Marsal, Juan F. "Sobre la investigación social institucional en las actuales circunstancias de America Latina" [On institutional social research in current Latin American circumstances]. *Revista latinoamericana de sociología* 6, no. 1 (1970), pp. 144–157. [2]
The main concern of the author is the impact on sociology of political forces of the left and right. These influences and the situation of the university as the only forum available for political opposition have led to strong ideological currents in sociology. Even scientific research institutes are not autonomous, as shown by Project Camelot. The author calls for autonomous research institutes, academic freedom, and theoretical pluralism.

Mendieta y Nuñez, Lucio. "La sociología y la investigación social" [Sociology and social research]. *Revista mexicana de sociología* 32, no. 5 (1970), pp. 1101–31. [2]
The author's basic concern is the relation between social theory and research methods. The author observes that empirical influences have had only a slight influence on Mexican sociology, which at the time is basically theoretical and humanistic. The author points out the importance of basing empirical studies on theory and of revising theory to fit empirical findings

Molina Chocano, Guillermo. "The Training Process and Research in Central America." *International Social Science Journal* 31, no. 1 (1979), pp. 70–80. [2]
The author discusses teaching university-level social science in the context of the theoretical and methodological variety that has resulted from different influences on Latin American social science. Professional social scientists can be trained most effectively through research-centered education programs. The author describes one such experimental program.

Moraes Filho, Evaristo de. "Sociologie du développement de l'Amérique latine" [Sociology of development of Latin America]. *Current Sociology* 18, no. 1 (1970), pp. 33–42. [2]

The author traces the shift in concern toward the solution of Latin American problems, beginning with the founding of CEPAL in 1948. He identifies nine themes in recent social research on Latin America and cites the literature on each theme.

Mora y Araujo, Manuel. "Cientificismo e ideologicismo: Un comentario sobre la lucha de clases, el imperialismo y otras variables ruidosas en la explicación de la sociología argentina" [Science and ideology: A comment on class struggle, imperialism and other "noisy" variables in the explanation of Argentine sociology]. *Revista paraguaya de sociología* 15, no. 35 (1978), pp. 59–69. [2]

Latin American social scientists occupy themselves more with the analysis of the development of the social sciences than with the general reality on which they are built. The argument that scientific activity is determined by structural characteristics and general social processes lacks solid empirical support. The development of Argentinian sociology has to be understood in terms of (1) its international linkages with other scientific circles and with international donor agencies, and (2) the scientific and societal origins of the "paradigms" rooted in Argentina's sociopolitical thought.

———. "La sociedad y la praxis sociológica" [Society and sociological praxis]. *Desarrollo económico* 11, no. 41 (1971), pp. 125–143. [1, 2, 3]

The author describes the relationship between the Latin American social-science community and the international social-science community and how the relationship has affected the former. Social scientists identified with external sociology are not generally concerned with the production of knowledge for use by society. This has resulted in a dependent sociology with little originality. This situation is changing, however, and the author discusses alternative roles for social scientists and the possibility of collaboration, which could be used to improve social science and reduce economic and scientific dependence.

Needler, Martin C. "The Logic of Conspiracy: The Latin American Military Coup as a Problem in the Social Sciences." *Studies in Comparative International Development* 13, no. 1 (1978), pp. 28–40. [2]

The author examines the Latin American military coup in the perspective of four modes of social-science analysis: behavioral analysis, development theory, class analysis, and the theory of bureaucracy. The military may serve as an instrument of class rule, but ultimately it pursues its own institutional and personal interests. No single approach can provide a comprehensive understanding.

Nichols, Glenn. "Ventura i desventuras no estudo da politica na America Latina" [Fortunes and misfortunes in the study of politics in Latin America]. *Revista brazileira de estudos politicos* 48 (1979): 47–83. [2]

The author reviews three main approaches to political research in Latin

America: pluralist, Marxist, and corporatist. He analyzes their weaknesses and lack of correspondence to regional political history. He proposes instead a further approach, namely, social fragmentation or anarchy, and illustrates its utility.

Oliveira Belchior, Elysio de. "A introducão das ideias de Adam Smith no Brazil" [The introduction of Adam Smith's ideas in Brazil]. *Revista brasileira de economia* 31, no. 1 (1977), pp. 21–30. [1, 3]
A survey of the introduction of Adam Smith's economic thinking into Brazil, from the 1790s to 1812. Smith's basic tenets against colonial monopoly had a significant effect on official Brazilian policies, leading, for example, to the opening of two ports to friendly nations in 1808.

Pasara, Luis. "Comment: Frank Fights Scientific Imperialism: An Essay Review." *Contemporary Crises* 1, no. 4 (1977), pp. 441–447. [1, 3]
The essay sympathetically reviews the book *Economic Genocide in Chile* (Nottingham: Spokesman Books, 1976), which consists of two open letters written by Andre Gunder Frank to University of Chicago economists who advise the military regime in Chile. Frank is concerned with economists' scientific role in the imperialist plan imposed on Chile and makes the theoretical and empirical case that Chile is not a case of capitalist development but of "economic genocide."

Podesto, Bruno. "Para una historia de la sociología en el Peru" [Toward a history of sociology in Peru]. *Cuadernos americanos* 6 (1978): 60–69. [1, 2]
The history of Peruvian sociology reproduces the evolution of the discipline in the Western world, from enlightenment, idealism, and rationalism to positivism and functionalism. The article reviews individual contributions of Peruvian thinkers and the role of the University of San Marcos.

Portes, Alejandro. "Trends in International Research Cooperation: The Latin American Case." *American Sociologist* 11, no. 3 (1975), pp. 131–140. [1, 2]
The author outlines historical trends and the current status of cooperation between Latin American and U.S. social-science communities. A period of low cooperation and high distrust has led to reform on the part of U.S. foundations and granting agencies, which the author notes. He presents the radical structural critique of social-science cooperation but finds that it leads to only one solution—no cooperation. The author believes that the problems presented Latin America by the sheer size, resources, and dynamism of U.S. social-science institutions can be overcome and that Latin Americans can benefit from cooperation while maintaining their identities and integrity.

Rivarola, Domingo M. "Notas preliminares sobre el desarrollo científico de las areas dificitarias de America Latina" [Preliminary notes on the

scientific development of deficient areas of Latin America]. *Revista paraguaya de sociología* 10, no. 26 (1973), pp. 141–149. [1, 2]
A descriptive overview of social sciences in Latin America, with specific policy prescriptions. Latin American social sciences are characterized as overly dependent on external resources and unevenly distributed through the hemisphere. The author believes international cooperative efforts are inadequate to improve the situation and makes specific proposals for increased communication and cooperation among Latin American social-science communities.

Riz, Liliana de. "Algunos problemas teórico-metodológicos en el analisis sociológico y político de America Latina" [Some theoretical-methodological problems in sociological and political analysis of Latin America]. *Revista mexicana de sociología* 39, no. 1 (1977), pp. 157–171. [2]
The author attributes the lack of social change in Latin America in part to theoretical and methodological deficiencies in sociological analyses. In a sophisticated epistemological argument, the author criticizes methodological rigor in the absence of sound theoretical bases and in closed analyses that do not reflect empirical social reality. She suggests means for moving forward in the construction of explanations of social phenomena.

Rodriguez Bustamante, Norberto. "Sociology and Reality in Latin America." *International Social Science Journal* 31, no. 1 (1979), pp. 86–97. [2]
The author discusses several issues involved in the politicization of social sciences in Latin America. Should the sociologist be committed to ideas or to political praxis? Is there a national sociology? Are techniques and methods from developed countries adaptable to less developed countries? The author is highly critical of sociology in Argentina since the military takeover in 1966. Earlier efforts to establish a first-rate sociology discipline in the national university have been destroyed. The replacement combines populism and Marxism and has become completely politicized even while it has attracted increasing numbers of students. The author is a member of the Facultad Latinoamericana de Ciencias Sociales (FLACSO) in Buenos Aires.

Schiefelbein, Ernesto, and Pujol, José Miguel. "Integración de métodos económicos y demográficos para projecta recursos humanos: El caso del Paraguay" [Integration of economic and demographic methods to predict human resources: The case of Paraguay]. *Revista paraguaya de sociología* 16, no. 14 (1979), pp. 165–183. [2, 3]
The author reviews the nature of data and data-collection methods of economics and demography. He discusses the potentialities and limitations of each, as well as basic information sources available in Paraguay. He describes a research project carried out as part of the Paraguayan national development plan, in which methods from both disciplines

were integrated to predict human resources and needs through the year 2000.

Sheahan, John. "Market-Oriented Economic Policies and Political Repression in Latin America." *Economic Development and Cultural Change* 28, no. 2 (1979), pp. 267–291. [3]

An examination, both theoretical and empirical, of the relation between the use of market-oriented economic policies and political repression in Latin America. After a useful definition of terms, an analysis of the implications of market criteria in five policy areas, and a cross-country comparison of policies and outcomes, the author addresses the issue of what kinds of economic policies are desirable if high value is placed both on economic performance and freedom from political repression.

Solís, M. Leopoldo. "Economía, ciencia e ideología" [Economics, science, and ideology]. *Foro internacional* 17, no. 3 (1977), pp. 327–337. [2, 3]

Neoclassical economics cannot explain the historical evolution of capitalism, and Marxism can explain little about efficient allocation of resources. Economics has sought a more general theory that would include the global equilibrium of neoclassical theory and the historical conscience of Marxism; yet the methodology for such an achievement is not yet available. Prebisch's structuralism failed on empirical grounds, but it inaugurated a tradition of logical rigor in Latin American economic thought. As to policy-relevance, Solís suggests that economics is in fact an instrument, not a substitute for a clear political ideology.

Strassmann, W. Paul. "La economía del desarrollo desde la perspectiva de Chicago" [The economics of development from the perspective of the Chicago school]. *Comercio exterior* 26, no. 7 (1976), pp. 1436–43. [3]

An analysis of the Chicago school approach to the economics of development and an evaluation of its policy recommendations, mainly with respect to international commerce, foreign aid, and improvement of market institutions. One of the principal limitations of that approach is its inadequate treatment of rationality and the process of learning.

Suarez, Francisco Martin. "Algunas reflexiones sobre los procesos de institucionalización de la sociología en la Argentina durante los últimos años" [Some reflections on the process of institutionalization in the sociology of Argentina during recent years]. *Revista mexicana de sociología* 35, no. 1 (1973), pp. 117–134. [2]

The author offers his impressions of the current state of sociology in Argentina. In the universities, the discipline is paralyzed by internal and external attacks from both the political left and right. Internally, the discipline is exclusively neopositivist, narrowly focused on technical and statistical analyses, inattentive to Latin American problems. The author recommends expanding curricula to include Marxist as well as idealistic perspectives. He reviews social research being done in universities and in research institutes and offers specific suggestions for future research.

Tobar, Carlos. "La sociología y el rol del sociólogo en la Argentina" [Sociology and the sociologist's role in Argentina]. *Revista paraguaya de sociología* 7, no. 19 (1970), pp. 117–128. [2, 3]
Since 1960, Latin American sociologists have been involved in problems of underdevelopment and inequality. In Argentina the position of sociologists is difficult because of the need to be employed and the identification of most potential employers with the status quo, a situation that threatens the professional independence of the sociologist. The author encourages social scientists to work toward social change in the direction of increased popular participation in government and more equitable distribution of wealth. Such objectives are best reached through an interdisciplinary approach and professional courage.

Trias, Vivian. "Las transnacionales y la influencia de la 'escuela de Chicago' en America Latina." [The transnationals and the influence of the Chicago school in Latin America]. *Nueva sociedad* 38 (1978): 5–19. [1]
The author maintains that within the Third World, Latin America has been the area most profoundly and systematically integrated into transnationalism, due to the development of peripheral capitalism. The article discusses the influence of "neoliberalism" and the Chicago school on Latin American thought, and the contradictions of the new model of development-dependency-underdevelopment. In the author's view, the crisis of the neoliberal model reflects the dialectic nature of dependent capitalist development, of which Latin America is the prime example.

Van Nickerk, Arnold. "La sociología latinamericana: Un testimonio epistemológico" [Latin American sociology: An epistemological testimony]. *Revista paraguaya de sociología* 12, no. 32 (1975), pp. 115–139. [1]
The essay is rooted in the spirit of Weber's *Verstehende Soziologie,* according to which it is not possible, for instance, to acquire an image of the reality of underdevelopment without previously obtaining an "image of the image" a Third World person has about his own reality. The Western paradigm cannot be transferred to Latin American reality. Empiricism has severe limitations. The author analyzes the complexities in the transfer and diffusion of several other theoretical frameworks from the developed to the underdeveloped world.

Veron, Eliseo. "Imperialismo, lucha de clases y conocimiento (25 años de sociología en Argentina)" [Imperialism, class struggle, and consciousness (twenty-five years of sociology in Argentina)]. *Revista paraguaya de sociología* 11, no. 30 (1974), pp. 93–146. [1, 2, 3]
In this historical description of the development of sociology in Argentina, the author concentrates on the effects of North American influ-

ence and the impact of Argentinian politics. The mid-1950s to the mid-1960s were years of major growth in students, programs, and research, and in U.S. imperialism. More recently, sociology is under attack by leftist and rightist political forces. Sociologists find it difficult to maintain objectivity. Sociology is becoming an applied science as sociologists are forced to look for contract research and consultancies to survive.

Vessuri, Hebe M.C. "La observación participante en Tucuman 1972" [Participant observation in Tucuman, 1972]. *Revista paraguaya de sociología* 10, no. 27 (1973), pp. 59–76. [2]

Two field studies are used to illustrate the importance and techniques of participant observation. The author places the examples in the general context of social science in Argentina and in Latin America and calls attention to the need for locally executed research. The author also discusses the complex role of the Latin American social scientist, who is responsible not only to an academic discipline but also to society, government, and other political forces.

Villa Aquilera, Manuel. "Los rasgos de la sociología crítica en Mexico" [The traces of critical sociology in Mexico]. *Revista paraguaya de sociología* 11, no. 30 (1974), pp. 7–56. [2]

An excellent historical account of the development of critical social theory in Mexico that links changing social thought to political and economic changes in Mexican society. It describes in detail the founding of the periodical *El espectador* in 1959 by a group of intellectuals who wished to refute both Soviet Marxist theory and official Mexican dogma. The author is encouraged by the focus and quality of recent social research and by increased financial support. Both will help assure a positive role for the social sciences in the solution of Mexican problems.

Wilhelmy, Manfred. "Desarrollo y crisis de los estudios de relaciones internacionales en Chile" [Development and crisis in the study of international relations in Chile]. *Estudios sociales* 17 (1978): 9–29. [2]

A discussion of domestic and international, political and economic variables that have influenced the institutionalization, growth, and crisis of academic activity in the field of international relations. The author analyzes the state of the field in Chile in relation to the general development of the social sciences and to specific peculiarities in the study of law and history, as well as in terms of Chilean institutional features (the decline of universities and the role of international and private organizations).

Wionczek, Miguel S. "Los problemas de la investigación sobre el desarrollo económico-social de América Latina" [The problems of research on the economic and social development of Latin America]. *Desarrollo Económico* 10, no. 37 (1970), pp. 127–153. [2]

A prominent economist and officer of the Mexican National Council on Science and Technology (CONACYT) writes of the problems associated with development research in Latin America: deteriorating political conditions, scarce statistical data, and dominance of the values of industrialized-country social science. Research is characterized as lacking a globally integrated focus, being either trivially technical or tending to grand theory unrelated to social reality, and emphasizing politically and economically advanced areas to the neglect of smaller countries. He offers suggestions for improvement.

About the Contributors

Jorge Balán, a sociologist, is senior researcher, Centro de Estudios de Estado y Sociedad (CEDES), Buenos Aires, Argentina. A specialist in urbanization, migration, and regional development, he is the editor of *Why People Move: Comparative Perspectives on the Dynamics of Internal Migration* (1981) and coauthor of *Men in a Developing Society: Geographic and Social Mobility in Monterrey, Mexico* (1973).

Edgardo Boeninger, an economist, is a private consultant in Santiago, Chile. He was formerly rector of the University of Chile, economic adviser to the Chilean Bureau of the Budget, and director of the budget of Chile. His writings include articles on economic and scientific planning and administrative and university reform.

Elizabeth J. Brooks is a political scientist. Her research interests include the international transfer of knowledge and technology, a topic on which she has presented papers at two annual meetings of the International Studies Association, "Transnational Diffusion of Social Science Knowledge" (1976) and "Social Science Cooperation across National Boundaries: Development or Dependence?" (1977).

David Court is The Rockefeller Foundation's representative in East Africa and a senior research Fellow at the Institute for Development Studies, University of Nairobi. A specialist on education in social and economic development, he is the author of a number of articles in scholarly journals and coeditor, with D.P. Ghai, of *Education, Society and Development: New Perspectives from Kenya* (1974).

Huan Xiang is vice-president of the Chinese Academy of Social Sciences. Between 1949 and 1978, he held a number of posts in the Chinese foreign service, serving as ambassador to Belgium, the European Community, and Luxembourg, and chargé d'affaires in Great Britain.

Warren F. Ilchman, a political scientist and Asia specialist, is vice-president for research and graduate studies, State University of New York at Albany. His recent publications include *Political Economy of Development* (1972) and *Policy Sciences and Population* (1975).

Akin L. Mabogunje, professor of geography at the University of Ibadan, Nigeria, is also chairman of the Nigerian Council for Management Development and a member of the board and vice-president of the Panafrican Institute for Development. His publications include *Urbanization in Nigeria* (1969) and *Regional Planning and National Development in Tropical Africa* (1977).

Kenneth Prewitt, a political scientist, is president of the Social Science Research Council, New York. He has had substantial teaching and research experience in East Africa, and his numerous publications (books, book chapters, and articles in scholarly journals) include *Introductory Research Methodology: East African Applications* (1975) and, with A. Stone, *Elites and American Democracy* (1973).

Paul Streeten, an economist, is professor of economics and director, Center for Asian Development Studies, Boston University. He has published books and articles on economics of development, including *Frontiers of Development Studies*, and is chairman of the editorial board of *World Development*.

Eduardo Venezian is head of the Department of Agricultural Economics, Catholic University of Chile. He is the author of *The World Food Shortage with Reference to Latin America* (1977) and coauthor, with W.K. Gamble, of *The Development of Mexican Agriculture: Structure and Growth Since 1950* (1968).

Myron Weiner is professor of political science and senior staff member, Center for International Studies, Massachusetts Institute of Technology. He has published books and articles on Indian politics, including *India at the Polls: The Parliamentary Elections of 1977* (1978).

About the Editors

Laurence D. Stifel, an economist, is vice-president and secretary of The Rockefeller Foundation. His overseas experience has included assignments in the Philippines, Burma, and Thailand; he was economic advisor to the Thailand National Economic Development Board (1964–1967) and The Rockefeller Foundation's social-science project leader in Thailand (1967–1974). He has contributed a number of articles to scholarly journals and is coeditor, with J.E. Black and J.S. Coleman, of *Education and Training for Public Sector Management in Developing Countries*.

Ralph K. Davidson, an economist, is deputy director, Social Sciences Division, The Rockefeller Foundation. On assignment from the foundation, he served for a year (1962–1963) as visiting professor of economics at Makerere University College, Kampala. His publications include articles in scholarly journals, and he is coauthor, with V.L. Smith and J.W. Wiley, of *Economics: An Analytical Approach*.

James S. Coleman is professor of political science and chair, Council on International and Comparative Studies, University of California, Los Angeles. He was the representative of The Rockefeller Foundation in East Africa (1965–1974) and in Zaire (1974–1978). He has published many articles in scholarly journals, is the author of *Nigeria: Background to Nationalism*, and editor of *Education and Political Development*.